GW00771366

THE RECORD SOCIETY OF LANCASHIRE AND CHESHIRE

FOUNDED TO TRANSCRIBE AND PUBLISH
ORIGINAL DOCUMENTS RELATING TO THE TWO COUNTIES

VOLUME CXLIII

The Society wishes to acknowledge with gratitude the support given towards
publication by

Lancashire County Council

© The Record Society of Lancashire and Cheshire
Walter J. King

ISBN 978 0 902593 78 7

Printed in Great Britain by 4word Ltd, Bristol

THE COURT RECORDS OF PRESCOT
1640–1649

Edited by Walter J. King

PRINTED FOR THE SOCIETY
2008

FOR THE SUBSCRIPTION YEAR 2005

COUNCIL AND OFFICERS FOR THE YEAR 2005

CONTENTS

ACKNOWLEDGEMENTS

I am deeply indebted to more people than are noted here.

The DDCs collection has been prepared for publication by kind permission of Tickle Hall Cross, solicitors at Prescot, and the DDKc/PC collection by kind permission of the Provost and Scholars of King's College, Cambridge.

No Record Office has a more professional and helpful staff than the Lancashire Record Office in Preston. To each and every one of them I owe more gratitude than these mere words can convey.

I wish to thank Mr T. Kevin Campbell, former head archivist at Bolton Archives Service, for his generous assistance in transcribing difficult passages, and Mr Keith Fitzpatrick for his very kind permission to investigate manuscripts still housed at Tickle Hall Cross.

Lachelle Fehr scanned and formatted the volume, and Dr Jerome Rosonke resolved several computer challenges. Dr DeLloyd Guth critically read a draft of the manuscript. To Dr Peter McNiven, General Editor of the Record Society, I owe much gratitude for his generous, professional and constructive editorial assistance. Any errors that remain are mine.

I am also grateful to Northern State University in Aberdeen, South Dakota, for providing a sabbatical in 2002 during which much of the research for the introduction was completed and for a Nora Staael Evert Research Stipend during the summer of 2003.

My understanding wife, Janet, made the late nights of writing seem short.

Walter J. King

ABBREVIATIONS

BIHR	Borthwick Institute of Historical Research, York
CRO	Cheshire Record Office, Chester
dec.	deceased
esq.	esquire
f.	folio
gent.	gentleman
husb.	husbandman
jun.	junior
LPRS	Lancashire Parish Register Society
LRO	Lancashire Record Office, Preston
m.	membrane of a roll of parchment
RSLC	Record Society of Lancashire and Cheshire
sen.	senior
THC	Tickle Hall Cross, Prescot
THSLC	*Transactions of the Historic Society of Lancashire and Cheshire*
TNA	The National Archives, Kew
wid.	widow
WRO	Wigan Record Office, Leigh
yeo.	yeoman

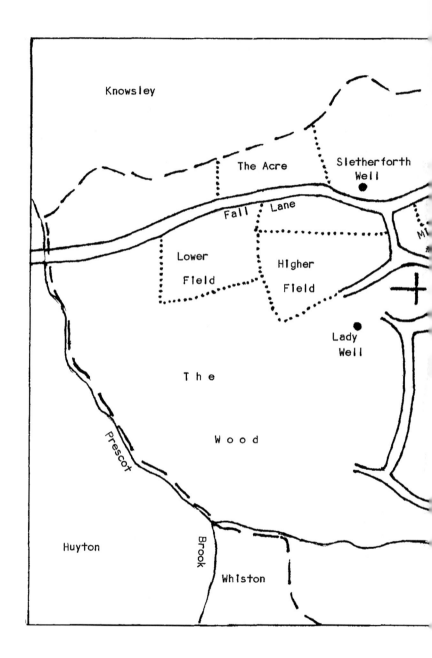

Knowsley

The Acre

Sletherforth
Well

Fall Lane

Lower
Field

Higher
Field

Lady
Well

The

W o o d

Prescot

Huyton

Brook

Whiston

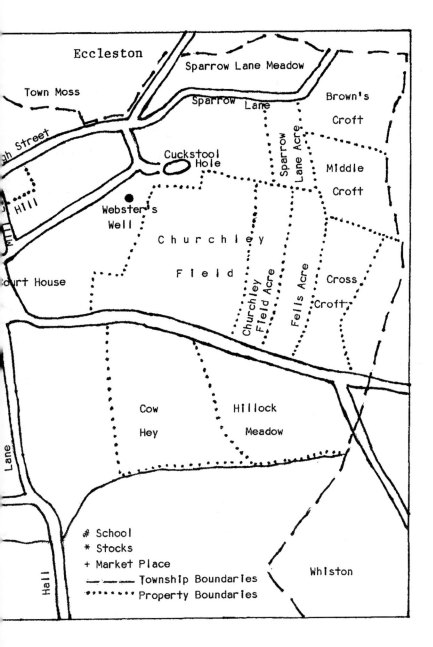

Eccleston

Town Moss

Sparrow Lane Meadow

Sparrow Lane

Brown's
Croft

gh Street

Cuckstool
Hole

Sparrow Lane Acre

Middle
Croft

HILL

Webster's
Well

Churchley

MILL

Field

Churchley Field Acre

Fells Acre

Cross
Croft

ourt House

Cow

Hey

Hillock

Meadow

Lane

\# School
* Stocks
\+ Market Place
—— Township Boundaries
•••••• Property Boundaries

Whiston

Hall

*Prescot: sites mentioned in the Court Records of the 1640s
(Based on Bailey, 1937, and Knowles, 1980. See p. xi, note 1.)*

*Dedicated to the residents of
Prescot during the seventeenth century*

INTRODUCTION

No attempt has been made here to write the history of Prescot, not even of the 1640s.[1] However, because the events in Prescot during the 1640s, as set down in these records of the court leet and court baron, occurred in a context and affected subsequent years, this introduction will provide some of that context and effect and therefore will range beyond the 1640s.

When in 1447 Henry VI granted to King's College in Cambridge the rectory of Prescot, which had descended to the Crown in 1399 when John of Gaunt's eldest son became Henry IV, the College became the lord of the manor of Prescot and so remained into the twentieth century. What has become known as the Prescot charter of 1447 contains privileges granted to the College's estates, including the manor of Prescot, though Prescot is not specifically mentioned.[2] On 29 March 1613 eleven residents of Prescot and the deputy steward gathered in the court house and agreed to assess on tenants and undertenants a tax of £10, or more if necessary, for confirming that charter. A year later on 24 June at another meeting one or two of the nineteen in attendance expressed disapproval at raising money to defend the privileges and liberties of Prescot, but they eventually 'Conformed', and in October 1614 James I issued a charter confirming Prescot's privileges.[3]

Since some of these privileges are recognizable in the court records transcribed here, it is appropriate to discuss a number of them. The residents of Prescot paid

---

1. For the history of Prescot see F.A. Bailey, ed., *A Selection from the Prescot Court Leet and Other Records, 1447–1600*, RSLC, lxxxix (1937); Bailey, 'The Court Leet of Prescot', *THSLC*, 84 (1932), pp. 63–85; Bailey, ed., *The Churchwardens' Accounts of Prescot, Lancashire, 1523–1607*, RSLC, civ (1953); Thomas Steel, ed., *Prescot Churchwardens' Accounts, 1635–1663*, RSLC, cxxxvii (2002); F.G. Paterson, *The History of Prescot* [n.p.p. (Prescot), 1908]; Robert A. Philpott, *Historic Towns of the Merseyside Area: a Survey of Urban Settlement to c.1800*, Liverpool Museum Occasional Papers No. 3 (Liverpool, 1988), pp. 21–34; P.J. Davey, *Prescot Action Area: an Archaeological View* (Liverpool, 1978); Dora Bailey, *Prescot Court Leet* [Liverpool, n.d.p. (1970s)]; E.P. Turton, *Bibliography of the Ancient Parish of Prescot, Lancashire, Including the Modern Boroughs of St. Helens and Widnes* [n.p.p. (1962)]; William Farrer and J. Brownbill, eds, *The Victoria History of the County of Lancaster*, 3 (London, Constable, 1907), pp. 353–4; and Jack Knowles, ed., *Prescot Records: the Court Rolls, 1602–1648 – from notes left by the late F.A. Bailey* (Huyton, 1980). Knowles devoted only four large sheets to selections from the paper books of 1640–48, while the original manuscripts contain 237 sheets and the parchment rolls twenty-four membranes. Statements such as for 1640 '*Absence*. 15 persons' and for 1647 '*Jury*. List of 23 names', without supplying those names, render this work of limited value.
2. Bailey, *Prescot Court Leet*, pp. 60–73.
3. LRO: DDCs/Paper Book and Parchment Roll/1614. For the charter, see LRO: DDKc/ 5213 which is a copy in Latin made in 1843 by William Beamont; Tickle Hall Cross (THC) in Prescot also has a copy. References for the paper books and parchment rolls of the 1640s deposited at the Lancashire Record Office will be found in this volume at the beginning of each year's records and are not usually repeated in these notes.

no tolls in the market at nearby Liverpool[4] and were exempt from jury service outside the manor, including at quarter sessions,[5] and they paid no fifteenth or county tax.[6] Prescot also enjoyed the right to appoint its own coroner (who elsewhere was selected in the county court) and to license its alehousekeepers (normally licensed by any two justices of the peace), and its court baron heard pleas in any sum, while other localities were restricted to under 40s.[7] Residents also claimed through custom the right not to pay an alienation fine to the manorial lord when they were admitted to land by the court baron as a result of descent or purchase, though they did pay rent.[8] In 1680 Prescot's jurors[9] confirmed that no fine was due, but in 1721 King's College disputed that custom and claimed that for many years lessees of the manor had appointed local men to be steward who mismanaged and did not collect fines that were legally due.[10]

Another privilege was the right to determine within Prescot 'all Matters... either of a publick or private nature' that arose on the manor.[11] In 1617 jurors ordered

4.   Bailey, *Prescot Court Leet*, pp. 62–3; 300, note 3. Liverpool disputed the exemption in 1646 and 1648. George Chandler, *Liverpool Under Charles I* (Liverpool, Brown, Picton and Hornby Libraries, 1965), pp. 359, 374, 411. However, at least as late as 1765 Prescot continued to claim the right to pay no tolls. THC: 'The Charities and Other Publick Affairs Concerning the Township of Prescott, 1754', ff.93–6. This volume measures 24.5 cms × 38 cms. Because the binding has decayed from damp, all sheets are loose and some text near the binding has been lost. While paginated to 122, most sheets are blank and unpaginated. The volume contains references to individuals, court actions and documents as far back as 1508, though mostly from 1754 on. While there is much material on the actions of the court leet, from 1778 the book merely lists surrenders; the last is dated 6 January 1815. I initially viewed this volume in 1973, before dampness damaged it, by the kind permission of W. Coombs, Senior, of (then) Henry Cross and Son of Prescot, and most recently in 2002 by the enormous generosity of Keith Fitzpatrick of Tickle Hall Cross. An undated typed manuscript at THC goes to sheet 87. I am very grateful to the staff at Tickle Hall Cross for their kind permission in 1994 to review Prescot's court records in their possession. These documents, mostly in thirty-seven chests, are uncatalogued except for several chests inventoried by the staff of Prescot Museum, and I can here provide only a date and title, usually on the cover. For centuries a member of this law firm often served as steward or deputy steward of Prescot's manor, which explains why so many of Prescot's records remain at Tickle Hall Cross. (Just before publication of this volume, Mr Fitzpatrick informed me that some of the documents had recently been transferred to the LRO.)
5.   LRO: QJI/1/32, Easter 1658 and *passim*.
6.   LRO: QSR/48, Wigan, Epiphany 1655.
7.   Apparently not everyone knew of this privilege. For example, in 1610 John Higham complained against John Leadbetter in four separate pleas of 39s 11½d each for trespass. In 1619 Henry Lake of Tarbock complained against William Mollynex of Prescot in six pleas of debt; the first five were for 39s and the sixth for 5s, or, as the record noted, a total of £10. The limitation was based upon Statute 6 Edw. I, c.8 from 1278. LRO: DDCs/Paper Books/1610 and 1619. For a summary of sixteenth-century pleas at Prescot, see Bailey, *Prescot Court Leet*, pp. 320–3.
8.   According to Bailey, *ibid.*, pp. 122 and 299, no alienation fine was paid in the sixteenth century. In 1666 at Clitheroe and in 1686 at the manor of Ightonhill, Burnley and Colne a fine was a year's rent. LRO: DP 482/la and DDB/42/4.
9.   LRO: DDCs/Paper Book/1680. Unless otherwise noted, 'jurors' refers to 'presentment Jurors' and not to jurors who served at the court baron, to jurors-between-parties or to jurors on a coroner's inquisition.
10. THC: 'Case between Kings Colledge in Cambridge and the Tenants of the Mannor of Prescott in County of Lancaster', August 1721.
11. THC: 'Charities', ff.17, 65. Also see Bailey, *Prescot Court Leet*, p. 70.

residents not to obtain warrants off the manor, without the consent of the steward or at least two of the Four Men, for serving within Prescot concerning matters that the manor itself could resolve.[12] Between 1600 and 1700 thirty-three residents obtained such warrants 'for tryfling businesse' or sued a fellow resident in the county court at Lancaster, for which Prescot's court amerced them either 3s 4d or 6s 8d. All such cases occurred between 1609 and 1632 with a cluster of twenty-five between 1626 and 1628.[13]

Prescot also claimed the privilege exempting its constables from appearing at the sessions of the peace to make presentments, though they could choose to appear, and did, including during the 1640s.[14] Justices of the peace in 1623 and 1661 unsuccessfully contested this privilege.[15] The issue arose again in 1693 when justices fined Prescot's constables for non-attendance. Prescot argued that the charter of 1614 had confirmed that exemption.[16] Although the justices at their Midsummer sessions in 1695 agreed that Prescot's constables were not required to attend 'att any succeeding sessions', the issue languished until 1738 when, up to 1750, it generated at least seventy-five items of correspondence, court documents and expense accounts for legal research that survive for every year except 1741.[17] This prolific correspondence reveals that a number of persons on both sides of the debate searched local records in Prescot and central documents in London. The privilege was still in dispute in late 1750 when the correspondence ended. Curiously, this exemption was not included among the privileges that in 1754 at 'a publick Meeting' in the court house leypayers resolved should 'be Supported and preserved' and was not mentioned in the 'Memorial' entered into the court record in 1759.[18] Yet in 1766 Prescot was still claiming exemption from making presentments to the quarter sessions.[19]

The court records of the 1640s show Prescot exercising some of these privileges by annually swearing in its own coroner, licensing its own alehousekeepers and not collecting alienation fines at admittances to land.

When discussing the history of any location it is vital to estimate the number of people we are talking about, for that estimate will affect our view of their

---

12. LRO: DDCs/Paper Book/1617. The accounts of constable Peter Kenwrick record for 1617 his ten trips conveying to justices of the peace persons served with warrants obtained by residents of Prescot. His expenses of at least 11s 4d fell upon the town, but in the future such expenses would be borne by the procurers of such warrants.
13. In 1725 and 1729 jurors ordered individuals obtaining warrants served within Prescot, with the exception of those for 'public offences', to reimburse the town for its expenses. LRO: DDKc/PC 4/49/Paper Books/1725 and 1729.
14. Commonly Prescot, Liverpool, Ormskirk, Wigan and Warrington and occasionally other towns in West Derby Hundred in constabulary lists had no marginalia indicating that their constables had attended the quarter sessions. See LRO: QJI/1, *passim*.
15. LRO: QSR/20, Wigan, Michaelmas 1623; and QJE/1/80, Ormskirk, Midsummer 1661. Also see QSR/86, Wigan, Epiphany 1693.
16. THC: 'Charities', f.32.
17. LRO: QSR/89, Ormskirk, Midsummer 1695; DDKc/PC 2/59. Also see THC: 'Charities', ff.34–6.
18. THC: 'Charities', ff.17–18 and 55–8.
19. THC: 'Charities', f.96.

behaviour, indeed of their very history. The manorial rental of 1635 (presented to the court in 1636) reveals about 140 households in Prescot, while the five extant call books for 1640–45, when non-residents are excluded, list an annual average of 174 tenants and undertenants.[20] Employing a multiplier of 4.6 individuals per household, we arrive at approximately 644 and 800 residents respectively.[21] Since Prescot's call books list individuals over twelve years of age owing suit and service and not households, population estimates based upon call books will be high; on the other hand, rentals and call books do not include the names of inmates and vagrants. Still, it would seem reasonable to estimate the population of Prescot for the 1640s at between 600 and 700. For comparative purposes, using the manorial surveys of 1592 (about 105 households) and 1721 (about 180) and the same multiplier, Prescot's population was approximately 483 and 828, respectively. The assessment in 1614 for defending Prescot's liberties listed about 134 households, which suggests a population of about 616.[22]

Finally, Prescot was an important marketing centre for the surrounding agricultural area, was situated on main roads between Liverpool and Warrington and Liverpool and Wigan, and was the site of the parish church serving seven other townships. Its role as a marketing centre is demonstrated by the diverse occupations noted in the court records of the 1640s: alehousekeeper, blacksmith, breadbaker, butcher, buttonmaker, carpenter, chapman, clerk, collier, currier, feltmaker, glover, hatter, hooper, husbandman, linenwebster, mason, mercer, miller, nailer, saddler, schoolmaster, shearman, shoemaker, skinner, slater, tailor, tanner, vintner, weaver, webster, wheelwright and whittawer. Many residents participated in commercial and industrial enterprises because Prescot's agricultural area was limited by the town's unusually small size; about 270 acres when Prescot Hall is included. But leet jurisdiction, which seems not to have extended to the Hall, covered approximately 120 acres.[23]

20. LRO: DDKc/PC 4/66/Paper Book/1636.
21. The choice of 4.6 for a multiplier is based principally upon Peter Laslett, 'Mean Household Size in England Since the Sixteenth Century' in *Household and Family in Past Time*, ed. Peter Laslett (London, Cambridge University Press, 1972), pp. 125–58; Laslett himself prefers 4.75 (p. 139). It is not possible to use the call books for 1646–48 because, while those of 1640–45 contain an annual average of twenty-eight female undertenants (eighteen of whom were widows), those for 1646–48 contain the name of just one female (Janet Futerell in 1646). Legal theory required that every male from twelve – or sixteen according to Sir William Scroggs, *The Practice of Courts Leet and Courts Baron*, 4th ed. (London, 1728), p. 18 – to sixty attend his court leet and answer to his name; certain males were exempt. William Sheppard, *The Court-Keepers Guide: or, A Plaine and Familiar Treatise, Needfull and Usefull for the Helpe of Many that are Imployed in the Keeping of Law Dayes, or Courts Baron*, 2nd ed. (London, 1650), p. 7. Presumably at Prescot by 1646 the decision was made to follow legal theory and drop the names of female undertenants from call books, though female names continued to be included in the list of tenants. In the 1650s the annual average number of female undertenants in call books was still only 5.5 (with only one in 1650 and 1651 and two in 1652). In 1591 the population of Prescot was 'at the lest iiij hundred soules.' Cited in Bailey, *Prescot Court Leet*, p. 300, note 1.
22. For the survey of 1592 see Bailey, *ibid.*, pp. 32–46; for the survey of 1721, LRO: DDKc/PC IV/69; for 1614, LRO: DDCs/Paper Book/1614.
23. Bailey, *Prescot Court Leet*, p. 314.

Prescot's position as a regional marketing centre is underscored in yet another way. In pleas of debt, trespass and damages between 1615 and 1635, when they cease to be recorded in these annual court records, 21 percent, or 217 of 1,047 cases, had one or two non-resident plaintiffs (208) and/or defendants (14). Not surprisingly some 42 percent of these non-residents came from the four contiguous townships of Whiston, Eccleston, Knowsley and Huyton. Still, a total of thirty-seven locations were represented; three individuals came from Cheshire and one from London. And individuals from as far away as Derbyshire, Lincolnshire and Yorkshire conducted business at Prescot's annual fair held on Corpus Christi.[24]

DESCRIPTION OF THE RECORDS

LOCATION. Both paper books (drafts of court proceedings) and parchment rolls (final copies of books) for the 1640s are at the Lancashire Record Office in Preston; document references will be found in this volume at the beginning of each year's material. DDKc/PC was deposited in 1971 by King's College in Cambridge, while DDCs was deposited in 1972 by Henry Cross and Son (now Tickle Hall Cross), solicitors in Prescot. Some records relevant to this decade remain at Tickle Hall Cross; and, because of their relative inaccessibility, I have referred to them in this introduction where relevant.

SIZE. Since the paper books for the 1640s have sheets that range between 9 cms × 10 cms (smallest) and 31.5 cms × 39.5 cms (largest), the size of each sheet has been noted in this volume; the average is 21 cms × 29 cms. The range for the parchment rolls is between 26.5 cms × 15 cms and 36 cms × 66 cms; the average is 30 cms × 61 cms. The books are sewn on the left and folded in half lengthwise, while the rolls are sewn at the top. Occasionally a large paper sheet was folded in half and sewn book-wise and is here treated as two sheets. A few sheets show signs of having been folded prior to being unfolded and sewn into a book.

LANGUAGE. During the 1640s in the paper books the presentments and orders were always written in English, while less than half of the surrenders were in Latin, though provisos, when present, were always in English. When in Latin, surrenders occasionally included the English equivalent for a key word or two. Lists of suitors and officers were most often in English, but lists of presentment jurors were most often in Latin. Marginalia were usually in Latin. In the parchment rolls surrenders were exclusively rendered in Latin with provisos in English.

HAND. So many individuals wrote the contents of paper books that, to avoid cluttering this volume, changes in handwriting are noted only when such a note is important for analysis of the text. Commonly, unless a folio's contents are

24. LRO: DDCs/Paper Books/1619, 1622 and 1637.

a continuation of the previous folio, hands change from folio to folio and sometimes even within the same folio.

Also noted in this volume is the number of hands that wrote the annual lists of jurors and presentment officers; several hands could indicate reluctance or inability to serve, as nominators went deeper and deeper into the pool of potential nominees. Annual lists of nominations for various offices were written by up to three different hands (as in 1647, for example) before the required number of officers had agreed to serve. In this volume those names deemed to have been written when the folio's heading and officers' titles were written have been assigned '1' (one). While it is not always easy to ascertain whether group '2' or '3' follows '1', it is possible to distinguish the two additional groups of nominees. Sometimes when a second and even a third set of nominees was added, the names were inserted above other names. Thus, since the order in the original documents has been retained here, '2' may appear in this volume above '1'. Finally, amercements and marginalia were usually written in a different hand, and many times in a different ink as well, from that of the presentments to which they relate.

The clerks of Prescot's court during the first half of the century were Edward Orme (1600–14), James Walthew (1615–34)[25] and Edward Stockley (1642–52). These are the years for which we are certain; a new clerk assumed his duties in 1635, but whether he was Stockley cannot be determined. While the clerk wrote the parchment rolls and undoubtedly other court records, occasionally the presentment officers wrote their own presentments. The handwriting of some of these local scribes reappears in churchwardens' accounts, wills and documents forwarded to the bishop in Chester and to the justices of the peace who met in Wigan (at Epiphany and Michaelmas) or Ormskirk (at Easter and Midsummer) or infrequently in Prescot (at Midsummer 1648, for example) for West Derby and Leyland hundreds.

TYPES OF DOCUMENTS. A 'typical' paper book for an annual court leet and court baron for the 1640s contains a call book of tenants and undertenants; nominations for the presentment jury; jurors' orders and presentments or informal charges of unlawful behaviour; presentments by other officers; nominations of officers for the following year; surrenders of or admittances to property; and occasionally miscellaneous documents such as accounts of the trustees of a charitable bequest, a coroner's inquest, and examinations of witnesses. During other decades of the seventeenth century, paper books may also contain nominations of jurors-between-parties and the pleas which they resolved, and occasional documents such

---

25. One James Walthewe was clerk of the manorial court at Upholland in 1599, 1608–11, 1613–15 and 1630. These are the years known from extant books. While the word 'clerk' was employed only in 1599, context suggests 'clerk' for the other years, too. LRO: DDHi/Paper Books/1599, 1608–09, 1609, 1613–15 and 1630. A James Walthewe also served in 1628 as clerk of the manorial court at Scarisbrick. LRO: DDSc/10/21.

as accounts of constables[26] and of surveyors of the highways, a rental or survey, or an account of transactions at the annual fair.

Unfortunately, personal actions of debt, trespass, breach of covenant and damages do not figure in the 1640s because they mysteriously disappeared from the records after 1635. Between 1602 and 1635 the jurors-between-parties annually heard an average of about fifty-three pleas, with a high of 102 in 1611. We know, however, that pleas continued to come before the court after 1635 because lists of jurors-between-parties are bound in paper books for 1653 and 1672. And about 1760 John Hodgkinson, steward at Prescot, composed 'The Method of Holding The Court Leet and Court Baron of Prescott' in which he related the procedure for plaintiffs and defendants in their 'plaints'.[27] Presumably, then, after 1635 pleas were still heard but entered into a separate book that has since been lost. Also noteworthy is that for the 1640s each year's extant court records have no missing sheets.

PRESERVATION AND IMPORTANCE OF PRESCOT'S COURT RECORDS

The court at Prescot was both a court leet and a court baron.[28] A court leet was a manorial or borough court held annually (as at Prescot on the Friday after Corpus Christi) or semi-annually that exercised limited civil and non-felonious criminal jurisdiction.[29] Because a court leet was a local royal court in private hands

26. Constables' accounts for Prescot survive at the LRO for 1605–06 (DDCs/Paper Book/1606), 1616–17 (DDCs/Paper Book/1617; accounts are for only one constable), 1617–18 (DDCs/Paper Book/1618; one constable, and accounts are torn), and 1682–83 (DDKc/PC 4/126/Paper Book/June 1683). The account year of 1664–65 is a document separate from court leet papers; LRO: DDKc/PC 2/22. Also, while detailed accounts are missing, late seventeenth-century leet records do contain jurors' reviews of those accounts. For the only extant sixteenth-century constables' accounts (1579), see Bailey, *Prescot Court Leet*, pp. 207–8.
27. THC: 'The Method of Holding The Court Leet and Court Baron of Prescott', in a book of forty-four sheets written about 1760 by John Hodgkinson, steward between 1754 and 1785; the book measures 20 cms × 19 cms.
28. Still valuable for a study of courts leet is F.J.C. Hearnshaw, *Leet Jurisdiction in England: Especially as Illustrated by the Records of the Court Leet of Southampton*, Southampton Record Society, 5 (1908). Also see John Kitchin, *Jurisdictions: or, The Lawful Authority of Courts Leet, Courts Baron, Court of Marshalseys, Court of Pypowder, and Ancient Demesne*, 5 editions (London, 1605, 1623, 1653, 1663, 1675); references below are to the 5th edition. Also useful are LRO: DDHo, Walton-le-Dale, 'Method of Keeping a Court Leet and Court Baron', 1744; DDK/Bundle 1532/1, 'The Charge of Mr Roberte Hanckinson', 1674 or 1675. Hanckinson was steward of the manor of Thornley near Ribchester. Extracts of John Wilkinson's *A Treatise...Concerning...the Method for Keeping of a Court Leet, Court Baron, and Hundred Court* (London, 1638) have been reprinted in William Farrer, ed., *The Court Rolls of the Honor of Clitheroe in the County of Lancaster*, 1 (Manchester, Emmott & Co., 1897), pp. xii–xx. Also see Sheppard, *Court-Keepers Guide*, pp. 1–94. For the types of offences presentable and punishable at the court leet in 1510 and 1650, including behaviour made a statutory offence in the sixteenth and seventeenth centuries, see Alan Macfarlane, *A Guide to English Historical Records* (Cambridge, Cambridge University Press, 1983), pp. 82–8.
29. Basing their claim on the Magna Carta, Tudor-Stuart writers of leet guides declared that a court leet could meet once or twice a year. For the relevant chapters of the charters of 1217 (ch. 42) and 1225 (ch. 35), see Harry Rothwell, ed., *English Historical Documents, Volume II: 1189–1327*

adjudicating petty crime in the name of the king or, in the 1650s, of another central authority, leet presentments were supposed to contain the phrase 'to the common annoyance of the king's subjects', but they almost never did (actually, less than one percent of the accusations before Prescot's leet). The headings on the lists of nominees for presentment jurors in the 1640s and 1650s charged jurors to inquire about wrongdoing for 'the sovereign lord the king', 'the Republic', 'the Commonwealth', or 'the Lord Protector', and for the lord or lords of the manor, who in Prescot's case were the Provost and Scholars of King's College.[30]

During the Middle Ages the leet derived from the frankpledge (a division of a community into ten men who shared responsibility for the behaviour of each other) and the sheriff's tourn (or court).[31] R.E. Latham lists 1086 as the date of a document in which he found '*leta*' first used.[32] The word 'leet' to describe a court came into frequent usage around the end of the thirteenth or early fourteenth century, as more and more courts assumed leet jurisdiction with or without a royal grant. But it was not until 1559 that Prescot's court was initially styled 'leet', although it may have been exercising leet jurisdiction during the fifteenth century.[33] The function of a court leet was to provide to the king's subjects local justice 'for the ease of the people...[so that they] should have...justice done unto them at their own doors without any charge or loss of time....'[34] Courts leet began to decline in the sixteenth century as more authority was bestowed on justices of the peace at quarter sessions.[35] During the first half of the seventeenth century some leets, including Prescot's, retained considerable power, but even they declined as the century progressed.

(London, Eyre & Spottiswoode,1975), pp. 337 and 345. A court baron could meet every three weeks. Of those seventeenth-century courts leet in northwest England with sizeable runs of extant documents, seven, including Prescot's, met once a year, while twenty-two met twice, and two others assembled twice but changed to once about 1650 and 1660. The records will be found at the LRO, Liverpool City Libraries Record Office, Manchester City Central Library, and Cumbria Record Office in Carlisle and Barrow-in-Furness; J.P. Earwaker, ed., *The Court Leet Records of the Manor of Manchester*, 2–6 (Manchester, pr. H. Blacklock & Co., 1885–88); Anthony Hewitson, *Preston Court Leet Records: Extracts and Notes* (Preston, pr. Toulmin, 1905); J.G. de T. Mandley, ed., *The Portmote or Court Leet Records of...Salford*, 2 vols, Chetham Society, 46 and 48, New Ser. (1902).

30.   In the court records of Prescot, 'lord of the manor' refers to King's College and 'lords of the manor' to the Provost and Scholars of King's College.
31.   Sir Frederick Pollock and Frederic William Maitland, *The History of English Law Before the Time of Edward I*, 2nd ed., 1 (Cambridge, Cambridge University Press, 1898, 1968), p. 580; Hearnshaw, *Court Leet of Southampton*, pp. 66–71; Sheppard, *Court-Keepers Guide*, pp. 3–4.
32.   R.E. Latham, *Revised Medieval Latin Word-List From British and Irish Sources* (London, Oxford University Press, 1965, 1994), p. 274.
33.   Bailey, *Prescot Court Leet*, pp. 73, 143.
34.   Edward Coke, *The Second Part of the Institutes of the Laws of England*, 1 (London, 1797), pp. 70–1.
35.   While late, a document at THC, 'Prescot Court Charge to the Jury, 26 May 1826', illustrates the extent of the decline. It contains much more material on the court baron than on the court leet, whose only charges are disturbances of the peace and the keeping of a list of all residents of the leet.

Enforcing the customs of the manor, a court baron was the private court of the lord and dealt with relations between lord and manorial residents, including the transfer of land.[36] Although early modern writers of leet manuals differentiated court leet from court baron, at seventeenth-century Prescot, as at other locations, the two courts were not usually distinguished at the annual court held in May or June. But in 1668, 1669 and 1672 the two courts held separate adjournments. During the 1640s headings employed in Prescot's paper books and parchment rolls included 'view of frank pledge with court baron' (most frequently used), 'court leet with view of frank pledge', 'court leet', 'Prescott court' and 'court baron'. During the 1640s five courts were styled 'court baron',[37] and they dealt only with admittances, except for the one in February 1642 which also fined William Webster of nearby Eccleston 10s for an enclosure 'upon a certaine Common'.[38]

During the seventeenth century most inhabitants of England who committed unlawful acts were brought before a court leet, not quarter sessions, assizes or another superior court. For example, between 1640 and 1648 (the presentments for 1649 have not survived), Prescot's leet adjudicated 927 alleged offences, including 183 individuals for affray or tussle, while only nine alleged misdeeds (two for theft, two by churchwardens for disobeying a sessions order and five for recusancy) by residents of Prescot came before justices of the peace.[39] Admittedly, leets only heard minor infractions. Still, the weight of sheer numbers would suggest that in order to know the daily life of the 'average' resident of seventeenth-century Prescot and of other localities researchers need to investigate the records of courts leet which touched more lives more often than did superior courts.

At Prescot the activities of the courts leet and baron were initially recorded on paper and later, after the court had adjourned, on parchment. The present volume is based upon the paper books with reference to the rolls when the two sources differ. Paper books are loose pieces of paper of various sizes; in some cases, they are 'scratch' sheets with non-relevant writing or tabulations on the reverse side of paper torn from a larger sheet. Written by many individuals and collected after the court had adjourned and sewn together on the left side, these loose papers were essentially worksheets to be discarded after accusations of wrongdoing, presented to the court at Prescot by eight sets of officers including jurors, had been

---

36. LRO: DDKc/Bundle 1532/14 for 1681, 'Articles to bee Enquired of att a Courte of Survey and Courte Baron for the Mannor of Thornley.' For forty-five orders made at the court baron of Little Crosby in 1658, see LRO: DDB1 48/6; and for the orders and by-laws of the manor of Cartmel, 1658–1721, LRO: DDCa 7/3.

37. Those five courts baron were held in February 1642, January 1643, January and October 1645 and July 1649. A court baron was also held in March 1640 but has not been included in this volume because it is an adjournment that dealt with a plea of land from the general court held in June 1639.

38. Besides dealing with property transactions, a court baron could also judge certain minor infractions and settle 'ease and quietness between Lord and tennant And lastly between tenant and tenant, neighbour and neighbour....' LRO: DDHo, 'Method of Keeping a Court Leet and Court Baron.'

39. Presentments and orders for 1649 have not survived. For 1640–48 leet presentments are 100 percent complete, while sessional records are 62 percent complete.

reviewed by jurors and amercements assessed by affeerors and guilty verdicts copied onto parchment, the final verdict of the court, by the clerk of Prescot's court. Only paper books contain marginalia and interlineations that reveal leet jurors to be conscientious, deliberative and even merciful and the leet judicial system as just and reasonable. In contrast, in the parchment rolls everyone accused of an offence was found guilty.[40]

In other words, present in the paper books but absent in the parchment rolls is the judicial process of give and take, of fact finding, of determining innocence or guilt. Fortunately, both books (drafts) and rolls (final copies of books) have survived for Prescot. For much of the Tudor period Prescot's court proceedings have been handed down to us on parchment and paper rolls and on rolls of both parchment and paper filed together. Beginning in 1598 both parchment rolls and paper books have survived. As already noted, in 1615 James Walthew assumed his duties as clerk of Prescot's court. It may not be a coincidence that 1614 is the last year that parchment rolls contain orders, presentments and pleas, except for the roll for 1662 that contains orders and presentments. Despite jurors ordering the clerk in 1631 to enroll each annual court's presentments and orders as well as surrenders, from 1615 through the rest of the century, with the exception of 1662, rolls contain only surrenders and, for forty years, a list of sworn officers.[41] For the 1640s besides surrenders the rolls contain in 1640 two presentments, in 1641 one presentment and seven orders, and in 1648 and 1649 a list of officers elected. With regard to surrenders, books provide data not in rolls: the paper books for 1640–48 contain 206 signatures and ninety-seven marks as well as some details dropped from the drafts when the surrenders were recopied in final form onto parchment. Still, the important point is that for Prescot a draft of most years' court proceedings has survived.

A comment on completeness of the records is in order. While leet records at other courts either have not survived or leets never met during the troubled 1640s,[42] Prescot's records of presentments, orders and surrenders for the 1640s are complete except for 1649 for which only surrenders have survived.[43] For researchers interested in criminal and other activity in Prescot during that decade, these court leet and court baron records are the only source for certain years. Because justices of the peace never assembled from Easter 1643 to Michaelmas 1645 inclusive, sessional rolls, petitions, recognizances, indictment books and rolls and

---

40. For a more detailed discussion of the differences between books and rolls, see Walter J. King, 'Leet Jurors and the Search for Law and Order in Seventeenth-Century England: "Galling Persecution" or Reasonable Justice?', *Histoire sociale – Social History*, 13 (November 1980), pp. 305–23.
41. LRO: DDKc/PC 4/161/Paper Book/1631; DDKc/PC 4/32/Parchment Roll/1662.
42. See p. lii *infra*.
43. The court leet records for Wigan that are loose sheets, some of which are badly damaged, are incomplete and for the 1640s have survived only for October and December 1640, March 1641, December 1647, and October and December 1649. WRO: CL/Wi.—5–7. Upholland's records of the courts leet and baron, in paper books, have fared no better, and for the 1640s only thirty-six pleas of debt from 1640 and sixty-four from 1641 have survived. LRO: DDHi.

estreats are only 62 percent complete for the 1640s.[44] Between 1640 and 1649 the assize rolls for the Prescot area are missing except for 1647.[45]

Prescot's extant court records begin in 1510 but do not become reasonably complete, as F.A. Bailey noted in 1937, until 1534.[46] Between that year and 1600 all or most court proceedings are missing for only five years: 1543–44, 1554, 1560 and 1600. For 1601–1700, because in some years the court baron met more than once, 108 paper books and 105 parchment rolls survive.[47] Paper books with presentments and orders are 85 percent complete and are missing only for 1601, 1603–05, 1612, 1649, 1656, 1661–66, 1673 and 1677.[48] Parchment rolls for 1601–1700 are 94 percent complete, with only 1601, 1611, 1613, 1677, 1681 and 1693 missing.

Of those fifteen paper books missing today, ten were missing when an abstract book of the court proceedings, ordered by jurors in 1642, was composed during the seventeenth and early eighteenth centuries, while the other five (1601, 1649, 1661–62 and 1673) existed then but have since been lost.[49] We know that some court proceedings were held for all fifteen years because the Abstract Book contains admittances, but, as one of the compilers noted for 1612, 'Noe orders nor presentments to bee found.'

---

44. Extant quarter sessions records at the LRO for the 1640s include Sessions Rolls (QSR/37–43), Order Books (QSO/2/15–22), Petitions (QSP/1–24), Recognizances (QSB/1/230–329), Indictment Rolls (QJI/1/17–23), Indictment Books (QJI/2/5 and 6), and Estreats of Fines (QJE/1/25–52). Some rolls of Estreats of Fines will be found at TNA: DL 50/8/9, 11 and 12 and DL 50/9/2.
45. TNA: PL 25/31. This roll, not well preserved, contains no reference to anyone from Prescot. A number of rolls of Estreats of Fines at the assizes have also survived for West Derby Hundred. TNA: DL 50/8/9 and 11.
46. Bailey, *Prescot Court Leet*.
47. For the seventeenth century the Abstract Book (see note 49 *infra*) predominantly employs 'Paper Rowle' and for only eleven years between 1652 and 1681 uses 'Paper Booke'.
48. All extant paper books for the seventeenth century are at the LRO except for 1682 which is at THC. Actually, some of the court proceedings in the missing paper books survive elsewhere. For example, pleas for 1604 are in the paper book for 1606. The paper book for 1612 contains no presentments and orders but does have four admittances and thirty-two pleas; however, presentments, a list of sworn officers and twelve pleas for 1612 are on paper filed with the roll for 1614.
49. The Abstract Book is at THC and measures 20 cms × 30 cms. It has been bound and on the spine titled 'Epitome of the Manor Rolls of Prescot Co. Lancs'. The first three sheets are blank and not paginated. An index on folio 4v, also not paginated, was made in 1740. Sheets 5 to 190 are paginated 1–186 at the top right. Of five additional sheets, only ff.188r and 188v, with an index, have writing. From f.5r (paginated 1): 'Prescott 20 April 1642. A perfect Abstract of all the Rowles of the Courtes held for the mannor of Prescott now remayninge in the Chest for that purpose provyded at the Charges of the towne with the orders and other proceedinges at every Court as hereafter Followeth.' LRO has a three-volume copy (DDX 480/20) of the Abstract Book transcribed by E.B. Driffield in 1905–06; volume 2 contains the 1640s. Bailey, *Prescot Court Leet*, relied heavily on the Abstract Book, though he did compare its contents with the original rolls. Upon the Abstract Book and other sources Driffield based his *Prescot Genealogies From the Rolls of the Court of the Manor of Prescot* (unpublished, 1918) at LRO: UDPr 4/1. That the compilers of the Abstract Book omitted many details must be kept in mind when using Driffield.

The Abstract Book has 195 sheets and covers 1510 to 1681; a second volume that continued to 1716 has been lost.[50] Clerks composing the Abstract Book abstracted, heavily, all surrenders but only an extremely small portion of the orders and presentments: for 1640–49, only seventy-five summarized orders and presentments, representing only a tiny fraction of the whole, were included in the Abstract Book. Because the paper book for 1649 has not survived, the Abstract Book is our only source for three orders, one presentment and one 'informacon against' made at the court held on 25 May. There is also a Lesser Abstract Book, but its mid-eighteenth-century composer focused entirely on orders and presentments and selected for 1640–49 only fourteen from the Abstract Book's seventy-five.[51]

For 1701–1800 there are thirty paper books (the last is for 1729) and 296 paper and parchment rolls, or rolls of paper with a parchment cover, and some folded paper items; many of these rolls contain paper that previously would have been sewn into the form of a book. In short, for Prescot from 1534 into the nineteenth century, paper books (1598 to 1729), paper rolls (to 1597 and from 1730 on) and parchment rolls form an almost unbroken and hence unique series and present to researchers an almost overwhelming amount of material.

As stated, we know that some of the books and rolls for the seventeenth century that are missing today have been so for some time. Tickle Hall Cross in Prescot has inventories made on 8 February and 6 June in 1748 by the steward and the Four Men that note which books and rolls for 1600–1747 are either in the town chest or are missing.[52] Missing in February are the books for 1600–05, 1656, 1661–66, 1730–33 and 1741–46; the same books are noted as missing in June except 1741–46 was changed to 1740–45. The second account also lists rolls missing for 1600–02, 1611 and 1613. Regarding the parchment rolls, at least one (1601) that existed when the Abstract Book was composed was missing in 1748 and remains missing today. Another three rolls (1677, 1681 and 1693) existed in 1748 but have since been lost. On the positive side, missing in 1748 but not today are the paper book and parchment roll for 1602.

The situation concerning which books and rolls were missing from the town chest was very fluid. The February inventory noted that Mr T. (Thomas) Barron

50. For 4 April 1 Henry VIII, the Abstract Book mistakenly assigns 1509.
51. I transcribed this small volume in 1972, but despite a valiant effort in 2002, the staff at the LRO could not locate it. In 1972 it was in a box marked '1606–24' in the uncatalogued DDCs collection. In 2002 I myself located in box '1606–24' only a paper book of six sheets with paper covers, measuring 18 cms × 26 cms, in a modern sleeve with modern writing: 'The Lesser Abstract Books of Prescot Court Rolls'; but this is not the item I transcribed in 1972. The original Lesser Abstract Book has on the front cover 'Abstract of the proceedings in Prescott Court comenceing Anno 1509 onding 1716' and on the reverse of the back cover '1775' and contains entries for seventy-nine of the years between 1600 and 1716. The item located in 2002 has only sixteenth-century material on the first five sides, the next five are blank, and the remaining two and the inside of the back cover contain undated material.
52. THC: 'An account of the rolls in Prescott Town Chest and belonging thereto taken by the Steward and Four men', 8 February 1748; 'An Account of the Rolls in Prescott Towns Chest taken by the Steward and the Four men', 6 June 1748.

and Mr E. (Edward) Deane had removed some twenty-two rolls from the chest for the years between 1685 and 1747, only five of which they had returned. Perhaps they were researching the dispute already mentioned over Prescot's privileges. The February inventory concluded with this statement: 'Those not marked (as returned) Mr Barron is accountable for as Steward for those years.'[53] On 25 February 1748 King's College wrote to Thomas Barron, steward from 1730–32 and 1740–45, and criticized him for not selecting a time, as requested in a previous letter, to meet at the town chest in order to return 'all the Surrenders, Rolls and papers that are due from you and the present Steward' and informed him that in four days the manorial lords expect him to meet them at 10 a.m. in the vestry in Prescot and surrender the records in his possession.[54] A similar letter, noting loud complaints from four copyholders, went to Edward Deane, steward from 1746 to his death in 1754.[55] Both the letters and the inventories may have been prompted by requests, beginning in May 1746 by four copyholders of Prescot, for the steward to deliver 'outstanding Rolls' to the town chest, which as late as March 1748 had not been done.[56] One imagines that these eighteenth-century researchers, as well as those in earlier centuries, took court books and rolls to their homes or other locations and, apparently, sometimes failed to return them. It is indeed fortunate that the court records of Prescot are as complete as they are.

Preservation of these court records was a concern in 1642 when the jury noted that Edward Stockley, clerk of the court, had in his keeping a chest that contained the rolls. The jury commended him for saving 'original paper records' from being lost and requested that he make 'a catolodge and Colleccon' of the surrenders, orders and customs in the paper books and parchment rolls; this catalogue became what we today call the Abstract Book. Past and future court records should be placed, the jury continued, in the chest that has several locks, and keys should be kept by the steward, clerk and two of the Four Men so that without all of them there was no access to the records. That chest should be kept in the court house or another convenient location selected by the steward and jurors.[57]

Earlier in 1616 jurors ordered Edward Orme, on pain of £20, to deliver to the steward and Four Men by Midsummer the court records in his possession.[58] The seventeenth century began with Orme as clerk of Prescot's court, a position he held until 1614. By 1615 James Walthew had assumed his responsibilities as clerk

53. Both Barron and Deane are styled gentleman. For an interesting account of the apparent shenanigans and carelessness that can result in mutilated or missing documents, see J.A. Twemlow. ed., *Liverpool Town Books: Proceedings of Assemblies, Common Councils, Portmoot Courts, etc., 1550–1862: Vol. 1, 1550–1571* (London, Constable, 1918), pp. clxxxiii–ccxvi. In May 1642 at Salesbury's court baron the jury ordered an inquiry to determine who 'did abuse the Court bookes by pulling, cuttinge or tereing out certaine leaves.' LRO: DDX/80/1.
54. LRO: DDKc/PC 4/154bis/Paper Roll/1745; this roll contains material for 1745–48.
55. LRO: DDKc/PC 4/138/Paper Letter/1748.
56. LRO: PR 3404/14/6 and 7.
57. In 1597 jurors ordered that a chest with five locks be made for storing court records. Bailey, *Prescot Court Leet*, p. 265.
58. LRO: DDCs/Paper Book/1616.

in which office he continued until 1634. Clerks who copied court proceedings onto parchment and undoubtedly wrote sections of the paper folios and who were responsible for preserving the records may have at times felt proprietary about these documents. In this case, Orme, a former clerk, was ordered to surrender to the new clerk the court records which he had retained. Given the importance of these records for the copyholders of Prescot, possession of them probably conveyed some element of power or influence. While the copyholder who paid 12d to the clerk of the court received a copy of his or her admittance written into the court rolls, the original rolls would further protect the claim to land if the copy became lost or damaged.

In 1629 jurors lamented that diverse orders and presentments at several courts had not been enrolled onto parchment 'but Contenew in loose papers'.[59] They ordered that the constables purchase a paper book for Walthew who would enter the said orders and presentments and the names of officers yearly elected, a directive that Walthew did not obey. The situation did not improve, and in 1631 jurors stated that some court records remained in the clerk's hands and had not been enrolled onto parchment and that presentments and orders as well as admittances for each annual court should be enrolled before the next court was held, as was the custom.[60]

The records reveal no more major concerns among jurors about the state of the court's documents until, as we have seen, in 1642. Nine years later the jury craved 'some setled course for keeping of the Court Rowles'.[61] Curiously, this comment was written on the last of sixty-one sheets in the paper book for 1651 and hints at frustration. Stockley was still clerk of the court in 1652 when jurors, concerned that he had retained custody of the town's records, chest and keys to that chest, ordered him to place the court rolls into the chest and give a key to the steward and each of the Four Men.[62] In 1680 jurors declared that 'many' rolls and books 'are wanting or mislaid and some are not inrolled in parchment as they ought to bee.'[63] Five years later jurors repeated their frequent order to the clerk: copy orders, presentments and leys into the paper book, presumably the one ordered to be purchased in 1629.[64]

The near completeness of Prescot's court records is testimony to an admirable and mostly successful effort to preserve them. That the parchment rolls beginning early in the seventeenth century and the Abstract Book focused on surrenders suggests that, as the court increasingly lost its jurisdiction over misdemeanours to the petty and quarter sessions, Prescot's court began to function primarily as a land registry, and that function became the main impetus for preserving the court records. In 1617 jurors directed the clerk of the court to enroll a surrender of 13

59. LRO: DDCs/Paper Book/1629.
60. LRO: DDKc/PC 4/161/Paper Book/1631.
61. LRO: DDKc/PC 4/112/Paper Book/1651.
62. LRO: DDKc/PC 4/112/Paper Book/1652; THC: 'Extract from the Minute Book of the Steward', 15 June 1759, f.3.
63. LRO: DDCs/Paper Book/1680.
64. LRO: DDCs/Paper Book/1685.

July 1610 missed in 1611 'by the negligence of the clearke'[65] and in 1651 ordered the clerk to add in a surrender copied onto parchment a line missed in 1632 when the messy paper surrender was presented to the court.[66] By these and similar actions jurors attempted to ensure that the court records would be available and accurate when needed to resolve a dispute over tenancy, mineral rights,[67] rights of way, the town's privileges, and 'betwixt the Lords and Tenants of this Manor and amongst the Tenants themselves'.[68]

Yet, as jurors directed in 1641, access to the town's records was not unlimited: copyholders were not to search court records except with the consent 'Jointly' of the steward and Four Men who had keys to the chest, the same five officers who possessed keys in 1759.[69] A case from about 1721 illustrates some of the problems that researchers could encounter. Those wanting to examine court records in the chest in order to locate evidence to support the claim by King's College that anyone admitted to land should pay an alienation fine complained that the five individuals with keys to the chest refused to assemble together.[70] The importance of preserving Prescot's manorial records is underscored by brief notes in some seventeenth-century paper books about searches made in these documents,[71] and by extant results of searches back to the sixteenth century made during the eighteenth and nineteenth centuries by claimants and their attorneys attempting to resolve disputed claims to property.[72]

Finally, I have investigated the court records of seventy-eight manors in Lancashire and thirty-four others in western and northern England, with only six of these 112 having no extant seventeenth-century material. The records of Prescot's court leet and baron are among the most complete and chronicle the

65. The paper book for 1617 (LRO: DDCs) contains the original surrender with the signatures of the surrenderer, John Gouldicar the younger, and two witnesses and immediately following on a separate sheet is another copy minus signatures. The parchment roll for 1617 (LRO: DDCs) introduces the surrender of 1610 with the jury's order to enroll.
66. LRO: DDKc/PC 4/161/Paper Book and DDKc/PC 4/69/Parchment Roll/1632; DDKc/ PC 4/112/Paper Book and DDKc/PC 4/56/Parchment Roll/1651.
67. Documents at THC from the early nineteenth century disagree as to whether copyholders of Prescot enjoyed a customary right to dig coal under their lands and to convert to their own use or whether King's College may enter lands, dig and remove coal and reasonably compensate tenants for the damage. Both sides supported their position with evidence derived from their search of Prescot's court records back to about 1600.
68. LRO: DDCs/Paper Book/1680.
69. THC: 'Charities', f.57.
70. THC: 'The Provost and Scholars of Kings College, Cambridge...Wm Tempest, Esq, and others, Defendants.' The document is undated, but internal evidence suggests a date of around 1721. About 1686 searchers at the copyhold manor of Ightonhill, Burnley and Colne faced the difficulty of obtaining keys to the chest containing manorial records, kept at the castle in Clitheroe, from three persons and paying each 1s. LRO: DDB/42/4.
71. For example, LRO: DDKc/PC 4/161/Paper Book/1632, final sheet.
72. For instance, THC: 'Abstract of Title (from the Court Rolls) to Lands in Prescot...called the Cow heys', 1828. Some thirty-five sheets, with writing on both sides, briefly summarize entries from court documents from the sixteenth century on; entries for the seventeenth century cover ten years including 1643 and 1647.

activities of one of the few leets which remained powerful into the period of the Civil War.[73]

COURT PROCEDURE

During the seventeenth century Corpus Christi fell on a Thursday between 21 May (1668) and 24 June (1641), the greatest range possible; the median was 8 June. About three weeks before a general court met on the Friday after Corpus Christi, the steward forwarded a precept to the bailiff, an undertenant[74] appointed by the steward (or deputy steward when the steward was the non-resident Earl of Derby), commanding him to summon residents and non-residents who owed suit and service to appear at the upcoming court, or to tender an excuse for absence in order to avoid an amercement, and to submit 'plaints' at least six days before the court met.[75] At Upholland the steward ordered the bailiff to give notice, on two Sabbaths during divine service, of an upcoming court.[76] At Prescot the bailiff attached a notice of this future court to the door of the court house that stood on the northern edge of the market place. Also prior to court day the bailiff prepared a list of nominations to the presentment jury on which only resident and non-resident tenants, or those who held property directly from the landlord (King's College), could serve, and from which the more numerous undertenants or subtenants who rented from tenants were excluded. In 1647 Robert Lyon of Eccleston was among those nominated for the lord's jury, but he was not sworn because, as the marginal note declared, he was 'noe tenant'. Of course he was not an undertenant either. The bailiff had also included his name in the call book among the tenants, an entry that he later cancelled.

The bailiff had other important responsibilities. He collected rents due to the lord of the manor.[77] When not paid within two days of the due date, the bailiff could distrain or seize goods which, if not redeemed within fifteen days, could be sold. Furthermore he collected fines imposed by the steward and amercements assessed by affeerors and distrained or impounded goods until inhabitants paid those amercements.[78] In addition he sealed measures used by sellers in the

73. See p. lxi *infra*.
74. Unusual is the case of Edward Darbishire, yeoman and innkeeper, of Prescot. Besides serving nineteen times in eight different leet offices, he was bailiff from 1656–59 and 1663–66. An undertenant, his name appeared in the top 10 percent of names until 1652 when, besides being listed among undertenants, his name was added on the side of the list of tenants. From then until his death in 1669, Edward's name appeared between 16 and 21 percent from the bottom of tenants' names, that is, fairly close to the beginning of undertenants. While he was a tenant between 1652 and 1669, he witnessed forty-one surrenders. Jill Drabble, ed., *The Registers of the Parish of Prescot, 1665–1726*, LPRS, 149 (2000), p. 81.
75. Bailey, *Prescot Court Leet*, p. 102.
76. For example, LRO: DDHi/Paper Books/1603, 1623 and 1631.
77. LRO: DDCs/Paper Books/1614 and 1622.
78. LRO: DDCs/Paper Books/1614 and 1626; DDKc/PC 4/66/Paper Book/1635. In only a few cases was 'fine' and not 'amercement' used in these records. In 1645 Thomas Browne, alefounder, was 'amerced' 40s for not submitting his presentments. When he belatedly did, the steward was 'pleased to spare his Fyne affouresaid and to remitt his Amerciment of xls affouresaid.' That

market, for which he was paid 4d per measure.[79] Except for the casual note in 1629 that John Walker was elected bailiff by the steward and for four annual lists of sworn officers,[80] all references to bailiffs in Prescot's seventeenth-century court records are incidental. Known from those manuscripts are the names of twenty-one bailiffs who served from one to fourteen years at the steward's (or deputy steward's) pleasure and who were undertenants who commonly came from the top half of the names of undertenants in call books.[81]

From 1453 until 1649 the Earls of Derby leased the rectory of Prescot from King's College and thereby became stewards of the manor and 'lord for the time being'.[82] The Earls renewed their lease seven times during the first half of the seventeenth century. Because the Earls' main residence was at Lathom House near Ormskirk and because they had interests and responsibilities far beyond Prescot,[83] they appointed local gentlemen to serve as deputy steward and preside at the annual court and adjourned courts where those gentlemen were variously titled 'steward' or 'deputy steward' and where the Earls were called 'chief steward'.

Between 1534 and 1603 six different individuals served as deputy steward. In 1604 Henry Stanley, esq., entered that position, which he held until 1636. By July Thomas Wolfall, esq., became the Earl's deputy, holding office until 1648, and in 1649 Arthur Borron, gent., succeeded him. It was also in 1649 that King's College cancelled the lease held by James, seventh Earl of Derby – because the conditions of the lease 'were never performed att all' – and the history of the

is, at Prescot the distinction between amercement imposed by affeerors and a fine set by the steward seems unclear. 'Fyne' was also employed in presentments of breaches of the peace for 1637 and 1640. LRO: DDCs/Paper Books/1637 and 1640.

79. LRO: DDCs/Paper Book/1621.
80. The paper book for 1629 (LRO: DDCs) has '*senescallum*' (steward), while the parchment roll (LRO: DDKc/PC 4/153bis) has '*subsenescallum*' (deputy steward). See note 101 *infra*.
81. These twenty-one and the known years that they served are James Case (1602), Thomas Pyke (1604, 1606–07, 1612), Ralph Stock (1609), William Helme (1610), William Radley (1612, 1614, 1617), George Tapley (1613, 1617), Robert Makynson (1618), Thomas Parr (1621, 1623–24, 1632–42), Henry Darbishire (1626–29), John Walker (1629, 1631), Henry Parr (1645, 1647–48), Henry Ashton (1650–54), John Poughtin (1652), Thomas Webster (1654, 1660), Edward Darbishire (1656–59, 1663–66), William Wood (1669), William Parr (1672), William Standish (1673–74, 1676, 1679–81, 1683–84), Peter Lawrenson (1687–89), David Robinson (1690–92) and William Woods (1697–98, 1700). For the accounts of a bailiff (W. Radley), see LRO: DDCs/Paper Book/1614.
82. King's College, Cambridge: Ledger Books, vols. 3–7 contain leases through to the end of the seventeenth century; vols. 4 and 5 have leases for the 1640s. For an analysis of the diverse responsibilities of the steward in late seventeenth-century England, see D.R. Hainsworth, *Stewards, Lords and People: the Estate Steward and his World in Later Stuart England* (Cambridge, Cambridge University Press, 1992).
83. For an overview of just how extensive the Earls of Derby's interests were, see Barry Coward, *The Stanleys, Lords Stanley and Earls of Derby, 1385–1672: the Origins, Wealth and Power of a Landowning Family*, Chetham Society, 3rd Ser., 30 (1983), especially Appendix B, pp. 200–12, where Prescot is mentioned on pp. 201, 205 and 208. The Earl of Derby was also the lord of the manor of Upholland. LRO: DDHi/Paper Books/1613–15, 1621–22 and 1641; DDK/1540/36 for 1678.

stewardship of Prescot manor took a different turn.[84] In 1649 the Earl, who had supported Charles I in the Civil War, was in exile on the Isle of Man, and in October 1651 at Bolton he was executed for his role in the 'massacre' in Bolton in 1644. From 1649 to 1699 the lease was renewed seventeen times, and all lessees were non-resident (from London, Middlesex or Shropshire), except for Edward Stockley, gent., clerk of Prescot's court, who leased from 1649 to 1651 (with Samuel Terrick of London), and William Tempest of Prescot, esq., who leased in 1695 and renewed in 1699. After the Earl's lease was cancelled, court records always described the officer presiding at the court leet as 'steward'. While between 1604 and 1648 only two individuals served as deputy steward to the non-resident Earls, between 1649 and 1699 eleven officiated as steward, sometimes appointing a local gentleman to preside as deputy steward at a court baron.

Throughout the seventeenth century, court records contain references to the steward who 'solely and secretly examined' wives when they and their husbands surrendered property, in order to ensure that wives concurred, and who was frequently consulted by jurors when they issued orders. It was also he who ultimately licensed alehousekeepers in Prescot, while for most other localities justices of the peace issued licences.[85]

On the Friday after Corpus Christi the steward or deputy steward and presentment jurors met in the court house above some shops, many of which were butcher shops; the court house was located east of the parish church and north of the market place. In that building the public gathered, as they had on 29 March 1613 and 24 June 1614, as we have seen, to discuss raising money to confirm the charter of 1447. The court house was frequently 'in greate decay and verie ruinous', and jurors ordered owners of shops beneath to finance repairs in proportion to their holdings. In 1669 six persons or couples and the heirs of Jane Turner, deceased, had eight shops; in 1740 three individuals owned those eight shops.[86] In six of the thirteen years from 1688 to 1700 jurors ordered repairs to the court house. Also in 1740 jurors commanded shop owners to repair the walls and roof of the court house and directed the constables to repair the windows as well as the benches and seats used by the steward and jurors and to add a new window and a new bench.

As court was being held on 26 May 1749, loud cracks were heard and, with suitors only half called, everyone immediately scampered out. The 'great pressure and weight of the people therein' caused 'the principal Beam' to become dislodged, and the building was 'not thought safe to be used again for the holding

---

84. King's College, Cambridge: Ledger Books, vol. 5, f.76.
85. Besides Prescot, in Lancashire Garstang and Upholland also licensed locally. LRO: QSP/26/1, Epiphany 1650; DDHi/Paper Books/1610 and 1621. Prescot's court amerced any resident 13s 4d who obtained an alehousekeeping licence from justices of the peace rather than from the steward. LRO: DDCs/Paper Books/1648 and 1650.
86. LRO: DDKc/PC 4/11/Paper Book/1669 and DDKc/PC 4/137/Paper Roll/1740.

of Courts'.[87] But the building continued to be used, and a proposal of 1755 to replace the court house, because it was 'insecure' and too small to accommodate the increase in the number of residents, described the building as being about fifteen by seven yards in size and built chiefly of timber with clay walls.[88] The 'First Stone' of the new court house was laid on 29 May 1755 where the old court house had stood, and on 4 June 1756 the annual court was held in the new court house, also used as the town hall 'for Transacting the Publick Business of the Manor'[89] and making binding decisions by a majority of those present. In 1771 it was noted that at such meetings over the past sixteen years 'deciding any difficult matters by a Majority of the Ley-payers present' had worked well, and the recommendation was to continue that practice.[90]

Apparently some town business was also conducted in small groups in homes of residents, as occurred in 1647 when John Alcocke, jun., was accused of entering the house, which also functioned as an alehouse, of John Pendleton where the constables and Four Men were meeting, giving 'uncivill speeches' and tussling with Edward Stockley, one of the Four Men.[91] Appropriately, John Pendleton was first mentioned in the court records of 1604 as one of twelve jurors-between-parties, an office he held for sixteen years (to 1634)[92] and for which he was nominated in four other years. Such frequent office-holding hints at a personality that could resolve rather than feed conflict between neighbours. John also served as a pledge for six tusslers and as a pledge in three pleas of debt. Additionally, he served as a constable four times, aletaster twice and burleyman once. Except for not ringing his swine in 1635, his neighbours never accused him of any offence not related to alehousekeeping, and his last in that category was in 1633, for allowing unlawful gaming.[93] John was clearly respected by his neighbours and in 1646 was one of twenty-five who the steward and constables thought should be permitted to keep an alehouse; in fact, his name was third from the top of the list.

So, sometime between the general courts of May 1646 and June 1647 the constables and Four Men met in John's alehouse, where over ale they conducted 'the townes business'. His alehouse was a logical choice: John had kept an orderly alehouse for the past thirteen years and was an active participant in the town's business, although as age crept up on him he participated less often.

87. LRO: DDKc/PC 4/54/Paper Roll/1749.
88. THC: 'Proposals for Rebuilding the Court House', 31 January 1755.
89. THC: 'Charities', ff.22, 42–3. Bailey, 'The Court Leet of Prescot', p. 84, incorrectly assigns the rebuilding of 'the ancient court house' to 1775.
90. THC: 'Charities', a loose, unpaginated printed sheet measuring 20 cms × 17 cms.
91. In 1664 or 1665 the Four Men met at the residence of George Webster to lay an assessment. At Rishton, Eccleston-with-Heskin, Winstanley and Bootle-cum-Linacre courts leet and baron, courts baron and adjourned courts assembled, sometimes regularly, in the houses of residents. LRO: DDKc/PC 2/22, DDPt/22, DDM/7/114, DDBa/Division 8/Bundle 12 and DDX/109/29.
92. Pleas of debt have not survived from 1636 on.
93. Also excluding the non-offence of breaking the assize of ale. See p. xxix *infra*.

After court was declared open by the steward or his deputy, possibly about 8 a.m.,[94] the bailiff began to call the names of the tenants and undertenants who owed suit and service and added to this list, prepared before court met, a mark next to the names of those in attendance or noted briefly the reason for absence, such as 'sick', 'out of county', 'at London', or 'in the publicke service'. While calling names of suitors may be traced back to the medieval frankpledge, now suitors were being asked, functionally speaking, to appear and acknowledge the court's jurisdiction over them. Between 1640 and 1648 call books listed an average of 170 residents and non-residents owing attendance at court, of whom an average of 16.5 defaulted in appearance and were amerced; with forty-one defaulters, 1645 had the highest number.[95] During the seventeenth century the amercement for non-attendance, which differed from year to year, ranged from 3d to the more common 12d. Most of those excused or essoined were tenants because all undertenants resided in Prescot and undoubtedly found it more convenient to attend court than did tenants living outside Prescot. Also, undertenants, with fewer responsibilities outside the county, were less likely to be outside Prescot or Lancashire when court met and, with less income, may have avoided being absent because they were less able to pay an amercement, however small. The last point is suggested by the actions of affeerors who amerced tenants 12d and undertenants 4d or 6d in forty of forty-two cases of non-attendance when seventeenth-century affeerors broke with the custom of assigning the same amercement to all defaulters. In sum, undertenants were more likely than tenants to fulfill their suit and service: during the 1640s 91 percent of undertenants' names have an attendance mark but a lower 72 percent of tenants' names do so.

Until there was a full jury of at least twelve, the bailiff next called the names of nominated presentment jurors, whom he (as instructed by the steward) had selected before the court met.[96] A foreman was sworn, and then the remainder of the jury, called 'the Grand Jury' in 1625 and 1628, was sworn in groups of four.[97]

---

94. The only known beginning times for courts at seventeenth-century Prescot are 7 and 8 a.m. for adjourned courts in 1651 and 1691. During the eighteenth and nineteenth centuries general courts typically opened between 9 and 11 a.m.; courts baron and adjourned courts began most often at noon or 2 p.m. After the seventeenth-century opening times would have been later when there was less deliberation and consequently less work because of a loss of jurisdiction to the petty and quarter sessions. Elsewhere during the seventeenth century general courts commonly met between 7 and 11 in the forenoon but especially at 9, while adjournments and courts baron assembled between 8 a.m. and 3 p.m. but most frequently in the morning. LRO: DDKc/PC 4/53/Paper Book/1691, DDHo, DDM/7/114, DDBa/Division 8/Bundle 12, and DDX/109/29; Shropshire Record Office: 4001/Box 193 and 194.

95. The years 1640–43 and 1645 had an average of 184 individuals owing attendance while 1646–48 had 148. See note 21 *supra*. John Hodgkinson, steward at Prescot between 1754 and 1785, offered a reason for suit and service in the past: ' that they might hear and learn the Law by which they were governed and also might here be Sworn to be true and loyal Subjects to the King.' THC: 'The Charge to the Jury at a Court Leet and Court Baron', about 1760, f.1, bound with 'The Method of Holding The Court Leet' in note 27 *supra*.

96. 'In the Court Baron the Jury may be less then [*sic*] twelve, but in the Court Leet never....' Sheppard, *The Court-Keepers Guide*, p. 3.

97. LRO: DDCs/Paper Books/1625 and 1628.

In each of the two decades preceding the 1640s, an average of twenty-one tenants were nominated; in the 1640s the average moved up to twenty-four and in the 1650s returned to twenty-one. The average number sworn during the 1640s was fourteen and during the 1650s it was sixteen. During the first four decades of the seventeenth century the average number sworn each decade ranged between 14.9 and 15.1; during the last four decades the range was 15.4 and 15.6. Because of adjournments and because some sworn jurors were non-residents, more than twelve were sworn in order to ensure that at least the legally required twelve would attend each session of the court.

All presentment jurors held land directly from King's College and were the more, but not the most, prominent inhabitants. All nine nominations, for instance, of esquires (the same three individuals for 1640–42) resulted in no sworn jurors, as did about half of the nominations of gentlemen between 1640 and 1648. Most jurors were quite active in the court leet in other capacities and held an above average amount of property, some of which they subletted to undertenants.

While jurors made presentments and orders that touched the lives of every resident to some degree, during the 1640s more and more non-residents served on the jury. During the 1620s an average of less than one juror (0.9) a year of the fifteen sworn was non-resident, during the 1630s the number was 2.6 of fifteen; the 1640s saw 5.5 of fourteen and the 1650s 7.9 of sixteen. Perhaps the size of the sworn jury was increased in the 1650s to accommodate the ever increasing number of non-residents on it. No non-resident served before 1623; the largest number was eleven of fifteen jurors in 1649 and eleven of seventeen in 1653. In 1649 four sworn jurors came from Prescot; three from Whiston; two from Knowsley; and one each from Eccleston, Huyton, Kirkby, West Derby, Windle and Woolfall Heath. In 1653 six sworn jurors came from Prescot; two each from Knowsley and Windle; one from Cronton, Huyton, Kirkby, Rainhill, Sutton, West Derby and Whiston; and Tarbock and Widnes each contributed one nominee who was not sworn, while Prescot had one nominee not sworn and three others whose names were cancelled.[98]

During the seventeenth century 186 individuals officiated as presentment jurors, an average of eight years or a median of five; 51.6 percent served five or fewer times, while 18.8 percent served only once. Almost 10 percent took their oath for between twenty and thirty-eight years. For the 1640s the numbers are an average of 3.2, median of 2.5, 81.8 percent five or fewer years, and 31.8 percent only once. As the century progressed the trend was towards serving more frequently: between the first and last decades of the century, median service more than doubled from 2.5 to six years, and the percentage of jurors serving only one year decreased from 33.3 to 11.1.

Not unexpectedly, certain families frequently filled the office of juror. Three generations of Alcock (William, John, sen., and John, jun.) served forty-eight years between 1604 and 1659; five of the six sons of John, sen., officiated but only John, jun., served more than five times. Nicholas Marshall sat on forty-four

98.   LRO: DDKc/PC 4/112/Paper Book/June 1653.

juries between 1594 and 1644. His two sons, Henry and John, between 1648 and 1672 took their oaths as juror a total of twenty-five times, and a grandson did twice. Nicholas's father-in-law, Henry Blundell, served on fourteen juries and his brother-in-law, William, on eight, whose son, William, jun., took five annual oaths of office. Henry's father-in-law, William Fletcher, served twenty-four years. While additional examples of frequent family service as juror could be provided (Kenwrick, Lyon, Webster, to name a few), it would be misleading not to point out that, as noted, many individuals sat on only a few juries.

These jurors and the steward or deputy steward constituted the court. The steward then proceeded to give jurors their charge, or what they were to inquire into;[99] indeed jurors submitted their own presentments to the court. Jurisdictional boundaries between the issues that jurors and other presentment officers submitted to the court were flexible, and these jurors covered some areas of behaviour usually reserved for other officers. At Prescot jurors presented defaulters in appearance, inmates, receivers of inmates, and inhabitants for non-payment of taxes, cutting timber in Prescot Wood without permission, enclosing, drinking beer at unlawful times, not cleaning ditches, making pits in the streets, removing soil or stones from those streets without filling in the holes, and not repairing buildings, gates or hedges. Jurors issued orders for the proper care of the court records and against laying dung on the Town Moss or in the lanes, and directed other officers to perform specific duties; they reviewed annual accounts of constables, overseers of the poor, feoffees of charitable bequests and surveyors of the highways; resolved disputes between inhabitants; ordered the town's debts to be paid and leys to be collected; and approved nominees who administered charitable bequests.

During the 1640s about fifty different individuals including jurors annually filled sixty-six slots as officers of Prescot's court. Annually there was an average of fourteen presentment jurors sworn,[100] fourteen jurors at the court baron (with some overlapping between the two juries), and almost certainly twelve jurors-between-parties. There was one deputy steward, bailiff,[101] doorkeeper for the presentment jury (called 'attender of the Jury' in 1654[102]), clerk of the court,[103] leygatherer and coroner; two constables, clerks of the market, burleymen, sealers of leather, alefounders or aletasters, and streetlookers and well lookers; and four affeerors and

99. THC: 'The Charge to the Jury at a Court Leet and Court Baron'; LRO: DDHo, 'Method of Keeping a Court Leet and Court Baron'; John Wilkinson, *The Manner and Forme How to Keepe a Courte Leet, or a Law-day* [(London) 1641]. Also see Kitchin, *Jurisdictions*.
100. Fifteen was the average sworn annually during the seventeenth century; the names of sworn jurors survive for every year except 1601.
101. Between 1601 and 1700, only for 1604, 1609, 1626, 1629 and 1681 is the bailiff included in the annual list of officers sworn. LRO: DDCs/Parchment Roll/1604; DDCs/Paper Books/1609, 1626 and 1629; DDKc/PC 4/120–136/Paper Book/1681.
102. LRO: DDKc/PC 4/112/Paper Book/May 1654, f.2r.
103. The court record of 1642 mentions 'Mr Stockley and his Clarke'. That is, Edward Stockley, clerk of Prescot's court, had an assistant who would constitute a sixty-seventh slot; that position of assistant clerk was never mentioned again during the seventeenth century.

the Four Men. Besides these sixty-six, occasional or temporary officers included a poundkeeper (sworn only for 1651–55), an average of fifteen jurors on a coroner's inquisition, and about nine toll-takers at the annual fair held on the Town Moss on the northeast side of Prescot in conjunction with the annual court held in May or June,[104] as well as householders required by constables to watch for suspicious individuals from sunset to sunrise between Ascension Day and Michaelmas, as required by the Statute of Winchester of 1285.[105]

Irregularly, constables also required the assistance of their neighbours, as constable Peter Kenwricke did in 1617 when he and two assistants conveyed the accused murderer William Smyth to the gaol in Lancaster, a damp round trip of five days.[106] In September 1639 Hamlet Whitfield, constable of Prescot, and vicar John Aldem charged William Houghton and Richard Mollineux, both of Prescot and labourers, to convey Richard Spencer, 'an idle and wanderinge person' apprehended and whipped in Prescot, to Eccleston where others would convey him ultimately to Newton, his place of birth.[107] Between 1620 and 1655 neither Houghton nor Mollineux served in any other leet or ecclesiastical office.[108]

Slightly more frequently constables hired individuals to guard suspected offenders, especially at night, in order to prevent their escape from 'prison'; Kenwricke hired four to assist him in watching Smyth the night before their departure for Lancaster. In 1691 Peter Marsh was amerced 13s 4d 'for refuseing to guard and attend men that were impressed for the Kings service.'[109] The greatest number at any seventeenth-century court to be charged with refusing to assist constables 'in the Execucon of their Office' was eleven in 1688.[110]

Associated with the court were the six feoffees or trustees (the vicar and five others) of the charitable bequest in the amount of £20 of Lawrence Webster, who died in 1608.[111] While Lawrence's will instructed surviving feoffees to nominate a replacement for a deceased feoffee, jurors at Prescot were supposed to review and possibly approve (and during the seventeenth century they never rejected) the nominee and to review the feoffees' accounts which would reveal how the profit or interest from investing the £20 was dispensed to relieve the poor of Prescot and Eccleston, Whiston and Rainhill. But until the troubled 1640s when a greater

104. For the accounts of toll-takers at the fair in June 1614, see LRO: DDCs/Paper Book/1614. Individuals refusing to serve as 'a Toll man being thereto Lawfully sumoned' were presented to the court leet. LRO: DDKc/PC 4/152/Paper Books/ 1711 and DDKc/PC 4/115/1707. In 1795 toll-takers collected from buyers 3d per bull, 2d per cow and 1d per calf. THC: Box 1/Bundle 42/1. In 1508 Ralph Eccleston of Eccleston, esq., granted land to Prescot that would become 'Prescott towne mosse'. Bailey, *Prescot Court Leet*, pp. 278, 281–3; THC: 'Charities', f.4.
105. Statute 13 Edw. I, c.4.
106. LRO: DDCs/Paper Book/1617.
107. LRO: QSB/1/222/38, Michaelmas 1639. This is Richard Spencer's only appearance in Prescot's manorial records.
108. The churchwardens' accounts for 1607–34 and 1636 are missing.
109. LRO: DDKc/PC 4/53/Paper Book/1691.
110. LRO: DDKc/PC 4/126/Paper Book/1688.
111. LRO: WCW/Prescot/1608/Lawrence Webster. Half of the interest on the legacy went to Prescot and half to Whiston, Rainhill and Eccleston.

need for charity arose, the court was not an attentive supervisor of the bequest. While the court did issue several orders requiring the submission of accounts, feoffees did not comply until 1627 when they submitted accounts for 1609–21. In November 1642 William Alcocke of Prescot established another charitable bequest that necessitated more feoffees, commonly the sons of deceased feoffees, but by the time he died in April 1645 he had reduced the amount from £40 to £25 'by reason of the trowblesomnes of these times'.[112] Although William's will stipulated that Prescot's jurors themselves should in the future choose a replacement for a deceased feoffee, this bequest is mentioned in the leet records of 1654, 1655, 1659 and 1660 and never again, and accounts of 1709, 1754 and 1772, describing all charities belonging to Prescot, note bequests by Webster and John Alcocke but not William's.[113] 'John Alcocke' refers to John Alcocke of nearby Eccleston, brother of the said William, who himself established in 1653 a third charitable bequest in the amount of £50 for the poor of Prescot and again required feoffees, five in number, who were sometimes nominated and always approved by jurors at Prescot.[114]

Since the parish church of St Mary was in Prescot, manorial residents also served in ecclesiastical offices. The parish church had a clerk, who in the 1640s was our Edward Stockley.[115] Annually on the Tuesday after Easter the vicar, some of the Eight Men[116] and up to a dozen other parishioners from the eight-township parish[117] elected churchwardens; during the 1640s Evan Garnett of Prescot was chosen four times. They then also elected two supervisors or surveyors of the highways within Prescot township whose accounts of receipts and disbursements were reviewed by the Four Men until 1670 and thereafter by leet jurors; five different residents of Prescot filled this office during the 1640s. Responsible for keeping streets in repair and, along highways, ditches cleaned and hedges trimmed, these supervisors were different from the streetlookers chosen annually at Prescot's leet. Supervisors also made presentments to leet jurors and ordered inhabitants 'to come

112. LRO: WCW/Prescot/1645/William Alcocke.
113. THC: 'Charities', ff.5, 7, 112–14. W. Alcocke's bequest is also not noted in *Endowed Charities (County of Lancaster): Parish of Prescot* (London, 1902).
114. For example, LRO: DDCs/Paper Book/1670. For John Alcocke's will, see TNA: PROB 11/226/98. The charities of John and Lawrence 'had been lost before 1828.' Farrer and Brownbill, *Victoria History*, 3, p. 346, note 7.
115. Between 1590 and 1607 in twenty-nine entries in the churchwardens' accounts Edward's father was paid 42s 7d for writing various parish documents; the accounts for 1607–34 are missing. Bailey, *Churchwardens' Accounts of Prescot*. Also see J. Perkins, ed., *The Registers of the Parish of Prescot, 1531–1595*, LPRS, 137 (1995), p. 253. The elder Edward died in 1614. F.V. Driffield, ed., *The Parish Register of Prescot, 1573–1631*, LPRS, 76 (1938), p. 188.
116. The Eight Men chose the churchwardens and examined their accounts. Steel, *Prescot Churchwardens' Accounts*, passim.
117. Before the 1640s the ancient parish of Prescot had divided into two sides. Prescot township was joined with Eccleston, Parr, Rainford, Rainhill, Sutton, Whiston and Windle, while the southern side consisted of Bold, Cronton, Cuerdley, Ditton, Great Sankey, Penketh and Widnes. Each side kept its own parish registers and churchwardens' accounts; those accounts for Prescot refer only to the Prescot side except for church leys paid by the southern seven townships for the upkeep of the parish church.

with there teames and hand laboure according to the Statute' and repair high-ways.[118] Highway repairs were funded by leys, by the sale of muck from the town midden, and by fees, usually 2d or 3d, collected from residents who had midden steads on the lord's waste or in or near streets.[119] For twenty of the years between 1678 and 1699 the court charged Cornelius Fells with having such a midden.

At that same meeting held in the parish church two overseers of the poor for the town were elected, and although they are not mentioned in court leet records until 1675, they are noted every year from 1687 to the end of the century.[120] The Eight Men were elected on St Luke's Day (18 October), and four inhabitants of Prescot served as many as three annual terms during the 1640s. Parishioners also then chose four wardens who served the grammar school in Prescot, located on modern Church Street.[121] In 1641 Edward Stockley was selected to serve from Prescot with three wardens from Eccleston, Rainhill and Whiston.[122]

There was some overlap, with the same person filling two or more offices in any given year. During the 1640s the affeerors (who assessed amercements) were always chosen from among the presentment jurors, and on average three of the Four Men were also jurors, and an annual average of two jurors served with both the Four Men and affeerors. Presentment jurors relied heavily on the Four Men, who 'have always beyond the Memory of Man' been chosen at the court leet, two by the steward and two by the jury.[123] Rather than perceiving this overlap as self-perpetuation, it may be more accurate to view the Four Men as a subcommittee of the full jury that was almost four times larger, a subcommittee that contained on average one outsider or non-juror.

In 1643 Edward Stockley was a presentment juror, coroner and clerk for both the court leet and baron and the parish church. Particular families were especially

---

118. LRO: DDCs/Paper Book/1638. Supervisors submitted their first presentments in 1671 and others in 1672, 1683 and 1694. For their accounts for 1631–36 see LRO: DDCs and DDKc/PC 4/66/Paper Books/1636 and 1637. Their accounts for 1749 will be found in LRO: QSP 1629/30, Epiphany 1750. For the duties of supervisors, see William Lambard, *The Duties of Constables, Borsholders, Tithing Men* (London, 1583; Da Capo Press, Theatrum Orbis Terrarum Ltd, Amsterdam and New York, 1969), pp. 52–61. The statute referred to was 2 and 3 Philip and Mary, c.8; also see 5 Eliz., c.13.
119. See, for example, these paper books at LRO: DDKc/PC 4/154/1674–76, DDCs/1678 and DDKc/PC 4/126/1683. In 1683 alone supervisors presented about fifty individuals for non-payment of leys for highway repair.
120. Overseers of the poor were first mentioned in the churchwardens' accounts of 1606–07. Bailey, *Churchwardens' Accounts of Prescot*, p. 154. During the 1640s justices of the peace issued quite a few orders to the churchwardens and overseers of the poor of the parish of Prescot to maintain specific individuals. LRO: QSR/37–43.
121. F.A. Bailey [to 1944], G. Dixon [1944–70] and J.C.S. Weeks [1971], *Prescot Grammar School, 1544–1971* [Birkenhead, n.d.p. (1970s)]; Bailey, 'Prescot Grammar School in Elizabethan Times: a Sidelight on the Reformation in Lancashire', *THSLC*, 86 (1934), pp. 1–20.
122. Knowsley Central Library in Huyton: PGS Archives 37, f.4. The appointment of four school-wardens was discontinued during the 1630s because those annually elected were 'Gentlemen of Fortune in the Neighbourhood of Prescot who paid little or no attention to the duties of the Office....' LRO: DP/377, ff.64–5.
123. THC: 'Minute Book', f.2; 'Charities', f.56; LRO: DDKc/PC 4/137/Paper Rolls/1731 and 1740.

active in Prescot's affairs. Between 1604 and 1659, only 1627 experienced no Alcock (William, his son John, sen., or his grandson John, jun.) serving as an officer of the court leet.[124]

In short, while some inhabitants each year served in several offices, the many and diverse positions required that a good number of residents and some non-residents participate in governing Prescot. As population increased, the pool from which officers could be selected enlarged as well, and in 1775 the court ordered 'for this Mannor that one person shall hold no more than One Office at one time.'[125]

The Four Men also constituted an oversight committee to see that jurors' orders were obeyed and constables' accounts reviewed. While the former duty must have kept the Four Men busy, the latter responsibility was not an inconsiderable task. Constables' accounts covering June 1664 to July 1665, for example, contain 113 entries dealing with receipts and disbursements and the names of 163 persons, with some repetition, for various unpaid taxes.[126] In addition, the Four Men reviewed the accounts of the surveyors of the highways and accepted security from anyone who took up residence in Prescot that they would not become financially burdensome to the town and would depart within three months of a notice from the Four Men. They gave permission to inhabitants to cut timber in Prescot Wood or to remove dung from highways, or to constables to dispense financial assistance to travellers. They also reviewed repairs to buildings, highways and wells and assessed leys. Obviously, they made presentments relating to the foregoing matters, and, with the steward, at least two of the Four Men possessed a key to the town chest containing the records of the court.

The officers most likely to be encountered by residents of Prescot were the two constables. Not surprisingly, this office was the most difficult to fill.[127] The twenty slots available between 1640 and 1649 were filled by eighteen individuals; only Nicholas Anderton and Peter Herefoote served twice. Moreover, for five of the ten years nominees had to be threatened up to three times with amercements as high as £5 to force them to take their oath of office. In 1644 Herefoote and John Parr took their oaths three months after the court had met in June and after they had defaulted three times and had been amerced 40s, then £3 6s 8d and finally £5; there is no indication that these amounts were ever cancelled. In 1645 a nominee, James Sadler, while ultimately not sworn, declined to serve and uttered 'scandalous words in open court' and was amerced 40s.

In comparison, between 1602 and 1659 eighty-four individuals filled 115 constabulary positions (in 1651 Lawrence Lathom died in office and was replaced in October by Henry Eaton). During those fifty-eight years (fifty-seven, actually, since the constables for 1607 are unknown), 75 percent of constables served only once.

---

124. LRO: DDCs/Paper Book/1627.
125. THC: 'Charities', f.23.
126. LRO: DDKc/PC 2/22.
127. A perusal of the records of quarter sessions and courts leet for seventeenth-century Lancashire located sixty-nine townships which chose constables by house-row, nine including Prescot by courts or specific individuals, and two townships which changed from nomination by individuals to selection by house-row. House-row involved rotation among occupiers of tenements.

While the position was always burdensome, it was more so during the troubled 1640s when residents were even more reluctant to serve.[128] Further, while four who served in the 1620s also officiated in the 1630s and while four who served in the 1630s also took their oath in the 1640s, only one (Thomas Walls) who served in the troubled 1640s returned in the next decade for another stint in office. Finally, in contrast to the 1640s when one nominee defaulted and seven were threatened with or assessed amercements designed to compel them to serve, in the 1630s the court threatened only one nominee and officers set an amercement of 40s on another who was never sworn.

The duties of a constable in Prescot included presenting for unlawful gaming, eavesdropping, harbouring persons of 'evill Cariadge' (who were usually women), refusals to quarter a soldier or to participate in the watch, and breaches of the peace, a very important function at Prescot where between 1602 and 1659 some 1,762 persons (counting recidivists) were so accused at Prescot's leet and an additional twenty-four were presented to the quarter sessions. Constables also conducted hue and cry, executed warrants sent to Prescot, conveyed alleged offenders to justices of the peace for examination and, if necessary, conveyed the accused to the house of correction in Preston (or to the house of correction in Wigan during the first two decades of the seventeenth century[129]) or to the gaol in Lancaster. Constables also kept in good condition the 'instruments of justice' and collected leys.[130]

Being a constable was an unpleasant and at times even dangerous task. At the 1645 general court Peter Hearefoote, whom we have already met as a reluctant nominee, reported having a piece of the end of his finger cut off with a pocket dagger when attempting to stop an affray. His fellow constable, John Parr, also reluctant to serve, had his head broken in a different affray when he tried to end a breach of the peace. In 1646 constable Ralph Plumpton reported to the court that fourteen named individuals had verbally abused him during his year in office, including Edward Booth, who had entered Ralph's house and abused him in words and deeds, and that two of these persons had struck him and his fellow constable. Both constables presented four more residents for slanderous words against them.

However, the principal disincentive to serving in the office of constable was financial. Whenever disbursements exceeded receipts, constables found it necessary after leaving office to request and often to fight for reimbursement. At Prescot between 1679 and 1699, 55 percent of the annual constables' accounts were in the red when presented to jurors for review. Reimbursement could depend upon

128. For examples of constables in Lancashire experiencing economic difficulties during the Civil War, see LRO: QSR/40, Wigan, Epiphany 1646; QSR/41, Ormskirk, Easter 1647; QSB/1/272/23, Easter 1646; QSP/23/29, Michaelmas 1649.
129. LRO: DDCs/Paper Book/1617.
130. For a critical and yet sympathetic evaluation of the duties of constables, see Joan R. Kent, *The English Village Constable, 1580–1642: a Social and Administrative Study* (Oxford, Clarendon Press, 1986).

the fiscal strength of tax-paying inhabitants.[131] At Prescot in 1643 jurors presented for taxes in arrears roughly one in seven who owed suit and service and in 1655 one in six. In 1647 leet jurors claimed that negligence on the part of constables led to taxes going uncollected.

Perhaps the relative difficulty of filling each type of office at Prescot during the troubled 1640s may be illustrated by noting how often the court exerted pressure to encourage nominees to take their oath of office and prodded sworn officers to attend general and adjourned courts. Twelve individuals nominated to the presentment jury were each amerced 6s 8d and not sworn; another nominee was amerced and then sworn; six more were sworn and amerced,[132] but five of these amercements were later cancelled; and three other nominees who were eventually sworn either 'denied' or failed to appear at an adjourned court. For the position of constable the court threatened two nominees (later sworn) with an amercement of up to £5; amerced two sworn constables up to £5 for not appearing at adjourned courts; amerced a nominee 40s for declining to take his oath and threatened to amerce for the same another nominee who eventually took his oath; and at a general court ordered two sworn constables to appear a week later at an adjourned court or pay 40s. But for all other officers only two sealers of leather and one leygatherer needed to be prodded into office by an amercement or the threat thereof.

Turning to the two sealers of leather, they presented traders who sold or attempted to sell unsealed leather or leather not sufficiently tanned and who mixed cow and horse leather. Sometimes they also presented buyers. Two clerks of the market presented individuals who forestalled the market or sold unlawful meat, including in 1648 beef not marketable because it was 'deade before of some desease' and in 1643 a calf not fit to be sold because it had died 'in guelding'.[133] The two burleymen presented owners and renters of property for unlawful hedges and hayments and unrung swine. Two streetlookers, sometimes called streetlookers and well lookers, presented those who polluted wells, did not clean the street in front of their house, and were careless with their midden near their front door.

The coroner, of course, with the assistance of a jury, investigated suspicious deaths. In the coroner's inquisition of 1642 sixteen jurors declared that James

---

131. At Manchester between 1612 and 1647 some 38 percent of constables' accounts were in the red when presented to the court leet. J.P. Earwaker, ed., *The Constables' Accounts of the Manor of Manchester*, 1 and 2 (Manchester, Cornish, 1891, 1892); computations are mine.
132. Possibly all but one may have been amerced for failing to attend an adjourned court.
133. On 20 June 1637 William Webster of Eccleston purchased one bay mare for £3 from Godfrey Shaw of Lincolnshire on Tuesday, the market day. LRO: DDCs/ Paper Book/1637. Tuesday remained the market day in 1795. John Aikin, *A Description of the Country from Thirty to Forty Miles Round Manchester*, 1st ed. (London, John Stockdale, 1795; New York, Kelley, 1968), p. 310. In 1836 the market days were Tuesday and Saturday. Edward Baines, *History of the County Palatine and Duchy of Lancaster*, 3 (London, New York & Paris, Fisher, Son & Co., 1836), p. 704. Also see G.H. Tupling, 'An Alphabetical List of the Markets and Fairs of Lancashire Recorded Before the Year 1701', Lancashire and Cheshire Antiquarian Society, 51 (1936), p. 104.

Lyon of Whiston had between 6 and 7 in the evening of 16 May 1642 acciden-
tally fallen into a well at the back of William Hough's house and drowned. The
inquisition of July 1628 found that Evan Pike, an exceptionally troubled young
man as the records of the 1620s demonstrate, had been the cause of his own death
and therefore had forfeited his possessions to the lord of the manor.[134] Either
John Alcock, sen., or John Alcock, jun., served as coroner between 1625 and
1657 except for the nine years that Edward Stockley filled that position.

Two alefounders or aletasters, called 'Overseers of the Weights of Bread and
Measures of Beer' in 1699,[135] enforced the assizes of ale and beer and bread.[136]
They were responsible for seeing that these commodities were of sufficient quality and quantity. In 1644 they accused John Hoole, his wife and two others of
refusing to allow them to taste their drink. In general they presented residents
who sold ale and beer not according to the assize, and year after year for the
most part they presented the same persons.[137] In every year between 1626 and
1695, except 1644, first Thomas Bond (died 1645), then his widow Ellen
('infirme' in 1658), after her death their son James (died 1690), and finally his
widow Margery (died 1709) were presented for 'breaking the assize of ale'.[138]
The amercement, usually 12d, essentially constituted a local licensing fee and
did not represent wrongdoing, which was submitted to the court in presentments
separate from this annual list.

In 1646 jurors, in consultation with the steward and constables, allowed eighteen males and seven females, including Ellen Bond, to be alehousekeepers. A
year later jurors complained that more than these twenty-five brewed and sold ale
and beer. In 1651 the jury proposed that the steward license twenty-seven
alehousekeepers; someone later added 'ly' for 'lycensed' next to all but three
names. Ellen and the other twenty-three entered into bonds of £10 each, supported by two sureties of £5 each, to keep an orderly alehouse.[139] After this list

134. LRO: DDCs/Paper Book/June 1629. Unfortunately, seventeenth-century coroners' inquisitions
    have survived only for 1602, 1618 (two) and 1642, and the paper book of 1629 refers to the
    inquest into the suspicious death of Evan Pyke. A volume covering 1746 to 1789 contains infor-
    mation on sixty investigations by coroners. F.A. Bailey, 'Coroners' Inquests Held in The Manor
    of Prescot, 1746–89', *THSLC*, 86 (1935), pp. 21–39.
135. LRO: DDKc/PC 4/53/Paper Book/1699.
136. Acts of 1495 (11 Hen. VII, c.2) and 1552 (5 and 6 Edw. VI, c.25) authorized any two justices
    of the peace to license alehousekeepers. By 1729 (2 Geo. II, c.28) statutory law required that
    the licence be issued by justices in the area of the prospective licensee. Annual licensing was
    required by a royal proclamation of 1619. James F. Larkin and Paul L. Hughes, eds, *Stuart
    Royal Proclamations, Volume 1: Royal Proclamations of King James 1, 1603–1625* (Oxford,
    Clarendon Press, 1973), pp. 409–13. Until 1753 (26 Geo. II, c.31) no statute required annual
    licensing, but by around 1600 it was becoming customary to license yearly. Until 1627 selling
    ale at fairs was legal even without a licence from justices. Prescot's court presented no fair
    brewers until 1669 and in only six more years down to 1700.
137. See Walter J. King, 'Regulation of Alehouses in Stuart Lancashire: an Example of Discretionary
    Administration of the Law', *THSLC*, 129 (1980), pp. 31–46.
138. No presentments of breakers of the assize of ale and beer have survived for 1649, 1656, 1661,
    1663–66, 1673 and 1677.
139. Those bonds survive at the LRO: DDKc/PC 4/6 and PR 3404/14/13. For the paper book for
    1651, see DDKc/PC 4/112.

of twenty-seven names was composed, on a different folio the foreman of the jury, John Alcocke, jun., in the name of all jurors entreated the steward to license Roger Man, too, for he and his wife were born in Prescot and were not burdensome, and, we might add as leet records reveal, he was law-abiding and a good candidate to keep an orderly alehouse. While Roger was not 'lycensed', between 1644 and 1660 he clearly kept an alehouse and beginning in 1645 was annually accused of breaking the assize of ale; in 1644 he was one of the 'poore houses that bruwe at severall times.'

This licensing fee explains why the Earl of Derby, as the lessee of Prescot manor to whom would go the annual fee disguised as an amercement, preferred to license more alehousekeepers than justices of the peace allowed. In 1646, for instance, the Earl or his deputy licensed, as we have seen, twenty-five alehousekeepers, seventeen more than allowed by justices in 1647.[140]

Between 1640 and 1648 an average of thirty-four persons annually were charged with breaking the assize of ale and beer; the range was a low of twenty-eight in 1643 and a high of forty in 1646. The averages for the preceding and following decades were thirty-five and thirty respectively. Assuming that in the 1640s Prescot had 600 to 700 inhabitants, excluding occasional sellers of ale and beer, the town had an alehouse for every seventeen to twenty residents.

As with the assize of ale, Prescot enjoyed the unusual authority to enforce the assize of bread. Two aletasters enforced both assizes and presented to the court leet bakers who sold bread in the market place without a licence from the steward and bakers who failed to follow the law regarding the wholesomeness and weight of bread sold publicly. As in many other localities, 'ineguality and incertentie of measures' was a problem in Prescot, as noted in jurors' orders in 1654 and 1667.[141] Even possessing a measure 'bigger then the standard considerably' was not allowed.[142] Statutory law required local authorities to test the weights and measures of tradespeople against the town's standards that in actuality might differ from the royal ones.[143]

While constables had the difficult responsibility of collecting leys, between 1637 and 1646 and in 1657 and 1660 the court swore in a leygatherer. He submitted no accusations of wrongdoing to the jury and was never ordered to submit presentments or financial accounts. In fact, outside the annual list of officers, he was never mentioned except in 1643 when jurors ordered thirty-four individuals,

140. LRO: QSB/1/288/20, Easter 1647. Here the justices indicated their view of the importance of Prescot as a market centre on a major highway. For the sixty locations in West Derby Hundred noted in the sessional order, only Ormskirk of the other fifty-nine was allowed more alehouses than Prescot's eight; one was permitted seven and three allowed six, and the rest permitted fewer. Justices allowed the other seven townships in Prescot parish a total of eight alehouses, the same number as permitted in Prescot.
141. LRO: DDKc/PC 4/112 and DDKc/PC 4/11/Paper Books/1654 and 1667.
142. LRO: DDCs/Paper Book/1680.
143. Statute 51 Hen. III, c.3; concerning common weights and measures, see 27 Edw. III, c.10; 8 Hen. VI, c.5; 11 Hen. VI, c.8; 7 Hen. VII, c.4; 11 Hen. VII, c.4; 16 Car. I, c.19. Bailey, *Prescot Court Leet*, p. 63.

including Edward Fynney, leygatherer, to pay their leys that were unpaid according to the constables' accounts. It is clear that the Four Men continued to assess leys and constables continued to collect. What exactly the leygatherer did is less clear.

To return to the procedure when the full court met each May or June, presentment jurors were sworn and given their charge, presentment officers, sworn a year earlier, submitted their presentments, and residents were asked to come forward and, under oath, provide information on unlawful, questionable and irritant behaviour that had come to their knowledge. In 1642 Hamlet Whitfeeld informed the steward about scandalous words uttered by Richard Taylor against the Right Honourable the Lord Strange, and at an adjournment held on 22 July three residents gave sworn testimony. Jurors occasionally required some inhabitants, who during the year of their 'own accord' had provided information on alleged wrongdoing to presentment officers, to repeat that information under oath in open court. Falsely accusing and refusing to repeat allegations under oath brought severe punishment.[144]

For the most part, though, jurors received information on alleged misbehaviour from fellow officers chosen by jurors at the previous annual general court. To judge by the date on a few folios containing presentments, some officers submitted their accusations after the general court had adjourned. Most presentments, however, were written up before court met and were probably copied from rough notes kept during the year; very rarely for the sevententh century both those rough notes and the version submitted to the court have survived in paper books.[145]

The court records make clear that some residents accused of unlawful activity were present in the court house. Their presence should not surprise us. Some suitors whose names had been called by the bailiff an hour or two earlier may have remained and a number of those with a surrender to submit to the court in the afternoon may also have attended the morning session. In addition, many of those about to be presented for alleged wrongdoing must have suspected their impending presentment and some attended to plead their cases. After all, since the last court, presentment officers had warned individuals, sometimes several times, to alter behaviour or risk presentment.

Also, not only had some residents of Prescot earlier in the court year verbally abused officers issuing warnings, but other inhabitants uttered 'undecent woordes' to officers and even to the steward in open court when presentments were read. At Upholland it was an offence to talk in the court house when the court was in session, except when called to answer a question from the court.[146] To underscore further that at least some residents knew of the impending charges against them, leet jurors at Wigan in 1649 continued to another day those cases involving

---

144. King, 'Leet Jurors', p. 316 and note 59.
145. The process of fact-finding is again revealed when these two lists of presentments are compared, and it is discovered that some names were dropped, presumably because the accusation was doubtful.
146. LRO: DDHi/Paper Books/1609 and 1610.

witnesses required to give evidence in court and involving persons accused of misdemeanours who had failed to attend court and ordered their attendance at a future date.[147]

The court next asked plaintiffs with pleas, submitted before court met, and the defendants to approach. During the three weeks between the bailiff's call for 'plaints' to be submitted and the meeting of the court, from 1615 to 1635 individuals sent 1,047 pleas to the court. Of the 893 with a recorded decision, in 380 or 42.6 percent plaintiffs and defendants reached an agreement; in the remaining 513 cases, or 57.4 percent, jurors-between-parties imposed a settlement. These jurors always numbered twelve, though between 1615 and 1635 the bailiff annually nominated an average of nineteen individuals. While tenants including non-residents served as presentment jurors, residents, commonly subtenants, officiated as jurors-between-parties.

Having accomplished a great deal of work, court adjourned until the afternoon. Presentment jurors, officers and (deputy) steward walked to a nearby alehouse and dined at the expense of the ratepayers of Prescot. The court at Prescot ordered in 1757 and restated in 1772 that officers and jurors each be allowed one shilling for their dinners and directed that 'the ale or porter shall be equally bore and paid by the Officers and Jurymen', while those choosing other alcoholic drinks 'shall pay for it themselves'.[148] At a public meeting in 1767 those present resolved that future juries on every general court day shall dine in 'the Town hall'.[149] Bills for this meal have survived for 1901–13 when in eleven years participants dined at the King's Arms Hotel and in one year (1907) at the Royal Hotel; in the other (1909) the list did not specify the location. The number of diners ranged between fourteen and nineteen, with an average of sixteen. Besides a meal, on average each person enjoyed 70 percent of a bottle of alcohol (sherry, claret, brandy, whisky, wine, champagne and port) as well as a glass of liquor, and drank one cup of coffee and smoked two and a half cigars.[150] Obviously, the type of alcohol consumed would have been different in the seventeenth century, and at Upholland in 1609, 1622 and 1630 ale constituted about 20 percent of the total average expense for such meals for the steward and leet jurors; over a four-day period in 1609 they consumed 144 quarts of ale.[151]

Back in the court house the jury, now sequestered, discussed their presentments and those of other officers in order to eliminate the doubtful and the false. This process of sifting accusations, revealed, as has been noted, only in paper books, is demonstrated by marginalia, cancelled entries and actual statements by jurors. Between 1615 and 1678 at Prescot jurors decided that ninety-two accusations were doubtful and added in the margin 'quere (inquire) for evidence', 'respited because

147. WRO: CL/Wi.—7.
148. THC: 'Charities', ff.44–5 and 105.
149. THC: 'Charities', f.97.
150. Bills are at THC. At Wigan in 1672 the court prohibited the taking of tobacco into the room where and when jurors assemble. WRO: CL/Wi.—35.
151. LRO: DDHi/Paper Book/1609.

doubtfull', 'respited till further examination', or 'respited until next Court'. When neighbour was judging neighbour, these jurors were deliberative and reasonable, not galling, and they were quite concerned to avoid slandering the accused.[152] Ultimately, of those ninety-two presentments, jurors determined that sixty-nine were true, and affeerors later assessed amercements, while the other twenty-three individuals incurred no punishment. Some of these decisions, of course, may have been made at adjournments.

During the afternoon discussion some lively debate occurred and occasionally a juror departed in a huff before all certain verdicts had been reached and was later amerced. Divulging 'the secrets' or deliberations of jurors, contrary to their oath, incurred an amercement. That jurors declared most accusations of wrong-doing true should not surprise us. The cancelled accusations in presentment chits submitted by various officers to the court demonstrate that some sifting had occurred before jurors began deliberating guilt or innocence. While deliberating between 1615 and 1678 jurors cancelled thirty-six of their own presentments.[153]

Besides railing against the court the accused could react to an accusation by pleading not guilty, as vicar John Aldem did in 1641 and as two other residents of Prescot did in 1642, the only obvious pleas of not guilty during the entire seventeenth century. During that century no one accused of misbehaviour by Prescot's court pleaded not guilty by entering a 'traverse', but traverses do appear in the court records at Upholland, Clitheroe and other courts leet.[154] It is possible that more not guilty pleas were made and not entered into Prescot's court records as traverses but, for example, as 'quere for evidence' or 'respited till further examined'.[155]

After the jurors had deliberated, the steward next administered oaths to the officers, including affeerors, nominated by jurors and the steward to serve until the next annual general court. The four affeerors (two before 1616) immediately began their task of assessing amercements.[156] During the 1640s affeerors always came from the presentment jurors and predominantly from the top half of the list of nominees for jury duty and almost always included the foreman of the jury. These

---

152. For a more detailed discussion of this assessment of jurors and other officers, see King, 'Leet Jurors'.
153. The thirty-six are in addition to the ninety-two and exclude presentments struck out because they duplicate those by other officers.
154. LRO: MBC/163 for 1593; MBC/196 for 1653; MBC/256 for 1699; DDHi/Paper Book/1609; Cl/Parchment Roll/1660. At Etchells in Cheshire five residents entered traverses in 1667 alone, three of whom ultimately were found not guilty. Manchester City Central Library: M10/20/2b.
155. Regarding the legality of traversing a leet presentment, see King, 'Leet Jurors', p.321 and note 84.
156. Affeerors were 'jurors sworn to *affeere...*the *general* amercement according to the *particular* circumstances of the offence and the offender.' William Blackstone, *Commentaries on the Laws of England*, 4 (Oxford, 1769; Chicago, University of Chicago Press, 1979), p. 373. At Upholland 'the affearinge of the verdicte' occurred on the last of four days of court meetings. LRO: DDHi/Paper Books/1626 and 1630. Muchland in Lancashire held two annual courts leet in April or May and October, generally one court baron in January or February, and an 'affearing court' in September or October. Cumbria Record Office in Barrow-in-Furness: BD/HJ/202/8–20.

four individuals had already spent much time and energy with their fellow jurors deciding guilt or innocence, and the deliberations of the full court continued after adjournment among these four regarding uncertain accusations. The process was fluid, as demonstrated when some amercements were decided but later cancelled and new ones, usually lower, were added. Some of the accused, against whose presentments jurors had added 'not certainly knowne' and similar notations, were presumably found innocent by affeerors who never assessed an amercement. Between 1615 and 1678 affeerors voided fifty-three punishments. For instance, in 1654 jurors accused eight residents of refusing to pay an assessment for laying their muck on the lord's waste, and affeerors later amerced each 13s 4d. But a spark of uncertainty remained, and later still someone added 'quere for evidence' in the margin, and eventually the court cancelled the punishments.[157] After deliberating, affeerors assessed amercements on those who had been found guilty either at the full court or as a result of their investigations and added the amounts above the name of the guilty or at the end of the presentment. Sometimes, as if to justify their decision to amerce, affeerors added 'upon warninge', that is, the presentment officer had warned to no avail that behaviour needed to be altered. The few accusations that remained doubtful could be resolved at future adjournments.

In 1682 and 1683 jurors accused William Plombe of bringing into Prescot Elizabeth Birchall, wid., and her child and failing to give bond to prevent the town from suffering financially. No amercement was ever imposed, but in the margin next to the presentment for 1683 was added: 'The afferers are satisfyed that the Jury were misinformed as to this presentment.' This year's four affeerors were also the first four sworn jurors, and, as if to demonstrate the close relationship between affeerors and jurors, these affeerors mistakenly began their marginal note with 'The Jury', which they cancelled.[158]

Wrongdoers in Prescot were almost always assessed an amercement which the bailiff collected; failure to pay could result in the guilty being placed in the stocks or in the distraining of their animals. Unfortunately, it is not possible to determine compliance with punishment, as it is at the leets at Walton-le-Dale and Upholland where officers added 'done' or 'not done', 'performed' or 'not performed', 'punyshed', 'payed' (the amercement), 'pardoned by Mr Stewarde' or 'not to be founde' in the margin next to or at the end of many orders for punishment and next to threats to punish if certain behaviour continued.[159] Occasionally, the 'not' was later struck through. In 1609 the court at Upholland appointed eight persons including the bailiff to assist constables and churchwardens in executing orders for punishment and reporting to the next court whether amercements had been collected and corporal punishments carried out.[160]

157. LRO: DDKc/PC 4/112/Paper Book/1654. Also see DDKc/PC 4/112/Paper Book/1651.
158. LRO: DDKc/PC 4/126/Paper Book/June 1683.
159. LRO: DDHi for Upholland and DDHo for Walton-le-Dale. Upholland's court records are parchment rolls and paper books containing some loose and pinned papers.
160. LRO: DDHi/Paper Books/1607, 1610 and 1612.

While not informing us whether punishments were performed, Prescot's court records do contain numerous references to individuals, presented and amerced at a previous court, continuing misbehaviour that merited another and larger amercement. In 1650 jurors reduced a number of uncollectable amercements from previous years to smaller but presumably collectable amounts,[161] but again, the court records do not inform us whether the bailiff was able to collect the new amercements.

At Prescot 'Instruments of Justice' included stocks, pillory, ducking stool, cuckstool and rogues' post. The 'Ducking stoole' was not mentioned until 1700 and was then only noted by constables as being in good repair in a list in which in previous years the word 'cuckstool' had been employed instead.[162] Hence, though the two stools were originally different, by 1700 at Prescot the terms may have become synonymous.[163] The ducking stool was next mentioned in 1750 when it was moved from 'Prescott Moss' to the far end of Sparrow Lane where there was 'a constant Supply of water the Year about.'[164] The 'cuckstool pit', also a watering place for cattle during the seventeenth century, was located at the far east end of modern Eccleston Street.[165]

Although specific individuals were in 1609 and 1621 threatened with their use and on a number of occasions constables reported to juries that they were in good repair, court leet records for the seventeenth century yield no evidence that at Prescot the pillory, both stools and whipping post were ever used; in their account year of 1664–65 constables paid 6d 'for a whipp by the stewards appointment', which likewise had no documented use; nor did a cuckstool that jurors in 1676 ordered to be constructed.[166] While the missing constables' accounts might contain notes on their use, the five extant accounts only mention spending, besides 6d for a whip, 3d 'for mendinge the cockstole' in 1605–06.[167]

The stocks, however, were used, and in 1616 the court ordered Evan Finny to sit in them for six hours on two Sundays or pay 2s for collecting underwood in Prescot Wood.[168] Between 1614 and 1669, when the first and last imprisonments were mentioned in the court records of the seventeenth century, twenty-six persons

---

161. LRO: DDCs/Paper Book/1650.
162. LRO: DDKc/PC 4/115/Paper Book/1700.
163. Leet jurors at Upholland sometimes offered offenders the choice of paying an amercement or being 'wasshed in the water upon the Cookestoole.' LRO: DDHi/ Paper Books/1602 and 1607, for example.
164. LRO: DDKc/PC 6/151/Paper Roll/1750.
165. Where it was still located in 1772. LRO: DDKc/PC 6/230/Parchment Roll. Also see DDCs/Paper Book/1678.
166. LRO: DDCs/Paper Books/1609 and 1621; DDKc/PC 2/22/1664–65; and DDKc/PC 4/154/Paper Book/May 1676. However, justices of the peace ordered residents of Prescot to be branded in 1632 and whipped in 1639 and 1652. LRO:QJI/2/4, Ormskirk, Midsummer 1632; QSB/1/222/38, Wigan, Michaelmas 1639; QSR/45 and QJI/1/25, Wigan, Epiphany 1652.
167. LRO: DDCs/Paper Book/1606.
168. LRO: DDCs/Paper Book/1616.

were 'imprisoned', including eight during the 1640s.[169] Eight of these twenty-six entries indicate that the prison was the court house, which contained a pair of stocks in which offenders, commonly those in need of restraint, were placed. The court placed one misdemeanant in the stocks or prison for one hour, another for four, and a third for ten hours, and five for a whole night. Escapes from these stocks and/or the court house occurred in 1614, 1622 (two persons), 1634 (three persons), 1639, 1644 and 1657. A second pair of stocks was located in the market place where the whipping or rogues' post also stood.[170]

In addition to these twenty-six, the court placed two other persons in the stocks, set two in the stocks in the court house, and 'punished' nine more; in a few cases 'punished' seems to have meant set in the stocks. These thirty-nine individuals are the only misdemeanants in seventeenth-century Prescot to have received a recorded punishment other than monetary. Some thirty-five of these thirty-nine were accused of breach of the peace. Commonly those so charged supplied another person who pledged 'to answeare the Fyne if an Assalt was proved' and if found guilty were assessed an amercement of 12d, or 3s 4d if blood was drawn.[171] When in 1657 Henry Cheshire and Thomas Birchall, both of Burtonwood, about seven miles to the east, tussled on the fair day and could not locate pledges in Prescot, the steward forced them to pay 12d upfront, that is, before they were presented at the next general court and possibly found guilty, which ultimately they were. Since only two of these thirty-five offered a pledge to constables, perhaps we may conclude that corporal punishment and/or imprisonment replaced the pledge. In 1644, for instance, Richard Angsdale, one of these two, was set in the stocks in the court house, and only after Gilbert Heyes became his 'bayle' did the court release him.[172]

In 1616 jurors charged the wife of Richard Taylyer with 'uncyvill and ill manered speeches' against Mrs Tarbock. Because her husband was of 'pore estate', jurors recommended that the steward decree corporal punishment. It is tempting to conclude that Prescot's relative prosperity as a market centre for the area contributed to the clear preference for monetary over corporal punishment.[173]

---

169. While Edward Coke is sometimes cited as denying courts leet the right to imprison (Bailey, 'Court Leet of Prescot', p. 73), Coke did allow leets to imprison for offences committed in court. Edward Coke, *The Compleate Copy-Holder* (London, 1641), pp. 39–43. At Wigan 'Dangerous prisoners' were imprisoned in 'the Counsell house in the Moath hall', which had a pair of stocks. WRO: CL/Wi.—7; also see CL/Wi.—3 and 38.
170. At Wigan seventeenth-century leet records provide evidence that there the cuckstool and especially the stocks were employed, while whippings and wearing the bridle were rare; the court amerced most offenders. WRO: CL/Wi.—1–84 (to 1700). The court leet at Upholland offered many offenders the choice of paying an amercement or being placed in the stocks. LRO: DDHi/Paper Books/*passim*.
171. LRO: DDCs/Paper Book/1637.
172. 'Bayle' was employed four times in 1685 in the constables' presentments of tussles. LRO: DDCs/Paper Book/1685.
173. LRO: DDCs/Paper Book/1616. Earlier in 1570 jurors ordered that 'younge men... which have noe money to paye theire amerciaments' for disturbing the peace shall be set in the stocks. This order hints of a preference for monetary punishment. Bailey, *Prescot Court Leet*, p. 177.

These transcriptions of the court records of the 1640s reveal a number of individuals appearing nearly year after year accused of various offences. A question that begs to be asked is: How effective were the court leet at Prescot and leets elsewhere at controlling misbehaviour?[174] A colourful yet tragic example is that of Evan Pyke. The court that met on 13 June 1623 charged him with twenty-five affrays and tussles with, or mostly on, twenty-seven different individuals and with six other incidents of foul words, abuse or drunkenness for which affeerors amerced him the considerable sum of £3 13s; he was drunk in twenty-one of these thirty-one cases. Verbally abused in open court by Pyke, the steward on that same day wrote to 'Sir William' that Prescot 'Rather desire(s) his absence then otherwyse to be dayly in troble with hym.' 'Sir William' may be William Norris of Speke, knight, a justice of the peace. A justice of the peace did bind Evan in a recognizance to appear in July at the sessions of the peace, but Evan defaulted.[175] Before the court in 1629 reported Evan's suicide in late 1628, annual courts accused him of another thirty-one breaches of the peace.

Limited in the severity of punishment they could dispense, courts leet must have occasionally experienced great exasperation. Leet jurors at Wigan in 1663 declared that they 'can find noe way to punish (Richard Crosse, labourer, for assault) according to his desert.' They temporarily imprisoned him in the 'Moot hall' and entreated the mayor of Wigan, a justice of the peace, to send him to the house of correction in Preston. Jurors made similar requests regarding other offenders in 1678, 1679 and 1681.[176]

Finally, having sworn in a new set of presentment officers, the steward accepted surrenders made 'out of court' since the last annual court or that were being made at the current court. Since surrenders consumed a fair amount of the court's time and constituted 53 percent of the sheets in paper books between 1640 and 1648, a few comments about them are in order. One or more surrenderers appeared out of court before up to seven witnesses (as in 1644) but more commonly three and for a variety of reasons (money, 'love and affection', 'good reasons') surrendered property to the lord of the manor who regranted it back to the surrenderer or another for rents and services that may or may not be specified. Usually manorial rents were due on the feasts of the Nativity of St John the Baptist and the Nativity of Our Lord in equal portions. A tenant by copyhold could pass land to his family or to another acceptable to the manorial lord.

When the surrender was presented in open court, the bailiff asked whether anyone objected to the admittance, and if no one came forward to object, admittance

---

174. For a well researched study of this issue during an earlier period, see Marjorie Keniston McIntosh, *Controlling Misbehavior in England, 1370–1600* (Cambridge, Cambridge University Press, 1998). Also see Keith Wrightson and David Levine, *Poverty and Piety in an English Village: Terling, 1525–1700* (Oxford, Academic Press, 1979, 1995), ch. 5, 'Conflict and Control: the Villagers and The Courts', pp. 110–41.
175. LRO: DDCs/Paper Book/1623; QSR/20, Ormskirk, Midsummer 1623.
176. WRO: CL/Wi.—20, 45, 46 and 49.

was granted.[177] But if someone pleaded in bar, a day was given for pleading. The court records of the 1640s also contain several 'recoveries' or fictitious actions to protect property.[178] Once the steward and jurors had approved the admittance, the clerk of the court enrolled the surrender onto parchment, then on paper that may have contained corrections or insertions, placed the parchment roll containing all surrenders into the town chest, and for a fee of 12d,[179] and because Prescot manor was copyhold, gave at the next court a copy of the admittance to the individual admitted.

In some cases the surrendered property was employed as security for a loan, and if the original amount or principal and sometimes an additional amount or interest were paid, then the surrender was void. The surrender by Thomas Halsall in August 1648 actually employed the word 'principall' and declared the surrender void if a year later he paid £13 10s, of which £12 10s was principal. Other surrenders were intended to pass property to children after the death of parents or to the wife, if she became a widow.

Lastly, during the seventeenth century, when Prescot's courts leet and baron regulated the behaviour of up to approximately seven hundred residents, court officials probably struggled to complete the court's business in one day, business that took the steward and jurors four days at Upholland. Since some presentments still required more investigation, additional courts were held by adjournment so that jurors could 'perfect their verdict'. Prescot's courts adjourned an average of three times each year between 1640 and 1648; one year (1644) experienced eight, while another (1641) witnessed six. Between 1637, when the first adjournment was recorded, and 1660, the average number of adjournments per year was also three. At the court held on 30 May 1651 jurors were ordered to meet and perfect their verdicts on 22 July and to deliver those verdicts to the steward by 7 in the morning on 1 August. Jurors were further adjourned to 22 August and then to 3 October, each time on pain of 13s 4d.[180] By the 1680s and 1690s the court also employed adjournments to swear in one or more officers.

---

177. For what constitutes 'a good Surrender [and]...a good Admittance', see Charles Calthrope, *The Relation Betweene the Lord of a Mannor and the Coppy-Holder His Tenant* (London, 1635; New York, Da Capo Press, 1972), pp. 56–64. In 1666 at Clitheroe a surrender was void if made out of court and not presented to the court within nine months, and if the copyholder was not of 'sound memory' at the time of the surrender. LRO: DP 482/la. Similar customs prevailed in 1686 at the manor of Ightonhill, Burnley and Colne. LRO: DDB/42/4.
178. For 'common recovery' or 'plea of land', see A.A. Dibben, *Title Deeds: 13th–19th Centuries*, The Historical Association No. 72 (London, 1968, 1971), pp. 19–21; Blackstone, *Commentaries*, 2, pp. 117, 357–64, and 4, p. 422.
179. LRO: DDCs/Paper Book/1628. For a calendar of thirty fees charged at the court leet and borough court at Clitheroe in 1666, including 2s 6d for a parchment copy of an admittance, see LRO: DP 482/1a. For a table of fees at courts baron, see LRO: DDK/Bundle 1505/11 for 1733 at Bootle-cum-Linacre, DDBa/ Division 8/Bundle 12 for 1733 at Winstanley, and for 1774 at Prescot see THC: 'A Table of the Fees for the Court Baron of Prescot.' In 1774 a commentator claimed that this table of fees, based on 'the Character of the writing', appeared to be over sixty years old. THC: *ibid.*
180. LRO: DDKc/PC 4/112/Paper Book/1651.

THE CIVIL WAR

The first direct reference in Prescot's court records to the troubled times of the 1640s will be found in the proceedings of the adjourned court held on 22 July 1642 when four residents affirmed that on 3 July Richard Taylor of Prescot, 'a dissolute yonge fellow', had declared, 'Let my Lord Strange kisse my Arse' and 'that the Right honorable the Lord Strange had taken away all the Armor and Amunition from Liverpoole and from Manchester and was an upholder of papist.' Actually, Richard was only partially correct: while in June 1642 Lord Strange secured for the king the ammunition and weapons at Liverpool, in June and later in September he tried but failed at Manchester.[181] By the end of the year, however, some did regard Lord Strange as a leader of 'the Popish faction'.[182]

Richard Taylor was born in 1610 to Richard and Elizabeth, who were recusants and poor.[183] When we examine the full names of Richard's accuser and the three witnesses against him – Hamlet Whitfeeld,[184] John Urmeston,[185] Jane Angsdale[186] and Thomas Standish[187] – we find a Thomas Standish, tailor, of nearby Eccleston in lists of recusants from 1630, 1633 and 1640 and a Hamlet Whitfield, a recusant who lived in Prescot in 1604.[188] When we look at only the

---

181. George Ormerod, ed., *Tracts Relating to Military Proceedings in Lancashire During the Great Civil War*, Chetham Society, 2 (1844), pp. xxiv, 16; William E.A. Axon, ed., *The Annals of Manchester: a Chronological Record from the Earliest Times to the End of 1885* (Manchester, J. Heywood, 1886), p. 54; Ernest Broxap, *The Great Civil War in Lancashire (1642–1651)* (Manchester, Manchester University Press, 1910), pp. 16–19.
182. Ormerod, *Tracts*, p. 64.
183. TNA: E/179/131/318 (f.21); CRO: EDV 1/12b (ff.147v and 152v), /13 (f.143r), /14 (ff.103r, 119v and 121r) and /15 (ff.116r and 119v). BIHR: V.1595–6/CB.2 (f.20r). In 1616 his father was described by leet jurors as 'in pore estate'. LRO: DDCs/Paper Book/1616. Richard's widowed mother, Elizabeth, received a subsidy in 1628. TNA: E/179/131/332.
184. A blacksmith, alehousekeeper and yeoman in Prescot, Hamlet was an undertenant whose service to his community included acting as pledge in fourteen breaches of the peace between 1612 and 1638, but his relationship with his neighbours was not always amicable: he himself was before the court for ten breaches of the peace and in twenty-two pleas of debt as plaintiff or defendant. He died in 1646. Robert and Florence Dickinson, eds, *The Register of Prescot Parish Church, Part II: 1632–1666*, LPRS, 114 (1975), p. 96.
185. Between 1611 and 1624 Prescot's court leet charged John with six breaches of the peace and at the quarter sessions with another, and between 1606 and 1628 he was a plaintiff or defendant in fourteen pleas of debt or trespass. Additionally, in 1618 constables accused him and his wife Em of indecent speeches in the street, and in 1620 and 1621 leet officers presented Em for uncivil words. While John's service to and appearances before the court leet occurred before 1642, the data still reveal a person unlikely to remain quiet if he disliked Richard Taylor's remarks. John died in December 1646. LRO: QSR/19, Wigan, Michaelmas 1622; LPRS, 114, p. 97.
186. Jane was married to James Angsdale. See p. 47, note 133 *infra*.
187. The only other reference in the manorial records of the seventeenth century to this Thomas Standish appeared in 1621 when the Four Men charged him with cutting burdens of tinsel in Prescot Wood. A different Thomas Standish appeared in lists of undertenants from 1667–71 and in 1670 was accused of receiving inmates.
188. For Standish, see LRO: QJI/1/17, Epiphany 1641; BIHR: V.1629–30/CB (f.114v) and V.1632–3/CB.2B (f.379v); for Whitfield, CRO: EDV 1/13 (f.132r). Hamlet W. of Prescot died

surnames of the accuser and witnesses, we discover within Prescot recusants with the surnames of Whitfield, Angesdale, Standish and Taylor, in Eccleston with the surnames of Standish and Teylor, in Whiston with Whitfeild, in Windle with Taylor, and in Parr with Teylor and Whitfeild.[189]

James (husband of Jane Angsdale), Hamlet and John were fairly similar in social standing. In lists of individuals owing suit and service at Prescot's manorial court, James's name appeared in the top half of undertenants and as high as third from the top; Hamlet's name also appeared in the top half including first in 1646 and second in 1645. John entered Prescot in 1599 as an inmate, and by 1605 he, his wife Em and daughter Ann rented a cottage on Hall Lane from John Gouldicar. By 1638 his name had risen in lists of suitors from typically in the middle of undertenants to commonly near the bottom of tenants. All three served in a similar number of leet offices: eleven, twelve and eleven respectively. All three experienced some verbal and even physical combat with their neighbours: court leet officers charged James with twenty-six breaches of the peace, Hamlet with ten and John with six. They were also before the court as plaintiff or defendant in pleas of debt and trespass: fourteen, twenty-two and fourteen pleas respectively. In short, that these three individuals shared some time together probably was not unusual, and their temperament may have encouraged some lively discussion that on 3 July included Richard's remarks about Lord Strange.

Concerning Standish and Taylor, except for a Thomas Standish of Prescot who in 1621 was amerced 12d for cutting tinsel in Prescot Wood, this reference in 1642 is the only reference to a Thomas Standish in the manorial records between 1596 and 1666.[190] Richard Taylor does not appear more frequently: except for this entry and another also in 1642, for removing timber from Prescot Wood, Richard does not appear in these manorial records except for three tussles between 1636 and 1640.

Since the evidence is suggestive but far from conclusive, we resort to speculation. Richard Taylor spent part of Sunday, 3 July 1642, at the home of Jane and James Angsdale. Later Hamlet Whitfeild reported Taylor's remarks to 'the Steward' who in 1642 was Thomas Wolfall, esq. On 22 July three sworn witnesses gave evidence about what they and Jane's children had heard Richard say. Because there is no evidence that further legal action was taken against Richard either locally or at the sessions of the peace, perhaps he was just visiting friends, possibly fellow recusants, on a Sunday and the conversation turned to the recent

in March 1646. LPRS, 114, p. 96. Catholicism was quite strong in early seventeenth-century Lancashire, and the manor of Prescot 'was a stronghold of Catholic recusancy.' J.J. Bagley, *A History of Lancashire*, 5th ed. (Henley-on-Thames, Darwen Finlayson, 1970), p. 32; R.C. Richardson, *Puritanism in North-West England: A Regional Study of the Diocese of Chester to 1642* (Manchester, Manchester University Press, 1972), pp. 5–6, 168–9; J.K. Walton, *Lancashire: a Social History, 1558–1939* (Manchester, Manchester University Press, 1987), p. 91. In December 1640 the names of 337 recusants on the Prescot side of Prescot parish were reported to justices of the peace. LRO: QJI/1/17, Epiphany 1641.
189. CRO: EDV 1/12a, 12b, 13–15, 19 and 34; LRO: QJI/1/17, Epiphany 1641; TNA: E 179/131/318.
190. See note 187 *supra.*

military movements of Lord Strange. Richard uttered a few comments that met with some disapproval in Prescot where sympathy for the king was strong.[191] One suspects that during the divisive 1640s such conversations in Prescot, and in the whole of England for that matter, occurred fairly often, and sometimes with similar reactions.

At the next general court of 2 June 1643 jurors ordered constables to demand that inhabitants pay their unpaid leys for soldiers and for arms for the town's use. Immediately prior to that order jurors ruled that the thirty-four individuals who had not fully paid their taxes since the last court of a year ago should do so by 24 August. It was also in 1643 that Nicholas Anderton reluctantly began his year as a constable. Perhaps he perceived trouble ahead. At that same court in 1643 the constables going out of office presented Anthony Prescott and affeerors amerced him 3s 4d because, while drunk, he entered the shop of Anderton and called him a 'traytor' and beat on his window or door. Anderton came forth, assaulted Prescott and drew blood, and Prescott assaulted him back. While it was common to amerce those who assaulted even in self-defence, Anderton was not amerced but Prescott was, in the amount of 3s 4d.

Nothing in the court records stands out as a possible cause of Prescott calling Anderton 'traytor'. We know that it was night and Prescott was drunk. Possibly as he returned home from a night of drinking and conversing about king and Parliament (as reflected locally, of course), he may have made a deliberate effort to arrive at the shop of Nicholas, described in 1641 and 1647 as a mercer. Apparently, Anthony entered, made his remark about 'traytor', left and began to beat at the shop's window or door.

Prescott's behaviour may hint at a person capable of taking a strong position on issues: between 1626 and 1660 affeerors amerced him 25s for ten tussles or affrays, and he was bound at the quarter sessions in 1628 and 1656 in two recognizances to keep the peace.[192] Nicholas, on the other hand, may have been the type who avoided confrontation, as suggested by his behaviour: in 1643 he reluctantly accepted the office of constable, and in 1646 when Evan Hereffotte threw a candlestick at Nicholas and drew blood from his brow, 'Nicholas was houlden and did not stricke.'[193] In contrast to Anthony's twelve breaches of the peace, Nicholas was amerced for only one tussle.[194]

---

191. Because the ringers at Prescot continued into the early 1640s to ring the parish bells on 27 March (the anniversary of the accession of Charles I), because the king's arms were not taken down from the parish church until 1650, and because on the last day of May 1660 the bells were rung before and after the sermon until eight in the evening to celebrate the restoration of Charles II, it is reasonable to conclude that there was some genuine sentiment in Prescot parish for the monarchy. Steel, *Prescot Churchwardens' Accounts*, pp. 69, 85, 143, 198–9, 207.
192. LRO: QSR/25 and QSB/1/38/2, Easter 1628; QSR/50 and QSB/1/1656/16, Michaelmas 1656.
193. Evan, an undertenant, was a shoemaker and alehousekeeper who served his community as sealer of leather for nine years and aletaster for three. Besides this breach of the peace, in 1659 Evan tussled with his brother Thomas and assaulted Edward Darbishire, bailiff, an unusually low number of breaches of the peace. Evan died in 1684. LPRS, 149, p. 111.
194. LRO: DDKc/PC 4/66/Paper Book/June 1639. However, in 1646 the court did charge Nicholas with verbally abusing a constable whom he threatened to strike.

Any civil war encourages the attitude that 'You are either with me or against me.' If, to continue the speculation, Nicholas did not make clear his position on the civil strife then occurring around Prescot, while Anthony was solidly on one side, then we need look no further for a cause of Prescott labelling Anderton 'traytor', especially when alcohol is added to the emotional mix.

Moving on to 1644, there is something different about the paper book for 21 June. Though the officers' titles are plural (clerks of the market, alefounders, and so forth), only one nominee was listed and two of the customary four affeerors, that is, a second group of nominees was never added to the list of officers to serve for the following year. Since constables were not sworn until 13 September, something during late spring and summer of 1644 interrupted the process that usually occurred at Prescot's annual leet. That 'something', of course, was the crossing from Cheshire into Lancashire by Prince Rupert, nephew of Charles I, in late May, the 'massacre of Bolton' on 28 May when royalists under the Prince stormed Bolton, and the Prince marching to Liverpool, which fell to him in mid-June after fierce fighting that took the lives of about 360 inhabitants.[195] On 19 June the Prince left Liverpool for Ormskirk and later the Ribble Valley and the battle of Marston Moor near York on 2 July; by 22 July he was back in Liverpool and in a couple of days he left for Chester.[196]

There are other indicators of something amiss when court met on 21 June 1644. Between 1640 and 1643 problems with swearing in presentment jurors occurred with only one nominee, but in 1644 eight of the fifteen jurors initially defaulted; and, though they eventually took their oaths, six needed persuasion in the form of a threatened amercement of 6s 8d. Also, since between 1640 and 1648 the average number of adjournments was three, even the eight adjournments for the court year 1644–45 was unusual.

In addition, the names of suitors were not called, the only year between 1640 and 1648 when they were not. Furthermore, excluding courts baron meeting at other times of the year, the records of the general courts that met the day after Corpus Christi between 1640 and 1648 averaged twenty-seven sheets, while the record for 1644 has only seventeen, the smallest of the nine paper books. Also, with only three surrenders submitted to the court in June 1644, this general court reviewed the lowest number of any court held in May or June during the decade; the highest was nineteen surrenders recorded in the parchment roll of 1649, while the 1640s as a whole averaged ten per year (excluding admittances following a death).

Interestingly, those officers (two of the Four Men, clerks of the market and streetlookers) who at the 1645 court had 'sworn before' (that is, sworn at the previous court) next to their names had actually been sworn in 1643. Those officers

195. E.B. Sexton, 'Losses of the Inhabitants of Liverpool on the Taking of the Town in 1644', *THSLC*, 91 (1939), pp. 181–91.
196. That 'something' may have added to vicar Richard Day's decision to be absent from Prescot between April 1644 and October 1645. Steel, *Prescot Churchwardens' Accounts*, pp. xxxvii and 109, note 153. Also, it is no coincidence that Prescot's monthly Communion was not observed in July, August and September during 1644. *Ibid.*, p. 105.

with only 'sworn' (one each of burleymen, sealers of leather and alefounders and two affeerors) had been nominated but not sworn in 1644. In other words, the customary assortment of officers was not sworn for the 1644–45 court year. At the court held in 1645 jurors charged the alefounder, Thomas Browne, with not making his presentments; his sworn partner, William Molyneux, was deceased. Those two individuals had been sworn at the 1643 court. It is possible that Browne did not realize that the customary year of service could extend in these unusual times to a second year, or until a replacement had been chosen.[197] Rather than pay an amercement of 40s he belatedly made his presentments, which consisted only of the perfunctory list of breakers of the assize of ale and beer and assize of bread. The only other officers who submitted presentments in 1645, besides jurors, were constables and sealers of leather. Either inhabitants were unusually law-abiding, which can occur during times of war when lawfulness and patriotism are often linked, or the 1644–45 court was barely functioning.

Furthermore, the call books indicate that a number of suitors had left the area. Between 1640 and 1648 an annual average of five were 'out of county' when the court met, but ten, the highest number for any year during the 1640s, were elsewhere when the court met in 1645; and defaulters in appearance to do suit and service annually averaged 10.4 in the 1630s and 7.3 in the 1650s, but a much higher 16.5 in the 1640s.

If Prescot's court was struggling to function in 1644 and possibly in 1645 as well, elsewhere courts did not meet at all. At Walton-le-Dale, for example, there is no evidence that the court leet, which met twice a year, had assembled after October 1642 and before October 1645 when jurors declared that:

Item wheras the distractions of these tymes have occationed the slowing and parte of neclecte *[sic]* in the service requyred by us, And for that wee have not att this tyme receive *[sic]* evident proofe against offendors within this our enquyrie....[198]

Between 1643 and 1645 or 1646 manor courts also did not meet at West Derby, Rishton, Westby-with-Plumptons, Salesbury, Urmston, Newton-with-Scales, Lytham, Salford and Manchester and undoubtedly at other locations as well.[199] We have also already noted that the Lancashire quarter sessions did not meet during the period 1643–45 either. That Prescot's court met and accomplished even minimal work appears atypical.

At the general court that met at Prescot on 6 June 1645 jurors seemed to admit that all was not well. Previous orders, they claimed, for preserving gates, hedges, fences and houses lately had not been enforced by the appropriate officers, and no presentments made, and they therefore ordered enforcement. The context

---

197. At the Epiphany sessions of the peace in 1646 Robert Hesketh and Richard Sumpner of Scarisbrick complained to the justices that they had been unsuccessful in obtaining from the manor court a discharge from their constableship which they had served for two and a half years and requested a discharge from the justices, which was granted. LRO: QSR/40, Wigan, Epiphany 1646.
198. LRO: DDHo for 1645.
199. LRO: QSR/40, Ormskirk, Easter 1646 (West Derby); DDPt/22 (Rishton); DDC1/1141 (Westby

for lax enforcement of by-laws was the housing of royalist prisoners in the parish church in Prescot after the fall of Ormskirk in August 1644, the surrender of Liverpool in November to Parliamentarians[200] and the on-again, off-again siege of Lathom House by Parliamentary forces about a dozen miles to the north.

The general court that met on 29 May 1646 saw more activity relevant to the Civil War. Jurors pointed to 'divers Complayntes...made of the multiplicitie of Alehowses in this towne', complaints that could hint at the existence in Prescot of complainers or reformers who may or may not have had sympathies with 'puritanism'. As we have seen, in 1646 the steward licensed twenty-five inhabitants to keep alehouses, a number which reformers probably thought too many. Jurors next stated that the town owed money to two individuals for three muskets and furniture and owed 24s to Ralph Plumpton for keeping a sick soldier and his father for twenty-four days.

Perhaps most colourful at the 1646 court is the case of John Hoole, his wife Eleanor and their daughter Ellen. We are told that when 'the Princes forces' were in the county in 1644 John brought four soldiers of Sir Thomas Gardner to the house of William Blundell, gent.[201] Upon entering, they forced Mrs Blundell out of her childbed, called her 'Divell and Roundhead whore', and took two silver

and Lytham); DDX/80/1 (Salesbury); QSB/1/277/53, Midsummer 1646 (Urmston); QSP/62/18, Easter 1652 (Newton-with-Scales); Mandley, *Salford*, 2, pp. 73, 80, 102; Earwaker, *Court Leet Records of the Manor of Manchester*, 4, p. 1, note 1.

200. Steel, *Prescot Churchwardens' Accounts*, p. 106. A similar concern about these by-laws was voiced at the 1643 court.

201. Between 1635 and 1660 William Blundell, gent., commonly appeared in the top 20 percent in lists of tenants in call books. He married Margaret, daughter of John Orme of Bold, yeo., in 1627, and to judge by the rental of 1635 and his surrenders in the 1630s, 1640s and 1650s, he was a substantial landowner. Between his first appearance in the manorial records as an officer of the court in 1635 and his last in 1652, he served as presentment juror in seven years, juror at a court baron twice, one of the Four Men seven times, affeeror in seven years, and once each as constable and surveyor of the highways. He also functioned as a feoffee for a charitable bequest and was a witness in twenty-three surrenders. As a prominent parishioner, he served his parish by reviewing churchwardens' accounts for two years, electing officers of the parish once, and twice approving the collection of church leys. His neighbours indicated the high esteem with which they viewed him by nominating him fifteen additional times for service as a manorial officer and for the grand jury at three sessions of the peace. Besides serving as a high constable for West Derby Hundred in 1652, the justices also appointed him in 1649, with Edward Stockley and Henry Marshall, to review the accounts of Prescot's constables for the past seven years. As William gradually reduced his participation in manorial affairs and last served in a leet office in 1652, his son and heir, William, one of eight children, began to serve in various capacities in that same year. In 1661 William the son married Sarah, daughter of Edward Stockley, clerk of Prescot's court. According to the manorial paper book of June 1660, William the father died after the court held in June 1659. While William the father supported Parliament in the Civil War, clearly his political preferences did not adversely affect his participation in the affairs of Prescot where a number of residents strongly favoured the king. LRO: DDCs/Paper Books/DDCs and DDKc/PC 4/11/1637 and 1660; QSR/42, Wigan, Epiphany 1649; QSR/46, Ormskirk, Easter 1652; QJI/1/30, Midsummer 1656 and Epiphany 1657; QJI/1/33, Easter 1659. Steel, *Prescot Churchwardens' Accounts*, pp. 150, 154–5, 157–8; LPRS, 76, p. 126; LPRS, 114, p. 69.

spoons, a hat and 2s in cash and threatened to carry her to the Prince.[202] Mrs Blundell claimed that on other occasions Eleanor had called her 'a Parlyament queane', while Ellen had labelled her 'a Cutt'.

Mrs Tyrer[203] testified that about a month ago John had called her a whore, and Eleanor, who would not let her pass in the street, had called her a 'Parlyament whore', and had criticized the wife of Ralph Houghton[204] for nursing 'a Parlyament whores child'. Giving hearsay evidence from Margaret Oliverson,[205] Mrs Tyrer continued that Ellen had declared that 'If ever the Cavelleers came againe shee would cutt throates as fast as ever shee cutt sheaves of bread.' The constables in turn presented Eleanor for slandering them many times, and the affeerors amerced her 3s 4d.

Why did Blundell, Tyrer and Oliverson wait about two years to report such behaviour to Prescot's court? In June 1645 Parliamentarians defeated royalists at Naseby in Northamptonshire, in September 'the last formal battle of the war'[206] occurred just outside Chester, and in December royalists at Lathom House surrendered. By the time Prescot's court met on 29 May 1646, the king had surrendered to the Scots three weeks earlier. Although at the time people may not have realized that the first Civil War was over, many, including these women, probably only now felt sufficiently secure to bring their complaints against the Hooles, royalists in an area where the king enjoyed considerable support, to the attention of Prescot's court leet. In addition, the record seems to indicate that problems with the Hooles may have worsened in recent months.

---

202. Margaret had most recently given birth to John, who was baptized in January 1641. Several baptisms, possibly as many as eight, for December 1643 have been lost, and 'childbed' may refer to a birth (the recording of which has not survived) or stillbirth. LPRS, 114, p. 30.
203. Probably Margaret Alcock, who in 1625 married Richard Tyrer styled gentleman, clerk and schoolmaster. His name and later her name appeared at or close to 25 percent from the top of tenants' names in call books. That is, the Tyrers and Blundells were reasonably close in social status. William Fergusson Irvine, ed., *Marriage Licences Granted Within the Archdeaconry of Chester in the Diocese of Chester, Vol. III: 1624–1632*, RSLC, lvii (1909), p. 30.
204. There are several Ralph Houghtons in Prescot and Whiston mentioned in the court records who today are not easily distinguished. What appears fairly certain is that this Ralph Houghton entered Prescot around 1634 when jurors noted that he, an inmate, had been 'entertained' and required that he provide security to the Four Men. Between 1635 and 1655 his median position, among a median number of 117 undertenants listed in call books, was tenth from the end, which suggests that he was low on the economic and social spectrum. He always attended the general court when suitors' names were called. Described as a 'wooddenheele maker' in 1651, he resided in a cottage that belonged to the free school of Prescot. He served as an aletaster in 1653 and could not sign his name. Ralph died in 1657, and his wife is not referred to in these court records beyond this one note in 1646. Her wet-nursing another's infant was a means of contributing to the family's income. LRO: DDKc/PC 4/161/Paper Book/1634; DDKc/PC 4/112/Paper Books/1651 and 1653; DDKc/PC 4/54/Paper Book/1658; LPRS, 114, p. 115.
205. For the only other reference in Prescot's manorial records to Margaret Oliverson, see 1645, f.12r, p. 84 *infra*. Her husband, John, was an undertenant always in the bottom fourth in call books between 1638 and 1652 who rented property from Edward Stockley, clerk of Prescot's manorial court. He served in only two manorial offices: as burleyman in 1649 and doorkeeper at the general court in 1650. John was buried in September 1652. LPRS, 114, p. 109.
206. J.P. Kenyon, *The Civil Wars of England* (London, Weidenfeld & Nicolson, 1988), p. 151.

John Hoole first appeared in Prescot's court records in 1619 when he was amerced 12d for a tussle, and in 1620 the court amerced John Appleton for allowing Hoole and his wife, without the consent of the Four Men, to dwell in a house he held of Peter Wyke.[207] John seems to have been a below average participant in the affairs of his adopted town: he served thirteen times as a pledge for persons accused of a breach of the peace, as streetlooker once (1626) and as a juror-between-parties once (1622), but was another five times nominated (1623–28) and apparently declined to serve. He was not a particularly violent individual, and leet officers accused him of tussling only in 1619, 1624, 1627 and 1642 but never of drawing blood. His other offences between 1623 and 1645 were fairly common to his neighbours: defaulting in appearance at the annual court, annoying sink, unlawful gaming in his alehouse, gravel in the street, neglecting the watch, scouring the watering pool, obtaining a warrant from the justices of the peace without local consent, not paying his leys, selling bread in his alehouse that was too light, and not allowing alefounders to taste the ale he sold.[208] John is described as an alehousekeeper, husbandman and once as a yeoman. To judge by his unpaid tax of 9d in 1643, he was not wealthy: the range for the thirty-four persons so accused was 8d to 34s, with an average of 4s 11d.

John may have had a personality that did not accept authority, a personality that would not have been compatible with a period when people were taking very strong positions on issues. While it was certainly not unheard of for presenting officers to state that a warning had gone unheeded, and hence the necessity of the presentment, it is still noteworthy that John did not obey a warning about his sink, and the streetlookers, to whom he gave uncivil words, had twice warned him about the gravel in the street. Going against court leet orders and obtaining a warrant from a justice to be served within the town may hint of a person who 'marches to his own drummer', as does not allowing alefounders in 1644 to taste his and his wife's ale and declaring that there was no law that required him to do so.

As might be expected for the seventeenth century, Eleanor Hoole, as a female, was somewhat invisible. In 1626 John's unnamed wife was amerced 6d for washing calf's meat in the Lady Well. In that same year justices bound Eleanor at the sessions in a recognizance for good behaviour.[209] In 1633, though warned, Eleanor 'annoyed' a well with barrels.[210] While Ellen, their daughter, was bound at the sessions in a recognizance of peace in 1642,[211] leet records do not bring her to our attention until 1646. In that year constables accused her mother of numerous

---

207. Five more times between 1616 and 1624 the court accused Appleton of allowing other individuals to inhabit his house without the consent of the Four Men. Styled a yeoman and a gentleman, John's name in call books appeared in the top 25 percent of undertenants. Interestingly, in every year between 1608 and 1627 except 1621 he was involved in pleas as a plaintiff (twenty-four cases) or defendant (twenty-three cases).
208. LRO: DDCs/Paper Books/1619–28.
209. LRO: QSR/22, Wigan, Epiphany 1626.
210. LRO: DDKc/PC 4/161/Paper Book/1633.
211. LRO: QSB/1/269e/5, Epiphany 1643.

instances of slander and of 'words as we Cannot well expres', for which affeerors amerced her 3s 4d; she was amerced a further 6d for foul words against one of the constables. The personalities of John and Eleanor appear to have been well matched.

In 1646 John's name was missing from the call book and from the twenty-five persons allowed to operate an alehouse. John, too, was becoming invisible, or at least some inhabitants preferred him to be. At the 1646 general court that met on 29 May, jurors ordered the three Hooles, because of their 'notorious abuses', to leave Prescot before 24 June on pain of 3s 4d each per night, and anyone who sheltered them was also ordered to forfeit 3s 4d per night.

Though John never reappeared in the court records,[212] his wife and daughter remained in Prescot, jurors stated in 1647, for forty nights in a house of Nicholas Marshall and therefore forfeited £6 13s 4d, while Nicholas and his wife Margaret forfeited £13 6s 8d for sheltering them. In 1648 the court again ordered the two Hooles to leave, this time before 1 September on pain of 26s 8d. Actually, at that court Eleanor's name was also included in a list with the names of thirty-six other alehousekeepers. The name 'Hoole' last appeared in the leet records in 1651 when the court amerced Nicholas Marshall 6s 8d for receiving an inmate into the house late in the holding of Eleanor Hoole, widow.[213]

This case and some others noted in this introduction illustrate that in the final analysis courts leet, including Prescot's, were sometimes relatively weak when it came to enforcing their orders. The Hoole case also shows the troubled times known to us as the Civil War or the English or Puritan Revolution being experienced on a personal level in the homes and lanes in Prescot. Furthermore, the situation with the Hooles demonstrates the existence in Prescot of some sentiment for both Parliament and the monarchy. While Charles I was executed in January 1649, parishioners in the town did not take down the king's arms from the church until about a year and a half later and appear to have genuinely celebrated the restoration of Charles II in 1660 by restoring the king's arms and ringing the church bells.[214]

Besides many references to the Hooles, the paper book for 1646 also mentioned three residents amerced 6d each for refusing to quarter a soldier. Except for the court's continued difficulty with encouraging nominees to fill certain offices in 1647 and 1648, there is no other obvious hint of troubled times. At the 1650 court Roger Dey petitioned that when Thomas Lytherland and Nicholas Anderton were constables (for the court year 1643–44) they took from him a horse worth at least £6 for the use of Captain Hugh Henley and the town's service. He requested reimbursement which jurors approved in 1651.[215]

212. John was buried on 7 February 1647. LPRS, 114, p. 97.
213. LRO: DDKc/PC 4/112/Paper Book/1651.
214. See note 191 *supra*.
215. LRO: DDCs/Paper Book/1650 and DDKc/PC 4/112/Paper Book/1651. Captain Hugh Henley (Hindley) fought for Parliament. William Beamont, ed., *A Discourse of the Warr in Lancashire*, Chetham Society, Orig. Ser., 62 (1864), p. 43. In early 1644 he participated in the siege of

In still other ways the Civil War affected Prescot. Call books for 1640–43 annually list an average of seven non-resident tenants, while call books for 1645–48 contain at 19.5 nearly three times as many. Dislocation and a higher than normal death rate of residents may have created an opportunity for non-residents to lease property from King's College and thereby enjoy Prescot's privileges.[216] This change affected the makeup of the presentment jury, as we have seen, and hence of town government as represented by the court. The percentage of non-residents on the jury increased from 39 percent in the 1640s to 49 percent in the 1650s. Without an increase in the size of the jury (from fourteen to sixteen sworn members), that percentage would have increased even more in the 1650s.

No non-resident served as foreman of the presentment jury until 1642 when George Deane of Rainhill was selected to be foreman; this service was his first and last as foreman. Actually, he may not have been the bailiff's first choice (which only paper books can reveal). The names of eight residents, none of whom was sworn, preceded his name on the list of nominations. Because the line that usually extended from the nominee's name to 'sworn' on the right side of the folio was next to Nicholas Marshall's name (and not next to any of the other seven names), he may have been the bailiff's preferred choice for foreman. But he was not sworn, and his refusal to serve probably surprised everyone, for Nicholas was a very active member of his community. Between 1594 (his first time sworn as a presentment juror) and 1644 (last time), he served as a juror for forty-four of the fifty years (no record survives for 1601), eight times as a juror on a court baron between 1627 and 1645 and three times as a juror on a coroner's inquest between 1602 and 1618. Also, between 1600 and 1653 he was a witness for 198 surrenders, and for a variety of reasons his signature appears 183 times in the court records between 1600 and 1654. He served as one of the Four Men in thirty years between 1602 and 1647, affeeror in twenty-one years between 1602 and 1640, sealer of leather thirty times between 1602 and 1638, and constable in 1604 and 1637. From 1608 to his death in the 1650s,[217] he was also a feoffee for the charitable bequest of Lawrence Webster. While this position probably did not involve a great deal of work, his appointment by Webster, to serve with the vicar and four other influential tenants, attested to his prominence in Prescot.[218]

Lathom House. Broxap, *Great Civil War*, p. 99. In October 1648 'Obediance', daughter of Captain Hugh Hindley, was baptized. K.T. Taylor, ed., *The Registers of Hindley, 1644–1814*, LPRS, 138 (1995), p. 3.

216. For instance, between 1630 and 1641 burials at Prescot averaged thirteen per year. Not unexpectedly, burials increased to nineteen per year during the war-torn years of the 1640s. LPRS, 114.

217. The parish register for the 1650s is in poor condition and contains no burial entry for Nicholas. The call books for 1657 and 1658 have 'dead' next to his name. LRO: DDKc/PC 4/112/Paper Books/1657 and 1658.

218. In 1624 Nicholas married Margaret, daughter of Henry Blundell of Prescot, yeo. LPRS, 76, p. 124. Henry, his wife Ann and their daughters Margaret and Jane were recusants. CRO: EDV 1/14, f.103, for 1605, and /15, f.116, for 1608. Nicholas had two sons, Henry (b. 1625) and John (b. 1628). Henry served on the presentment jury and as one of the Four Men and an affeeror, while John focused on the position of clerk of the market. The Marshall family was fairly active in the governance of Prescot.

Nicholas was described as a shoemaker and yeoman, and the rental of 1635 has him possessing a respectable amount of property in Prescot. His position in the community, and the community's sense that Nicholas was dependable, can be gauged by his median position in twenty-nine lists (1611, 1617–46) of nominated presentment jurors: sixth of twenty-five nominees; that is, he was among the first to be nominated. He may have had a rather peaceful temperament useful on juries: of the 1,724 persons (including recidivists) accused at Prescot's court of breach of the peace between 1602 and 1655, Nicholas was accused just once, and his one incident (in 1610) was very brief and minor as indicated by affeerors amercing both tusslers only 6d when the usual amount was 12d.

Nicholas last served as a juror in October 1645 at a court baron, when he put in his only stint as a foreman. Although the work at that court must have been light – the court dealt only with a revocation of a former surrender and then a surrender of that property to another individual – he may have had a bad experience, although that is unlikely. Alternatively, perhaps long-term poor health contributed to his reluctance in 1642 to lead a presentment jury. In 1646 next to his name on the list of nominees to the presentment jury is 'pardoned'; and call books contain the following notes next to his name: 'infirme' (1647, 1652, 1654, 1655) and 'dead' (1657, 1658).[219]

Why Nicholas never served as a foreman except at one court baron is puzzling. But while his reason may have been personal, the point, though, is that the first non-resident (George Deane) to sit as foreman of Prescot's court may have served because of the reluctance of a resident (Nicholas) to serve in that position.

Besides George Deane, another non-resident, John Alcocke of Eccleston, gent., also served as foreman (in 1649 and 1650). The name of Thomas Sorrocold, gent., resident of Prescot, appears above that of Alcocke in the list of nominees for the presentment jury in 1650.[220] The first appearance of Thomas's name in Prescot's records was in the call book of 1638.[221] He was amerced for not appearing at all courts between 1640 and 1647, except in 1641 when he 'appeared by Wm Hough tenent'. Though he was not amerced for absence in 1648, the bailiff did not place an attendance mark next to his name. Before 1649 he was nominated for the jury only in 1646 and 1647, but he did not serve. To judge by his position in the list of tenants – either seventh or eighth from the top during the 1640s – Thomas was a prominent resident of Prescot. During the 1640s every tenant from Sorrocold to the top of that list nominated for the jury did not serve. In other words, it appears that the list of nominees in 1650 for the presentment jury may have been designed to ensure that John, a non-resident, would be in a position to become foreman, because the resident (Thomas), whose name was the only one above John's, was usually absent from court, had never served as a juror and presumably was not expected to serve.

219. LRO: DDKc/PC 4/112/Paper Books/1652–58.
220. The paper book for 1649, with its list of nominees, has not survived. LRO: DDCs/Paper Book/1650.
221. LRO: DDCs/Paper Book/1638.

Otherwise from 1602 to 1699 all other foremen of the presentment jury were residents of Prescot. It was surely no coincidence that, of 254 non-resident jurors between 1623 when the first served and 1684 when the last officiated, only three were chosen foreman. To put it another way, in only three of fifty-four years when non-residents served on the jury was a non-resident elected foreman, and on only one of the eleven occasions when non-residents constituted a majority of sworn jurors (1649) was a non-resident elected foreman.

Since there was considerable overlap among jurors, Four Men and affeerors, we should not be surprised that some non-residents served in the latter two offices as well. Indeed during the 1640s non-residents filled nine of thirty-four slots among affeerors and one of forty among the Four Men. Five of these ten came from Whiston and one each from Huyton and Rainhill, localities near Prescot, and three from Widnes. Presumably logistics compelled non-resident jurors from relatively distant townships to avoid offices that required a more frequent presence in Prescot than did the office of juror. All sworn jurors were tenants.

During the 1640s all other principal offices (constable, coroner, clerk of the market, burleyman, sealer of leather, aletaster, streetlooker and leygatherer) were filled by residents. Tenants occupied all slots for coroner. While burleyman and streetlooker each had five tenants, clerk of the market and aletaster had one each. Only undertenants occupied the other three offices.

After the Civil War and Commonwealth periods, the residents of Prescot slowly regained full governance of their town. In call books the number of non-residents, which had jumped from an annual average of 6.2 for 1635–43 to 18.3 for 1645–59,[222] declined from an average of 15.2 in the 1660s to 8.1 in the 1670s, to 3.4 in the next decade, and to 2.4 in the 1690s. Not surprisingly the number of non-residents on the presentment jury, after annually averaging 5.5 in the 1640s and 7.9 in the 1650s, followed a similar pattern of decline from 7 in the 1660s to 1.6 in the 1670s, less than one (0.9) in the 1680s and none in the last decade of the seventeenth century. In short, one change in Prescot contemporary with the Civil War and which may have been assisted by the troubled times – increased participation by non-residents in the affairs of Prescot – was greatly diminished after the 1660s.

The consequence of increasing numbers of non-residents in Prescot can be seen in still another area: charges of affray, tussle and bloodwipe. At the 1645 court William Ackers the younger of Whiston and Robert Nelson of Knowsley were accused of an affray on each other. John and Thomas Worrall of Whiston came to Ackers's assistance. When constable John Parr commanded all to keep the peace, Ackers broke the constable's head. Non-residents were especially numerous around the time of the annual fair; the case of Cheshire and Birchall of Burtonwood in 1657 has already been mentioned. In the 1620s only 1.6 percent (8 of 498) of offenders against his majesty's peace were from outside Prescot; in the 1630s, 8 percent (26 of 327); in the 1640s, 18 percent (33 of 183); and in the 1650s, 20.7 percent (24 of 116). Over these four decades some 28.6 percent of

---

222. As previously noted, names of suitors were not called in 1644.

non-residents accused of breach of the peace came from nearby Whiston alone and 18.7 percent from Eccleston. These ninety-one non-resident offenders came from twenty-two localities, a number that again underscores Prescot's important economic position as a market centre for the area.

Between 1640 and 1648 Prescot's court accused thirteen other non-residents of violations of laws, mostly regarding meat and leather. During the 1650s sealers of leather charged six non-residents with misdemeanours relating to leather, and jurors presented two others for removing timber and soil without the permission of the Four Men. These twenty-one offenders came from ten localities.

Of course, some residents of Prescot travelled to nearby townships. If we look at affrays and tussles during the early seventeenth century, we find inhabitants of Prescot so accused at Upholland in 1613, West Derby in 1625 and 1626, and Liverpool in 1617 and 1628.[223] During the reign of Charles I some fifteen residents of Prescot were accused of market violations in Liverpool.[224]

AFFRAYS, TUSSLES AND BLOODWIPES

Finally, offences that appear with some frequency in Prescot's court records are affrays, tussles and bloodwipes. Between 1640 and 1648 constables and in 1648 jurors accused 176 males and seven females; forty of these individuals drew blood. This writer has reviewed seventeenth-century court records for over one hundred localities in western and northern England, and the single most important indicator that a local court had retained some measure of authority over misdemeanants, that had yet to pass to petty and quarter sessions, is the number of affrays and tussles brought before it.[225] The number at Prescot for 1640–48 – 183 individuals accused in ninety-six cases – is sizeable and demonstrates that the court leet at Prescot had not yet become decadent as so many leets had by the seventeenth century. But by the end of that century the leet at Prescot, too, had lost much of its former power, and some officers submitted presentment chits with the declaration that they had nothing to present. During the 1690s a mere twenty-one cases of breach of the peace involving thirty-nine alleged offenders came before leet jurors;

223. See for Upholland, LRO: DDHi; for West Derby, see Liverpool Central Libraries, Record Office: 920/SAL 1/135 and 136; and for Liverpool, see George Chandler, *Liverpool Under James I* (Liverpool, Brown, Picton and Hornby Libraries,1960), p. 192, and *Liverpool Under Charles I*, p. 141.
224. Chandler, *Liverpool Under Charles I*, pp. 138, 141, 170, 185, 193, 219, 239 and 348.
225. While riots, or fighting by three or more persons, could be punished only at a royal court superior to the leet (1 Mary, c.12), between 1602 and 1700 Prescot's court adjudicated 309 cases of breach of the peace involving one offender, 680 with two and 92 with between three and seven offenders. Breaches of the peace between two individuals, with or without blood drawn, could be inquired about and punished at both quarter sessions and courts leet. For a discussion of leet jurisdiction over affrays and bloodwipes, see Hearnshaw, *Court Leet of Southampton*, pp. 112–13. For the definition of affray, see Michael Dalton, *The Countrey Justice* (London, 1618; Amsterdam and Norwood, New Jersey, 1975), p. 29. In 1625 two male residents of Prescot met 'at the place of Chalince', tussled and drew blood from each other. '[P]lace of Chalince' was never mentioned again during the seventeenth century. LRO: DDCs/ Paper Book/1625.

during the last five years of that decade they judged a paltry two cases involving three persons.

Tussles and affrays fascinate because we crave to understand the cause of conflict between individuals and even families. One interesting tussle occurred in Prescot in 1647 between John Alcocke, jun., and Edward Stockley, both of whom were quite prominent in Prescot.[226] Between 1631, when John first appears in the court records, and 1647, the year that they tussled, both served often as presentment juror, affeeror, one of the Four Men and coroner. While John also served as a juror on eight courts baron, Edward was clerk of the manor court, surveyor of the highways within Prescot and feoffee for the charitable bequest of Lawrence Webster. Between 1631 and 1647 in seven wills of residents of Prescot, Edward was either executor or witness, and in two inventories he served as an appraiser of property; John was a witness to a codicil.[227] Between 1633, when John's signature first surfaces in the court records, and 1647, his signature appears some fifty-one times while Edward's for those same years occurs forty-eight times, both mostly as witnesses to surrenders. The activity of both individuals extended beyond Prescot manor. Each served their parish church;[228] and, as already noted, Edward served as a schoolwarden for the parish school located in Prescot township. Edward was also steward of the manor courts at Knowsley, Rainford, Eccleston, Halewood, Little Woolton and Upholland.[229]

The perceived importance and social status of Alcocke and Stockley may be roughly gauged in lists, written by bailiffs, of suitors who were called at each annual general court. Lists of 1619 and 1621 have William Alcocke, grandfather

---

226. Edward was born in 1592 (LPRS, 76, p. 15; LPRS, 137, p. 141) and married Jane, daughter of Richard Harrington of Prescot Hall, gent., in 1615 [LPRS, 76, p. 121; William Fergusson Irvine, ed., *Marriage Licences Granted Within the Archdeaconry of Chester in the Diocese of Chester, Vol. I: 1606–1616*, RSLC, liii (1907), p. 194]; she died in 1628 (LPRS, 76, p. 213), a month after giving birth a sixth time. In 1630 Edward married Sarah Broom (*ibid.*, p. 128), and they had four children. She died in October 1643 (LPRS, 114, p. 91). The parish register gives the marriage date of Edward and Katherine Brettergh as 1 February 1634 (*ibid.*, p. 59), but that is an error for, possibly, 1 February 1644 or any time between Sarah's death in 1643 and Edward's surrender of 1645. That surrender, presented to Prescot's general court on 6 June 1645, notes that Katherine is Edward's wife and summarizes his surrender of 1641 that had mentioned Sarah. He died in September 1665 (LPRS, 149, p. 73), was buried in the parish church (LRO: PR 2880/4/3) and left over £213 in property according to the appraisors of his inventory (LRO: WCW/Prescot/1665). Katherine was buried on 22 September 1670 at Childwall (Robert Dickinson, ed., *The Registers of the Parish of Childwall, Part I: 1557–1680*, LPRS, 106 (1967), p. 173).
227. The wills are at LRO for Oliver Lyme (1631), Jane Bruen (1634), William Alcock (1642), Thomas Parr the elder (1645), Alexander Webster (1646), Ann Webster (1646) and Elizabeth Fletcher (1647).
228. Steel, *Prescot Churchwardens' Accounts, passim*; LRO: 2880/4/1 and 2 (churchwardens' accounts, 1663–64 and 1664–65).
229. See at LRO for Knowsley: QSP/27/47, Epiphany 1650; Rainford: QSP/55/37, Michaelmas 1651; Eccleston: QSP/67/57, Midsummer 1652; QSP/151/38, Michaelmas 1657; QSP/159/28, Easter 1658; QSP/179/45, Midsummer 1659; QSP/191/42, Easter 1660; Halewood: QSP/159/40, Easter 1658; Little Woolton: QSP/171/48, Epiphany 1659; QSP/175/48, Easter 1659; Upholland: QSP/159/37, Easter 1658.

of John, jun., appearing in the ninth and eleventh positions and John, sen., in tenth and twelfth, while Edward Stockley was lower at sixteenth and seventeenth.[230] Between 1636 and 1642 the position of Edward ranged between sixteenth and twentieth, while the range for John, jun., was between tenth and twelfth.[231]

Lists of nominees to the presentment jury are another rough indicator of the relative social importance of individuals, at least to the bailiff. For ten of the eleven presentment juries for 1619–29, Edward and either William or John, sen., or both were nominated, and the bailiff always nominated an Alcocke ahead of Stockley. Edward served on ten consecutive juries (1616–25) and his median nomination was fifth. In 1626 John Alcocke, sen., was sworn and became foreman, and sometime later his name was cancelled, and Edward, whose name was immediately below John's, became foreman for the first time. In contrast to Edward's slow rise to foreman, John, jun., in 1632 on his first nomination to the jury was the first to be nominated and accepted the position of foreman; Edward was the second nominee.[232]

In 1633 Edward again became foreman when the bailiff nominated him first. Initially, however, Edward's name was immediately below that of John, jun., but was cancelled and by the same hand that wrote the list of nominations but in a different ink (which indicates at a later date) was added at the top of the list. That move took the position of foreman from John, who then became the second to be sworn, and gave it to Edward and may have set in motion a process that would result in the tussle in John Pendleton's alehouse in 1647.[233]

For the following year, John, jun., became foreman, and Edward, though the second sworn, was the fourth nominee. Edward was not again nominated to the presentment jury until 1643 and between 1635 and 1642 served in no major leet office except that of coroner, which is very unusual behaviour for a person of his demonstrated strong preference to be involved in civic affairs; he, for example, was sworn to every presentment jury from 1616–34 except 1628. John, on the other hand, between 1635 and 1644 was foreman of six annual general courts and six courts baron and served on two other general courts and two courts baron.

In 1643 something unusual occurred. Edward sat on the presentment jury for the first time since 1634 and became foreman, was coroner and one of the Four Men, while John did not attend court and served in no leet office. Also, in the list of suitors, Edward curiously jumped from seventeenth in 1642 to eleventh in 1643, right behind John.[234] Of the six tenants ahead of Edward in 1642, only John Aldem, vicar, had died (late 1642), and the remaining five were in 1643 now below

---

230. While 'junior' and 'senior' were not always employed in the records to distinguish Edward the father from Edward the son, their signatures do set apart father and son, and that of Edward the son first appeared in the leet records of June, just prior to the death of Edward the father in December 1614. LPRS, 76, p. 188.
231. After 1621 the next extant list of suitors is actually in 1635 where curiously Edward's name is in the fifty-fourth position, while John junior's is twelfth.
232. LRO: DDCs/Paper Book/1626 and DDKc/PC 4/161/Paper Book/1632.
233. LRO: DDKc/PC 4/161/Paper Book/1633.
234. Strictly speaking, the cancelled name of Edward Devisse, gent., came after that of John, jun.

Edward. Between 1645 and 1647 John was not nominated to the jury, while each year Edward served as foreman.

Except for an affray by Edward in 1619 with John Hoole, the only charge of breach of the peace against both John, jun., and Edward occurred in 1647 when they tussled in Pendleton's alehouse.[235] We may never know whether John sought out Edward or just happened to enter the alehouse to enjoy some ale and discovered Edward and other court officers (for the year 1646–47 when John went unnominated to the presentment jury) conducting the town's business. Presumably John did not enjoy his chosen or forced recent lack of involvement in Prescot's affairs. Perhaps they were both on edge because of a strained relationship that went back many years. Bailiffs may have known about their strained relationship because for some time they had avoided nominating both to the same jury.

For John, jun., and Edward their strong personalities, ambition and desire to be involved in community affairs may have been the root cause of their conflict. By the early 1630s Edward may have concluded that no matter how much time and energy he devoted to Prescot's affairs, he would continue to be viewed as 'inferior' to John, sen., and John, jun., as demonstrated by his lower position in lists of suitors and often in lists of nominees to the presentment jury. John, jun., on the other hand, may have felt threatened by Edward's attempts to put himself forward. Given the foregoing context, the tussle in 1647 becomes explainable and almost expected.

This publication of the records of Prescot's courts leet and baron reveals individuals from the seventeenth century behaving as humanly as this writer and the reader. On occasion they became angry, fought and swore, when they were not reticent, cheerful or altruistic; they had fears and aspirations; they worked hard to keep body and soul together, and some occasionally took unlawful shortcuts to that end. Many of us can sometimes become dazzled by our quantifications and analyses and fail to perceive the humanity and uniqueness of the very individuals we aggregate and later attempt to describe. This volume unmasks the interests, hopes, values and dignity as well as the weaknesses of a few elite but mostly ordinary human beings residing in Prescot during the very stressful decade of the 1640s.

EDITORIAL CONVENTIONS

Because of extensive repetition in the original documents, particularly in surrenders and breaches of the peace, the decision was made not to publish a verbatim transcript of the 246 sheets in the paper books for 1640 to 1649. The 1640s were chosen because of their importance in English history. Every subject, person, place, date and amount has been included and retained in its original sequence in the books which sometimes differs from the order in the rolls; also retained are all cancellations of consequence and marginal notes and checking marks, which may

---

235. LRO: DDCs/Paper Book/1619.

indicate attendance by suitors at the general court held in May or June and attendance by jurors at general and adjourned courts. While not a verbatim transcription, the present volume is more complete than a calendar and is presented as a substitute for the manuscripts themselves.

Except where indicated, spelling, punctuation, place names and forenames have been modernized, while full names in signatures and marks and all surnames elsewhere have been retained in the original; also noted are whether marks, when not a circle, cross or haphazard mark, comprise one or both initials. Inverted commas set off material that retains original spelling. Dates are in New Style, that is, the year begins on 1 January. Contractions have been extended and Latin translated. Square brackets contain words in italics and numbers that have been supplied which are not in the manuscript. Significant differences between paper books and parchment rolls are here placed within rounded brackets and introduced by 'parchment' in italics. To avoid interrupting the flow of the text, some differences have been placed in footnotes. Rounded brackets also contain amercements and, for breaches of the peace, names of pledgers. Cancelled material will be found in angled brackets.

For clarity the heading at the beginning of a court and at the beginning of each set of presentments has been set off by upper-case letters. Folio numbers, which do not appear in the original, have been added on the left side of the printed page and refer to paper books, except for 1649 for which membrane numbers refer to the parchment roll because no book with presentments and orders has survived for that year. In order to distinguish surrenders, they have been numbered.

THE COURT RECORDS OF PRESCOT 1640–1649

1640

[Paper Book: DDCs¹]   [Parchment Roll: DDKc/PC 4/67 ²]

[f.1r: 19 cms × 30 cms³]
(*Parchment*: **VIEW OF FRANKPLEDGE WITH COURT BARON OF PRESCOT** in the county of Lancaster held there according to the custom of the manor of Prescot aforesaid before Thomas Wolfall,⁴ esq., steward of the manor and court aforesaid, on Friday, the day after Corpus Christi, 5 June, 16 Charles, 1640.)

SUITORS OF THE COURT OF PRESCOT:⁵

Sir William Gerrard, baronet	○ William Alcocke, gent.	
Thomas Eccleston, esq.	○ John Alcocke, sen., gent.	
○⁶ Henry Ogle, esq.	○ John Aldem, clerk ⁸	
○ Henry Lathom, esq.	○ John Alcocke, jun., gent.	
○ Thomas Woolfall, esq.	○ William Lyme	out of
○ Richard Eltonhed, gent. out of⁷	Richard Woodes	
<the heirs of James>	○ William Kenwricke	out of
Thomas Sorrocold	○ Henry Webster of Knowsley	

1. Originally bound on the left side, folios are now loose but the paper book appears complete. Several large sheets are folded in half, and here each half has been given a separate folio number.
2. Sewn at the top, this parchment roll has two membranes that measure 32 cms × 62 cms. Sewn to the foot of the second membrane is another, with writing on one side that is not relevant to 1640, which serves as a cover for the roll.
3. Unless otherwise noted, measurements refer to paper books.
4. Steward of Prescot manor from 1637 to 1648.
5. Headings, such as that above, have been taken from the parchment roll whenever the paper book either lacks a heading or has a brief one, such as this heading for 1640. Regarding suit and service, see Introduction, p. xiv, note 21, and p. xxx, note 95.
6. Presumably, these marks and those next to the names of jurors for the lord indicate attendance at court.
7. 'Extra' (out of, i.e. out of Prescot) and other notes in Latin were usually added to the right of names after the list was composed by the bailiff.
8. Aldem was vicar of Prescot between 1616 and his death in 1642, and his name regularly appears in lists of tenants owing suit and service and elsewhere in these court records. But the name of his successor, Richard Day, who did not always reside in Prescot during his tenure between 1643 and his death in 1650, never appears in these manorial records. Steel, *Prescot Churchwardens' Accounts*, pp. xiv–xv; Paterson, *History of Prescot*, pp. 31–3; W.A. Shaw, ed., *Minutes of the Committee for the Relief of Plundered Ministers and of the Trustees for the Maintenance of Ministers; Relating to Lancashire and Cheshire, 1643–1660, Part 1: 1643–1654*, RSLC, xxviii (1893), pp. 11, 33–5, 37, 41, 47, 52, 56–8.

- George Lyon
- Edward Stockley, gent.
- William Aspia   essoined
- Henry Woodes of Widnes   dead [9]
- John Glover   out of
- Nicholas Marshall
  <Margaret Garnett, wid.>
- Jane Pyke, wid.
  Edward <Devias> Davies, gent.
  William Blundell, gent.
- John Webster
  Edward Symond
  George Croston, gent.
- Robert Wainwright
- Peter Kenwricke, sen.
- George Lyon of Eccleston
- George Deane of Rainhill
- Richard Molynexe
  William Parr
  James Houghton
- Thomas Webster
- William Lyon of Thingwall
- George Lyon, jun., of Whiston
  John Lyon, skinner
- Edward Orme
  George Tarleton
  <John Leadbeter>
  Richard Mercer
- John Webster, nailer
- Henry Crosse
- Richard Litherland
- William Sutton
- Henry Woodes of Whiston
- William Fletcher
  Richard Tarbocke
- Thomas Devias
- James Ditchfield
- Hugh Ward
  <Richard Gill>
- Henry Pinnington   essoined

- John Urmeston
- William Coppall
- Ann Lodge, wid.

Tenants:[10]
  William Hardman   dead[11]
- Anthony Prescott
- James Angsdale
- Anne Ackers
  <Ellen> William Stocke <wid.>
- John Ashton
- John Taylor
- Anne Shawe, wid.
- Thomas Knowles
- Thomas Eaton
- Isabel Hey
- Jane Boulton
- James Taylor
- Thomas Caldwell
- Thomas Parr
- Thomas Wood
- William Hough
- Margery Shuttleworth
- Thomas Neylor   infirm
- Mary Haward, wid.
- John Cowper
- Nicholas Renicars
- George Standistreet
- Cecily Hill
- Anne Lodge, wid.

[f.1v]
  Anne Ditchfield, spinster
- Margaret Goodicarr
- Thomas Goodicarr
- Janet Winstandley
- Thomas Heas
  <Alice Birtchall, wid.>
- John Einsworth
- George Wright
- John Hoole

---

9. Henry, a yeoman, was described as 'ill' in the call book of 14 June 1639 and was buried on 15 February 1640. LRO: DDKc/PC 4/66/Paper Book/1639; Robert Dickinson, ed., *The Registers of Farnworth Chapel in the Parish of Prescot, Part II: 1612–1698*, LPRS, 97 (1958), p. 70.
10. Actually, undertenants or subtenants.
11. Of Prescot, buried on 25 September 1639. LPRS, 114, p. 83.

o William Standish, gent.
o Jane Fletcher, wid.
o Edward Rylandes
   Ellen Rylandes, wid.
o Thomas Horneby
o Elizabeth Man, wid.
o Peter Garnett
o Roger Dey
o Richard Chorleton
o William Fletcher, glover
o John Houghland
o Ralph Parr
o Peter Herefoote
o Evan Garnett
o Thomas Aspe
o Ellen Halsall, wid.
o Margery Browne, wid.
o Anne Harrocke, spinster
o Hamlet Whitfield
   Alexander Webster
o Ralph Halsall
o Nicholas Anderton
o John Wade
o John Pendleton
o Henry Garnett
o William Ewood
o Henry Parr
o William Rose
o George Kirkes   sick
o Alexander Rylandes
o Thomas Mobberley
o Elizabeth Webster, wid.
o John Parr
o Edward Fynney
o Robert Kennion
o John Huson
o Edward Bate
o Richard Woolfall
o James Houghton
o John Walker
o Richard Banner
o Cecily Houghton, wid.

o Barbary Story, wid.
o Anne Giller
o Thomas Garnett
   Richard Ditchfield
o Anne Miller
o Richard Marshall
o James Sadler
o Anthony Litherland   sick
o William Standish <gent.>
o Janet Orrell, wid.
o Edward Webster
o William Aspe
o William Molynex
o John Strettell
   Thomas Ditchfield
o John Sutton
o Anne Molynexe, wid.
o John Rainford
[f.2r: 19 cms × 30 cms]
o Edward Lyon
o Henry Atherton   dead [12]
o John Stevenson, gent.   out of
o Thomas Litherland
o Thomas Bond
o Thomas Walls
o Henry Darbishyre
o Jane Greene, wid.
o William Houghton
o Alice Houghton, wid.
o John Poughton
o John Oliverson
o Richard Aspshawe
o Robert Hatton
o Margaret Angsdale, wid.
o Peter Kenwricke, jun.
o John Frodsome
   Katherine Stevenson, wid.
o Henry Prescott
o Hugh Ward
o Margaret Houlden, wid.
o Thomas Browne

12. The parish register contains no burial entry. He and his wife and family were inmates in Prescot in 1638, 1639 and 1640. LRO: DDCs/Paper Book/1638 and DDKc/PC 4/66/Paper Book/1639.

- ○ Thomas Fletcher
- ○ Richard Angsdale
- ○ Richard Higginson
- ○ Jane Fennowe, wid.
- ○ Henry Kirkes
- ○ Ralph Plumpton
- ○ John Rigby
- ○ Thomas Kenwricke
- ○ Edward Lowe

- ○ Ellen Parr, wid.
- ○ Ralph Houghton
- ○ Robert Woosie
- ○ Margery Whitesyde, wid.
- ○ William Swift
- ○ Ralph Hall
- ○ Katherine Norres, wid.
- ○ Robert Bolton, gent.
- ○ Adam Bate

[f.2v, blank]
[f.3r: 19 cms × 30 cms]
JURORS FOR THE LORD, 5 June 1640:[13]

Thomas Eccleston, esq.		James Houghton	
John Lancaster, esq.		George Lyon of Whiston	sworn
Henry Lathom, esq.		Henry Webster	sworn
<John Alcocke, gent., sen.>		<William Aspe>	
John Alcocke, gent., jun.	sworn	Henry Crosse	sworn
Nicholas Marshall	sworn	Richard Litherland	
John Webster	sworn	Robert Wainwright	sworn
George Deane	sworn	John Lyon, skinner[14]	
William Lyonn	sworn	Thomas Webster	sworn
William Fletcher	sworn	John Webster, nailer	sworn
James Ditchfield	sworn	Peter Kenwricke, sen.	
Henry Woodes	sworn	William Coppall	
William Parr		Edward Orme, gent.[15]	sworn

[f.3v, blank]
[f.4r: 20 cms × 32 cms]
VIEW OF FRANKPLEDGE WITH COURT BARON OF PRESCOT in the county of Lancaster held there according to the custom of the manor of Prescot aforesaid before Thomas Wolfall, esq., steward of the manor and court aforesaid, on Friday, the day after Corpus Christi, 5 June, 16 Charles, 1640.

JURORS SAY AND PRESENT upon their oaths as follows.
Richard Angsdealle of Prescot, collier, on last 15 May at Prescot 'By force and Armes' against the peace of our sovereign lord the king 'broke open and entred' the shop of John Taylor, shoemaker, at Prescot and 'feloniously stoole and carryed away' one pair of black leather shoes worth 20d.[16]

---

13. All names appear to be in the same hand except the last name which may have been added by a different hand.
14. Between 1633 and 1644, John Lyon, skinner, a tenant, was eleven times nominated to the presentment jury but served only in 1638.
15. There is no 'gent.' in the parchment roll.
16. The parchment roll continues: The bailiff of the manor aforesaid is directed to seize all Richard's possessions in order that he answer concerning the same to the lord of this

[f.4v, blank]
[f.5r: 16 cms × 27 cms]
  Owe suit to this court and made default (12d each):

William Gerard, baronet	George Tarlton
Thomas Eccleston, esq.	Richard Mercer
Richard Woodes	Richard Tarbock
Thomas Sorowcold	William Stock
William Blundell	Anne Ditchfeild
Edward Symond	Thomas Ditchfeild
George Croston	Katherine Stevenson, wid.
William Parr	

  We present that Ralph Fletcher (26s 8d) has not removed Henry Atherton, his wife and family as ordered by the previous court.[17]

[f.5v]

manor. Because Richard was accused of a felony (theft above 12d), this case was forwarded to the quarter sessions where Richard was found not guilty. For 1640, LRO: QSR/37, Ormskirk, Midsummer; QSB/1/234/31, 43, 44, Midsummer; QJI/1/17, Midsummer. Dalton, *Countrey Justice*, p. 229. At Michaelmas 1641 (QSR/38, Wigan) and Epiphany 1652 (QSR/45, Wigan; QJI/1/25; QJI/2/6) Richard was again at the quarter sessions and both times found guilty and ordered to be whipped for stealing barley. In 1672 he was accused of wrongfully removing trees and hedgewood from land belonging to Thomas Eccleston of Eccleston, esq. (QSB/1/1672, Michaelmas). Richard was an undertenant whose name in call books between 1635 and 1681 appeared in the bottom half and who failed to serve in any manorial office except as streetlooker in 1666. Six times between 1632 and 1655 Prescot's court accused Richard, an alehousekeeper, of not paying his taxes or fees and between 1620 and 1652 he was accused of fifteen breaches of the peace. He outlived two wives (Jane died in 1649 and Margery in 1677) and died in 1682 at about the age of 88. CRO: EDC 5/3 (1680); LPRS, 114, p. 104; 149, pp. 99, 108.

17. In this volume amercements have been placed within rounded brackets immediately after the name to which they relate, but in the manuscripts they will be found either above the name or at the end of the presentment. For not removing Henry and family, who were inmates, general courts amerced Ralph 6s 8d in both 1637 and 1638 and 13s 4d in 1639. An inmate was an individual unable or unwilling, or perceived to be unable or unwilling, to provide for himself or herself; that person lodged with an inhabitant or in an unoccupied dwelling belonging to another. Regulating inmates was inquirable and offences punishable at both quarter sessions and courts leet. Between 1615 and 1700 Prescot's leet dealt with 274 presentments and issued fifty-eight orders not associated with a presentment that concerned inmates, but only four presentments and one order about rogues and vagabonds. Those 274 presentments mentioned roughly 550 different individuals who had provided no bond of £10 and for whom no other person had offered a bond that the inmates would not become a financial liability and would depart from Prescot within three months of a notice from the Four Men. Stated differently, Prescot had about nine inmates annually between 1615 and 1639, approximately seven during the 1640s and 1650s and about six from 1660 to 1700. Those leet records contain another thirty-one presentments and seven orders against anyone erecting a building for inmates or converting an existing house, barn, oven house, outhouse or shippon into lodging for inmates. The principal relevant statutes are 31 Eliz. I, c.7 (1589) and 43 Eliz. I, c.2 (1601). LRO: DDCs/Paper Books/1618, 1637–38; DDKc/PC 4/66/Paper Book/1639; DDP/172, 'Articles to bee given in Charge at the Sessions of the Peace', c.1610; and Laslett, *Household and Family*, pp. 34–6.

We order the said Ralph Fletcher to remove them from the said house before next St James Day and not allow the said house to be used as a cottage for inmates, on pain of 20s.

We present John Sutton (6s 8d) for converting the lower end of his house into a cottage and receiving Thomas Fletcher the younger and his wife as inmates, though forewarned by the Four Men.

We order the said John Sutton to remove the said Fletcher and his wife and to use the said cottage as formerly or forfeit 20s.

[f.6r: 16 cms × 27 cms]

We present Jane Greene[18] (3s 4d) 'for harbouringe misordered company to bee Conversant in her howse to drinke att unseasonable tymes in the night' and allowing William Ward, an apprentice, to sit and drink several times in the night to the great annoyance of neighbours.[19]

We present that the said Jane Greene (6s 8d) harbours as inmates in some part of her house Thomas Sumner and a woman supposed to be his wife.

We order her to remove them from her house before next 1 August and to enjoy the same as formerly it has been, on pain of 20s.

We present that Henry Darbishire[20] (6d) has pulled up 'stoopes'[21] in Fall Lane and threw them into a ditch to the great annoyance of the highway.

[f.6v]

We order the said Derbishire to replace the 'stoopes' at his charge before the feast of St James the Apostle, on pain of 10s.

We present that James Angsdale (13s 4d), though warned by one of the Four Men not to, sold two bays of building to young William Browne of Whiston who took them out of this manor to his house in Whiston. Angsdale 'peremptoryly

18.   Jane married John Green, tailor, a subtenant who died in 1637, while she lived until 1675. At the Epiphany 1638 sessions of the peace, justices ordered the churchwardens and overseers of the poor of the parish of Prescot to maintain Jane, a widow, and her children, and some allowance to Jane continued at least until 1643. Probably to supplement her income as an alehousekeeper, Jane took in lodgers in 1640 and 1641. LPRS, 114, p. 78; 149, p. 93; LRO: QSR/34, Wigan, Epiphany 1638; Steel, *Prescot Churchwardens' Accounts,* pp. 65, 70, 79, 84, 92.
19.   Statutory law prohibited drinking at an alehouse more than an hour a day and during divine service on the Sabbath and fast days or 'festyvall dayes', except by the sick and lodged travellers who remained all night. While no statute fixed the hours of opening and closing until the nineteenth century, justices of the peace during the seventeenth century set closing time at nine in the evening or 'after daylight'. The proclamation of James I in 1619 also established nine as closing time. At Prescot from 1615 to 1700 the court leet, which exercised jurisdiction over its alehousekeepers, adjudicated only three cases (1628, 1637 and 1640) of alehousekeepers allowing drinking at unlawful times. Statute 1 Jac. I, c.9; Larkin and Hughes, *Stuart Royal Proclamations,* p. 411; LRO: QSR/3, Manchester, Midsummer 1592; QSR/9, Ormskirk, Easter 1606; QSR/17, Wigan, Epiphany 1621; QSR/28, Ormskirk, Easter 1631; QJI/1/24, Ormskirk, Midsummer 1650; DDCs/Paper Books/1628 and 1637.
20.   Knowles, *Prescot Records,* p. 33, incorrectly has 'Derbyshire'.
21.   Stoop: 'a post or stake set in the ground, esp. as a mark, *e.g.* to show where refuse may be thrown.' Twemlow, *Liverpool Town Books,* p. 401, note 3.

avouched that hee wold defend any question that should bee made concerninge the sale thereof' on 9 July 1639.[22]

We order that anyone who lays dung in the lane from Hamlet Whitfeilde's house to 'the Platt neare the hillocke' shall not henceforth lay any more there or 'showe up any earth or soyle', on pain of 6s 8d.[23]

[f.7r: 20 cms × 30 cms]

Whereas at the court held on 9 June 1637, it was found that diverse inhabitants had not paid their taxes for repairing the highways, and each had forfeited 3s 4d which was to be employed to repair the highways. That order was not observed, and we now order that the forfeited sums shall be paid to the surveyors of the highways to repair the highways, or each of those inhabitants not paying shall forfeit 6s 8d towards the reparation of the said highways.

[f.7v, blank]
[f.8r: 20 cms × 30 cms]
5 July 1640. **PRESENTMENTS BY THE CONSTABLES** for last year 1639.

We present Richard Walker (12d, John Hoole[24]) for a tussle on Jeffrey Molynex.

Richard Walker (12d, imprisoned) for a tussle on John Taylor, jun., and Taylor (12d, his father James Taylor) on him again.

Ralph Ledbeter (12d, James Parker) for a tussle on James Angsdale, and Angsdale (12d, himself) on him again.

John Taylor (12d, himself) for a tussle on William Whytehed, and Whytehead (12d, Ralph Halsall) on him again.

William Houghton (3s 4d, William Standish) for an affray with blood on Thomas Ditchfield, and Ditchfield (12d, himself) on him again.

Henry Fletcher (12d, Richard Marshall) for a tussle on Richard Taylor, and Taylor (12d, punished) on him again.

James Angsdale (12d, himself) for tussling on Thomas Fletcher, son of Ralph Fletcher, and Thomas Fletcher, son of Thomas Fletcher (for both Fletchers: 12d each, their fathers).

Henry Ackers (12d, Henry Garnett) of Whiston for tussling on James Garnett, and Garnett (12d, Thomas Bond) on him again.

James Angsdale (12d, himself) for tussling on William Houghton, and Houghton (12d, Thomas Wood) on him again.

James Angsdale (12d, himself) for tussling on William Standish, and Standish (12d, imprisoned) on him again.

Nicholas Lyme (12d, Henry Garnett) for tussling on William Houghton, and Houghton (12d, William Standish) on him again.

22. In 1639, 9 July fell on a Tuesday, the market day. See Introduction, p.xxxviii, note 133.
23. Statutory law authorized both quarter sessions and courts leet to inquire about and punish those causing highways to be obstructed or in disrepair. 2 and 3 Philip and Mary, c.8; 5 Eliz. I, c.13; 18 Eliz. I, c.9 and 10; 29 Eliz. I, c.5.
24. To conserve space, for breaches of the peace the amercement or other punishment and the name of the pledge have been placed within rounded brackets next to the person to whom they relate.

[f.8v, blank]
[f.9r: 20 cms × 30 cms]
   Ralph Parr (12d, Thomas Woodes) for tussling on Henry Parr, and Henry Parr (12d, himself) on him again.
   John Halsall (12d, his father) for tussling on Peter Dey, and Dey (12d, his father) on him again.
   William Ackers, jun. (12d, William Sutton), for tussling on William Futerell <and Futerell>.
   Thomas Wood (3s 4d, himself) for an affray with blood on Richard Molynexe, and Molynex (12d, imprisoned) on him again.
   Richard Molynex (12d, William Houghton) for a tussle on Thomas Fletcher, son of Ralph Fletcher, and Fletcher (3s 4d, Thomas Fletcher the elder) for blood on him again.
   Oliver Frodsome (12d, his father) for tussling on Edward Brundreth, and Brundreth (12d, George Wright) on him again.
   Richard Angsdale (12d, himself) for tussling on Gilbert Heas, and Heas (12d, Richard Banner) on him again.
   Richard Angsdale (12d, himself) and his son Edward (12d) for tussling on <W Edward> William Futerell, and Futerell (12d, Gilbert Heas) on them again.
   John Ackers, sen., of Whiston (12d, William Sutton) for tussling on William Forrest, and Forrest (12d, himself) on him again.
   George Lyon, jun., of Whiston (12d, himself) for tussling on William Forrest.
   George Thomasson of Whiston (12d, himself) for tussling on William Jackson, and Jackson (12d, himself) on him again.
   Thomas Lawranson of Whiston (6s 8d, himself) for affray with blood on Walter Laton.

[f.9v]
   We present Thomas Wood (6d) for keeping unlawful gaming in his house twice.[25]
   For keeping unlawful gaming: Richard Litherland (12d) and Isabel Hey (12d).
   William Ackers, jun., of Whiston for tussling on <Wm Ackers> James,[26] and William Ackers on him again. Pledge: themselves.[27]
   William Ackers, jun., of Whiston (12d, himself) for tussling on James Angsdale, and Angsdale (12d, himself) on him again.

[f.10r: 20 cms × 19 cms]
1639. **PRESENTMENTS BY THE CONSTABLES**.
   Richard Mollyneux (3s 4d, William Houghton) for affray with blood on John Leadbeter, and Leadbeter (12d, Richard Marshall) tussled on him again.

---

25.   As an alehousekeeper licensed at Prescot by the steward of the manor, Thomas agreed not to allow in his house any unlawful games, such as bowling, dicing and carding. Unlawful games came under the jurisdiction of both quarter sessions and courts leet. The relevant statute was 33 Henry VIII, c.9 from 1541. The court at Little Crosby permitted gaming only 'in the Christenmas tyme'. LRO: DDBL/48/1 for 1616.
26.   'James' is interlined above the cancelled 'Wm Ackers'.
27.   Marginated in the same hand and ink: 'voided because afterwards', that is, the scribe had incorrectly written this presentment, which he immediately rewrote.

Richard Mollyneux (12d, William Standish) tussled on Thomas Webster, and Webster (12d, John Wade) on him again.

Edward Halsall of Litherland (12d, Richard Litherland) and his neighbour, one Goolden (12d, said Richard Litherland), tussled on a stranger.

John Ashton <and Henry> of Prescot (12d) and one <Henry Taylor> Ralph Naylor (12d, Ralph Halsall 'who received twelve pence to satisfy the Fyne') for a tussle.

Thomas Heyes (3s 4d, Edward Lyon) <tussled> for a fray with blood on John Leadbeter.[28]

Mary Heyes,[29] spinster (3s 4d), 'for beinge an Evesdropper [30] and soweing sedition amongst neighbours.'

[f.10v]

Hugh Whitestones (3s 4d, promised to give pledge but neglected to do it) for affray with blood on Richard Molyneux.

[f.11r: 20 cms × 15 cms]

PRESENTMENTS BY THE CLERKS OF THE MARKET, Hamlet Whitfield and James Angsdale.

Have forestalled[31] the market by buying butter on a market day before it was brought to the cross: Ann (6d), wife of Anthony Litherland;[32] Margaret (6d), wife of Edward Webster; Elizabeth, wife of Thomas Fletcher the elder (12d).[33]

Thomas Webster, butcher (12d), for opening and stuffing a calf.[34]

Ellen Kildale alias Poughten (12d) for selling stinking herrings.

28. Marginated in the same hand and ink: 'respited'.
29. Knowles, *Prescot Records*, p. 34, incorrectly has 'Mary Eaves'. This is the only reference to Mary Heyes in Prescot's court records.
30. An eavesdropper listened under walls, windows or eaves for news to spread to others, leading, it was feared, to slander of and quarrels between neighbours. The offence was presentable and punishable at quarter sessions and courts leet. During the sixteenth and seventeenth centuries Prescot's court leet accused only five persons, all female, of eavesdropping. Blackstone, *Commentaries*, 4, p. 169; LRO: DDK/Bundle 1532/1, 'The Charge of Mr Robte Hanckinson', 1674 or 1675; DDCs/Paper Books/1622–23, 1640; DDKc/PC 4/126/Paper Book/1684; Bailey, *Prescot Court Leet*, pp. 109–10.
31. To judge by a jury's order of 1671, Prescot's market opened exactly at twelve o'clock when a bell was rung; leet records of 1628, 1644, 1648 and 1683 also refer to the town or common bell. To purchase goods intended for the market before that time and later to resell for a profit was to forestall. Related offences were engrossing, or the purchase of large quantities of agricultural products in order to monopolize and resell at a profit, and regrating, or the reselling in the same market or in one within four miles. The law, however, did allow licensed badgers, or dealers in corn, and drovers of cattle to engross. Both quarter sessions and courts leet could inquire about and punish offenders. At Prescot between 1615 and 1700 the clerks of the market presented twenty-five individuals for forestalling or regrating, and jurors themselves presented the only four persons accused of engrossing. LRO: DDCs/Paper Book/1628; DDKc/PC 4/154/Paper Book/1671; DDKc/PC 4/126/Paper Book/1683; William Sheppard, *An Epitome of All the Common and Statute Laws of this Nation Now in Force* (London, 1656), p. 614; 5 and 6 Edw. VI, c.14 and 5 Eliz. I, c.12.
32. Knowles, *Prescot Records*, p. 33, incorrectly has Anthony Litherland but not Ann.
33. The amercement for Elizabeth is above 'Thomas Fletcher', whose name is underscored; the other two amercements were added at the end of the presentment.
34. Two clerks of the market inspected meat to determine whether it was wholesome, or inflated by blowing air into it. Offenders were presentable and punishable at both quarter sessions and courts leet. Statute 51 Henry III.

[f.11v, blank]
[f.12r: 15 cms × 10 cms]
PRESENTMENT BY THE STREETLOOKERS AND WELL LOOKERS,
Hugh Ward and Thomas Browne.

We present Jane Greene (5s) for setting 'a stound' into Slutterforth Well,[35] which was not fit to stand and which the streetlookers took out.

[f.12v, blank]
[f.13r: 12 cms × 17.5 cms]
PRESENTMENTS BY THE BURLEYMEN, Thomas Webster and James Sadler.

We present Ellen Halsall, wid. (2s), for not making her hayment between John Webster and her 'uppon warninge.'[36]

We present the said Ellen Hallsall (4s) for the said fault.

We present Jane Greene (6d) for not making her hayment between Henry Darbisheere and her.

[f.13v, blank]
[f.14r: 20 cms × 32 cms]
5 June 1640. **PRESENTMENTS BY THE ALEFOUNDERS**, Richard Litherland and Alexander Rylandes.

For breaking the assize of ale and beer (12d each):

William Sutton	John Wade
Thomas Parr	John Pendleton
Thomas Woodes	Thomas Bond
William Houghe	Henry Garnett
Thomas Naylor	William Stocke
Nicholas Rannykers	Nicholas Marshall
Ann Ditchfyld	Henry Parr
Janet Winstanley, wid.	William Rose
John Houle	Edward Booth
Ellen Halsall, wid.	Alexander Rylandes
Hamlet Whitfield	Thomas Maberley
Ralph Halsall	Margaret Angsdale
Isabel Fearnes	James Ditchfield
Jane Boulton	Peter Kenwricke
Henry Darbyshyre	Jane Fenney, wid.
Thomas Walles	Richard Angsdale
Richard Litherland	Ralph Plumpton

35. Besides private wells, Prescot had three public wells: Slutterforth Well on Fall Lane, Lady Well near the church and a well sunk by Lawrence Webster in 1606, at the east end of modern Eccleston Street, and surrendered to the town in 1629 by his grandchild, John Webster. Leet authorities decreed orders and issued punishments relating to the quality of well water at twenty-three of the forty-four annual courts held between 1615 and 1660 for which records survive.
36. Probably the affeerors added 'uppon warninge' when the amercement was added because both are in the same hand and ink which are different from the presentment.

For breaking the assize of bread (12d each):

John Poughton	James Houghton
Jane Fenney	Thomas Wood
Thomas Fletcher 'the eldest'	James Taylor

[f.14v, blank]
[f.15r: 20 cms × 32 cms]
5 June 1640. **OFFICERS ELECTED** and sworn for this year:

Constables	*[1]* Ralph Halsall	sworn
	[2³⁷] Nicholas Anderton	sworn
Four Men	*[1]* John Alcock	sworn before
	[1] William Fletcher	sworn before
	[1] James Ditchfeild	sworn before
	[1] Nicholas Marshall	sworn before
Coroner	*[1]* Edward Stockley	sworn
Clerks of the	*[1]* John Parr	sworn
market	*[2]* Hamlet Whitfeild	sworn
Burleymen	*[1]* Alexander Rylandes	sworn
	[2] John Poughten	sworn
Sealers of leather³⁸	*[1]* Thomas Kenwricke	sworn
	[2] Thomas Ackers	sworn
Aletasters	*[2]* Henry Garnett	sworn
	[1] <James Sadler>	
	[2] William Sutton	sworn
Streetlookers and	*[1]* Peter Kenwricke, jun.	sworn
well lookers	*[2]* William Aspia	sworn
Leygatherer	*[1]* Ralph Hall	sworn
Affeerors of the court	*[2]* John Alcocke	sworn
	[2] Nicholas Marshall	sworn
	[2] John Webster	sworn
	[1] William Fletcher	sworn

[f.15v]
Thomas. Therefore the said Thomas Woodes is admitted tenant.

[f.16r: 20 cms × 31.5 cms]
[SURRENDERS AND ADMITTANCES]
  [1] And the jurors further say and present that at a court held on Friday after
Corpus Christi, 9 June 13 James,³⁹ Henry Woodes of Widnes and Margaret his

---

37. Here and in other lists of officers and jurors a '*2*' indicates a name that was added after
    the initial list had been compiled; a name with a '*3*' was added later yet. Because the
    order in the documents has been retained, a '*2*' precedes a '*1*' and a '*3*' a '*2*' when the
    name, subsequently added, was squeezed above the name it was replacing.
38. Marginated on the left: '3s 4d a peece'.
39. 1615.

wife surrendered their messuages, lands, tenements and all rents reserved on surrenders by them formerly made to the said Henry Woodes and Margaret for their lives and the life of the survivor. After their decease, to Thomas Woodes, second son of the said Henry and Margaret, and the heirs of the said Thomas Woodes. For lack of issue, to Joan Woodes, daughter of the said Henry Woodes. For want of issue, to Eleanor Woodes and Mary Woodes, grandchildren of the said Henry Woodes and daughters of William Woodes and the heirs of the said Eleanor and Mary. For lack of issue, to the right heirs of the said Margaret Woodes forever. Jurors further say that the said Henry Woodes and Margaret are both dead.[40] And the said Thomas Woodes is 'in full lyffe' and asks to be admitted.

William Woodes pleaded in bar and a day was given until 7 August for pleading.

A further day was given until 18 September; on which day the said William Woodes made default and says nothing. The said William Woodes on 9 October appeared and says that the messuage, occupied by Jane Fenney and never surrendered or in any way recovered at any time, was inhabited by the said Margaret, at the rent of 2s owed by the said Margaret and her heirs. Therefore the said William says that the said Thomas, with regard to the said rent of 2s and the said messuage in occupation of Jane Fenney, should not be admitted tenant, and concerning the rest the said William says nothing in bar of the admittance.

[f.16v, blank]
[f.17r: 16 cms × 26.5 cms]
[2] James Houghton of Prescot, tailor, is now possessed of one burgage, cottage or dwelling house heretofore in the tenure or occupation of Edward Houghton for the lives of the said Edward Houghton and Elizabeth, wife of the said Edward, and the survivor.

Now on 10 March 15 Charles[41] the said James Houghton out of court came before Nicholas Marshall and Thomas Devias and for £3 10s to him paid by John Webster of Knowsley, nailer, surrendered forever to the said John Webster the said burgage, cottage or dwelling house.

Acknowledged before us: *[signed]* James Houghton
   [signed] Nyc Marshall
   [signed] Thomas Devies[42]

[f.17v, blank]
[f.18r: 19 cms × 30 cms]
[3] On 2 March, 15 Charles, 1640 John Aldem, clerk, bachelor of theology and vicar of the parish church of Prescot, out of court came before Nicholas Marshall and Henry Woodes, and for £180 to him paid by William Fletcher of Prescot, mercer, surrendered to the lord that one close and parcel of land, meadow and pasture commonly called 'Le Cow hey' containing two acres and three rood land of land of the large measure. The lord to regrant the said close, parcel of land and premises to the said William Fletcher forever. Paying yearly to the lord the rent of 2s.

---

40.   For Henry see note 9 *supra*. Margaret was buried in November 1640. LPRS, 97, p. 72.
41.   1640.
42.   The paper book has no 'proclaimed' and 'admitted', and the parchment roll has no 'is admitted' statement; see the following note.

Acknowledged before us: proclaimed   *[signed]* John Aldem
   [signed] Nyc Marshall   admitted
   [signed] Henry Woodes

(*Parchment:*[43] And upon this came the aforesaid William Fletcher in his own person here in open court aforesaid before the steward aforesaid and homage there and prayeth to be admitted tenant thereon. And thereupon proclamation was made and so forth. And because and so forth. Therefore the said William Fletcher is admitted tenant thereof by the steward aforesaid according to the custom of the manor aforesaid to hold to him the said William Fletcher, his heirs and assigns forever in manner and form aforesaid.[44])

[f.18v, blank]
[f.19r: 19 cms × 30 cms]

   [4] On 23 January 15 Charles,[45] Edward Symond of Elton, gent., son and heir of Richard Symond, late of Elton, dec., and George Croston of Bury, gent., son and heir of Mary Croston, late his mother, dec., out of court came before William Alcocke, gent., and Edward Stockley and for £10 to them paid by William Blundell of Prescot, gent., surrendered to the lord those two bays of building near the dwelling house of the said William Blundell and that parcel of land on which the said two bays stand containing twelve yards in length and six yards in breadth. The lord to regrant the said two bays of building and parcel of land to William Blundell and Margaret his wife for their lives. After their decease, to the heirs and assigns of the said William Blundell forever. Paying yearly to the lord the rent of 1d.

Acknowledged before us: proclaimed   *[signed]* Edward Simond
   [signed] Willm Alcock   admitted   *[signed]* Geo Croston
   [signed] Edw Stockley

(*Parchment*: The said William Blundell and Margaret his wife are admitted.)

[f.19v]

   Surrender from Edw Symond and Geo Croston to Will Blundell, gent.

[f.20r: 20 cms × 32 cms]

   [5] On 27 March, 16 Charles, 1640 Edward Stockley, gent., and John Walker [46] out of court came before John Alcocke, jun., James Ditchfeild and Peter Kenwricke,

---

43. While paper books almost always have only 'proclaimed' and 'admitted', parchment rolls contain the following or a slightly altered version.
44. Hereafter to conserve space this long version will be shortened to 'The said William Fletcher is admitted forever.' In this volume *'admissus est (sunt)'* has been rendered 'is (are) admitted' and not 'was (were)' or 'has (have) been admitted' because from 1651 to 1660, when surrenders were enrolled in English, approximately 98 percent have 'is (are) admitted' rather than 'was (were) admitted'.
45. 1640.
46. A subtenant who worked as a cutler, pettychapman and alehousekeeper, John served as constable (1627–28), bailiff (1629–31), burleyman (1636), leygatherer (1637), aletaster (1638) and surveyor of the highways (1640). He petitioned the justices of the peace in 1641 for assistance in caring for his three grandchildren abandoned by his daughter, Ann, and her husband, Tom Radley of Eccleston. John died in late 1646. CRO: EDC 5/99 (1631); LRO: QSR/31, Wigan, Epiphany 1635; QSB/1/242/59, Epiphany 1641 and QSP/3/25, Midsummer 1648; Steel, *Prescot Churchwardens' Accounts*, pp. 51 and 71; LPRS, 114, p. 97.

sen., and for good considerations surrendered to the lord that messuage and tenement with a garden in the upper part of High Street leading toward Eccleston late
in the tenure or occupation of the said John Walker. The lord to regrant the said
messuage, tenement and premises to James Houghton of Prescot, tailor, and Isabel
now his wife for their lives and the survivor. The said James and Isabel pay yearly to the said Edward Stockley the rent of 5s. The remainder after the said term
ended to the said Edward Stockley forever.

Provided that if the said yearly rent or part thereof be unpaid by twenty days
after due, then the said Edward Stockley may repossess.

Acknowledged before us: proclaimed   *[signed]* Edw Stockley
   [signed] John Alcock Jn   admitted   *[signed]* John Walker
   James Ditchfeild *[mark]*
   [signed] Peter Kenwricke

(*Parchment*: And upon this came the said James Houghton and Isabel his wife in
their own persons here in open court aforesaid before the said steward and homage there and ask to be admitted tenants by the steward aforesaid according to the
custom of the said manor to hold the said messuage, land and premises to him
the said James Houghton and Isabel his wife in the manner and form aforesaid.[47])

[f.20v, blank]
[f.21r: 19 cms × 30 cms]

   [6] On 30 January, 15 Charles, 1640 Margaret Goodicar of Prescot, wid., out
of court came before James Ditchfeild and Peter Kenwricke and for the yearly
rent hereafter mentioned and reserved surrendered to the lord that one messuage
or dwelling house which the said Margaret now inhabits and one garden and one
hemp yard to the same messuage belonging. The lord to regrant the said messuage
or dwelling house, garden, yard and premises to Thomas Goodicar of Prescot,
slater, son of the said Margaret, for forty years to be completed if the said Margaret
Goodicar so long lives. Paying yearly to the said Margaret Goodicar rent of 10s
as follows: 2s 6d on the feast of the Annunciation of the Blessed Virgin Mary, 2s
6d on the feast of St John the Baptist, 2s 6d on the feast of St Michael the
Archangel, and 2s 6d on the Nativity of Our Lord.

Acknowledged before us: proclaimed   Margrett Goodicar *[mark]*
   James Ditchfeild *[mark]*   admitted
   [signed] Peter Kenwricke senior

(*Parchment*: The said Thomas Goodicar is admitted.)

[f.21v, blank]
[f.22r: 20 cms × 31.5 cms]

   [7] On 4 June 1640 Henry Ogle, esq., out of court came before Edward Stockley
and William Fletcher[48] and for good reasons surrendered to the lord the messuages,

47.   The parchment roll does not contain an 'are admitted' statement. In that the other usual
      statements (about coming to court, asking to be admitted and holding in manner and form
      aforesaid) are present, the clerk may have inadvertently omitted the 'are admitted tenants'
      material by jumping, when copying the paper book, from 'ask to be admitted tenants' to
      the words that follow 'are admitted tenants'.
48.   The names of ES and WF were added in a blank in the same hand and ink as the rest of
      the surrender.

cottages, gardens and premises. The lord to regrant to Cuthbert Ogle, gent., son and heir apparent of the said Henry, for his life. After his decease, to Elizabeth Ogle, wife of the said Cuthbert, for her life. After her decease, to the said Cuthbert and his male heirs by Elizabeth. For lack of issue, to Cuthbert and his male heirs. For lack of issue, to the said Henry Ogle, father, and his male heirs. For lack of issue, to the right heirs of the said Henry Ogle forever. Paying yearly to the lord the rent of 2s 9d.[49]

Proviso that the said Henry Ogle may surrender the said premises or part thereof to any person for twenty-one years or less or for term of one, two or three lives.
Acknowledged before us: proclaimed   *[signed]* Henry Ogle
   [signed] Edw Stockley   admitted
   Willm Fletcher *[mark – initials*[50]*]*
(*Parchment*: The said Cuthbert Ogle is admitted.)

[f.22v, blank]
[f.23r: 19.5 cms × 31.5 cms]
   [8] On 4 June late 11 James of England and 46 of Scotland,[51] Henry Ogle, esq., surrendered to the lord that messuage or tenement in the tenure or occupation of Richard Gleast of Prescot, husb., to Margery Devias, Elizabeth Devias and Ann Devias, daughters of Roger Devias late of Huyton, clerk, dec., and the life of the longest liver under the yearly rent of 4s 8d to the said Henry Ogle on the Nativity of St John the Baptist and the Nativity of Our Lord in equal portions.

Now on 2 June, 16 Charles, 1640 the said Henry Ogle, esq., out of court came before Edward Stockley and William Fletcher[52] and for <30s> 40s to him paid by William Plombe of Knowsley, yeo., surrendered to the lord the said messuage now occupied by Alexander Rylandes and one croft and parcel of land and that messuage or burgage now occupied by Thomas Moberley. The lord to regrant the said messuages and premises to the said William Plombe who will have the said several messuages and premises immediately after the decease of the said Margery Devias, Elizabeth and Ann for eighty years to be completed if Mary Plombe, daughter of the said William, lives so long. Paying yearly to the said Henry Ogle rent of 4s 8d on the Nativity of St John the Baptist and the Nativity of Our Lord in equal amounts.
Acknowledged before us: proclaimed   *[signed]* Henry Ogle
   [signed] Edw Stockley   admitted
   Wm Fletcher *[mark – initials]*
(*Parchment*: The said William Plombe is admitted.)

[f.23v, blank]
[f.24r: 20 cms × 31 cms]
   [9] On 20 June, 15 Charles, 1639 William Gerard of Brynn, knight and baronet, and John Chadocke of Parr, blacksmith, out of court came before Henry Ogle, esq., and Edward Stockley and for 40s to him the said William Gerard paid

---

49. The parchment roll mentions no amount.
50. Here and subsequently the last vertical stroke of the 'W' and the two horizontal strokes of the 'F' are joined.
51. 1613.
52. The names of ES and WF were added in a blank in a different hand but the same ink.

surrendered to the lord that dwelling house which Ellen Stocke, wid., now inhabits, late in the occupation of John Taylor, and heretofore in the tenure or occupation of Richard Mathewson alias Wilcocke, dec. The lord to regrant the said
dwelling house to the said John Chadocke for the lives of the said John Chadocke;
John Chadocke, jun., son of the said John Chadocke; Alice Chadocke, daughter
of the said John Chadocke; and the survivor. Remainder after the said term ended
to the said William Gerard forever. Paying yearly to the lord 12d in rent. And
paying yearly to the said William Gerard rent of 12d.

Acknowledged before us: proclaimed   *[signed]* Wil Gerard
  [signed] Henry Ogle   admitted   John Chadocke *[mark – initials]*
  [signed] Edw Stockley
(*Parchment*: The said John Chadocke is admitted.)

[f.24v]
  John Chaddock his surrender.

[f.25r: 20 cms × 31 cms]
  [10] Edward Lyon of Prescot, glover, holds to himself for his life and the life
of Thomas Lyon his son or either of them that messuage or cottage containing
two buildings on the east side of the messuage and dwelling house of Nicholas
Marshall under the yearly rent of 13s 4d paid to George Lyon, jun., of Whiston,
as by a surrender acknowledged by the said George Lyon to the said Edward Lyon
and presented at the court held on 21 June 9 Charles.[53]

  Now on 28 April 16 Charles[54] the said Edward Lyon out of court came before
William Blundell and James Ditchfield[55] and for £4 15s to him paid by Nicholas
Marshall of Prescot, yeo., surrendered to the lord the said messuage or cottage on
the east side of the dwelling house of the said Nicholas Marshall. The lord to
regrant the said messuage or cottage and premises to the said Nicholas Marshall
and Margaret his wife for the lives of the said Edward Lyon and Thomas Lyon
his son and the survivor. Paying yearly to the said George Lyon rent of 13s 4d.

Acknowledged before us: proclaimed   Edw Lyon *[mark]*
  [signed] Will Blundell   admitted
  Ja Ditchfield *[mark]*
(*Parchment*: The said Nicholas Marshall and Margaret his wife are admitted.)

[f.25v, blank]
[f.26r: 31.5 cms × 39.5 cms]
  [11] Anthony Litherland of Prescot, chapman, now possesses, for the lives of
himself the said Anthony Litherland, Ann his wife and Elizabeth Litherland,
daughter of the said Anthony and Ann, and the survivor, those two bays of buildings on the west side of the dwelling house of Henry Lyon and by him lately built,
and a parcel of land on the north side of the said two buildings containing in
breadth seven yards, and also a shippon with a passage to the said building between

53. 1633.
54. 1640.
55. The names of WB and JD were added in a blank in the same hand and ink as the surrender.

the dwelling house late in the occupation of Ann Ewde and the dwelling house late in the occupation of Jane Washington, and all under the rent of 3s 4d to the said Henry Lyon and the rent of 2d to the lord; that building on the east side of the dwelling house of the said Anthony and one parcel of land lying lengthwise on the north side of the said building under the yearly rent of 12d to the said Henry Lyon; also that land with a bay of building on it, and the same building is situated on the upper end of High Street leading toward Eccleston heretofore used for 'a worke howse' under the yearly rent of 12d to the said Henry Lyon; and that croft and parcel of land now occupied by the said Anthony on the north side of the dwelling house of the said Anthony and called Lyon's yard, under the rent of 12d to the said Henry Lyon. All as by four surrenders made to the said Anthony Litherland by the said Henry Lyon.

Now on 26 May, 16 Charles, 1640 the said Anthony Litherland out of court before Edward Stockley and William Fletcher for good causes surrendered to the lord the said buildings, workhouse and premises. The lord to regrant to the said Anthony Litherland for the life of the said Anthony. After his decease, to Ann, wife of the said Anthony, for her life. After her decease, to John Litherland, son of the said Anthony and Ann, during the said term of grant to the said Anthony by the said Henry Lyon. Paying yearly to the said Henry Lyon rents totalling 6s 4d. And to the lord the rent of 2d.

Acknowledged before us:

[signed] Edw Stockley

Willm Fletcher [mark – initials]

Elizabeth Hey pleaded in bar [and time was given until the next court], but on which day the said Elizabeth made default. Therefore the said Ann and John are admitted.[56]

(*Parchment*: The said Ann Litherland and John are admitted.)

[f.26v, blank]
[f.27r: 18.5 cms × 29 cms]

[12] To this court came John Alcocke of Eccleston near Knowsley, gent., in open court before the steward and homage and surrendered to the lord a parcel of land on the upper end of High Street leading toward Eccleston and now in the possession of Edward Stockley of Prescot and by him used as a midding stead. Heretofore the copyhold inheritance of the said Edward Stockley, the parcel contains in length twenty-two feet and in breadth $11^1/_2$ feet and is surrendered to the said Edward Stockley forever in exchange for so much of the land of the said Edward Stockley on the western side of the said midding stead and on which the dwelling house of Richard Banner is now erected.*

proclaimed   [signed] John Alcock
admitted

(*Parchment*: The said Edward Stockley is admitted forever.)

---

56. 'Elizabeth Hey pleaded...Ann and John are admitted' was added in a different hand.
*   The parchment roll adds: paying yearly to the lord the rent and services due.

[13 ⁵⁷] To this court came the said Edward Stockley who in open court before the steward and homage surrendered to the lord one parcel of land heretofore used as part of a midding stead and upon which the said John Alcocke has built part of a house and part of a shippon now occupied by Richard Banner, tailor, containing in length 20½ feet and in breadth eight feet. Surrendered to the said John Alcocke of Eccleston, gent., forever in exchange for so much of the land of the said John Alcocke and before surrendered to the said Edward Stockley forever.*

proclaimed   *[signed]* Edw Stockley
admitted

(*Parchment*: The said John Alcocke is admitted forever.)

[f.27v, blank]
[f.28r: 19.5 cms × 32 cms]

[14] To this court came John Alcocke of Eccleston near Knowsley, gent., and in open court before the steward and homage and for 20s to him paid by Richard Banner of Prescot, tailor, surrendered to the lord that messuage or cottage in High Street leading toward Eccleston containing three bays of building and one garden on the north side of the same now occupied by the said Richard Banner.The lord to regrant the said messuage, cottage, garden and premises to the said Richard Banner for the lives of the said Richard Banner, Katherine his wife, William Banner his son and the survivor. Remainder after the said term ended to the said John Alcocke forever. Paying yearly to the said John Alcocke the rent of 13s 4d on the feasts of the Nativity of Our Lord and of St John the Baptist in equal amounts. And one able reaper to reap a corn field within two days of being demanded. Also paying to the lord the yearly rent of 3d.

(*Parchment*: The said Richard Banner is admitted.)

[f.28v, blank]
[f.29r, blank: 24 cms × 32 cms]
[f.29v]

Prescot. 5 June 1640. Extract delivered to Thomas Parr, bailiff.⁵⁸ Sum total: £10 4s⁵⁹ 10d.

---

57. This surrender is in the same hand and ink as the previous one.
58. The unknown clerk of the court wrote the extract. An undertenant (commonly in the top 12 percent of all undertenants in call books) and alehousekeeper who was also described as yeoman and badger, Thomas was bailiff for at least 1621, 1623–24 and 1632–42. He also served as schoolwarden in 1626 and 1628, surveyor of the highways in 1631 and 1640–43 and as one of the Eight Men for the parish in 1642, 1644 and 1645. Thomas was buried on 12 December 1645, not quite two weeks after his wife Ellen (Wilcock), 'a woman full of good works', was buried. His inventory reveals a rather tidy sum of over £103 in property. Not uncommon for this period, Thomas and Ellen had seven children between 1625 and 1637, only three of whom survived into adulthood. For Thomas as badger, see LRO: QSB/1/70/1, Easter 1630; QSB/1/82/54, Epiphany 1631; QSB/1/122/81, Midsummer 1633; QSB/1/158/72, Michaelmas 1635; QSB/1/186/80, Midsummer 1637; QSB/1/202/91, Midsummer 1638; QSB/1/219/71, Midsummer 1639. For Ellen see Irvine, *Marriage Licences...1624–1632,* p. 22; and LPRS, 114, p. 95. For Thomas's inventory see LRO: WCW/Prescot/1645/Thomas Parr. For their children, LPRS, 76, pp. 83, 88, 94, 98, 215; 114, pp. 4, 12, 72, 98, 120; 137, p. 179.
59. Knowles, *Prescot Records,* p. 33, incorrectly has 'IIIs'.

1641

[Paper Book: DDKc/PC 4/66]   [Parchment Roll: DDKc/PC 4/164⁶⁰]

[f.1r: 30.5 cms × 39.5 cms]

(*Parchment*: **VIEW OF FRANKPLEDGE WITH COURT BARON OF PRESCOT** in the county of Lancaster held there according to the custom of the manor of Prescot aforesaid before Thomas Wolfall, esq., steward of the manor and court aforesaid, on Friday, the day after Corpus Christi, 24⁶¹ June, 17 Charles, 1641.⁶²)

[SUITORS:]

o Sir William Gerrard,
    baronet   appeared by⁶³
o Thomas Eccleston, esq.
    John Lancaster, esq.
o Henry Lathom, esq.
o Thomas Woolfall, esq.
o Richard Eltonhed, gent.
o Thomas Sorrocold, gent. appeared
           by William
           Hough,
           tenant⁶⁴
o William Alcocke, gent.
o John Alcocke, sen., gent.
o John Aldem, clerk
o John Alcocke, jun., gent.
    Edward <Devisse> Davies, gent.
o William Lyme
    Richard Woodes   out of
o Henry Webster of Knowsley
o George Lyon of Eccleston
o Edward Stockley, gent.
o William Aspia
o <Henry> Thomas Woodes of Widnes
o John Gloover   out of
o Nicholas Marshall
o Jane Pyke, wid.
o William Blundell, gent.

o John Webster
o Edward Symond
o George Croston, gent.
o Robert Wainwright
o Peter Kenwricke, sen.
o George Lyon, jun., of Whiston
o George Deane of Rainhill
o Richard Mollynexe   out of
o William Parr
o James Houghton
o Edward Orme
o William Lyon
o John Lyon, skinner   pardoned
    George Tarleton
    William Leadbeter
o John Leadbeter
o Dorothy Mercer, wid.
o John Webster, nailer
o Henry Crosse   pardoned
o Richard Litherland
o William Sutton
o Henry Woodes of Whiston
o William Fletcher
o Richard Tarbocke   infirm
o Thomas Devias
o James Ditchfield

60. Two membranes (30 cms × 61 cms) with writing on both sides and a scrap (30 cms × 36 cms) at the bottom, with writing on one side, that serves as a cover.
61. A mistake for 25 June.
62. 'Prescott' is the only heading in the paper book.
63. The name or initials are smudged or erased and unreadable. That person would have presented the excuse for the suitor not attending court, which caused the bailiff to place an attendance mark next to Sir William Gerrard's name.
64. Actually, Hough is an undertenant.

- o Henry Pynnington   within age[65]
- o John Urmeston
- o William Coppall
- o Hugh Ward

Tenants:[66]
- o Ferdinand Parker
- o Katherine Stevenson, wid.
- o Anthony Prescott
- o John Frodsome
- o James Angsdale
- o Anne Ackers
- o John Ashton
- o John Taylor
- o Thomas Knowles
- o Thomas Eaton
- o Isabel Hey
- o Jane Bolton
- o James Taylor
- o Thomas Caldwell
- o Thomas Parr
- o Thomas Wood
- o William Hough
- o Thomas Ackers
- o Emeline Neylor, wid.
- o Mary Haward, wid.
- o John Cowper
- o George Lyon
- o Nicholas Renicars
- o George Standistreete
- o Anne Lodge
- o Anne Ditchfield, spinster
- o Margaret Goodicare, wid.
- o Thomas Goodicarr
- o William Futerell
- o Richard Holmes
- o John Strettell
- o William Birtchall
- o John Hoole
- o John Walker
- o John Einsworth

- o George Wright
- o <Mr> William Standish, gent.
- o Jane Fletcher, wid.
- o Edward Rylandes
- o Ellen Rylandes, wid.
- o Thomas Horneby
- o Elizabeth Man, wid.
- o John Huson
- o Peter Garnett
- o Roger Dey
- o Richard Chorleton
- o William Fletcher, glover
- o John Houghland
- o Ralph Parr
- o William Jackson
- o Peter Hearefoote

[f.1v]
- o Evan Garnett
- o Thomas Aspe
- o Ellen Halsall, wid.
- o Margery Browne, wid.
- o Hamlet Whitfield
- o Ralph Halsall
- o Nicholas Anderton
- o John Wade
- o John Pendleton
- o Henry Garnett
- o William Stocke
- o William Ewood
- o Henry Parr
- o Thomas Parr, jun.
- o William Rose
- o George Kirkes
- o Margery <Shuttleworth>
     Houghland, wid.
- o Alexander Rylandes
- o Thomas Mobberley
- o Henry Astley
- o Elizabeth Webster
- o John Parr
- o Edward Fynney

65. While *'infra etatem'* may be translated 'under age', it is here rendered 'within age', since 'within age' was always employed in the call books of 1651–60 when English replaced Latin in these records.
66. Actually, undertenants.

o Robert Kennion
o John Huson
o Edward Bate
o Richard Woolfall
o James Parker
o James Houghton
o Cecily Houghton, wid.
o Barbary Storie, wid.
o Anne Giller
o Thomas Garnett
o Richard Ditchfield
o Anne Miller
o Richard Marshall
o James Sadler
o Anne Litherland, wid.
o William Standish
o Richard Banner
o Janet Orrell
o Edward Webster
o William Abshall
o William Mollynexe
o Thomas Ditchfield
o Thomas Fletcher, jun.
o John Sutton
o Anne Mollynexe, wid.
o John Rainford
o Thomas Heas
o John Stevenson, gent.
   Ralph Fletcher
o Thomas Litherland
o Thomas Bond
o Thomas <Bond> Walls

o Henry Darbishire
o William Houghton
   Jane Greene, wid.
o Alice Houghton, wid.
o John Poughton
o John Oliverson
o Richard Aspshawe
o Robert Hatton
o Robert Woosie
o Peter Kenwricke, jun.
o Henry Prescott
o Ralph Stocke
o John Wainwright
o Thomas Browne
o Thomas Fletcher, sen.
o Richard Angsdale
o Richard Higginson
o Jane Fennow, wid.
o Henry Kirkes
o Ralph Plumpton
o John Rigby
o Thomas Kenwricke
o Edward Lowe
o Ellen Parr, wid.
o John Massie
o Ralph Houghton
o Margery Whytesyde, wid.
o Mr Bolton
o William Swift
o Katherine Norres, wid.
o Adam Bate

[f.2r: 19.5 cms × 30 cms]
JURORS FOR THE LORD, 24 June 1641:

Thomas Eccleston, esq.
Henry Lathom, esq.
John Lancaster, esq.
Richard Eltonhed, gent.
John Alcocke, sen., gent.
[2[67]] <William Parr of Cronton>

67. *'[2]'* indicates a name added after the initial list had been compiled. Also, the alignment
     of circles, dashes and crosses may indicate who attended adjourned courts with which
     colleagues.

+ John Alcocke, jun., gent.	sworn	
[2] William Parr		
Nicholas Marshall		
John Webster		
– George Deane of Rainhill	sworn	–
William Lyon		
– + William Fletcher	sworn	– –
James Ditchfield	sworn	–
– ○ Henry Woodes of Whiston	sworn	–
<William Parr>		
– ○ James Houghton	sworn	–
– + George Lyon, jun., of Whiston	sworn	–
	<denied [68]>	
○ Henry Webster of Knowsley	sworn	+ –
William Aspia	sworn	–
Henry Crosse		
– + Richard Litherland	sworn	
– ○ Robert Wainwright	sworn	–
– ○ Edward Orme	sworn	–
John Lyon, skinner		
[2] <William Lyme>		
John Webster, nailer		
Peter Kenwricke, sen.		
– + [2] Thomas Woodes	sworn	
– ○ [2] Thomas Devias	sworn	+ –
– + [2] William Coppall	sworn	+ –

The said jury adjourned to perfect their verdict at the next court under pain of 3s 4d each.

On 16 July 1641 the said jury further adjourned to perfect their verdict at the next court under pain of 3s 4d each.

On 27 August 1641 the jury adjourned to perfect their verdict at the next court under pain of 3s 4d.

On 17 September 1641 the jury further adjourned to perfect their verdict on 29 October under pain of 3s 4d.

On 29 October 1641 the jury further adjourned to perfect their verdict on 19 November under pain of 3s 4d.

On 19 November 1641 the jury made default. The steward nevertheless further adjourned the jury to perfect their verdict on 10 December under pain of 6s 8d.

[f.2v, blank]
[f.3r: 20 cms × 31 cms]
VIEW OF FRANKPLEDGE WITH COURT OF PRESCOT held on Friday, 25 June, 17 Charles, 1641.

68. Since '*negatus*' appeared after '*juratus*', George, sworn, may have initially refused to appear with his fellow jurors.

INQUISITION TO INQUIRE FOR THE LORD on the oaths of:

John Alcock, jun., gent.
George Deane of Rainhill
William Fletcher
James Ditchfeild
Henry Woodes of Whiston
James Houghton
George Lyon, jun., of Whiston
Henry Webster of Knowsley

William Aspia
Richard Litherland
Robert Wainwright
Edward Orme
Thomas Woodes
Thomas Devias
William Coppull

THE JURORS SAY AND PRESENT on oath that the following owe suit unto this court and this day made default (12d each):

John Lancaster, esq.
Edward Davies, gent.
George Tarlton
Ralph Fletcher
Jane Greene

We present John Sutton (6s 8d) 'for Convertinge his Oven howse into a Cottage and receivinge Raph Parr Butcher to live in the same as an Inmate without Consent of the 4 men.'

We order that the said John Sutton shall remove the said Ralph Parr out of the said house and likewise not use the same otherwise than formerly it has been, at or before the feast of St Michael the Archangel under pain of 13s 4d.

We present that according to an order of the last court Jane Greene, wid., was ordered to remove at or before 1 August last 'one Thomas Sumner and a woman supposed to bee his wife' out of her house who lived there as inmates, but she has not performed the same and therefore has forfeited a fine of 20s.

[f.3v]

We present Margaret Goodicar (3s 4d) for receiving Henry Kirkes, wife and family into the lower end of her house to live as inmates.

We order the said Margaret Goodicar to remove the said Kirkes out of the said lower end of her house at or before the feast of St Michael the Archangel next under pain of 13s 4d.

We present Mr Aldem for falling twenty-one poles in the Wood[69] without consent of the Four Men, which poles he did cleve into rails and posts and employed

69. Taking timber from the manorial lord's Wood, west of the parish church, was regulated by a by-law made at Prescot's court: no one was to cut trees or collect wood without the permission of the Four Men, or of the overseers of the Wood or woodlookers as they were called in the sixteenth century. Bailey, *Prescot Court Leet, passim*. Vicar Aldem had been before the court on a similar charge in 1619 (when he cut seventy-two trees), 1623 (cut 'timber'), 1624 (three poles), 1625 (diverse poles), 1629 (four poles) and 1630 (fifty poles). During the 1640s thirteen named individuals cut and removed twenty-three poles and unspecified amounts of timber or employed the same for unapproved purposes; two other persons removed pricks or underwood. In the 1650s three persons removed or misemployed thirty-seven saplings and unspecified timber. Earlier in the seventeenth century the

some for railing the fence along the brook and the residue for railing the hedge between the Wood and the delves. Amerced.[70]

We present John Rainforth and Adam Bate for not paying some part of the money taxed for their houses for the highways within this manor for last year. Each 2s.

We order the said John Rainforth and Adam Bate to pay what they were behind unto the now surveyors for this year at or before the feast of St <James the Apostle> Bartholomew next under pain of 2s each.

[f.4r: 20 cms × 31 cms]

'Whereas according to the Custome of this mannor the recordes within the same after they are enrowled by the Clarke of this Court have beene accustomably putt into the Chest appointed for that purpose and the keyes of the said Chest kept by the steward for the tyme beinge and 4 men. Wee now therefore order that from henceforth the said recordes shalbe putt into the said Chest and that the keyes shalbe delivered into the Custody of the said steward and fower men as formerly it hath beene accustomed and likewise that after they are yearely enrowled and putt into it noe search shalbe made by any Copiholder of this mannor without the privity and Consent of the said steward and 4 men Jointly upon payne of every one offending Contrary to this order to forfait xls.'

In 1631 the jury then issued an order concerning all who had timber, which was delivered to them out of the Wood by the Four Men but which was lying either in the streets or in their backsides and which was not by them employed at or before the feast of St Michael the Archangel then next following and is since that time not employed according to the uses by the said Four Men granted. That timber was to be redelivered by the said officers unto such persons in a reasonable manner for reparation of their houses as they should think most needful and convenient. We now order that any such timber remaining undisposed of, according to the uses before expressed that does either lie in the streets or backsides of any copyholder of this manor or in the Wood, shall be by those to whom it is granted put to use at or before the last day of <August> September next. If they or any of them neglect, the said Four Men shall deliver such timber unto such as shall then have need to repair their housing in such proportions as they shall think fit. Likewise

problem was much greater. In the 1610s twenty-four named individuals removed or misemployed two hundred poles and diverse other trees, while eleven took pricks, windings or tinsel. In the 1620s the numbers were forty persons, fifty-six poles and five individuals; in the 1630s thirty-eight, 107 and one, respectively. We have no record of the number of trees removed with permission. The adverse effect on Prescot Wood was obvious, and in 1759 the court stated that the timber in the Wood 'has been destroyed long since.' For Aldem see LRO: DDCs/Paper Books/1619, 1623–25, 1629; DDKc/PC 4/161/Paper Book/1630. THC: 'Extract from the Minute Book of the Steward', f.3.

70. Added in Latin at the end of the presentment: 'The said John Aldem appeared and pleaded not guilty.' Marginated in English: 'Also the said Mr Aldem hath this day Apealed to the Lord.' Both notes are in the same hand and ink but compared to the presentment are in a different hand but the same ink.

[f.4v]
the Four Men shall not grant any more wood to be fallen to any person before such time as the said timber is employed by those to whom it was granted and by the said former order limited to have been repaired before the said feast of St Michael in 1631 as aforesaid.

We further order that any copyholder within this manor, who shall have any timber lying in the places before mentioned that is not put to use at or before the said last day of <August> September next and who shall refuse obstinately to give 'liberty' to the said Four Men to come into their backsides to view such timber as they have lying there not employed or shall resist them if they come to deliver the same as is declared in the former order, shall, for every such time as they shall so obstinately refuse or resist the said officers in delivering the said timber not employed as aforesaid, forfeit to the lord of this manor a fine of £3 6s 8d each of them.

[f.5r: 20 cms × 31 cms[71]]
We order that the said Dorothy Mercer[72]shall reedify the said barn as formerly it was and that the said Robert Wainwright shall have recompense for such damage as he shall sustain by himself or his tenants by reason of the laying of the same open to the street. The repair or reedifying shall be done at or before the next court, under pain of 40s.

We order that the gate standing by the house of Cecily Houghton, wid., leading into Churchleys shall be repaired by the owners and occupiers of land within the said Churchleys who claim a way to their lands enclosed out of the same, and they shall contribute proportionally to the charge of maintaining the said gate.

[f.5v, blank]
[f.6r: 20 cms × 30 cms]
There is a parcel of waste ground called 'Prescott towne mosse' lying on the northeast side of the said town which the lord of this manor and his tenants in his right 'have tyme out of the memorie of man had and used to have Comon of Pasture and also libertie for theire sportes and exercyces upon the same both for shooting and other wise and also the Lord for keepinge of his horse Fayre[73] theire and which to the prejudice of the Lord of this mannor is now hindered.' We present that <William Lyme of Prescot> William Webster of Eccleston has about April last made or caused to be made one enclosure[74] with a cop and a ditch upon the

---

71. The hand that wrote the jurors' presentments on folios 3–5 continues on folio 7v. Folio 5 is out of order and should follow folio 7v. A different hand wrote folios 6r, 7r and the top several lines of folio 7v.
72. Dorothy, daughter of Thomas Layton, gent., was the widow of Richard Mercer of Kirkby, gent., who died in September 1640. Arthur Smith, ed., *The Registers of the Parish Church of Walton-on-the-Hill: 1586–1663*, LPRS, 5 (Wigan, 1900), p. 140. In call books Richard's name appeared in the bottom fourth of tenants; he never served in any leet office.
73. For the account of the sale of six geldings, two horses and three mares at the fair in 1618, see LRO: DDCs/Paper Book/1618.
74. Not surprisingly at Prescot, a market centre, the court records for 1615 to 1700 contain few accusations of enclosing, or restricting access to land held in common, by erecting fences or hedges. A more significant problem was encroachment, commonly on the waste

said Town Moss without consent of the steward and Four Men. Therefore <they are amerced either of them> he is amerced 2s.

We order that the said <William Lyme and> William Webster shall put down the same cop and ditch and lay the same even again by putting in the earth first and laying the 'greene[75] sodes' upon the same and so make the same even again before 'Christmas' next on pain of <either of them> 10s.

[f.6v, blank]
[f.7r: 20 cms × 30 cms]

We further order that if the said <William Lyme and> William Webster shall make default in evening the same as aforesaid, then the constables shall at the town's charge put down the same as aforesaid at or before Candlemas next under pain of 10s. And we pray that the charge of evening the same may be had out of the forfeitures made by the said <William Lyme and> William Webster if there be any.

Whereas it appears to us by evidence that certain parcels of land called Churchleys are now divided into severalty, and the way into Churchleys has been at the upper end through the gate at the house of Cecily Houghton and so along at the north end thereof. All occupiers thereof ought to leave a way for the other owners of the Churchleys to go to their parts that way which, as we are given to understand, has been heretofore hindered by John Webster of Prescot. We therefore order that both the said John Webster and all other owners and occupiers shall leave a convenient passage at the upper end

[f.7v]

thereof two yards broad for the necessary occupation of the rest of the said Churchleys, upon pain of everyone making default 3s 4d.

And whereas a hedge standing between the lands of Edward Stockley and John Leadbetter[76] is in decay and leans upon the inheritance of the said Edward Stockley, we order that the said John Leadbetter or his tenants shall set the said hedge upright as formerly it was at or before the feast of the Purification of the Blessed Virgin Mary next under pain of 6s 8d.

We present that a barn standing between the lands of Thomas Woodes of Widnes and the lands of Henry Latham, esq., being the inheritance of Dorothy Mercer, wid., is in decay, and the timber lying upon the said ground where it stood lays waste to the street. A garden belonging to the house of the inheritance of the said Henry Lathom is now in the holding of Robert Wainwright of Tarbock. The barn is to be repaired by the said Dorothy Mercer <wid.> who is in mercy 12d.

> and more frequently occurring during the final two decades of the seventeenth century. Encroachment involved altering the boundary of one's property to one's advantage by extending a building, wall, fence or hedge into a highway or onto the property of a neighbour or the waste. Such behaviour without the consent of the lord of the manor was presentable and punishable at Prescot's court; however, provided an annual rent was paid, the lord might approve of the enclosure of or encroachment onto common land.
>
> 75.   The right edge of the paper book is tattered and only 'gree' survives; 'greene' is from the parchment roll.
> 76.   While the parish registers contain no baptismal and burial entries for John, he was alive in 1613 when his father, John, senior, surrendered property to him but had died by 1652 or 1653 when the latter year's call book noted that he was dead. Uncharacteristically for a resident tenant, John the son filled no manorial or parish office. LRO: DDCs/Paper Book/1613; DDKc/PC 4/112/Paper Book/1653.

[f.8r: 20 cms × 22.5 cms]

PRESENTMENTS made by us this year for assaults and frays.

Richard Angsdell (3s 4d) and Edward Standish (3s 4d) made affray with blood against Thomas Laton, and Laton (12d, William Hough) tussled with them again.

William Houghton (3s 4d) an affray with blood against Edward Standish, and Standish (12d, his father) tussled with him again.

Robert Prescott (12d, Henry his brother) for a tussle on Henry Standish, and Standish (12d, imprisoned) on him again.

Ralph Parr (3s 4d, William Rose) an affray with blood against James Winstandley (12d, Thomas Parr, jun.), Henry Lathom (12d, Edward Lyon) and John Tunstall (12d, William Yeaud).

William Webster of Roby (12d, William Coppall) for affray against Lawrence Harrison, and Harrison (12d, Robert Hatton) tussled with him again.

John Lowranson (12d, Ralph Halsall) a tussle <with> against Thomas Laton, and Laton (12d) with him again.

James Angsdell (12d) for a tussle against Thomas Webster.

Thomas Ackeres (12d) made a tussle against John Strettell, and Strettell (12d) on him again.

William Ackeres, butcher (12d), tussle against John Knowles.

John Taylor, sen. (3s 4d), affray with blood against Thomas Bound.

[signed] Raphe Halsall   *[signed]* Nicholas Anderton

[f.8v]

We present Jane Greene (6s 8d) for 'harboringe and entertayninge a woman greate with a Basterd Child as wee weare enformed.' The said Jane had notice to remove her but did not.

Edward Holland of Windle (12d) tussled on Richard Haward of Whiston, and Haward (12d) tussled on him again.

Lawrence Harrison, slater (12d), tussled on the said Richard Haward, and Haward (12d) tussled on him again.

John Lawrenson of Huyton (12d) tussled on Thomas Ackers of Whiston, collier, and Ackers (12d) tussled on him again.

[f.9r: 19 cms × 24 cms]

25 June 1641. **PRESENTMENTS BY THE ALEFOUNDERS**, William Sutton and Henry Garnett, for the year now past.

We present these persons for breaking the assize of ale and beer (12d each):

Thomas Parr	Hamlet Whitfield
William Sutton	Ralph Halsall
Thomas Wood	Isabel Hey
William Hough	Jane Boulton
Em Naylor, wid.	Henry Darbishyre
Ann Ditchfield	Richard Litherland
William Futrall	John Pendleton
John Houle	Thomas Walls
Ellen Halsall, wid.	Thomas Bond

Henry Garnett
Nicholas Marshall
Henry Parr
William Rose
Edward Booth
Alexander Rylandes
Thomas Maberley
Ralph Plumpton

Jane Fenney
Richard Marshall
Richard Angsdale
James Ditchfield
John Waynwright
Jane Huntte
Ursula Teylor, spinster

[f.9v]
We present for breaking the assize of bread:

John Poughton (12d)
Jane Fenney, wid. (12d)
Thomas Fletchar, sen., two several times (2s)
James Houghton (12d)
Thomas Wood, two several times (2s)
John Cowper (12d)
James Teylor (12d)

[f.10r: 15 cms × 18 cms]
PRESENTMENTS by John Parr and Hamlet Whitfield,[77] one of the town clerks for Prescot 'this presant yeare 1640.'

We[78] present for selling unlawful meat openly in the market myself John Parr (6s 8d).[79]

We present for the like offence Richard Webster of Rainhill (6s 8d).

We present the same Richard Webster (12d) for opening meat.

We present James Angsdell of Prescot (6s 8d) for selling unlawful meat.

We present Henry Pare of Prescot (12d) for opening meat.

[f.10v, blank]
[f.11r: 16 cms × 22.5 cms]
PRESENTMENTS BY THE BURLEYMEN, Alexander Rylandes and John Poughten, for 1640.

We present Thomas Heyes (2s) 'for sufferinge his heyment to lye downe' between William Aspe and him, though several times warned by the burleymen.

We present Ellen Halsall, wid. (2s), for suffering her sow to trespass in the grass of John Webster several times, though she had warning to make her hayment sufficient which she neglected to do in time.

[f.11v, blank]
[f.12r: 9 cms × 10 cms]
PRESENTMENTS BY THE STREETLOOKERS this year.

77. '[A]nd Hamlett Whitfield' is interlined. This and the following two changes were written in a different ink but probably the same hand.
78. In these entries by the clerks of the market, 'We' was written over 'I'.
79. 'John Parr. Therefore, etc. vjs 8d' was added later.

Thomas Fletcher, jun. (12d), for keeping clay and dung in the streets a quarter of a year and having warning to clean it would not.[80]

Thomas Heyes (12d) and John Rainforth (12d) for the like.

[f.12v, blank]
[f.13r: 20 cms × 31 cms]
25 June 1641. **OFFICIALS ELECTED** and sworn for this year:

Constables	[1] Peter Herefoote	sworn
	[2] Alexander Rylandes	sworn
Four Men	[1] John Alcocke	sworn before
	[1] William Fletcher	sworn before
	[1] James Ditchfeild	sworn before
	[1] Nicholas Marshall	sworn before
Coroner	[1] Edward Stockley	sworn before
Clerks of the market	[1] James Angsdall	sworn
	[2] Ralph Halsall	sworn
Burleymen	[1] John Cowper	sworn
	[2] William Sutton	sworn
Sealers of leather	[1] Roger Dey	sworn
	[2] Thomas Ackers	sworn
Aletasters	[1] Ralph Plumpton	sworn
	[2] Thomas Aspe	sworn
Streetlookers and well lookers	[1] William Eaud	sworn
	[2] Ralph Houghton	sworn
Leygatherer	[1] Richard Marshall	absent; therefore 6s 8d which is respited to next year, and if then elected and sworn, another respite may be made.
	[2] William Birchall	sworn
Affeerors of the court	[1] John Alcock	sworn
	[1] William Fletcher	sworn
	[2] Henry Woodes	sworn
	[2] Richard Litherland	sworn

[f.13v, blank]
[f.14r: 16 cms × 27 cms]
[SURRENDERS AND ADMITTANCES]

[1] On 10 July, 16 Charles, 1640 Edward Davyes of London[81] out of court came before William Fletcher and Henry Parr and for £30 from Richard Tyrer of

---

80. A by-law passed and enforced by Prescot's court allowed inhabitants to pile solid human and animal waste on the street side of their dwellings, for a fee that went for street repair, for up to a week in 1580 and up to a month in 1678. Sellers and buyers of that waste piled near dwellings also paid a fee that went to the supervisors of the highways for highway repairs. Bailey, *Prescot Court Leet*, p. 212; LRO: DDCs/Paper Book/1678.

81. The parchment roll does not contain 'of London'.

Knowsley, clerk, surrendered that messuage or dwelling house near the church gate,[82] heretofore occupied by John Garnett, mercer, dec., and now in the hands of the said Edward Davyes, with one shop and cellar under the same. The lord to regrant to the said Richard Tyrer forever. Yearly rent of 2s to the lord.

Acknowledged before us and sealed: admitted[83]   *[signed]* Edward Davis
  William Fletcher *[mark – initials]*
  [signed] Henrey Parr   *[seal]*
(*Parchment*: The said Richard Tyrer is admitted forever.)

[f.14v, blank]
[f.15r: 16.5 cms × 27 cms]
  [2] On 17 June, 17 Charles, 1641 William Blundell of Prescot, gent., out of court came before John Alcock, jun., William Fletcher and Nicholas Marshall, and for £7 8s from John Houghton of Prescot, linenwebster,[84] surrendered that burgage or parcel of land in Churchley Field, heretofore in the holding of the said William Blundell and now in the occupation of the said John Houghton. The lord to regrant to the said John Houghton for the lives of the said John Houghton and Margery Houghton, sister of the said John Houghton, and life of the survivor of them. The remainder after the estate ended to the said William Blundell forever. To the lord the yearly rent of 8d at the usual feasts in equal portions and to the said William Blundell yearly rent of 4s in one payment on 1 August.

Acknowledged before us: admitted   *[signed]* Will Blundell
  [signed] John Alcock Jn
  Willm Fletcher *[mark – initials]*
  [signed] Nyc Marshall
(*Parchment*: The said John Houghton is admitted.)

[f.15v, blank]
[f.16r: 20 cms × 31 cms]
  [3] On 4 June, 17 Charles, 1641 William Coppoole of Prescot, husb., out of court came before John Alcocke, jun., Nicholas Marshall and William Fletcher, and for £10 to the said William Coppoole paid by John Webster of Prescot, wheelwright, surrendered that messuage or cottage commonly called 'le little Cookestoole howse' with one garden or yard lying on the north side. The lord to regrant to the said John Webster forever. Annual rent of 8d to the lord.

Acknowledged before us: admitted   Willm Coppoole *[mark]*
  [signed] John Alcock Jn
  [signed] Nyc Marshall
  Willm Fletcher *[mark – initials]*
(*Parchment:* The said John Webster is admitted forever.)

[f.16v, blank]
[f.17r: 20 cms × 31 cms]

---

82. For 'near the Church gate' in English in the paper book and in Latin in the parchment roll, the Abstract Book has 'dwelling howse standinge neare the porch leading into the Church yoard'.
83   Occasionally the paper book does not have 'proclaimed' but only 'admitted'.
84. Parchment: linenweaver.

[4] On 3 June, 17 Charles, 1641 George Deane of Rainhill, yeo., out of court came before John Webster, wheelwright, and Peter Kenwrick, and for £20 paid by Richard Webster of Sutton, butcher, surrendered that messuage and tenement heretofore occupied by William Fearnes, now dec., late in the occupation of Thomas Hey, and now occupied by Isabel Hey, wife of the said Thomas. The lord to regrant to the said Richard Webster for the lives of John Webster, George Webster and Cecily Webster, children of the said Richard and the longest liver of them. The remainder of the term when finished to the said George Deane forever. To George Deane the annual rent of 2s and to the lord the annual rent of 2s.

Acknowledged before us: admitted   *[signed]* George Deane

    [signed] John Webster

    [signed] Peter Kenwricke

(*Parchment*: The said Richard Webster is admitted.)

[f.17v, blank]
[f.18r: 19 cms × 29.5 cms]
At the court of Prescot held on 26[85] June 1641, the day after Corpus Christi.

[5] To this court came Edward Stockley who in full court before the steward and homage surrendered that messuage and tenement which the said Edward does now inhabit and two fields called Higher Hey and Lower Hey belonging to the said messuage and three messuages or cottages now in the occupation of Robert Hatton, Richard Aspshawe and John Oliverson, being all of the yearly rent to the lord of 12s 2d. And those closes called Brown's Croft, Middle Croft and Cross Croft – which Cross Croft, now in one croft, was heretofore in three crofts – and that messuage or cottage now in the occupation of William Fletcher, glover, and the midding stead in the upper end of the street leading towards Eccleston, being of the yearly rent of 11s 6d. And those three other messuages and tenements now in the occupation of James Houghton, John Strettell and Richard Holmes[86] of the yearly rent of 3s. To the use of the said Edward Stockley during his life and after his decease to Sarah, wife of the said Edward Stockley, during her life if she remains a widow and unmarried. After the determination of her estate, then to the male heirs of the said Edward Stockley. If no issue, to Jane Stockley and Sarah Stockley, daughters of the said Edward Stockley and their heirs. If no issue, to the right heirs of the said Edward Stockley forever. They respectively paying to the lord the aforesaid several yearly rents amounting to 26s 8d on the feasts of the Birth of Our Lord and the Nativity of St John the Baptist in equal portions.

Provided that it shall be lawful for the said Edward Stockley during his life to surrender the said premises in the occupation of the said Robert Hatton, Richard Aspshaw, John Oliverson, James Houghton, John Strettell and Richard Holmes to any person or persons for any term reserving the

[f.18v]
rents and services due.

Provided also that if the said Edward Stockley at any time in the presence of two or more copyholders of this manor of Prescot pays to the said copyholders

85. In 1641 the day after Corpus Christi was 25 June.
86. The Abstract Book has 'Hoomes'.

or any other person or persons 6d and declares his intent to void this surrender, then it shall be voided.

admitted   *[signed]* Edw Stockley

[signed] Tho Wolfall

(*Parchment*: The said Edward Stockley is admitted.)

[f.19r: 20 cms × 31 cms]
View of frankpledge with court of Prescot held on Friday, the day after Corpus Christi, 25 June, 17 Charles, 1641.

    [6] To this court came John Alcocke of Eccleston near Knowsley, gent., before the steward and homage and for the annual rent hereafter reserved surrendered to the lord that messuage and tenement now occupied by John Stevenson, gent., and Nicholas Anderton of Prescot, mercer. The lord to regrant to the said Nicholas Anderton to hold from 1 May[87] last for term of twenty-one years.[88] Paying yearly rent to the lord of 18d and to John Alcocke the annual rent of £4[89] at the feast of St Michael the Archangel.[90] The remainder after the said term ended to the said John Alcocke forever.

    Provided that if the said rent of £4[91] be unpaid within ten days after due, then John Alcocke may re-enter and repossess the said messuage.[92]

admitted   *[signed]* John Alcock

(*Parchment*: The said Nicholas Anderton is admitted.)

[f.19v, blank]
[f.20r: 20 cms × 31 cms]
View of frankpledge with court of Prescot on Friday, the day after Corpus Christi, 25 June, 17 Charles, 1641.

    [7] Afterwards to this court came John Webster of Well, wheelwright, in open court before the steward and homage and in consideration of a certain rent hereafter reserved surrendered to the lord that messuage or cottage called 'le little Cookstoole howse' and one garden or yard lying on the north side. The lord to regrant to William Coppoole of Prescot, husb., and Elizabeth his wife for their lives and the life of the survivor. Yearly rent of 8d to the lord and to the said John Webster the yearly rent of 2s 8d. The remainder after the said term ended to the said John Webster forever.

admitted   *[signed]* John Webster

(*Parchment*: The said William Coppoole and Elizabeth his wife are admitted.)

[f.20v, blank]
[f.21r, blank: 19.5 cms × 31 cms]
[f.21v]
Prescot. Court held there on 25 June 1641. Extract delivered to Thomas Parr.[93]
Sum total within: £7 13s 4d.

---

87. '[F]rom the First Day of May' was added in a blank by the same hand and in a different ink.
88. Added as above: twenty-one years.
89. Added as above: £4.
90. Added as above: feast of St Michael the Archangel.
91. Added as above: £4.
92. Marginated by the same hand in a different ink: 6 August 1641.
93. Delivered by the unknown clerk of the court to Parr, bailiff.

February 1642

[Paper Book: DDKc/PC 4/41]   [Parchment Roll: DDKc/PC 4/146bis [94]]
[f.1r: 16 cms × 15.5 cms]
[SUMMONS TO HOLD COURT]
   Thomas Wolfall, esq., steward of the manor, liberty and court of Prescot in the county of Lancaster to the bailiff of the said manor, liberty and court, greeting: I do command that you forthwith warn the customary tenants of the said manor, both resident and non-resident, to be before me at the next court baron to be held at Prescot on Friday, 11 February, to do their suit and to execute all other things which to them shall appertain. And this you may not omit. Dated 1 February, 17 Charles, 1642.
   [signed] Examined[95] by me, Edw Stockley, clerk of the said court.

(*Parchment*: **COURT BARON OF PRESCOT** in the county of Lancaster held there according to the custom of the manor of Prescot aforesaid before Thomas Wolfall, esq., steward of the manor and court aforesaid, on Friday, 11 February, 17 Charles, 1642.)

[f.1v, blank]
[f.2r: 19 cms × 28 cms]
JURORS FOR THE LORD on 11 February 1642:[96]

John Alcocke, sen., gent.	sworn	Edward Orme	
John Alcocke, jun., gent.	sworn	Henry Webster of Knowsley	sworn
Nicholas Marshall		Thomas Devias	sworn
William Parr of Cronton	sworn	William Sutton	sworn
George Deane of Rainhill	sworn	Henry Crosse	
George Lyon, jun., of Whiston	sworn	Robert Wainwright	sworn
James Ditchfield	sworn	Henry Woodes of Whiston	sworn
John Webster of Well	sworn	Richard Litherland	sworn
William Fletcher		John Webster, nailer	sworn
James Houghton	sworn		

[f.2v, blank]
[f.3r: 16 cms × 27.5 cms]
   On 22 January 17 Charles,[97] Thomas Wolfall of 'le Dam howse' in Huyton, gent., son of Thomas Wolfall of Wolfall, esq., and Christian, wife of the said Thomas Wolfall the son – the said Christian being solely and secretly examined by the steward – came before John Alcock, jun., gent., James Houghton and Thomas Devias[98] and for good considerations surrendered to the lord a messuage

94. One long membrane (36 cms × 66 cms) with writing on both sides.
95. Based upon a similar summons below for 8 October 1645, the abbreviated Latin '*Ex*', for '*Examinatus*', has been here rendered 'Examined'.
96. All names appear to be in the same hand and ink.
97. 1642.
98. 'John Alcock...Thomas Devias' was added in a blank in the same hand and ink.

and tenement commonly called 'le new Hall', being hereditary or land customary of Thomas Wolfall the son and now occupied by Thomas Litherland of Prescot. The lord to regrant to Edward Stockley of Prescot, gent., and Thomas Walles of Prescot, shearman, forever. Paying to the lord the annual rent of <2s> 4s.

admitted   Christian Wolfall *[mark – initials[99]]*
[signed] Thomas Wolfall

[f.3v]
Acknowledged before us:
  [signed] John Alcock Jn
  James Houghton *[mark]*
  [signed] Thomas Devies
The said Christian Wolfall was solely examined by the steward.
  Witness:
  [signed] Tho Wolfall steward
  Witnesses:
  [signed] Willm Alcock
  [signed] John Alcock Jn
  Tho Litherland's surrender.
(*Parchment*: The said Edward Stockley and Thomas Walles are admitted forever.)

[f.4r: 19 cms × 29.5 cms[100]]
COURT BARON held on 11 February, 17 Charles, 1642.

Whereas William Wesber *[sic]* of Eccleston 'was ordered to putt downe an enclossure which hee had made upon a certaine Common[101] upon which the tenantes of this mannor have had Common of pasture' and whereas he has made default in observing the former order made at the last court leet, therefore he has lost a fine of 10s to the lord of this manor.

Whereas there was a further order that the constables were at this town's charge to put down the same enclosure before Candlemas <next> last, but they have not done so and have forfeited 10s.

We further order the said constables to level and even the said enclosure at the town's charge, as expressed in the said former order, at or before the next Annunciation of the Blessed Virgin Mary under pain of 13s 4d.

[f.4v, blank]
[f.5r: 26.5 cms × 32 cms]
PLEA AMONG OTHER THINGS AT THE COURT BARON OF PRESCOT held before the said steward on Friday, 11 February, 17 Charles, 1642.

To this court came William Lyme and Henry Garnett in full court before the steward and homage and complain against Edward Stockley, gent., and Thomas Walles in a plea of land, that is, of one messuage, one garden, one orchard and half an acre of land in Prescot. And they have made protestation to prosecute their plaint

---

99. The 'W' is inverted.
100. Attached by adhesive is a small piece of paper (9 cms × 2.5 cms), probably eighteenth century in date.
101. The Abstract Book has 'the towne mosse.' Also see note 74 *supra*.

aforesaid in the form of a writ of entry upon disseisin in the post at the common law according to the custom of the manor aforesaid. And they have pledges, that is, John Doe and Richard Roe, to prosecute their plaint, and they request process against the said Edward Stockley and Thomas Walles which is granted.

But the said Edward Stockley and Thomas Walles are present in court and pray that the said William Lyme and Henry Garnett, upon the said plaint in form of the said writ against them, may declare.

[f.5v, blank]
[f.6r: 26.5 cms × 32 cms]
Whereupon the said William Lyme and Henry Garnett do declare against them and demand the said premises wherein the said Edward Stockley and Thomas Walles have no entry but by disseisin which Hugh Hunt has unjustly made to them the said William Lyme and Henry Garnett within the past thirty years. They say that they have been seised of the said premises and bring their suit.

The said Edward Stockley and Thomas Walles appear and defend their right and call to warrant Thomas Wolfall, gent., son of Thomas Wolfall, esq., who is in court and warrants.

The said William Lyme and Henry Garnett demand against the said Thomas Wolfall, gent., who comes and defends his right and further calls to warrant Edward Darbishire who is also present in court and warrants.

[f.6v, blank]
[f.7r: 26.5 cms × 32 cms]
The said William Lyme and Henry Garnett demand against the said Edward Darbishire and bring their suit.

The said Edward Darbishire came and defends his right and says that the said Hugh Hunt has not disseised the said William Lyme and Henry Garnett of the tenements aforesaid as the said William Lyme and Henry Garnett by their said declaration have supposed. He puts himself on the country.

The said William Lyme and Henry Garnett pray leave to imparl until the second hour. Granted. And the same hour is given to the said Edward Darbishire. Afterwards at the second hour the said William Lyme and Henry Garnett return but the said Edward Darbishire does not but defaults. The court decides that the said William Lyme and Henry Garnett shall recover the said premises against the said Edward Stockley and Thomas Walles, and that the said Edward Stockley

[f.7v, blank]
[f.8r: 26.5 cms × 32 cms]
and Thomas Walles shall have of the lands of the said Thomas Wolfall the son to the value of, and so forth. And the said Thomas Wolfall the son shall have of the lands of the said Edward Darbishire to the value of, and so forth. The said Edward Darbishire shall be amerced.

To the same court on the same day came the said William Lyme and Henry Garnett and ask that a precept be directed to the bailiff of the manor of Prescot aforesaid – being minister of this court – in the nature of a writ at the common law, giving them possession of the said property. Granted.

Afterwards the bailiff, Thomas Parr, appears and certifies that, by virtue of the said precept directed to him, he has given full possession of the said premises to the said William Lyme and Henry Garnett.

And upon this the said William Lyme and Henry Garnett came in court before the said steward and homage, ask to be admitted tenants and

[f.8v, blank]
[f.9r: 26.5 cms × 32 cms]
are admitted forever. Paying to the lord yearly rent of 4s.

admitted   [signed] Tho Wolfall

And the jurors further say that the said recovery was of the said messuage and tenement called 'le new hall', recovered by the said William Lyme and Henry Garnett of one messuage, garden, orchard and half an acre of land to the sole use of the said Thomas Wolfall, gent., forever.

Now the said Thomas Wolfall, gent., and the said William Lyme and Henry Garnett in open court before the steward and homage for £60 to the said Thomas Wolfall, gent., by Thomas Litherland of Prescot, yeo.,

[f.9v, blank]
[f.10r: 26.5 cms × 32 cms]
paid surrendered to the lord the said messuage and so forth as recovered. The lord to regrant the same to the said Thomas Litherland for the lives of the said Thomas Litherland, Elizabeth Litherland, daughter of the said Thomas, and Katherine Lyme, daughter of Richard Lyme late of Eccleston, dec., and for the life of the survivor. Paying annually to the lord the rent of 4s. And paying annual rent of 6s to the said Thomas Wolfall, gent., at the Nativity of St John the Baptist and the Nativity of Our Lord in equal portions. Remainder of the said term to the said Thomas Wolfall, gent., forever.

[signed] Thomas Wolfall
[signed] Wil Lyme
[signed] Henrie Garnett

(*Parchment*: The said Thomas Litherland is admitted.)

[f.10v]
Prescot. Court there held on 11 February, 1642, 17 Charles. Extract made and delivered.[102] Enrolled.

May 1642

[Parchment Roll: DDKc/PC 4/150[103]]

[m.1r]

102. That is, to Thomas Parr, bailiff, by Edward Stockley, clerk of the court.
103. A single membrane that is 26.5 cms × 15 cms with writing on one side. Seventeenth-century Prescot coroner's inquisitions survive for 1602, two for 1618, a reference to another for 1629 and this one for 1642 and no more until 1746. This membrane contains no signatures or seals.

INQUISITION TAKEN AT PRESCOT on 17 May, 18 Charles, 1642 before Edward Stockley, gent., coroner of Prescot, on the view of the body of James Lyon, late of Whiston, chapman, who died within the liberty and town of Prescot, by the oaths of:

Henry Garnett	Ralph Hall
Nicholas Anderton	James Houghton
Nicholas Marshall	James Sadler
Ralph Halsall	Henry Astley
Hamlet Whitfeild	Edward Booth
Evan Garnett	Edward Finney, jun.
Henry Darbishire	Thomas Ackers
Richard Litherland	John Taylor, sen.

who say that the said James Lyon on 16 May 1642 between six and seven in the afternoon going on the backside of the house of William Hough of Prescot in a well commonly called Hough's well, within the liberty of Prescot, by misfortune accidently fell into the said well and drowned.[104] In witness both the said coroner and jurors have affixed their seals to this present inquisition on the day and year above written.

[m.1v, blank]

June 1642

[Paper Book: DDCs]   [Parchment Roll: DDKc/PC 4/118[105]]

[f.1r: 20 cms × 31 cms]
(*Parchment*: **VIEW OF FRANKPLEDGE WITH COURT BARON OF PRESCOT** in the county of Lancaster held there according to the custom of the manor of Prescot aforesaid before Thomas Wolfall, esq., steward of the manor and court aforesaid, on Friday, the day after Corpus Christi, 10 June, 18 Charles, 1642.)

[SUITORS:]

	Sir William Gerrard, baronet	○	Richard Eltonhead, gent.
	Thomas Eccleston, esq.		Thomas Sorrocold, gent.
○	John Lancaster, esq.	○	William Alcocke, gent.
○	Henry Lathom, esq.	○	John Alcocke, sen., gent.
○	Thomas Woolfall, <esq.> gent.		John Alcocke, jun., gent.

---

104. This is the only reference to James Lyon in Prescot's court records. For his burial on 17 May 1642 see LPRS, 114, p. 88.
105. One membrane (31 cms × 73 cms) with writing on both sides.

o John Aldem, clerk
Richard Tyrer, clerk
o William Lyme
Richard Woodes
Henry Webster of Knowsley
o George Lyon of Eccleston
o Edward Stockley, gent.
o William Aspia
<Henry> Thomas Woodes of Widnes
o John Gloover   out of the county
o Richard Marshall
o Jane Pyke, wid.
William Blundell, gent.
o John Webster of Well
o Edward Symond   sick
o George Croston   out of
o Robert Wainwright
o Peter Kenwricke, sen.
o George Lyon, jun., of Whiston
o George Deane of Rainhill
o Richard Mollynex   out of
o William Parr of Cronton
o James Houghton of Whiston
o Edward Orme   dead[106]
o William Lyon of Thingwall
o John Lyon, skinner   essoined
George Tarleton
o William Leadbeter
o Dorothy Mercer, wid.
o John Webster, nailer
o Henry Crosse   pardoned by steward
o Richard Litherland
o William Sutton[107]
o Henry Woodes of Whiston
o William Fletcher
Richard Tarbocke
o Thomas Devias

o James Ditchfield
o Henry Pinnington   essoined
o John Urmeston
<William Coppall>
o Hugh Ward

Tenants:[108]
o Ferdinand Parker
o Katherine Stevenson
o Henry Kirkes
o John Strettell
o Richard Holmes
o <James> John Taylor, jun.
o Anthony Prescott
o John Frodsome
o James Angsdale
o Anne Ackers
Jane Greene, wid.
o John Taylor, sen.
o Henry Eaton
o Thomas Knowles
o Isabel Hey
o Jane Bolton
o Thomas Parr
o Thomas Wood
o William Hough
o Thomas Ackers
Em Naylor, wid.
o John Cowper
o Mary Haward, wid.
George Lyon
Margery Standistreet
o <Jane> Nicholas <Kirkes>
Renicars   out of the county
o Anne Lodge, wid.
o Anne Ditchfield
o Margaret Goodicarr
o Thomas Goodicarr

106. Of Tarbock, buried on 6 March 1642. F.A. Bailey, ed., *The Parish Register of Huyton, 1578–1727*, LPRS, 85 (1946), p. 217.
107. In 1972 I transcribed the six names from Sutton to Ditchfield at the bottom of the left column in the paper book. Those names were missing in 2000 when I next visited this manuscript. 'Henry Pinnington' begins a new column on the right. The bottom of this folio would have extended beyond the other folios and apparently has become separated at the fold. Only one 't' of 'Wm Sutton' remains recognizable.
108. The following individuals are undertenants.

o William Futerall
o William Birtchall
o John Hoole
o John Walker
o John Einsworth
o George Wright
o William Standish, gent.
o Jane Fletcher, wid.
o Edward Rylandes
o Ellen Rylandes, wid.
o Thomas Horneby   pardoned by
                                    steward
o Elizabeth Mann
o John Huson, jun.
o Peter Garnett
o Roger Dey
o Richard Chorleton[109]
o William Fletcher, glover
o John Houghland
  William Jackson

[f.1v]

o Peter Heerefoot
o Evan Garnett
o Thomas Aspe
o Ellen Halsall, wid.
o Margery Browne, wid.
o Hamlet Whitfield
o Ralph Halsall
o Nicholas Anderton   sick
o John Wade
o John Stevenson, gent.
o John Pendleton   sick
o Henry Garnett
o Thomas Sumner
o Ellen Stocke
o William Ewood
o Henry Parr
o William Rose
o George Kirkes
o Margery Shuttleworth

o Alexander Rylandes
o Thomas Mobberley
o Henry Astley
o John Parr
o Edward Fynney, sen.
o Edward Fynneye, jun.
o John Huson, sen.
o Edward Bate   out of
o Richard Wolfall
o James Parker
o James Houghton
o Cecily Houghton
o Ralph Hall
  Barbary Storie, wid.
o William Coppall
o Anne Giller
o Thomas Garnett
o Richard Ditchfild
o Richard Marshall
o Anne Miller
o James Sadler
o Anne Litherland
o William Standish
o Richard Banner
o Janet Orrell, wid.
o Edward Webster
o William Abshall[110]
  Gilbert Heas
o William Mollynex
o Thomas Ditchfield
o Thomas Fletcher, jun.
o John Sutton
o Anne Mollynex, wid.
  Ralph Parr
o John Rainford
  Henry Smith
o Ralph Fletcher
o Thomas Litherland
o Thomas Bond
o Thomas Walls

109. The last four names from Chorleton to Jackson, at the bottom of the right column, are also now missing.
110. The four names from Abshall to Thomas Ditchfield inclusive, at the bottom of the left column, are missing. Of 'Willm Abshall', only the dot of the 'i' and the top of the attendance mark remain recognizable.

o Henry Darbishyre	o Richard Angsdale
o William Houghton	o Richard Higginson
o John Poughton	o Jane Fennowe, wid.
o John Oliverson	o John Tyrer
o Jacob Ashton	o Ralph Plumpton
o John Ashton	o John Rigby
o Robert Hatton	o Thomas Kenwricke
o Robert Woosie	o Ellen Parr, wid. sick
o Peter Kenwricke, jun.	o John Massie
o Henry Prescott	o Ralph Houghton
o Ralph Stocke	o Margery Whytesyde, wid.
o John Wainwright	o Robert Bolton, gent.
o Richard Dyson	o William Swift
o Thomas Browne	o Adam Bate out of
o Elizabeth Fletcher, wid.	

[f.2r: 11 cms × 30 cms]
JURORS FOR THE LORD, 10 June 1642:[111]

Thomas Eccleston, esq.	– o James Houghton of Whiston sworn
John Lancaster, esq.	<George Lyon of Whiston>
Henry Lathom, esq.	Henry Webster of Knowsley
Richard Eltonhed, gent.	– William Aspia of Kirkby sworn
<John Alcocke, sen., gent.>	Henry Crosse of Huyton
John Alcocke, jun., gent.	– o Richard Litherland sworn
Nicholas Marshall	– o Robert Wainwright sworn
John Webster of Well	John Lyon, skinner
– o George Deane of Rainhill sworn	– o John Webster, nailer sworn
– o William Lyon of Thingwall sworn	– o Peter Kenwricke, sen. sworn
William Fletcher	– o William Sutton sworn
– o James Ditchfield sworn	– o Thomas Devias sworn
– o Henry Woodes of Whiston sworn	– o George Lyon of Whiston sworn
William Parr of Cronton	

The said jury has been adjourned to perfect their verdict until next 1 July on pain of 3s 4d each.

[f.2v]
The jury was further adjourned to perfect their verdict until next 22 July on pain of 3s 4d.

[f.3r: 20 cms × 30 cms]
VIEW OF FRANKPLEDGE WITH COURT BARON OF PRESCOT in the county of Lancaster held before Thomas Wolfall, esq., steward of the manor and court aforesaid, on Friday after Corpus Christi, 10 June, 18 Charles, 1642.

111. All names appear to be in the same hand and ink.

INQUISITION taken there to inquire for the lord on the oaths of.[112]
THE JURORS SAY AND PRESENT that the following persons owe suit to this court but have this day made default (12d each):

Sir William Gerrard, baronet	Richard Torbocke
Thomas Eccleston, esq.	Jane Greene, wid.
Thomas Sorrocold, gent.	Em Naylor, wid.
John Alcocke, jun., gent.	George Lyon of Prescot
Richard Tyrer, clerk	Margery Standishstreete, wid.
Richard Woodes	William Jackson
Henry Webster of Knowsley	Barbary Storie, wid.
Thomas Woodes of Widnes	Ralph Parr
William Blundell, gent.	Henry Smith
George Tarlton	

[f.3v]
Edward Orme late of Tarbock died[113] since the last court seised of a shop and chamber over the same now occupied by William Ackers or his assigns. Paul Orme, younger brother of the said Edward, is heir and 'under Age' and asks to be admitted tenant.

proclaimed   admitted

[f.4r: 20 cms × 30 cms]
PRESENTMENTS BY THE CONSTABLES, Peter Hearefoote and Alexander Rylandes, at the court held for the manor of Prescot on Friday, the day after Corpus Christi, 10 June, 1642.

They present a tussle between William Houghton (12d, Anthony Prescott) and Edward Standish (12d, John Huson).

They present a tussle on the Sabbath at night between John Edleston of Windle (12d, William Houghton) and Richard Mollyneux (punished).

They present a tussle between William Rose (12d) and Richard Astley of Rainhill (12d, William Rose).

They present an affray between Edward Ratchdale of Knowsley (3s 4d, James Ditchfeild) and Thomas Wood of Prescot (3s 4d, John Ashton of Prescot) with blood drawn upon both.

They present a tussle between Richard Birch (12d) and Edward Standish (12d, William Standish his father).

They present an affray between John Strettell (3s 4d, Thomas Ackers) who drew blood and Henry Parr (12d).

They present a tussle by Henry Standish (2s, James Angsdale) at night on William Futerell 'when hee was appointed watchman.'[114]

---

112. The names of jurors sworn above are repeated here.
113. See note 106 *supra*.
114. The Statute of Winchester of 1285 (13 Edw. I, c.4) directed constables to keep watch annually between Ascension and Michaelmas from sunset to sunrise in order to apprehend

[f.4v]

They present a tussle between John Tyrer (12d, James Ditchfeild) and Thomas Doby of Huyton (12d, Thomas Bond).

They present a tussle between William Ballard (12d, Thomas Bond) and William Sayle of Huyton (12d, Thomas Moberley).

They present an affray between Richard Bold of Sutton (3s 4d, Ralph Halsall) and Henry Standish of Prescot (3s 4d, William Houghton).

They present an affray between John Holme (3s 4d, William Futerell) who drew blood and John Hoole (12d).

They present a tussle between Ellis Glest (12d, Ralph Halsall), son of Robert Glest,[115] and John Taylor, jun. (12d, John Taylor, sen.).

They present a tussle between Thomas Fletcher (12d), son of Thomas Fletcher, dec., and Robert Norres of Kirkby (12d, James Ditchfeild).[116]

They present an affray or tussle between James Angsdale (3s 4d) who drew blood and the said Robert Norres (12d, James Ditchfeild).

They present Peter Kenwricke the younger (3s 4d) who struck James Stockley of Knowsley with a cudgel and drew blood.

[f.5r: 20 cms × 30 cms]

We further present William Futerall (12d) who abused the watchmen.[117]

[f.5v, blank]
[f.6r: 15 cms × 19 cms]

PRESENTMENTS BY THE SEALERS OF LEATHER, Thomas Ackers and Roger Dey.

We present for working horse leather: John Taylor, sen. (12d), and Thomas Kenwricke (12d).[118]

---

strangers. During the seventeenth century Ascension Day fell between 30 April and 3 June, while Michaelmas Day always fell on 29 September. Both quarter sessions and courts leet could present and punish for lack of enforcement. Between 1636 and 1661 the court leet at Manchester ordered constables to hire two persons to walk about town from 10 p.m. to 4 (or 5) a.m. between about 1 November and Candlemas (2 February) in order to apprehend offenders and prevent fires. Occasionally courts leet established additional watches, as, for example, during times of plague. In October 1652 watchmen in Wigan did not allow James Aynsdale of Prescot, butcher (who appears frequently in these leet records of the 1640s), to attend the meeting in Wigan of the sessions of the peace, though he was bound in a recognizance to attend and answer questions put to him. James, it seems, had arrived from Prescot, then being ravaged by plague. Dalton, *Countrey Justice*, p. 257; J.P. Earwaker, ed., *The Court Leet Records of the Manor of Manchester*, 3 (Manchester, 1886), pp. 248, 319, 330; 4 (Manchester, 1887), pp. 12, 25–6, 107–8, 124, 145, 171, 272, 297; LRO: QSP/71/6, Michaelmas 1652; QSP/75/1, Wigan, Epiphany 1653; QSP/79/19, Wigan, Easter 1653.

115. 'xijd' above Robert Glest is cancelled.
116. In the left margin for this entry and the next two in the same hand and ink as the presentments: 'respited'.
117. The only presentment on either side of the folio and in the same hand and ink as the jurors' presentments on folios 3r and 3v. While this single presentment begins 'We further present', all on folios 4r and 4v begin 'They present'. See notes 126 and 129 *infra*.
118. Statute 1 Jac. I, c.22 regulated the quality and preparation of leather and leather products. Both quarter sessions and courts leet inquired about and punished offenders against this statute.

John Strettell, currier (6d), for dressing unsealed leather.

For currying their own leather: Thomas Kenwricke (6d) and Henry Prescott (6d).

Thomas Ackers (2s 6d) 'for puttinge Roundinges instead of soales.'

John Strettall (12d) 'for want of liquor in his leather.'

<'Item for Curryinge leather unsealed.'>

Roger Dey (12d) for mixing cow leather and horse leather together.

[f.6v, blank]
[f.7r: 10 cms × 13 cms]
PRESENTMENTS BY THE STREETLOOKERS, William Yeaud and Ralph Houghton.

We present John Strettle, currier, and Richard Holmes for a midding before their door.[119]

[f.7v, blank]
[f.8r: 15 cms × 9.5 cms]
PRESENTMENT BY THE STREETLOOKERS, William Eawde and Ralph Houghton, for 1641.[120]

We present John Webster of Well (6d) for laying dung between William Fletchar's and Nicholas Anderton's to the annoyance of the town.

[f.8v, blank]
[f.9r: 14.5 cms × 19.5 cms]
PRESENTMENTS BY THE CLERKS OF THE MARKET, Ralph Halsall and James Angsdale, 1641.

John Parr (6s 8d) for three times selling meat not marketable and unwholesome for man's body.

Elizabeth Houghton (3d) and Jane Swifte (3d) for 'for stoleing the markett and takeing up fruite and raysing the markett by selling the same on greater rates the same day.'

Richard Webster (12d) for opening one veal.

[f.9v, blank]
[f.10r: 20 cms × 30 cms]
AT THE VIEW OF FRANKPLEDGE OF PRESCOT held there on 10 June 18 Charles *[1642]*.

ALETASTERS, Ralph Plumpton and Thomas Abshall, present as follows.

Broke the assize of ale (12d each):

William Sutton	Em Naylor, wid.
Thomas Parr	Ann Dichfield
Thomas Wood	William Futerill
William Hough	John Hoole

119. Added in Latin in a different hand but the same ink: the defendants appeared and pleaded not guilty.
120. This folio appears to have been written by a person different from the writer of the previous presentments by streetlookers.

Hamlet Whitfield	Alexander Rylandes
Ralph Halsall	Thomas Moberley
Isabel Hey	Thomas Garnett
Jane Bolton, wid.	William Swift
Henry Darbishyre	Ralph Plumpton
Thomas Walles	Jane Fennowe
Richard Litherland	James Dichfield
Thomas Bond	John Wainwright
John Pendleton	
Henry Garnett	Broke the assize of bread (2s each):
Henry Parr	Jane Fennowe, wid.
Nicholas Marshall	John Poughten
William Rose	Thomas Wood
Edward Booth	James Houghton

Also, Thomas Fletcher the elder (2s) of Prescot, dec.,[121] did in his lifetime sell bread and broke the assize of bread.

[f.10v, blank]
[f.11r: 23 cms × 11.5 cms]
PRESENTMENT BY THE BURLEYMEN, William Sutton and John Cowper.
  We present that Jane Bolton, wid. (2s), has not rung her swine despite two warnings.

[f.11v, blank]
[f.12r: 16 cms × 23.5 cms]
'**A NOTE OF THE SEVERALL NAMES** of them were taxed for the repare of the high wayes and yett unpayed':

Thomas Eaton		<William Lyme>	
Mary Haward, wid.		Cecily Houghton	
Henry Kirkes		Anne Giller	
George Lyon		Richard Ditchfield	
George Standishtreet	dead[122]	Thomas Heas	
Anne Lodge, wid.		Alice Houghton, wid.	
Margaret Goodicarr, wid.		Richard Aspshawe	dead [123]
Jane Fletcher, wid.		Ralph Stocke	
Richard Chorleton		William Blundell, gent.	
John Houghland		Richard Higginson	
John Webster		Richard Angsdale	
Mr Stevenson			

'[F]or not payinge the money Taxed on them for Layinge theire dunge on the Lordes wast':[124]

121. Buried on 3 May 1642. LPRS, 114, p. 88.
122. Of Prescot, buried on 5 March 1642. LPRS, 114, p. 87.
123. Of Prescot, buried on 30 July 1641. LPRS, 114, p. 86.
124. For a fee, sometimes called a tax, that financed street repair, inhabitants could dispose of their human and animal excrement on the 'common ground' or waste. In 1681 the court

Richard Chorleton	Richard Angsdale
<Thomas Horneby>	Richard Higginson
Anne Lodge, wid.	Adam Bate

[For both the above groups:] 6d each for use of the king's highway.
Affeerors of the court:[125]
  <Henry Woodes>
  <Richard Litherland>
  <George Lyon>
  <William Sutton>

[f.12v, blank]
[f.13r: 18.5 cms × 29.5 cms]
[PRESENTMENTS BY THE JURORS[126]]
  James Sadler and Henry Garnett, late constables, petitioned unto us that they
have undertaken to pay £1 6s 10d for clothes and other necessaries bought from
William Fletcher of Prescot, mercer, 'for the furnishinge of a souldier prest[127] for
his majesties service.' But by their petition we understand that the town is indebted to them for 15s 10d, and we request that the Four Men order the constables
to pay the said 15s 10d to the said James Sadler and Henry Garnett out of the
first money they shall receive.[128]
  Fell and carried timber out of the lord's demesne lands and employed the same
about coal pits within the manor of Whiston (12d each):

Thomas Parr	William Hardman
Thomas Devias	Nathaniel Robinson
William Plombe	Thomas Lawrenson
William Sutton	Thomas Greenehoughe
George Shuttleworth	Richard Taylor
Henry Webster	

  John Sutton (13s 4d) has not removed Ralph Parr out of his house or kitchen
as formerly ordered by this court.

[f.13v, blank]
[f.14r: 19 cms × 29.5 cms[129]]
  The court rolls and records of the court have heretofore been kept in a chest,
made at the charges of the copyholders, with several locks, and the keys have

  charged twenty-one persons between ld and 12d for fifty-six middens on the waste.
  Purchasers of that excrement also paid a fee that financed street repair. LRO: DDKc/PC
  4/120–136/Paper Book/1681.
125. While 'sworn' is in the right margin, all names have been cancelled.
126. The folio is in the same hand and ink as the above jurors' presentments on folios 3r, 3v
  and 5r.
127. For impressment of soldiers by constables, see Kent, *English Village Constable*,
  pp. 180–5.
128. Sadler and Garnett were constables for the court year May 1638 to June 1639.
  Perhaps the reference is to the Bishops' Wars of 1639–40.
129. This folio is in the same hand and ink as the preceding folio, and both are in the same
  hand and ink as the jurors' presentments; that is, these folios are out of order.

been kept by the steward, Four Men and clerk. Recently the chest and rolls have been in the keeping of <Mr> Edward Stockley, clerk of this court, who has well preserved them and who obtained several original rolls which had not been engrossed onto parchment by former clerks. And by his solicitation and with the assistance of the homagers, he has made a rental of copyhold rents due to the lord of this manor which in former rentals were 'Confused and not well distinguished.'

Now the jury asks the steward to join them in requesting that the said Mr Stockley make 'a catolodge and Colleccon'[130] of the surrenders and orders and customs now useful and in force contained in the rolls and records that are in the chest as well as in the original paper records which he saved from being lost. And then for the benefit of the copyholders and their heirs, 'a true Copie of the said Catolougue or Colleccon And a perfect Rentall' with the original rolls by him obtained should then all be placed into

[f.14v]

the said chest. A key should be kept each by the steward, clerk and by two of the Four Men as they shall agree so that without all of them there is no access to the records. The chest from time to time shall be kept in the court house or another convenient location approved by the steward and jurors. The copyholders shall reimburse Mr Stockley and his clerk for the cost of writing the catalogue and rental 'soe as shall Content him and Mr Steward shall thinke Fitt.'

No inhabitants of this manor or any other person shall lay dung or earth on the Town Moss, Sparrow Lane or any part of the lord's waste or demesne without the consent of the Four Men on pain of 6s 8d.

[f.15r: 20 cms × 30 cms]
10 June 1642.   **OFFICERS** for this year:

Constables	[1] Thomas Walls	sworn
	[2] Evan Garnett	sworn
Four Men	[1] John Alcocke	sworn before
	[1] William Fletcher	sworn before
	[1] James Ditchfield	sworn before
	[1] Nicholas Marshall	sworn before
Coroner	[1] Edward Stockley	sworn before
Clerks of the market	[1] John Parr	sworn
	[2] William Sutton	sworn
Burleymen	[1] Richard Litherland	sworn
	[2] John Cowper	sworn
Sealers of leather	[1] Thomas Kenwricke	sworn
	[1] Thomas Ackers	sworn
Alefounders	[1] William Houghe	sworn
	[1] Henry Garnett	sworn
Streetlookers	[1] Thomas Mawberle	sworn
	[1] Robert Hatton	sworn

130. The 'catolodge and Colleccon' is known to us as the Abstract Book.

Leygatherer	*[1]* Edward Fynney, jun.	sworn
Affeerors of	*[1]* Henry Woodes	sworn
the court	*[1]* Richard Litherland	sworn
	[1] George <Litherland> Lyon	sworn
	[1] William Sutton	sworn

[f.15v, blank]
[f.16r: 17.5 cms × 24 cms]
22 July 1642. **AT COURT LEET OF PRESCOT ADJOURNED** to this day.

Hamlet Whitfeeld informs the steward that Richard Taylor of Prescot, 'a dissolute yonge fellow', did in the hearing of several witnesses 'use scandolous and uncivill wordes in depravacon of the Right Honorable the Lord Strange'[131] and prays that witnesses may be examined and said Taylor punished 'as the Steward shall fynd him to deserve.'[132]

John Urmeston sworn 'in open Court' at Prescot says that on Sunday, 3 July, at the house of James Angsdale[133] in Prescot the said Richard Taylor of Prescot in the presence of the said John <Ainsworth> Urmeston and others declared, 'Let my Lord Strange kisse my Arse.'

Jane Angsdale, wife of James Angsdale, deposes that the said Taylor on the day and place aforesaid spoke these words: '[T]he Right honorable the Lord Strange had taken away all the Armor and Amunition from Liverpoole and from Manchester and was an upholder of papist soe as hee would undoe all the Country'.[134] Her children have told her that the said Taylor stated: 'Lett my lord kisse my Arse or wordes to that effecte.'

Thomas Standish of Prescot, sworn, deposes that the said Taylor on the day and place aforesaid claimed that the Lord Strange 'was such an upholder of papist as hee would undoe all the Country therby.'

[f.16v, blank]
[f.17r: 20 cms × 30 cms]
[SURRENDERS AND ADMITTANCES]

[1] On 21 February, 17 Charles, 1642 Edward Stockley, gent., James Houghton of Prescot, tailor, and Isabel his wife – the said Isabel being solely and secretly examined by the steward – out of court came before John Alcocke the younger and James Ditchfeild and for good considerations surrendered to the lord that

131. Lord Strange became the 7th Earl of Derby upon his father's death on 29 September 1642.
132. The remainder of this folio is in the same hand and ink as the constables' presentments and in a different hand from and the same ink as the preceding paragraph about Whitfeeld. For more on Richard Taylor, see Introduction, pp. xlix–li.
133. James's name always appeared in the top half of lists of undertenants, as high as third from the top. Between 1629 and 1641 he served once as constable, twice as aletaster, three times as juror-between-parties and five years as clerk of the market. He operated an alehouse and was also a butcher who between 1627 and 1652 was accused of fourteen market violations. From Henry Ogle of Whiston, esq., and later Henry's son, Cuthbert of Whiston, he rented a house that adjoined the churchyard, and from Richard Tarbock two shops. The parish register contains no entry for his burial, but the manorial court record of 1655 describes him as deceased. LRO: DDKc/PC 4/112/Paper Book/1655.
134. See Introduction, pp. xlix–li.

messuage and tenement containing two bays of building, one of them being now occupied by Elizabeth Atherton, wid., and the other occupied by Henry Astley, nailer, and by him used as a smithy; and that garden or backside on the south side of the said messuage. The lord to regrant the said messuage, tenement, garden and premises to Ralph Hall of Prescot, chapman, and Ellen his wife, holding them during their lives and the life of the survivor. Paying to the said Edward Stockley yearly rent of 2s. The remainder after the said term expired to the said Edward Stockley forever.

Provided that if the said yearly rent of 2s or any part be unpaid within twenty days after due, the said Edward Stockley may re-enter the said premises.

Acknowledged before us: proclaimed   *[signed]* Edw Stockley
   [signed] John Alcock   admitted   *[signed]* James Houghton
   James Ditchfeild *[mark]*

The said Isabel solely examined by the steward.
   [signed] Tho Wolfall
(*Parchment*: The said Ralph Hall and Ellen his wife are admitted.)

[f.17v, blank]
[f.18r: 16.5 cms × 27 cms]

[2] On 7 June, 18 Charles, 1642 Henry Crosse out of court came before James Ditchfeild and George Lyon of Whiston and for £12 paid by George Cartwright of Huyton, shoemaker, surrendered to the lord that messuage or dwelling house now occupied by James Taylor, shoemaker. The lord to regrant the said messuage or dwelling house to the said George Cartwright forever. Paying annually to the lord 6d.

Acknowledged before us: proclaimed   *[signed]* Henry Crosse
   James Ditchfeild *[mark]*   admitted
   [signed] Geo Lyon Jn
(*Parchment*: The said George Cartwright is admitted forever.)

[f.18v, blank]
[f.19r: 20 cms × 30.5 cms]

[3] On 6 August, 17 Charles, 1641 William Aspe of Kirkby, yeo., out of court came before John Alcocke, jun., George Lyon the younger and William Sutton and for good considerations surrendered to the lord that messuage or dwelling house which Thomas Parr the elder of Prescot now inhabits, and one burgage or yard on the south side of the said dwelling house. The lord to regrant to the said Thomas Parr for the lives of Ellen Parr his wife, Thomas Parr and William Parr, sons of the said Thomas Parr, and the survivor, and also for term of twelve years to commence immediately after their respective decease. Paying to the said William Aspe during the said three lives the yearly rent of 17s, paying to the said William Aspe during the term of twelve years in reversion after the said three lives ended the annual rent of 2s, and paying to the lord the yearly rent of 2s 8d.

Provided that if the said William Aspe within the next three months after the decease of the said three lives pays to the said Thomas Parr £10, then this surrender to be

[f.19v]
void. Howbeit the said William Aspe agrees that if the said Thomas Parr pays the
rent yearly to the lord it shall be deducted out of the 17s payable to the said
William Aspe on the feasts of St Andrew the Apostle and Corpus Christi yearly.
Acknowledged before us: proclaimed   Willm Aspe *[mark]*
  [signed] John Alcock Jn   admitted
  [signed] Geo Lyon Jn
  [signed] William Suttonn
(*Parchment*: The said Thomas Parr, father, is admitted.)

[f.20r: 20 cms × 30.5 cms]
  [4] On 21 February, 17 Charles, 1642 Edward Stockley, gent., James Houghton
of Prescot, tailor, and Isabel his wife – the said Isabel being solely and secretly
examined by the steward – out of court came before John Alcocke the younger
and James Ditchfeild and for good considerations surrendered to the lord that messuage and tenement containing two bays of building with 'a downedubb' and a
kitchen adjoining to the same messuage now occupied by James Houghton, and
also with 'a Swynecoate' belonging to the same messuage; and that garden or the
backside belonging to the said messuage on the south side of the said messuage.
The lord to regrant to James Houghton and Isabel his wife for their lives and the
life of the survivor. Paying yearly to Edward Stockley rent of 3s. The remainder
after the term expired to the said Edward Stockley forever.
  Provided that if the said yearly rent of 3s or any part be unpaid within twenty
days after due, then the said Edward Stockley may re-enter the said premises.
Acknowledged before us: proclaimed   *[signed]* Edw Stockley
  [signed] John Alcock   admitted   *[signed]* James Houghton
  James Ditchfeild *[mark]*
The said Isabel solely and secretly examined by
  [signed] Tho Wolfall
(*Parchment*: The said James Houghton and Isabel his wife are admitted.)

[f.20v, blank]
[f.21r: 19 cms × 30 cms]
  [5] On 10 June, 18 Charles, 1642 George Lyon, jun., of Whiston, yeo., out of
court came before John Alcocke, jun., James Dichfield and Henry Woodes and
for £21 5s to the said George Lyon paid by Nicholas Marshall of Prescot, yeo.,
surrendered to the lord that messuage or cottage containing two bays or two buildings on the east side of the messuage and dwelling house of Nicholas Marshall,
which messuage or cottage was late in the occupation of Edward Lyon, glover.
The lord to regrant the said messuage or cottage and other premises to the said
Nicholas Marshall forever. Paying yearly to the lord the rent of 2d.
Acknowledged before us: proclaimed   *[signed]* Geo Lyon Jn
  [signed] John Alcock Jn   admitted
  James Dichfield *[mark]*
  [signed] Henery Woodes
(*Parchment*: The said Nicholas Marshall is admitted forever.)

[f.21v, blank]
[f.22r: 29 cms × 40 cms[135]]

[6] On <9> 10 June, 18 Charles, 1642 Henry Astley of Prescot, nailer, and Ellen his wife <said Ellen solely and secretly examined by the steward> out of court came before Edward Stockley, gent., and Nicholas Marshall and for good causes surrendered to the lord one messuage or cottage late in the tenure or occupation of Thomas Webster, dec., and now in the tenure or occupation of the said Henry Astley, and one garden on the south side of the same messuage. The lord to regrant the said messuage, garden and premises to John Hyndley of Hindley, nailer, holding for term of sixty years fully to be ended if the said Ellen lives so long. The remainder after the said term ended to the heirs of the said Thomas Webster forever. Paying to the lord the annual rent of 6d.

Provided and it is agreed between the said Henry Astley and John Hyndley that the said Henry Astley will pay to the said John Hyndley or 'his lawfull Attorney' £8 16s 4d as follows: 30s on next St Michael the Archangel and on the same feast 30s in 1643, 20s from 1644 to 1648 inclusive and the residue of 16s 4d in 1649. For these several payments the said Henry Astley stands bound to the said John Hyndley in £16 in one bond bearing the same date as this surrender, conditioned for payment of the said several sums in manner as aforesaid. If the said Henry Astley makes these payments, this present surrender and bond are to be void.

Provided also and it is agreed that the said Henry Astley and Ellen his wife shall enjoy the said messuage and premises and take the profits thereof until default be made in payment of any of the said sums.

Acknowledged before us: Henry Astley *[mark – initials]*
  [signed] Edw Stockley   Ellen Astley *[mark]*
  [signed] Nicholas Marshall

[f.22v]
Court held on 10 June 1642. Extract delivered to Thomas Parr.[136] Sum total within for the lord: £7; for use of the king's highway: 13s 6d.

1643

[Paper Book: DDKc/PC 4/41[137]] [Parchment Roll: DDKc/PC 4/118[138]]

[f.1r: 11.5 cms × 30.5 cms]
(*Parchment*: **COURT BARON OF PRESCOT** in the county of Lancaster held there according to the custom of the manor of Prescot before Thomas Wolfall, esq., steward of the manor and court aforesaid, on Friday, 6 January, 18 Charles, 1643.)

---

135. The following surrender appears only in the paper book which has no 'proclaimed, admitted'.
136. Bailiff; delivered by Edward Stockley, clerk of the court.
137. Four loose leaves fastened at the top by a modern paper clip.
138. This material for January 1643 is included with the parchment roll for June 1642.

JURORS FOR THE LORD on 6 January 1643:[139]

John Alcocke, jun., gent.	sworn	James Houghton of Whiston	sworn
Nicholas Marshall	sworn	Thomas Devias	sworn
John Webster	sworn	Richard Litherland	sworn
William Lyme	sworn	William Sutton	sworn
James Ditchfield	sworn	Peter Kenwrick, sen.	sworn
William Fletcher	sworn	Hugh Ward	sworn
George Deane of Rainhill	sworn	George Cartwright of Huyton	sworn
Henry Woodes of Whiston	sworn	Ellis Webster	sworn

2s imposed on James Taylor for bad conduct in court.

[f.1v, blank]
[f.2r: 29 cms × 27 cms]

On 19 August 18 Charles[140] John Aldem, clerk, bachelor of divinity and vicar of the parish church of Prescot, out of court came before William Blundell, gent., Nicholas Marshall and Peter Kenwrick and for good considerations surrendered to the lord one close and parcel of land, meadow and pasture containing about two large acres heretofore called Fletcher's two fields, together with the cottage thereupon standing. The lord to regrant to the said John Aldem for his life and after his decease to Rachel, daughter of the said John Aldem and now wife of Samuel Hynd, clerk, and heirs of the said Rachel begotten by the said Samuel Hynde. And for want of such issue, to the heirs of the said Rachel Hynd. And for want of such issue, to Samuel Hynde forever. Paying yearly to the lord the rent of 2s 6d.

[signed] John Aldem[141]

[f.2v, blank]
[f.3r: 29 cms × 17.5 cms]

Provided that if the said John Aldem at any time in the presence of two or more credible witnesses pays to the said Samuel Hynd and Rachel his wife or either of them or to any other person or persons 12d and declares his intent to void this surrender, then this present surrender will be void.

Acknowledged before us: *[signed]* John Aldem
   [signed] Will Blundell
   [signed] Nichola *[sic]* Marshall
   [signed] Peter Kenwricke senior

[f.3v, blank]
[f.4r: 27.5 cms × 23 cms [142]]

139. All names are in the same hand and ink.
140. 1642.
141. The bottom of this folio in the paper book has been intentionally removed; the top portions of some of the letters of the alphabet remain and indicate that the missing section contained writing. In that J. Aldem's signature appears squeezed, he may have been the one who cut off the bottom; but to judge by Aldem's signature, he probably did not write the surrender. The parchment roll contains nothing beyond the contents of the paper book.
142. This folio is in a different hand from preceding folios.

And the said jury further say that since the acknowledging of this surrender, the said John Aldem is dead[143] and that the said John Aldem in his life did not pay the said Samuel Hynd and Rachel his wife or either of them or to any other person or persons 12d to void the said surrender and that the said Rachel also is dead[144] without issue. And to this court came the said Samuel Hynd.[145]

admitted

[f.4v]
Prescot. Court baron there. 6 January 1643. Enrolled.
[Paper Book: DDKc/PC 4/41]   [Parchment Roll: DDKc/PC 4/18 [146]*]*

[f.1r: 19 cms × 29 cms]
(*Parchment*: **VIEW OF FRANKPLEDGE WITH COURT BARON OF PRESCOT** in the county of Lancaster held there according to the custom of the manor of Prescot aforesaid before Thomas Wolfall, esq., steward of the manor and court aforesaid, on Friday, the day after Corpus Christi, 2 June, 19 Charles, 1643.[147])

[SUITORS:]

Sir William Gerrard, baronet	out of ○ John Glover
Thomas Eccleston, esq.	○ Nicholas Marshall
John Lancaster, esq.	○ Jane Pyke, wid.
Henry Lathom, esq.	William Blundell, gent.
○ Thomas Woolfall, <esq.> gent.	○ John Webster
○ Richard Eltonhead, gent. essoined	Edward Symond
Thomas Sorrocold, gent.	George Croston
○ William Alcocke, gent.	○ Robert Wainwrighte
○ John Alcocke, sen., gent.	○ Peter Kenwricke, sen.
John Alcocke, jun., gent.	<George Lyon, jun., of Whiston>
<Edward Devisse, gent.>	○ George Deane of Rainhill
○ Edward Stockley, gent.	○ Richard Mollynex
○ Richard Tyrer, clerk	○ William Parr
<Peter Jackson, clerk>	○ James Houghton
William Lyme	of Whiston essoined
Richard Woodes	infant <Jeremiah> Paul Orme
○ Henry Webster of Knowsley	○ William Lyon
○ George Lyon of Eccleston	○ John Lyon, skinner sick
○ William Aspia	George Tarleton
○ <Henry> Thomas Woodes	○ William Leadbeter
of Widnes	○ Dorothy Mercer, wid.

143. Buried on 8 September 1642. LPRS, 114, p. 89. For his will, see LRO: WCW/Prescot/1642/John Aldem.
144. Buried on 26 December 1642. LPRS, 114, p. 90.
145. The parchment roll continues: 'and he is admitted . . . forever.'
146. Two membranes with writing on all sides; the roll is 34 cms × 64 cms (the second membrane is 2 cms longer).
147. 'Prescott' is the only heading in this paper book.

o John Webster, nailer
o George Cartwrighte
o Richard Litherland
o William Sutton
o \<Thomas\> Henry Woodes
   of Whiston   dead[148]
o William Fletcher
o Richard Tarbocke   essoined
o Thomas Devisse
o James Ditchfield
o Henry Pynnington
o John Urmeston
o Hugh Ward

Tenants:[149]
o Ferdinand Parker
o John Strettell
o Richard Holmes
o Katherine Stevenson, wid.
o Anthony Prescott
o Margaret Garnett, wid.
o John Frodsome
o James Angsdale
o Anne Ackers
o John Ashton
o James Taylor
o Henry Eaton
o Thomas Knowles
o Isabel Hey
o Jane Bolton, wid.
o Thomas Parr
o Thomas Wood
o William Hough
o Thomas Ackers
o Em Neylor
o John Cowper
o Mary Haward, wid.
[f.1v]
o George Lyon
o Nicholas Ranicars
o Margery Standistreet
o Anne Lodge, wid.
o Margaret Goodicarr

o Thomas Goodicarr
o William Futerall
o John Hoole
o William Birtchall
o John Walker
o Ellen Einsworth, wid.
o George Wright
o Mrs Standish
o Jane Fletcher, wid.
o Edward Rylandes
o Thomas Horneby
o Elizabeth Man, wid.
o Roger Man
o John Huson
o Peter Garnett
o Roger Dey
o Richard Chorleton
o Thomas Tyrer
o John Houghland
o Ralph Parr
o Peter Herefoot
o Evan Garnett
o Thomas Aspe
o Ellen Halsall, wid.
o Margery Browne, wid.
o Hamlet Whitfield
o Ralph Halsall
o Nicholas Anderton
o John Stevenson, gent.
o John Wade
o John Pendleton
o Henry Garnett
o Thomas Sumner
o John Taylor
o William Ewood
o Henry Parr
o William Rose
o George Kirkes
o Margery Shuttleworth
o Alexander Rylandes
o Thomas Mobberley
o Henry Astley
o John Parr

148. Buried on 15 May 1643. LPRS, 114, p. 90.
149. Actually, undertenants.

○ Edward Fynney
○ Robert Kennion
○ John Huson
out of Edward Bate
○ Richard Woolfall
○ Thomas Garnett
○ James Houghton
○ James Parker
○ Cecily Houghton, wid.
○ Barbary Story, wid.
○ Anne Giller <wid.>
○ Richard Ditchfield
○ Anne Miller
○ Richard Marshall
○ James Sadler
○ Anne Litherland, wid.
○ Richard Banner
○ Janet Orrell
○ Edward Webster
○ William Abshall
○ William Mollynex
○ Thomas Fletcher, jun.
○ John Sutton
○ Gilbert Heas
○ Anne Mollynex, wid.
○ John Rainford
○ Ralph Fletcher
○ Thomas Litherland
○ Thomas Bond
○ Thomas Walls
[f.2r: 19 cms × 29 cms]

○ Henry Darbishyre
○ William Houghton
○ Jane Greene, wid.
○ John Poughton
○ John Olliverson
○ Jacob Ashton
○ Robert Hatton
○ Robert Woosie
○ Peter Kenwricke, jun.
○ Henry Prescott
○ Ralph Stocke
○ John Wainwrighte
○ Richard Dyson
○ Thomas Browne
○ Elizabeth Fletcher, wid.
○ Richard Angsdale
○ Richard Higginson
○ Jane Fennowe, wid.
○ Henry Kirkes
○ John Tyrer
○ Ralph Plumpton
○ John Rigby
○ John Massie
○ Thomas Kenwricke
○ Ellen Parr, wid.
○ Ralph Houghton
○ Margery Whytesyde, wid.
○ Mr Bolton
○ William Swift
○ Adam Bate
○ William Hardman

[f.2v, blank]
[f.3r: 20 cms × 29.5 cms]
JURORS FOR THE LORD on 2 June 1643:[150]

   ○ ○ + ○   Edward Stockley, gent.   sworn
                  Richard Eltonhead, gent.
                  John Alcocke, sen., gent.
                  William Blundell, gent.
      ○ + ○   Nicholas Marshall   sworn
                  William Lyme

150. All names appear to have been written by the same hand except that of Ellis Webster, and all are in the same ink.

o + o	John Webster	sworn
	George Deane of Rainhill	
o o + o	William Parr of Cronton	sworn
o o + o	William Fletcher	sworn
+ o	James Ditchfield	sworn
o + o	Thomas Devisse[151]	sworn
+ o	William Sutton	sworn
o o o + o	Richard Litherland	sworn
	Henry Webster	
	William Aspia	
	Thomas Woodes of Widnes	
o o + o	Robert Wainwright	sworn
	James Houghton of Whiston	
	John Lyon, skinner	
	John Webster, nailer	
	George Cartwrighte	
o + o	Hugh Ward	sworn
o o o + o	Peter Kenwrick, sen.	sworn
	<Richard Thomas Woodes>	
	Ellis Webster	sworn

[f.3v]

27 October 1643. The jury adjourned to perfect their verdict to 29 December next under pain each of 3s 4d.

29 December 1643. Jury further adjourned to 24 May next under pain of 6s 8d each.

21 June 1644. Jury aforesaid further adjourned until 2 August 1644.

2 August 1644. Jury aforesaid further adjourned to 23 August 1644.

Jury aforesaid adjourned to 13 <August> September 1644 under pain of 6s 8d.

[f.4r: 20 cms × 30.5 cms]
[SURRENDERS AND ADMITTANCES]

[1] On 11 June, 18 Charles, 1642 John Lancaster of Rainhill, esq., out of court came before John Alcock, jun., Nicholas Marshall and William Fletcher and for £34 19s 10d paid to him by Thomas Litherland of Prescot, yeo., surrendered that messuage or dwelling house which Thomas Walles, vintner, now inhabits. The lord to regrant to the said Thomas Litherland forever. Yearly rent to the lord is 6s.

Acknowledged before us: proclaimed   *[signed]* John Lancaster
   [signed] John Alcock Jn   admitted
   Willm Fletcher *[mark – initials]*
   [signed] Nicholas Marshall
(*Parchment*: The said Thomas Litherland is admitted forever.)

---

151. The parchment roll has 'Devias'.

[f.4v, blank]
[f.5r: 20 cms × 30.5 cms]
    [2] On 8 December, 18 Charles, 1642 Henry Lathom of Mossborough, esq.,
out of court came before John Alcocke, jun., and William Lyme and in consideration of the annual rent heretofore reserved surrendered to the lord one building
called 'the Bay on the milne hill' now occupied by Thomas Litherland of Prescot,
yeo. The lord to regrant the said structure to the said Thomas Litherland for the
lives of the said Thomas Litherland, Elizabeth Litherland his daughter and
Katherine Lyme, spinster daughter of Richard Lyme late of Prescot, dec., and for
the life of the longest liver. Paying yearly the rent of 2d to the lord and to Henry
Lathom the annual rent of 2s 4d. The remainder after the said term ended to the
said Henry Lathom forever.

Acknowledged before us: proclaimed   *[signed]* Hen Latham
    [signed] John Alcock Jn   admitted
    [signed] Wil Lyme
(*Parchment*: The said Thomas Litherland is admitted.)

[f.5v, blank]
[f.6r: 20 cms × 30.5 cms]
    [3] On 5 July, 18 Charles, 1642 Richard Eltonhead, sen., gent., out of court
came before Edward Stockley and Nicholas Marshall[152] and for £20 16s paid to
him by Margaret Smyth of Knowsley, spinster, surrendered to the lord that messuage or cottage now in the tenure or occupation of John Parr, butcher; one garden, croft and parcel of land on the north side of the said messuage; two other
messuages or cottages now in the tenure or occupation of Ellen Parr, wid., and
Edward Lowe, mason; and that other messuage or cottage now in the tenure or
occupation of Anne Mollyneux, wid. To the use of the said Margaret Smyth forever. Paying yearly to the lord all rents and services due.
    Provided that if the said Richard Eltonhead pays to the said Margaret Smyth
£20 16s on the next feast of St Michael the Archangel, this surrender to be void.

Acknowledged before us: proclaimed   *[signed]* Rich Eltonhed
    [signed] Edw Stockley   admitted
    [signed] Nicholas Marshall
(*Parchment*: The said Margaret Smith is admitted forever.)

[f.6v]
    Surrender from Mr Eltonhed for security of £20 16s at Michaelmas 1642.

[f.7r: 27 cms × 33 cms]
    [4] On 21 July, 18 Charles, 1642 Thomas Woodes of Widnes, yeo., out of court
came before John Alcock, jun., and William Fletcher and for £5 paid to him by
Jane Fenney of Prescot, wid., surrendered to the lord that messuage or cottage
with burgage or parcel of land on the north side of the said messuage or cottage
heretofore occupied by William Fenney late of Prescot, dec., and now by the said
Jane Fenney. The lord to regrant to the said Jane Fenney for the lives of the

152. The names of ES and NM were added in a blank in a different hand and ink.

said Jane Fenney, Thomas Fenney and Richard Fenney, sons of the said Jane, and the survivor of them. When the term has expired, to the said Thomas Woodes forever. Paying yearly to the lord the rent of 18d, and to the said Thomas Woodes the yearly rent of 18s 6d.

Acknowledged before us: proclaimed *[signed]* Thomas Woods
   [signed] John Alcock Jn admitted
   Willm Fletcher *[mark – initials]*
(*Parchment*: The said Jane Fenney is admitted.)

[f.7v, blank]
[f.8r: 30 cms × 39.5 cms]
   [5] 16 February, 18 Charles, 1643.
   John Alcock of Eccleston is seised to him and his heirs by copy of court roll of several messuages and cottages, that is, of one messuage and tenement against the court house now occupied by Nicholas Anderton or his undertenants and assigns; another messuage and tenement against the watering pool called 'the signe of the Eagle and Child' now occupied by Hamlet Whitfeeld, innkeeper,[153] or his assigns; a messuage, tenement and tanhouse in Hall Lane now occupied by George Lyon[154] or his assigns; two messuages and tenements in the lane leading from Mill Hill to the Town Moss, one occupied by Ralph Plumpton or his assigns and the other occupied by John Rigby or his assigns; a cottage towards the upper end of the street leading to Eccleston now occupied by Richard Banner or his assigns; a cottage adjoining to the south side of the churchyard now occupied by Anne Akers, wid., or her assigns; the moiety or one half of a cottage and meadow in Sparrow Lane called Sparrow Lane Cottage and Meadow and the moiety or one half of two crofts called Nell Milner's crofts adjoining to Fall Lane; and one close called Goodicar's acre now occupied by Peter Herefoote. The said John Alcock of Eccleston did this present day, 16 February, 18 Charles, 1643 out of court and in the presence of William Alcock, Edward Stockley, William Fletcher, Peter Kenwricke and John Alcock the younger surrender to the lords all the before mentioned properties. The lords to regrant the said two messuages, the one occupied by the said Nicholas Anderton and the other in the holding of the said Hamlet Whitfeeld or their assigns, and the acre of land held by the said Peter Herefoote and the moiety of the said cottage and meadow in Sparrow Lane and the moiety of Nell Milner's crofts to the said John Alcock of Eccleston. For want of such issue, to John Alcock 'his Cozen whom hee hath Educated as his Child', being son of John Alcock of Prescot. For want of such issue, to the right heirs of the said John Alcock of Eccleston forever.

[f.8v, blank]
[f.9r: 30 cms × 39.5 cms]
   And in like manner regrant the said two messuages and tenements occupied by Ralph Plumpton and John Rigby to the said John Alcock of Eccleston. For want

153. Not in the parchment roll: 'innkeeper'.
154. The Abstract Book has 'George Lyon tanner'.

of such issue, to William Alcock, son of the said John Alcock of Prescot. For want of such issue, to the right heirs of the said John Alcock of Eccleston forever.

And regrant the said messuage, tanhouse and premises occupied by George Lyon[155] to the said John Alcock of Eccleston. For want of such issue, to Thomas Alcock, one other son of the said John Alcock of Prescot. For want of such issue, to the right heirs of the said John Alcock of Eccleston forever.

And regrant the said two cottages occupied by the said Richard Banner and Anne Akers to the said John Alcock of Eccleston. For want of such issue, to Richard Alcock, one other son of the said John Alcock of Prescot. For want of such issue, to the right heirs of the said John Alcock of Eccleston forever.[156] Paying respectively to the lords the rents and services due.

Provided that if the said John Alcock of Eccleston pays 12d to any of his cousins before named or to any other person and in the presence of two or more credible witnesses declares his desire by such payment to revoke this surrender, then the whole surrender or such part or parts as he declares revoked shall be voided.

Acknowledged before us: *[signed]* John Alcock senior

> *[signed]* Willm Alcock
> *[signed]* Edw Stockley
> Willm Fletcher *[mark – initials]*
> *[signed]* Peter Kenwricke
> *[signed]* John Alcock Jn

At the court leet held on Friday, 10 June, the day after Corpus Christi, 1653. 'Proclaimed. And admittance given to John Alcocke the sonne as unto the messuages and premises to him limitted by this Surrender <reserving all other estates>.'[157]

(*Parchment:*[158] And afterwards at the court leet held on 10 June 1653, before Arthur Borron, gent., steward, came the said John Alcocke the son in open court before the same steward and homage. And the said John Alcocke of Eccleston being dead,[159] the said John Alcocke the son prays to be admitted as tenant to the several messuages, tenements and premises limited to his use in the said surrender. Proclamation was made and so forth. Therefore the said John Alcocke the son is admitted as tenant to hold in manner and form aforesaid.)

[f.9v]

Mr John Alcock's surrender 'by which he hath estated his Copihold Land in Prescott.'

[f.10r: 29 cms × 39.5 cms]

[6] To this court came William Sutton of Prescot, yeo., and Ann his wife – she being solely and secretly examined by the steward – in open court before the

---

155. The Abstract Book has 'George Lyon tanner'.
156. Marginated in the same hand and ink: 'The rent to be reserved particulerly.'
157. 'At the court leet...<reserving all other estates>' is in a different hand and ink from the surrender.
158. Written in English in the same hand and ink as the rest of the parchment roll.
159. Gent., buried on 12 June 1653. LPRS, 114, p. 111. For his will, see TNA: PROB 11/226/98.

steward and homage and for £13 9s 4d to the said William and Ann Sutton paid by William Webster of Eccleston near Knowsley, yeo., surrendered that messuage and tenement now occupied by the said William Sutton. The lord to regrant to the said William Webster to hold from 1 May next during the term of forty years to be ended if the said William Sutton and Ann his wife or either of them live so long. Paying yearly to the lord the rent of 4s. [160]

Provided that the said William Sutton and Ann or either of them or their lawful attorney do pay to the said William Webster £13 9s 4d in manner following: 40s on each 1 May in 1644 to 1649 inclusive and the remainder of 29s 4d on 1 May 1650. After fully paid, this surrender to be void.

Acknowledged in open court before   proclaimed   *[signed]* William Suttonn
the steward and homage; said Ann   admitted   Ann Sutton *[mark]*
being solely and secretly
examined by the steward:
　[signed] Tho Wolfall
(*Parchment*: The said William Sutton is admitted.)

[f.10v, blank]
[f.11r: 27.5 cms × 32 cms]
View of frankpledge with court baron of Prescot held on Friday, the day after Corpus Christi, 2 June, 19 Charles, 1643.

[7] To this court came William Fletcher of Prescot, mercer, and in open court before the steward and homage surrendered to the lord several messuages, that is, a messuage or dwelling house now in the tenure or occupation of James Parker; a messuage or cottage now occupied by Margaret Goodicar, wid.; a messuage or cottage late in the tenure or occupation of Ann Ditchfeild, spinster, now dec.; a messuage or dwelling house now occupied by Thomas Akers, shoemaker; one building called 'le barne' on the west side of the said messuage in the occupation of the said Thomas Ackers; four messuages or cottages lately built bordering on the said 'le barne'; and one close or parcel of land, meadow and pasture called 'le Cow hey' containing two acres and three rood land of land. The lord to regrant all to the said William Fletcher during his life and after his decease a third of all the said premises to Elizabeth Fletcher now his wife during her life. After her death, to Elizabeth Fletcher, daughter of the said William Fletcher, and the heirs of the said Elizabeth. For want of such issue, to Ellen Marshall, wife of Henry Marshall, and her heirs.

[f.11v, blank]
[f.12r: 27.5 cms × 32 cms]
For want of such issue, to Thomas Fletcher, son of John Fletcher of 'le outwood' within Pilkington, and the heirs of the said Thomas Fletcher. For want of such issue, to the right heirs of the said William Fletcher forever. The lord to regrant the remaining premises immediately after the death of the said William Fletcher to the said Elizabeth Fletcher, daughter of the said William, and her heirs. For want

160. 'iiijs' was added in a blank in a different hand and ink.

of such issue, to the said Ellen Marshall and her heirs. For want of such issue, to the said Thomas Fletcher and his heirs. For want of such issue, to the right heirs of the said William Fletcher forever. Paying 12d yearly to the lord for the said messuage occupied by the said James Parker, for the said close called 'le Cow hey' annual rent of 2s, and for the remaining premises the yearly rent of 19s 6d.

Provided that if the said William Fletcher in the presence of two or more copyholders of Prescot manor pays to the said copyholders 6d and declares his intent to void this surrender, then this surrender to be void.
Acknowledged in open court   proclaimed William Fletcher *[mark – initials]*
before the steward and homage: admitted
    Witness: *[signed]* Tho Wolfall
(*Parchment*: The said William Fletcher is admitted.)

[f.12v, blank]
[f.13r: 27.5 cms × 32 cms]
    [8] That whereas William Fletcher of Prescot, mercer, stands lawfully possessed by copy of court roll for the lives of Elizabeth Fletcher, wife of the said William Fletcher, and of Ellen Marshall, daughter of the said William Fletcher and now wife of Henry Marshall, and of the survivor of them in the messuage and tenement heretofore occupied by Edward Bolton, dec., and now occupied by the said William Fletcher; also the barn in the upper end of the street leading towards Eccleston containing three bays of building with one cottage and garden and two crofts and parcels of land on the east side of the said barn containing one acre of land of the large measure. Under the yearly rent of 3s 2d to the lord and to John Glover of Rainhill the yearly rent of 10s, as in a surrender made to the said William Fletcher from the said John Glover now among the manorial records may appear.

Now to this court came the said William Fletcher and in open court before the steward and homage surrendered the before-mentioned messuage and tenement with the said barn, cottage, garden and two crofts at the east end of the said barn. The lord to regrant all the said messuage and premises to the said William Fletcher during his life if the term before mentioned continues. After his decease one shop and warehouse over it and the chamber next adjoining – being parcel of the said messuage and tenement – to Elizabeth, wife of the said William Fletcher, during her life if she so long keeps the said shop and trading within the same. But if the said Elizabeth happens to leave off keeping the shop and trade, then the said shop, warehouse and chamber to the use of the said Ellen Marshall during the remainder of the said term. Paying a proportionable part of the said rent due for the whole premises hereby granted. The rest of the premises immediately after the death of the said William Fletcher to the said

[f.13v, blank]
[f.14r: 27.5 cms × 32 cms]
Elizabeth Fletcher during her life. After her decease to the said Ellen Marshall during the remainder of the said term. She the said Ellen Marshall paying yearly 30s upon twelve coats for the clothing of twelve poor children within the townships of Prescot, Eccleston and Sutton, that is, six within Prescot and three each in Eccleston

and Sutton, such as the said Ellen Marshall shall think most useful. Paying yearly to the lord the rent of 3s 2d, and to the said John Glover yearly rent of 10s.

Provided that if the said William Fletcher in the presence of two or more copyholders pays to the said copyholders or any of them 6d and declares his intent to void this surrender, then this surrender shall be void.

Acknowledged in open court   proclaimed   William Fletcher *[mark – initials]*
before steward and homage: admitted
   Witness:
   [signed] Tho Wolfall
(*Parchment*: The said William Fletcher is admitted.)

[f.14v, blank]
[f.15r: 19.5 cms × 29.5 cms]
[9] The jurors further say and present upon their oaths that Henry Woodes who held to him and his heirs by copy of court roll certain messuages, cottages and lands in Prescot hereafter mentioned, that is, one close and parcel of land containing about two large acres of land commonly called Prescot Meadow and certain houses, yards, orchards and gardens belonging or heretofore enclosed from the same, and also one messuage and tenement now in the tenure, holding or occupation of Ralph Halsall[161] being all of the yearly rent to the lord of 7s 9d; one burgage or parcel of land in Churchley Field of about a rood land of land with one messuage or dwelling house thereupon standing now occupied by Thomas Aspe, mason, being of the yearly rent to the lord of 6d; and one messuage or tenement occupied by John Walker being of the yearly rent to the lord of 3s.

The said Henry Woodes died[162] seised since the last court held here. And we find that Thomas Woods is son and next heir of the said Henry Woodes and is seventeen years old or thereabouts.

        proclaimed
        admitted saving the right of Margaret Woodes his mother
(*Parchment*: The said Thomas Woodes is admitted tenant, saving always the right of Margaret Woodes, wid., in the said premises. Paying yearly to the lord the said several rents aforementioned, in total 11s 3d.)

[f.15v, blank]
[f.16r: 20 cms × 31 cms[163]]
[PRESENTMENTS BY THE JURORS]
We present the following persons who 'owe suite of Court unto this Court and this day made default in apparence' (6d each):

Sir William Gerard, baronet	Thomas Sorocold, gent.
Thomas Eccleston, esq.	John Alcocke, jun., gent.
John Lancaster, esq.	William Lyme
Henry Lathom, esq.	Richard Woodes

161. The parchment roll has 'Raph Halsall blacksmith'.
162. See note 148 *supra*.
163. The top half of the folio is blank.

William Blundell   George Croston
Edward Symon   George Tarlton

[f.16v]

Whereas diverse leys have been laid this past year for the town's use and diverse taxations have been unpaid as by the constables' accounts appear, we order that the persons undernamed shall pay the sums hereafter mentioned to the new constables for the town's use at or before the feast of St Bartholomew next upon pain of 6s 8d each.

Henry Ogle, esq.	34s	Cecily Houghton	4s 9d ob
Hamlet Whitfeild	8d	Thomas Fletcher, jun.	21d
Ralph Halsall	2s 11d	Gilbert Heyes	3s 10d ob
John Tayler, sen.	18d	Henry Darbishyre	12d
George Kerkes and		Jane Bolton	21d
Edward Booth	2s 6d	John Chadock	19d ob
Thomas Maberley	2s 1d	James Angsdale	3s 6d ob
Henry Astley	2s 11d	Richard Webster	2s 11d
Richard Marshall	3s 1d ob	William Hough	9d
Ann Miller	13d ob	John Hoole	9d
John Houghton	2s 1d	Peter Heirefoote	2s ob

[f.17r: 20 cms × 31 cms]

William Blundell, gent.	27s 9d ob	Richard Tyrer, clerk, and	
Thomas Browne	9d	William Edwardson	17d ob
Richard Angsdale	2s 11d	William Blundell, gent.,	
Widow Whytesyde	8d ob	for a taxation	13s 4d
John Travers	14d ob	Alexander Webster	5s
Henry Eaton	17d	Edward Fynney, leygatherer	30s
William Ackers, butcher	4s 4d ob		

Upon perusal of the constables' accounts, we find that the town is indebted to them in the amount of 30s 11d which we order the new constables to pay Thomas Wall,[164] one of the former constables, out of the first money that they shall receive for the town's use.

164. Thomas Walls, innkeeper, was also styled vintner, clothmaker and shearman. In call books his name commonly appeared in the top half of lists of undertenants. Thomas rented a house on Sparrow Lane from Thomas Lancaster of Rainhill, esq., and after Lancaster's death from his son John until 1642 and thereafter from Thomas Litherland of Prescot, yeoman. Walls served his parish as churchwarden and one of the Eight Men, and fellow parishioners elected him surveyor of the highways, and for payment he supplied wine for Communions at the parish church and at chapels in Rainford and 'St Ellens' in Windle. Between 1627 and 1653 he served in ten manorial offices, including three terms as constable. He himself was not the most law-abiding resident of Prescot: excluding the so-called charge of breaking the assize of ale and beer, between 1628 and 1659 leet officers accused him of twenty offences consisting of seventeen different types. He died before 16 November 1660, the date of the inventory of his goods. Steel, *Prescot Churchwardens' Accounts, passim;* LRO: WCW/Prescot/1661/Thomas Walls. Also see note 249 *infra.*

We further present that the town is indebted to:

Edward Stockley	29s 2d
Ralph Halsall	43s 4d
Thomas Litherland	16s
Edward Darbishyer	3s 4d

We further order that the constables shall demand that the persons who have not paid the three double leys laid for the furnishing of soldiers and provision of arms for the town's use, as noted in the ley book, shall pay the same upon their demand or forfeit 3s 4d each.

[f.17v]

Whereas at diverse courts heretofore various orders have been made for the preservation of gates, hedges and fences of the tenants of this manor as also of the houses already made. Those orders have been very much neglected of late by the officers for that purpose appointed and the presenting of the breach of the said orders 'altogeather omitted to the greate hinderance of the Lord of this mannor and the Inhabitantes theireof and the utter subvertion and overthrow of all good order'. We therefore order that the constables and Four Men and all other officers shall henceforth take care to the performance of the said orders within their charge and that all hedge breakers and all others of that nature to be punished by the constables according to the direction of the said orders. And the Four Men shall from time to time present the breach of all orders wherein they are concerned and especially shall present what cottages or houses of habitation have been erected within the past eleven years and since the order made for restraining thereof and what houses made and built for other uses have been turned to houses of habitation and by whom. And they shall give an account at the next court leet upon pain that they making default shall forfeit for every default 20s each.

[f.18r: 20 cms × 30 cms]

1643. **ALETASTERS**, Henry Garnett and William Hough.

We present the following persons for breaking the assize of ale and beer (12d each):

Thomas Parr	Alexander Rylaunce
William Sutton	Nicholas Marshall
Thomas Wood	Thomas Bond
William Hough	Richard Litherland
Em Naylor	Thomas Walles
William Futerell	Henry Derbisheere
John Hoole	Jane Bolton
Hamlet Whitfeild	Isabel Hey
Ralph Halsall	Ursula Taylor
John Pendleton	John Wainewright
Henry Garnett	James Ditchfeild
Henry Parr	Wife Fennow
William Rose	Ralph Plumpton
Edward Booth	William Swift

[f.18v]

We present the following persons for breaking the assize of bread (12d each):

James Houghton
John Poughten
Wife Fennow
Wife Fletchar
Thomas Wood
Ursula Teylor

[f.19r: 28 cms × 16 cms]

2 June 1643. **PRESENTMENTS BY THE CONSTABLES**, Thomas Walles and Evan Garnett.

They present that William Rose (12d) made a tussle upon Ralph Plumpton, and Plumpton (12d) on him again.

<They present that Nicholas Anderton made an affray on Anthony Prescott and on him drew blood, and the said Anthony tussled with him again.>

They present that William Wood of Glugsmore[165] (3s 4d) made a tussle on Thomas Wood, butcher, and on him drew blood, and the said Thomas Wood (12d) tussled on him again.

They present that John Taylor the younger (12d) made a tussle on Richard Banner, and Banner (12d) on him again.

They present that John Houghton of Prescot (3s 4d, Cecily Houghton his mother) made an affray before the steward on Richard Wolfall and drew blood.

They present that William Sutton (12d) made a tussle on William Lyme, and Lyme (12d) tussled with him again.

[f.19v]

They present that William Sutton (3s 4d) made an assault on William Rose and drew blood.

We[166] present that Anthony Prescott (3s 4d), drunk, in the night time entered the shop of Nicholas Anderton and 'in a very vyle and uncivill manner with base wordes' abused the said Nicholas Anderton calling him 'traytor' and beating at his window or door with a cudgel. Upon which the said Nicholas Anderton came forth and assaulted the said Prescott and drew blood, and the said Prescott assaulted him again.[167]

[f.20r: 15 cms × 20 cms]

2 June 1643. **PRESENTMENTS BY THE CLERKS OF THE MARKET**, John Parr and William Sutton.

We present Edward Fintch (12d) for opening <and stuffing> one veal. Pledge for Fintch, John Poughten.

---

165. Within Eccleston.
166. This presentment, in a different ink, might have been added later, although the amercement is in the same hand and ink as the other amercements for the constables' presentments.
167. See Introduction, pp. li–lii.

We present Thomas Knowles of Ditton (12d) for opening one veal. Pledge for Knowles, William Standish.

We present Henry Parr (12d) for opening one quarter of mutton contrary to the statute. We present Henry Parr (12d) for suffering unwholesome meat to be sold in his shop.

We present James Justice of Whiston (12d) who 'brought into the markett at Prescott to be sold a Calf which wee suspect was unfitt to be sold by reason of ites dyinge in guelding', and we further present that Thomas Wood, butcher (12d), bought the same calf and 'uttered it all which wee leave to the Consideracon of the Court.'

[f.20v, blank]
[f.21r[168]]
PRESENTMENTS BY THE STREETLOOKERS, Robert Hatton and Thomas Moberley.

We present Richard Webster, butcher (6d), for not dressing and cleaning the street before his shop, though warned.[169]

We present Robert Birchall of Rainford (6d) for the like before his shop.

[f.21v[170]]
[f.22r: 19 cms × 30 cms]

2 June 1643.   **OFFICERS ELECTED** to serve for the year following:

Constables	[1] Thomas Litherland	sworn
	[1] Nicholas Anderton	\<at the oath taking he continued to make default; therefore\> sworn
Four Men	[1] John Alcocke	sworn
	[1] Richard Litherland	sworn
	[1] \<John Webster\>	
	[1] Nicholas Marshall	sworn
	[1] Edward Stockley	sworn
Coroner	[1] Edward Stockley	sworn before
Clerks of the market	[1] \<Hamlet Whitfeild\>	
	[2] Ralph Halsall	sworn
	[1] John Parr	sworn
Burleymen	[1] \<Richard Litherland\>	
	[1] John Raynforth	sworn
	[1] Hugh Ward	sworn

168. The top portion, constituting 12 cms, was cut off, possibly after this book was sewn. The remaining portion is 19 cms × 19.5 cms.
169. In 1686 jurors ordered residents to clean the street in front of their residence every week, stated in 1688 to be Saturday, and to remove what is raked up within three hours, changed to five hours in 1692. LRO: DDKc/PC 4/126/Paper Books/1686 and 1688; DDKc/PC 4/53/Paper Book/1692.
170. Contains numerical additions.

Sealers of	[1] Roger Dey	sworn
leather	[1] Thomas Ackers	sworn
Alefounders	[1] William Molyneux	sworn
	[1] Thomas Browne	sworn
Streetlookers	[1] William Eaud	sworn
	[1] Hugh Ward	sworn
Leygatherer	[1] Richard Marshall	sworn

Affeerors of the court *[blank]*

[f.22v]
Court leet. 2 June, 1643, 19 Charles. Extract made and delivered.[171] Sum total within: £3 7s 4d.

1644

[Paper Book: DDKc/PC 4/41]   [Parchment Roll: DDKc/PC 4/182[172]]

[f.1r: 29.5 cms × 19 cms]
(*Parchment*: **VIEW OF FRANKPLEDGE WITH COURT BARON OF PRESCOT** in the county of Lancaster held there according to the custom of the manor of Prescot aforesaid before Thomas Wolfall, esq., steward of the manor and court aforesaid, on Friday, the day after Corpus Christi, 21 June, 20 Charles, 1644.)

PRESCOT. JURORS FOR THE SOVEREIGN LORD KING AND THE LORD OF THE MANOR at the court held there on 21 June 1644: [173]

	•	John Alcocke, sen.		
–	•	John Alcocke, jun. [174]	sworn [175]	default; therefore 6s 8d
– ○		William Parr	sworn	default
○	•	Nicholas Marshall	sworn	default
– ○	•	William Fletcher	sworn	

171. Delivered by Edward Stockley, clerk of the court, to the bailiff who was either Thomas Parr, bailiff for 1621, 1623–24 and between 1632 and 1642, or Henry Parr, bailiff for 1645, 1647 and 1648; the records do not reveal who was bailiff in 1643 and 1644. Thomas and Henry were the sons of Brian Parr and Katherine Getter. LPRS, 76, pp. 13, 21, 109; also see notes 235 and 245 *infra*.
172. The parchment roll contains records of courts held in June 1644 and January 1645 on two membranes, or one for each court, with writing on all sides except the verso of the first. Membranes measure 31 cms × 59 cms and 31 cms × 61.5 cms.
173. All names appear to have been written at the same time except that of William Parr (third name from the top squeezed between two names and added by another hand) and William Sutton (added later at the bottom of the list); all names are in the same ink.
174. The parchment roll also has 'gent.'
175. All persons listed as sworn in the paper book were also described as sworn in the parchment roll.

–	○	●	Peter Kenwricke, sen.	sworn
–	○	●	Richard Litherland	sworn
	○	●	John Webster of Well	sworn
		●	Thomas Devias	
		●	\<William Parr of Cronton\>	
–	○	●	James Houghton of Whiston	sworn	\<default; 6s 8d\>
		●	James Ditchfeild	sworn	default \<6s 8d\>
–		●	Hugh Ward	sworn	default \<6s 8d\> afterwards he agreed
–		●	Thomas Woodes of Whiston	sworn	\<default; 6s 8d\>
		●	Henry Webster of Knowsley	
–	○	●	Robert Wainwright of Tarbock	sworn
–	○	●	John Webster, nailer	sworn
			Thomas Woodes of Widnes	
		●	Ellis Webster	
–		●	William Lyon of Thingwall	sworn
			John Lyon, skinner	
			Robert Lyon of Eccleston	
		●	William Aspia of Kirkby	
			Paul Orme	
			Richard Torbocke	
–			William Sutton	sworn	default \<6s 8d\>

Jury adjourned until 2 August.
Jury further adjourned until 23 August 1644.
Jury further adjourned until 13 September.
Jury further adjourned until 15 November under pain of 6s 8d each.
Jury further adjourned until 27 December on pain of 6s 8d each.

[f.1v]
 Jury adjourned until 7 February 1645, on which day they appeared. Imposed on John Webster for bad conduct in court – 20s.
 Jury further adjourned until 21 March on pain of 3s 4d each, on which day they defaulted.
 And further adjourned until 11 April on pain of 3s 4d each.

Constables [176]	Peter Hearefoote	default; therefore 40s [177]
		default; therefore £3 6s 8d
	John Parr, butcher	default; therefore £5

[f.2r: 20 cms × 29.5 cms]
[SURRENDERS AND ADMITTANCES]
 [1] On 18 July, 19 Charles, 1643 Richard Kenwrick, inhabitant and mercer of London, son and heir of Richard Kenwrick late of Eccleston near Knowsley, yeo.,

---

176. The material on constables is in the left margin in the same hand and ink as the jurors' list.
177. The three notes on default apply to both persons.

dec., out of court came before John Alcocke, jun., Thomas Devias and Thomas Litherland and for money paid to him by Edward Kenwrick of Eccleston, yeo., second son of the said Richard Kenwrick the father, surrendered to the lord one shop and two rooms above the said shop late in the occupation of Thomas Eaton, shearman, and now occupied by Henry Eaton his brother. The lord to regrant the said shop and premises to the said Edward Kenwrick forever. Paying yearly to the lord the rent of 12d.

Acknowledged before us:	proclaimed	*[signed]* Richard Kenwricke
[signed] John Alcock Jr	admitted	
[signed] Thomas Devies		
[signed] Tho Litherland		

(*Parchment*: The said Edward Kenwricke is admitted forever.)

[f.2v, blank]
[f.3r: 20 cms × 30 cms]

[2] About August 1643 John Webster of Knowsley, husb., came before John Alcock, jun., and Richard Litherland and for £20 paid to the said John Webster by William Webster[178] of Eccleston surrendered to the lord those messuages and cottages hereafter mentioned, that is, one messuage and cottage heretofore occupied by James Parker and now occupied by Thomas Garnett, one other messuage or cottage now occupied by Edward Bate, another cottage occupied by John Huson, and one other cottage now occupied by Richard Wolfall. The lord to regrant the said messuages and cottages to the said William Webster forever. Paying yearly rent of 7d to the lord.

Provided that if the said John Webster shall pay to the said William Webster £23 4s on the next Corpus Christi, then this surrender to be void.

Acknowledged before us:	proclaimed
[signed] John Alcock Jn	admitted
Ric Litherland *[mark – initials]*	

(*Parchment*: The said William Webster is admitted forever.)

[f.3v, blank]
[f.4r: 20 cms × 30 cms]
At the court leet with view of frankpledge of Prescot held on 21 June 1644, 20 Charles.

[3] To this court Thomas Litherland of Prescot, yeo., came in open court before the steward and homage and for good and valuable considerations surrendered to the lord that messuage or dwelling house which Thomas Walles, vintner, now inhabits. The lord to regrant the said messuage and dwelling house to John Walles, son of the said Thomas Walles, forever. Paying 6s yearly to the lord.

Provided that if the said Thomas Litherland does in the presence of two or more copyholders pay 6d to the said John Walles and declares his intent to void this surrender, then the surrender is void.

[signed] Tho Wolfall	proclaimed	*[signed]* Thomas Litherland
	admitted	

178. The Abstract Book has 'William Webster his brother'.

(*Parchment*: The said John Walles is admitted.)

[f.4v, blank]
[f.5r: 20 cms × 30 cms]
OFFICIALS ELECTED to serve for the year following:[179]

Constables	Peter Herefoote	sworn 13 September 1644
	John Parr	sworn 13 September 1644
Four Men	William Fletcher	
	John Alcock	
	Thomas Woodes	
	Richard Litherland	
Coroner	John Alcock, jun.	
Clerks of	Hamlet Whitfeeld	
the market		
Burleymen	Robert Hatton	
Sealers of	Thomas Layton	
leather		
Alefounders	Thomas Knowles	
Streetlookers	James Houghton	
Leygatherer	John Poughten	
Affeerors of	John Alcock	
the court	William Fletcher	

[f.5v]
[ORDERS BY THE JURORS]

Whereas diverse persons within this manor have committed and do daily commit waste in the Wood by cutting down young oak plants which if preserved might later be useful, we now therefore order that no inhabitant may cut down any such plants or make any waste within the same on pain of 10s for every offence.

Whereas there is a watercourse between the copyhold lands of William Lyme and James Houghton of Whiston which has anciently divided the lands and is wrecked up with dung and filth, which watercourse is to be cleansed by the said William Lyme or such as enjoy that estate. We therefore order that the same shall be done at or before next 1 May on pain of 13s 4d.[180]

[f.6r: 20 cms × 30 cms]

There is another sough or gutter between the copyhold lands of Nicholas Marshall and Richard Litherland which annoys the lands and housing of Richard Litherland. We therefore order the said Nicholas Marshall to cleanse and scour the said gutter and the said Richard Litherland to make good the hedge as far as

179. All names appear to have been written in the same hand and ink.
180. Seventeenth-century Prescot was a maze of private ditches running from buildings sheltering humans and animals to the public ditches in the middle of streets. While residents intended ditches to carry excess rain water, ditches illegally functioned as open sewers and sometimes became blocked by dung and filth and, when rain fell, overflowed into streets and wells. Prescot's court frequently charged individuals with not 'scouring' their ditches and occasionally with refusing to help clean public ditches.

it belongs to him. If the said Nicholas Marshall fails to cleanse the same at or before next 1 May, he will forfeit 6s 8d. If the said Richard Litherland or his tenant John Rainforth fails to make the hedge between them at or before the said 1 May, he will forfeit 6s 8d.

[f.6v, blank]
[f.7r: 19 cms × 30 cms]
PRESENTMENTS BY THE CONSTABLES, Thomas Litherland and Nicholas Anderton, at the court leet held on 21 June 1644.

On or about 18 July last a tussle was made between William Mellinge of Whiston <12d> and Thomas Walles (12d). And Mellinge 'who gave the First offence was imprisoned about one hower.'

On or about 30 July an assault was made by Thomas Fletcher (12d, Ralph Fletcher, jun.), son of Ralph, upon Thomas Bond and John Wainwright, and Wainwright (12d, Thomas Bond) tussled on Fletcher.

'Informacon was geven' that there was an assault or affray between Richard Marshall and William Webster (3s 4d) his servant one upon the other, and repairing to Richard Marshall's house there he was found bleeding and his head broken in two places but by whom was unknown to the constable. William Webster was then not to be found within the town.

'Informacon was given' by Ellen Marshall, wid., that John Walker had assaulted her and drawn blood from her face, and repairing to the said John Walker (12d) he confessed that he had struck her.

William Forrest (12d, Richard Litherland) made an assault on William Webster.

On 3 December 1643, the Sabbath, James Angsdall (6s 8d), drunk, did, as Richard Litherland and some others affirmed, in the house of the said Richard Litherland assault Henry Lathom, skinner, and some others and drew one of their swords or rapiers and cut off a part of Henry Lathom's finger and injured some of his other fingers and drew blood from John Tunstall by breaking his head, threw another man into the fire and burned his clothes and was in danger to have run through the said Richard Litherland with the sword or rapier.

On the same Sabbath day the said James Angsdall (6s 8d) after in the street with a cudgel struck at women and children. Disobeying one of the constables who commanded him in his majesty's name to keep the peace, he was brought to the court house where he still disobeyed and resisted

[f.7v]
both constables and struck them and uttered very many foul words. And the said Angsdall was set in the stocks in the court house but escaped and in the night time rung the town bell, and either he or whoever assisted in his escape took the chain belonging to the said bell, for it was missing the next morning and has since not been found.[181]

181. Between 1625 and 1652 Prescot's leet amerced James £3 8s 4d for twenty-six breaches of the peace, including eleven between 1640 and 1645. In 1628 and 1652 he was before the sessions of the peace for assaults and between those years had six recognizances against him for good behaviour. For 1628 see LRO: QJI/1/5, Easter, and QJE/1, Midsummer; for 1652, LRO: QJI/2/6, Midsummer, and QSR/46, Ormskirk, Midsummer. Also see note 133 *supra*.

On or about 30 December 1643 Nicholas Rennicars (3s 4d) 'voluntarily confessed' that he and his brother-in-law, Henry Kerkes (3s 4d), had made an affray and drew blood one upon the other.

On 1 January 1644 Richard Angsdale (3s 4d) and Edward Angsdale (6s 8d) his son violently broke down part of the cottage in Prescot inhabited by Richard Higginson and threatened to strike and kill him and his wife. Though commanded by the constables to keep his majesty's peace, they persisted in their menacings and uttered many grievous oaths. Imprisoned in the court house, the said Richard Angsdall offered to break down part of the wall; and the said constable took hold of him to stock him, but he drew his knives and endeavoured to stab one of the constables. He was set in the stocks, and because Gilbert Heyes became 'his bayle to answeur his said misdemeanors', he was released. Pledge for Edward Angsdale, the said Richard his father.

On 8 April 1644 William Wetherby, miller (3s 4d, Ralph Plumpton), and John Taylor (3s 4d, John Birchall), son of James, made an assault and drew blood on each other.

[f.8r: 15.5 cms × 19.5 cms¹⁸²]

5 August 1643. Assault on the constable, Nicholas Anderton, by James Angsdall (6s 8d) 'who was with out rule or goverment despising all outhoretie and violenly striking those who came in to the asistance of the Constable.'

5 September 1643. Affray with blood between John Taylor, jun. (3s 4d), and William Futrell (3s 4d). Pledge for Taylor, his father James. For Futrell, none 'for hee overwent us.'

The same day a tussle between the said Futrell (12d) and Evan Heward (12d) without blood.

[f.8v, blank]
[f.9r: 13 cms × 16 cms]
PRESENTMENT BY THE BURLEYMEN, John Rainforth and Hugh Ward.

They present John Walker (12d) for neglecting to make his hayment sufficient between his croft and the Hall Meadow according to the burleymen's appointment.

[f.9v, blank]
[f.10r: 14 cms × 19.5 cms]
PRESENTMENTS BY THE CLERKS OF THE MARKET, Ralph Halsall and John Parr.

    Henry Parr (12d) for stuffing veal two times.

    James Angsdall (12d) 'for Rubing and beating of meate.'

    John Parr (12d) 'his boy for Rubing and beating on *[one]* time.'

[signed] Raph Halsall
John Parr *[mark]*

---

182. The folio is in a different hand and ink from those of folios 7r and 7v.

[f.10v, blank]
[f.11r: 18 cms × 30.5 cms]

PRESENTMENTS BY THE ALEFOUNDERS, Thomas Browne and William Mullenex.

We have found good and sufficient bread of a reasonable size of '2 poundes 1d' for the most part and also of ale and beer, but they say not at all times sold according to the statute.

We present that John Hoole[183] (12d) and his wife 'denied us to tast of theire drinck and saide there was no lawe and wee had nothinge to do thire with.'

William Hough's (12d) wife and James Dichfelde's (12d) wife did the like.

The names of the alehouses:

Thomas Parr	James Houghtone's
Thomas Woodes	Nicholas Marshall
William Hough	Richard Litherland
Mrs Boulton	Thomas Walles
Hamlet Whitfilde	Henry Darbishire's
Ralph Hallsoll	Jane Boultone's
William Futurel	Isabel Fearne's
John Pendelton	John Poughtine's
John Berchall	John Wayneright's
Henry Parr	Jane Fenne's
William Roose	Ralph Plumtone
Edward Booth	Jane Swifte
Alexander Rilandes	Richard Marshall

'The names of poore houses that bruwe at severall times':

William Sootton
Thomas Knowes
Richard Webster
Roger Man
Richard Jacson
\<Thomas\> Richard Jacson[184] in Webstar's house
Henry Kearkes
Thomas Garnet

\<'Divers of these peti ale houses seles accordinge to the statute.'\>
For breaking the assize of ale (each 12d).[185]
Breadbakers who broke the assize of bread (12d each):

---

183. The names of J. Hoole, W. Hough and J. Dichfelde are underscored, and amercements are above their names.
184. 'Jacson' was written by the same hand both times, while the second 'Richard', interlined, could have been written by the same hand as the first, but may be in a different ink.
185. Refers to the preceding.

John Poughten
Thomas Woodes
Richard Jackson of the Hillock
Jane Hunt
Jane Fenney

[f.11v]
Court leet of Prescot held on 21 June 1644. Extract made and delivered.[186] Sum total within: £5 6s 4d.

[f.12r: 20 cms × 30 cms]
(*Parchment*: **COURT BARON OF THE MANOR OF PRESCOT** in the county of Lancaster held there according to the custom of the said manor before Thomas Wolfall, esq., steward of the manor, liberty and court of Prescot aforesaid, on Friday, 17 January, 20 Charles, 1645.)

JURORS FOR <THE SOVEREIGN LORD KING AND> THE LORD OF THE MANOR AT COURT BARON OF PRESCOT held on Friday, 17 January 1645:[187]

John Alcocke[188]
William Parr
Nicholas Marshall
Peter Kenwricke [189]
Richard Litherland
William Fletcher
James Houghton

Thomas Woodes
Hugh Ward
Robert Wainwright
John Webster, nailor
William Lyon
William Sutton

[f.12v, blank]
[f.13r: 20 cms × 30 cms]
[SURRENDERS AND ADMITTANCES]
    [1] On 16 July 20 Charles,[190] Samuel Hynd, clerk, bachelor of divinity, out of court came before Nicholas Marshall, James Ditchfeild, Peter Kenwricke, sen., William Parr, William Lyme, Richard Litherland and Thomas Litherland and for £60 already paid by John Ashton of Whiston, yeo., did surrender to the lord one close, meadow and pasture containing about two large acres of land[191] heretofore commonly called Fletcher's two fields, together with one cottage thereupon standing consisting of two bays of building. The lord to regrant the said close, cottage and premises to the said John Ashton forever. Paying yearly to the lord the rent of 2s 6d.

---

186. By Edward Stockley, clerk of the court, and delivered to the bailiff. See note 171 *supra*.
187. All jurors' names were written at the same time and all were sworn.
188. The parchment roll also has 'jun., gent.'
189. The parchment roll also has 'sen.'
190. 1644.
191. Parchment roll: 'two acres of land of the large measure or thereabouts'.

Acknowledged before us: proclaimed   [*signed*] Sam Hinde
     [*signed*] Nic Marshall   admitted
     James Dichfield [*mark*]
     [*signed*] Peter Kenwrick senior
     [*signed*] William Parr
     [*signed*] Wil Lyme
     Ric Litherland [*mark – initials*]
     [*signed*] Tho Litherland
(*Parchment*: The said John Ashton is admitted forever.)

[f.13v, blank]
[f.14r: 20 cms × 23.5 cms]
At the court baron of Prescot on 17 January 1645.
     [2] To this court came Richard Litherland   (*P*: [192] of Prescot, tailor), Cecily
his wife – being solely (*P*: and secretly) examined by the steward – Jane Pyke (*P*:
of Prescot), wid., and John Rainforth (*P*: of Prescot, husb., before the steward and
homage) and for 30s paid to (*P*: the said) Richard Litherland and Cecily his wife[193]
(*P*: by Thomas Rainforth, son of the said John Rainforth), surrendered to the lord
the messuage and cottage (*P*: now occupied by the said John Rainforth) and one
croft and parcel of land thereto belonging called Leadbeter's croft now occupied
by John Rainforth. (*P*: The lord to regrant) to (*P*: the said) Thomas Rainforth (*P*:
son of the said John Rainforth) for the lives of the said Thomas Rainforth, William
Rainforth his son, and Ellen, wife of Thomas[194] Hitchin, lately called Ellen
Rainforth (*P*: sister of the said Thomas Rainforth) and for the longest liver. (*P*:
Paying yearly to the lord) the rent of 10d. Rent to <Ric> Jane during her life and
(*P*: after her decease) to (*P*: the said) Richard and Cecily (*P*: his wife) of 3s 4d
(*P*: yearly on the feasts of the Nativity of St John the Baptist and the Nativity of
Our Lord in equal portions. '[T]o be drawne up in due Forme and enrowled
accordingly.'
The said Cecilia solely and   proclamation made   Jane Pyke [*mark*]
secretly examined: admitted   Ric Litherland [*mark – initials*]
     Witness: Cicely Litherland [*mark*]
     [*signed*] Tho Wolfall steward   John Rainforth [*mark*]
(*Parchment*: The said Thomas Rainforth is admitted.)

[f.14v]
Surrender from Mr Hynde to John Ashton.[195]

[f.15r: 19.5 cms × 29 cms]
Court baron of Prescot held before Thomas Wolfall, esq., steward, on Friday, 17
January, 20 Charles, 1645.

192. '*P*': parchment roll.
193. '[A]nd Cicely his wyef' is not in the parchment roll.
194. '[W]ife of Thomas' is not in the parchment roll.
195. Refers to the preceding surrender.

[3] To[196] this court came John Ashton of Whiston, yeo., and in open court before the steward and homage for £60 paid by Edward Stockley of Prescot, yeo., surrendered to the lord one close, meadow and pasture containing about two acres of land of the large measure commonly called Fletcher's two fields and one cottage on the same close containing two bays of building. The lord to regrant the same to the said Edward Stockley forever. Paying annual rent of 2s 6d to the lord.

[signed] Tho Wolfall   admitted   *[signed]* John Ashton
(*Parchment*: The said Edward Stockley is admitted forever.)

[f.15v, blank]
[f.16r: 19.5 cms × 30 cms]

[4] On 16 September, 20 Charles, 1644 John Webster of Prescot[197] out of court came before William Fletcher and Richard Litherland[198] and for good considerations surrendered to the lord the messuage and tenement which the said John Webster now inhabits, one close at the east side of the said messuage, the burgage in Churchley Field being the ancient copyhold inheritance of the said John Webster, and two crofts near Sparrow Lane in Prescot. All which premises are the ancient copyhold inheritance of the said John Webster and[199] are all of the yearly rent to the lord of 13s; the croft, heretofore the copyhold inheritance of John Goodicar, of the yearly rent to the lord of 6d; and that burgage[200] in Churchley Field now occupied by the said John Webster and one cottage now occupied by Barbary Storey, wid., being both of the yearly rent of 16d. The lord to regrant the said messuage, cottage and lands to the said John Webster for his life, and after his decease to Edmund Webster of Knowsley, blacksmith, son of Thomas Webster, dec., forever. Yielding to the lord the several yearly rents aforesaid being in the whole 14s 10d. Charged with the sum of £20 to be paid as follows: to Henry Webster, brother of the said Edmund Webster, £10; to John Webster, William Webster, George Webster, Thomas Webster, Robert Webster and Margaret, wife of Robert Nelson, brothers and sister of the said Edmund Webster, £10 equally to be

[f.16v]
divided among them. The said £20 is to be paid in manner aforesaid within six months after the decease of the said John Webster of Prescot.

Provided that if the said Edmund Webster shall fail to pay the said £20 in manner aforesaid, then the said messuage and lands to the use of the said Henry Webster, John Webster, William Webster, George Webster, Thomas Webster, Robert Webster and Margaret Nelson until they shall have taken the said £20 with damages from the clear profits of the premises. And afterwards to remain to the said Edmund Webster forever.

---

196. In the parchment roll this surrender follows the first one and begins 'And afterwards to this court came John Ashton....'
197. Added in the parchment roll: 'wheelewright'.
198. The names of WF and RL were added in a blank in the same hand and ink as the surrender.
199. '[A]ll which premisses are the anncyent Coppihold inheritance of the said John Webster and' is not in the parchment roll.
200. The parchment roll has 'that other burgage'.

Provided that if the said John Webster of Prescot pays to any copyholder of the manor of Prescot 6d and declares his mind to void this present surrender, then this surrender to be void.

Acknowledged before us: proclaimed   John Webster of Prescott
   William Fletcher *[mark – initials]*   admitted   *[mark – initials]*
   Richard Litherland *[mark – initials]*
(*Parchment*: The said Edmund Webster is admitted forever.)

[f.17r: 19.5 cms × 30 cms]
[5] On 16 September, 20 Charles, 1644 John Webster of Prescot, wheelwright, out of court came before William Fletcher and Richard Litherland[201] and surrendered to the lord one cottage now occupied by William Coppow of Prescot. The lord to regrant the said cottage to the said John Webster for his life. And after his decease, then to the use of Roger Billinge of Upholland, skinner, forever. Yielding yearly to the lord the rent of 8d.

Provided that if the said John Webster pays to any copyholder of Prescot 6d and declares his mind to void this surrender, then this surrender is void.

Acknowledged before us: proclaimed John Webster *[mark – initials]*
   William Fletcher *[mark – initials]* admitted
   Richard Litherland *[mark – initials]*
(*Parchment*: The said Roger Billinge is admitted.)

[f.17v]
Court baron of Prescot held 17 January 1645. Prescot. 21 June 1644.[202]

1645

[Paper Book: DDKc/PC 4/41]   [Parchment Roll: DDKc/PC 4/105[203]]
[f.1r: 20 cms × 31 cms]
VIEW OF FRANKPLEDGE WITH COURT BARON OF PRESCOT in the county of Lancaster held according to the custom of the manor and liberty of Prescot aforesaid before Thomas Wolfall, esq., steward of the manor and court aforesaid, on Friday, the day after Corpus Christi, 6 June, 21 Charles, 1645.

201. The names of WF and RL were added in a blank in the same hand and ink as the surrender.
202. 'Prescott. 21 June 1644' was added in a different hand.
203. This roll has three membranes, with writing on all sides except the verso of the second and third membranes, which measure 31.5 cms × 64 cms, 30.5 cms × 15 cms, and 31.5 cms × 64 cms.

SUITORS OR CUSTOMARY TENANTS:

Sir William Gerrard, <knight> baronet
Thomas Eccleston, esq.   dead[204]
Henry Ogle, esq. out of the county
John Lancaster, <gent.> esq.
Henry Lathom, <gent.> esq.
Richard Eltonhead, gent.
o Thomas Wolfall, gent.
Thomas Sorrocold, gent.
William Alcocke, gent.   dead[205]
o John Alcocke, sen.
o John Alcocke, jun.
o Edward Stockley
William Blundell out of the county
Richard Tyrer,
 clerk   out of the county
o William Lyme
Mris Margaret Smyth dead[206]
William Parr of Cronton
Edward Symond   dead[207]
George Croston out of the county
Henry Pinnington within age
o William Lyon of Thingwall
William Kenwricke
    out of the county
Edward Kenwricke
George Deane of Rainhill
<George> Robert Lyon of <Windle>
 Eccleston
o John Lyon of Windle sick
Thomas Woodes of Widnes
o James Houghton of Whiston
o Thomas Woodes of Whiston
Henry Webster of Knowsley
o John Webster of Knowsley
o Robert Wainwright of Tarbock

William Leadbeter, jun.
Henry Parr out of the county
Dorothy Mercer, wid.
Richard Mollyneux
o William Webster of Eccleston
William Aspia of Kirkby
John Glover
 of Rainhill out of the county
George Tarleton of Liverpool
Richard Torbocke
 of Windle   dead[208]
Paul Orme of Tarbock
Richard Woodes of Rainford
o Roger Billinge essoined by Ric
 of Upholland Lith*[erland]*
o Thomas Devias of Huyton
o George Cartwright
o William Fletcher
James Ditchfeild   dead[209]
o Edmund Webster
o Peter Kenwricke the elder
o Nicholas Marshall
o Richard Litherland
 <Dorothy Mercer>
Ellis Webster
o Hugh Ward
o William Sutton
o Ann Litherland
o Ann Lodge

Subtenants and inhabitants:
o George Lyon
o Hamlet Whitfeild
o Ralph Halsall
o Nicholas Anderton

204. Of Eccleston, buried on 25 December 1644. LPRS, 114, p. 93.
205. Of Prescot, buried on 26 April 1645. LPRS, 114, p. 94. His will survives at the LRO:
  WCW/Prescot/1645/William Alcocke.
206. Of Knowsley, buried on 6 November 1644. LPRS, 85, p. 142.
207. Of Elton, gent., buried on 25 March 1644. Rev. W.J. Lowenberg and Henry Brierley, eds,
  The Registers of the Parish Church of Bury... 1617–1646, LPRS, 10 (1901), p. 343.
208. Buried on 24 November 1644. LPRS, 114, p. 93.
209. Of Prescot, buried on 28 November 1644. LPRS, 114, p. 93.

o William Futerill
Jarvis Symonett
o John Pendleton
o Widow Garnett
o John Birchall
o Henry Parr
[f.1v]
o William Ewde
o William Rose
Edward Booth
o Alexander Rylandes
Thomas Moberley
o Thomas Somner
o Robert Kenion
o Edward Finney
o John Huson, sen.
Edward Bate
o Richard Wolfall
o Thomas Garnett
o James Houghton
o Ralph Hall
James Parker
o John Houghton
o Henry Houghton
o Barbary Storey
o William Coppow
Richard Ditchfeild
o Ann Miller
Richard Marshall
o James Sadler
o Richard Banner
o Widow Orrell
o Edward Webster
o Gilbert Heyes
o wife of William Mollyneux
Thomas Fletcher
o Henry Kirkes
o Widow Stocke
John Sutton   out of
o Widow Mollyneux
o <John> Thomas Rainforth
<Nicholas Marshall>
o Ralph Fletcher
o Thomas Litherland
o wife of Thomas Bond

o Thomas Walles
o Henry Darbishire
o Isabel Hey
o Jane Bolton
Richard Webster
William Hough
o Thomas Knowles
John Haddocke
o Ann Akers
o James Angsdale
o John Frodsham
o Margaret Garnett
o William Hardman
Henry Standish
Anthony Prescott   out of
o Ferdinand Parker
o Thomas Parr
o Thomas Wood
o Widow Naylor
o Widow Haward
o John Cowper
o Thomas Ackers
o Mris Bolton
o William Birchall
o John Walker
o Edward Brundreath
o Widow Browne
o Widow Halsall
o Thomas Aspe
o Evan Garnett
o Peter Hearfoote
o John Parr, butcher
o <Michael> Ann Wattne
Richard Jackson on the Hillock
o John Houghland
o Widow Fletcher
o Edward Rylandes
o John Huson, jun.
o Widow Mann
o Peter Garnett
o Roger Dey
o Richard Chorleton
William Houghton   out of
o Robert Hatton
o Richard Hoomes

○ John Oliverson
○ John Poughten
○ Robert Woosie
○ Peter Kenwricke the younger
○ John Wainwright
  Thomas Kenwricke
  John Hoole
○ Richard Birch
○ Ralph Houghton
○ Widow Fennow
○ John Tyrer
  Richard Angsdale
○ Richard Jackson, webster

○ Thomas Browne
○ Richard Higgonson
○ Ralph Plumpton
[f.2r: 20 cms × 31 cms]
○ Widow Whyteside
○ John Wade
○ John Massie
○ John Rigby
○ Widow Swift
○ Robert Bolton
  Thomas Webster
  <Ellen Bate> Henry Rigby
○ Henry Prescott

[f.2v, blank]
[f.3r: 20 cms × 31 cms]

JURORS FOR THE SOVEREIGN LORD KING AND LORD OF THE MANOR OF PRESCOT at the court held on Friday, after Corpus Christi, 6 June 1645:[210]

Henry Lathom, gent.
Richard Eltonhead, gent.
John Lancaster, gent.
○ Edward Stockley   sworn
○ William Fletcher   sworn
  <Nicholas Marshall>
  Nicholas Marshall
○ William Lyon of Thingwall sworn
○ James Houghton of Whiston sworn
○ Edmund Webster   sworn
  Richard Litherland
  Edward Kenwricke
  Thomas Woodes of Widnes

○ Thomas Devias of Huyton sworn
  George Deane of Rainhill
○ John Lyon of Windle sworn
  Henry Webster of Knowsley
  William Aspe of Kirkby
○ Peter Kenwricke the elder sworn
○ Robert Wainwright
  of Tarbock sworn
○ Thomas Woodes of Whiston sworn
○ Hugh Ward sworn
  Ellis Webster
○ George Cartwright sworn
  Roger Billinge

[f.3v, blank]
[f.4r: 18 cms × 29.5 cms]

[SURRENDERS AND ADMITTANCES]

[1] On 1 May, 21 Charles, 1645 Richard Tyrer, clerk, out of court in the presence of Edward Stockley and Henry Parr[211] and for £30 paid to him by Margaret Tyrer, spinster sister of the said Richard, surrendered to the lord a messuage and tenement late in the occupation of John Garnett, dec., and now occupied by William

---

210. All names appear to be in the same hand and ink.
211. The names of ES and HP were added in a blank in the same hand and ink as the surrender.

Hough and Thomas Parr the younger. The lord to regrant to the said Margaret Tyrer forever. Paying yearly to the lord the rent of 2s.[212]

Acknowledged before us: *[signed]* Rich Tyrer
   [signed] Edw Stockley
   [signed] Henry Parr
   Katherine, wife of Richard Tyrer, pleaded in bar, and a day was given until 27 June of this month.
   8 August: the said Katherine pleaded nothing in bar. Therefore the said Margaret is admitted.
(*Parchment*: The said Margaret Tyrer is admitted forever.)

[f.4v, blank]
[f.5r: 20 cms × 31 cms]
   [2] On 4 June, 21 Charles, 1645 Edward Stockley out of court came before William Fletcher, Thomas Devias and Thomas Woodes[213] and for good considerations surrendered to the lord the messuage or cottage which John Oliverson now inhabits, with a garden belonging. The lord to regrant to John Oliverson the younger, son of the said John Oliverson, to hold immediately after the death of the said John Oliverson the father, for four score years if the said John Oliverson the son lives so long. Paying yearly to the said Edward Stockley the rent of 12s on the Nativity of St John the Baptist and the Nativity of Our Lord in equal portions and to the lord all other rents and services.
   Provided that if the said yearly rent of 12s is partially or wholly unpaid at any feast day within twenty days after due, then the said Edward Stockley may repossess the said messuage and premises and this surrender to be void.
Acknowledged before us: admitted   *[signed]* Edw Stockley
   Wm Fletcher *[mark – initials]*
   [signed] Thomas Devies
   [signed] Thomas Woods
(*Parchment*: The said John Oliverson the son is admitted.)

[f.5v, blank]
[f.6r: 19.5 cms × 29.5 cms]
   [3] On 23 January, 20 Charles, 1645 John Lyon of Windle, yeo., out of court came before Edward Stockley, Nicholas Marshall and Richard Litherland and in consideration of the yearly rent of 20s herein hereafter reserved to be paid to the said John Lyon did surrender to the lord one messuage or dwelling house with a yard or certain parcel of land on the north side heretofore occupied by William Aspe. The lord to regrant to Gilbert Heyes of Prescot, feltmaker, for the lives of the said Gilbert Heyes, Elizabeth his wife and William Heyes their son and the longest liver. Paying yearly to the said John Lyon the rent of 20s on the Nativity of St John the Baptist and the Nativity of Our Lord in equal portions. Yielding to the lord yearly the rent of 14d.

---

212. The paper book has a blank that is empty, while the parchment roll has 2s.
213. The names of WF, TD and TW were added in a blank in the same hand as the surrender but in a different ink.

Provided that if the said yearly rent of 20s be unpaid in part or in whole to the said John Lyon at any feast day when due within twenty days after due, then the said John Lyon may enter the said premises and this surrender to be void.

admitted   John Lyon *[mark]*

[f.6v]
Acknowledged before us:
   [signed] Edw Stockley
   [signed] Nicholas Marshall
   Richard Litherland *[mark – initials]*
(*Parchment*: The said Gilbert Heyes is admitted.)

[f.7r: 20 cms × 31 cms]
View of frankpledge with court of Prescot held on Friday, after Corpus Christi, 6 June, 21 Charles.
   [4] William Alcocke, late of Prescot, gent., dec., held to him a messuage or tenement heretofore in the tenure or occupation of Matthew Sutton, dec., and now in the tenure of John Pendleton, of the annual rent to the lord of 4d; another messuage or cottage and one yard or parcel of land, late in the holding or occupation of Margaret Angsdale, wid., dec., and now occupied by Robert Woosey of the annual rent to the lord of ld; and another close or parcel of land commonly called 'the acre' late in the occupation of George Lyon next to a messuage or cottage which John Houghland lately inhabited at the annual rent to the lord of 2s. He said William Alcocke at the time of his death was seised of the same. The jury further says that John Alcocke of Prescot, gent., is son and next heir of the said William Alcocke and is of the full age of twenty-one years old and more.
   Now to this court came the said John Alcocke and prays to be admitted and is admitted to hold the said premises forever. Paying to the lord of the manor several annual rents totalling 2s 5d at the usual feasts in Prescot in equal amounts.[214]

proclaimed
admitted

[f.7v, blank]
[f.8r: 20 cms × 30 cms]
   [5] To this court came Edward Stockley, and whereas the said Edward Stockley at a court held on Friday, 4 June, 17 Charles, 1641 in open court surrendered his messuages, tenements and lands hereafter mentioned, that is, that messuage and tenement which the said Edward Stockley now inhabits and those two fields and parcels of land called Higher Hey and Lower Hey thereunto belonging; three messuages or cottages now occupied by Robert Hatton, John Oliverson and Richard Holmes *; closes and parcels of land called Brown's Croft, Middle Croft and Cross Croft – which Cross Croft was heretofore in three crofts; one parcel of land called the midding stead in the upper end of High Street leading towards Eccleston; and

---

214. From 'and is admitted' to 'equal amounts' is from the parchment roll.
*   The parchment roll has 'Hoomes'.

those messuages or cottages now or late heretofore in the occupation of James Houghton, Ralph Hall, William Fletcher, glover, John Strettill and Richard Holmes* or some of them. To the use of the said Edward Stockley during

[f.8v]
his life and after his decease to other uses in the said surrender mentioned with proviso that if the said Edward Stockley should in the presence of two or more copyholders pay to the said copyholders or any other person or persons 6d and declare his intent to void the said surrender, then the surrender shall be void.

Now the said Edward Stockley in open court before the steward and homage did not only pay 6d to William Fletcher, James Houghton and Peter Kenwricke, copyholders, and then did declare his intent to void the said surrender, but also for good considerations surrendered to the lord the messuage and tenement which the said Edward Stockley now inhabits, those two closes and fields called the Higher Hey and the Lower Hey belonging to the said messuage, and three messuages or cottages

[f.9r: 20 cms × 30 cms]
now occupied by Robert Hatton, Richard Holmes* and John Oliverson or their assigns of the yearly rent to the lord of 12s 2d.

Also that close and parcel of land called the Lowest Field, sometimes [215] the copyhold inheritance of Ralph Fletcher and called Fletcher's Field, and all houses now standing on the same, being of the yearly rent of 2s 6d; and those three closes and fields called Brown's Croft, Middle Croft and Cross Croft – Cross Croft being now one croft but heretofore was three crofts – and the messuage or cottage heretofore in the occupation of William Fletcher, glover, and that parcel of land called the midding stead in the upper end of the street leading towards Eccleston being of the yearly rent of 11s 6d.

And those messuages, cottages and lands now or late in the occupation of James Houghton, Ralph Hall, John Strettell and Richard Holmes* being of the yearly rent of 3s to the said Edward [216]

[f.9v]
during his life. After his decease, to Katherine Stockley, now wife of the said Edward Stockley, during her life. After her decease, to the male heirs of the said Edward Stockley upon the body of the said Katherine. For default of such issue, to the male heirs of the said Edward Stockley. For default of such issue, to the said heirs of Edward Stockley upon the body of the said Katherine. For want of such issue, to Jane Stockley and Sarah Stockley, daughters of the said Edward Stockley and the heirs of their [217] bodies. For default of such issue, to the right heirs of the said Edward Stockley forever. Paying to the lord the several yearly rents, being in the whole 29s 2d.[218]

215. The parchment roll has 'formerly'.
216. The parchment roll adds 'Stockley'.
217. A new hand finishes this surrender in the paper book.
218. Blank in the paper book, but 29s 2d is in the parchment roll.

Provided that it shall be lawful for the said Edward Stockley to surrender those premises now in the several occupations of Robert Hatton, Richard Hoomes, John Oliverson, James Houghton and Ralph Hall, and those two messuages or cottages lying below the churchyard

[f.10r: 20 cms × 31 cms]
on the south side, being heretofore in the several occupations of John Strettell and Richard Hoomes, to the use of any person or persons for any term of copyhold, reserving the rents and services to the lord.

Provided also that if the said Edward Stockley during the life of the said Katherine now his wife with her consent or if the said Edward Stockley shall outlive the said Katherine Stockley his wife and afterwards in the presence of one or more copyholders of this manor pays to any copyholder or to another person or persons 6d and declares his intent to void this surrender, then this surrender shall be void.

                     admitted   *[signed]* Tho Wolfall
(*Parchment*: The said Edward Stockley is admitted.)

[f.10v, blank]
[f.11r: 20 cms × 31 cms]
[PRESENTMENTS BY THE JURORS]
We present that the following persons owe suit to this court but today made default in appearance (6d each):

Sir William Gerard, baronet	Richard Woodes
Henry Ogle, esq.	Ellis Webster
Henry Lathom, esq.	Jarvis Symonett
Thomas Sorocold, gent.	Edward Booth
William Blundell, gent.	Thomas Moberley
William Parr	Edward Bate
George Croston	James Parker
Henry Pynington	Richard Dichfeild
William Kenwricke	Richard Marshall
Edward Kenwricke	Thomas Fletcher
George Deane	Richard Webster
Robert Lyon	William Hough
Thomas Woodes of Widnes	John Chadocke
Henry Webster of Knowsley	Henry Standish
William Leadbeter	Richard Jackson of the Hillock
Henry Parr of London	Thomas Kenwricke
Dorothy Mercer, wid.	John Hoole
Richard Molyneux	Richard Angsdale
William Aspia of Kirkby	Thomas Webster
George Tarlton of Liverpool	Henry Rigbie
Paul Orme	

We present that Thomas Eccleston, esq., late of this manor who held to him and his heirs one messuage and tenement now or late in the holding or occupation of George Kerke of the yearly rent to the lord of 2s 3d died[219] since the last court, and that Henry Eccleston, esq., is son and heir to the said Thomas and is five years or thereabouts.

[f.11v]

Margaret Smith, spinster, late of this manor who held forever one messuage and tenement occupied by John Parr, butcher, and two cottages near adjoining, likewise in the occupation of the said John Parr, and one messuage and tenement occupied by Ann Molyneux, wid., of the yearly rent to the lord of 16d, died [220] seised since the last court. Elizabeth Smith, spinster sister of the said Margaret, is her heir and of full age.

proclaimed

admitted

Richard Torbocke, late of Windle, who held two shops under the court house of the yearly rent to the lord of 9d, died[221] since the last court seised thereof, and John Torbocke his son is his heir and about the age of *[blank]* years.[222]

James Dichfeild at a former court surrendered the messuage and tenement, occupied by Robert Bolton of the yearly rent to the lord of 3d, to himself and Ellen his wife for their lives and after their deaths to George Lyon the younger of Whiston and Jane his wife and the heirs of the said Jane. For want of such

[f.12r: 20 cms × 31 cms]

issue, to the right heirs of the said James Ditchfeild forever. The said James Dichfeild is dead[223] since the last court.

We present that John Oliverson and Margaret his wife have taken diverse burdens of pricks from Prescot Wood without consent of any of the Four Men and have carried the same out of the town to several places. Amerced 6s 8d.

John Rigbie and wife Elizabeth for the same. Amerced 6s 8d.

We order that neither the said persons before named nor any other person shall take any pricks or underwood from the said Prescot Wood without the consent of the Four Men on pain of 2s for every burden of pricks or underwood.

Whereas William Lyme or such as enjoy his estate was at the last court ordered to cleanse a watercourse between the said lands and the lands of James Houghton of Whiston before last 1 May on pain of 13s 4d. Since he has not done so, the pain is forfeited. We further order that the same watercourse shall be cleansed by the said William Lyme or such as enjoy his estate before next 1 August on pain of 26s 8d.

---

219. See note 204 *supra.*
220. See note 206 *supra.*
221. See note 208 *supra.*
222. John was baptized on 15 February 1631. LPRS, 76, p. 100.
223. See note 209 *supra.*

[f.12v]
Whereas the watercourse between the house of Nicholas Marshall and the stable of John Raynford is stopped so that rain water cannot pass, we order the said Nicholas Marshall to open the said watercourse on pain of 6s 8d. We further order that after it is done the Four Men shall investigate and present any default by either party at the next court.

<We present that the alefounders have neglected to make their presentments.>
We present that Thomas Browne, one of the alefounders – the other being William Molyneux who is dead[224] – has not come to make his presentments. Amerced 40s. 'Yet afterward came and made presentment wheireupon Mr steward is pleased to spare his Fyne affouresaid and to remitt his Amerciment of xls affouresaid.' [225]

We order that Thomas Litherland and Nicholas Anderton, constables for 1643, and also Peter Heirefoote and John Parr, constables for last year, shall make their accounts of all money they have received as constables to the Four Men at or before next 3 July on pain of 40s each.

[f.13r: 20 cms × 31 cms]
The jury further present that Edward Symond, gent., held to him and his heirs 'by coppy of Court Rowle accordinge to the Custome of the said mannour' the moiety or one half of two messuages or tenements, one now occupied by Ralph Houghton and the other in the several occupations of Henry Rigby and Thomas Webster. All are of the yearly rent of 2s 2d[226] to the lord. The said Edward Symond died[227] seised before this court here held. Jurors also say that Thomas Symond, gent., is son and next heir of the said Edward Symond and is of the full age of twenty-one years and more. The said Thomas Symond asks to be admitted and is admitted forever. Paying to the lord of the manor the moiety of the annual rent of 2s 2d.[228]
proclaimed
admitted
At previous courts orders were made for the preservation of the gates, hedges and fences of the tenants and of houses already made, but those orders have been very much neglected of late by the officers for that purpose appointed and the presenting of the breaches of the said orders omitted to the great hindrance of the lord of this manor and the inhabitants and 'the utter subvertion and overthrowe of all good order'. We therefore order that the constables and Four Men and all other officers shall take care that the said orders within their respective care and charge be performed and that all hedge-breakers and all others of that nature shall be punished by the constables according to the direction of the said orders. And the Four Men shall present the breaches of all orders with which they are concerned

---

224. Of Prescot, buried on 12 April 1645. LPRS, 114, p. 94.
225. From 'Yet afterward' to 'xls affouresaid' was squeezed by the same hand between the preceding and following presentments.
226. 'ijs ijd' was added in a blank in the same hand and ink as the surrender.
227. See note 207 *supra*.
228. From 'of twenty-one' to '2s 2d' is only in the parchment roll.

and especially present what cottages or houses of habitation have been erected within this manor within the past eleven years and since the order made for restraining thereof, and what houses formerly made and built for other uses have been turned into houses of habitation and by whom.

[f.13v]
And all shall give an account at the next court leet on pain of 20s each.

[f.14r: 19 cms × 30 cms]
PRESENTMENTS BY THE CONSTABLES, Peter Hearefoote and John Parr.
   They present an affray made on the Sabbath at time of divine service by Roger Mollyneux[229] (6s 8d), William Parkinson (3s 4d) and Gawther Breres (3s 4d) all of Rainhill on Lawrence Lathom of Eccleston. Whereupon Peter Hearefoote, constable, coming to command the peace, had a piece of the end of his finger cut off with a pocket dagger which Roger Mollyneux did violently draw through his hand. Pledge for the Rainhill men, Richard Jackson of the Hillock. Lawrence Lathom went his way, and whether he offered any violence they know not.
   They present that James Angsdale (3s 4d) made an assault on Hamlet Whitfeild and his wife, with blood drawn on Hamlet's wife.
   They present that an affray was made between William Ackers the younger of Whiston <6s 8d> (3s 4d) and Robert Nelson of Knowsley (12d) the one with the other and that John Worrall (12d) and Thomas Worrall of Whiston (12d) came to assist the said William Ackers. Whereupon John Parr, constable, commanding peace among them, was struck down by the said William Ackers (3s 4d) and his head broken. Pledge for William Ackers, William Sutton. The two Worralls suffered imprisonment. For Nelson, no pledge.

[f.14v, blank]
[f.15r: 19 cms × 30 cms]
PRESENTMENTS BY THE SEALERS OF LEATHER.........   [230] and Roger Dey.
   We present John Massie (12d) for selling leather unsealed and not sufficiently tanned.
   William Gill of Halewood (12d) had leather brought to the currier not sufficiently tanned and 'beinge spoken to about it confessed the same.'
   John Lyon of Woolfall Heath (12d) for selling leather in this town not well tanned.
   John Barker of Halewood for selling leather not well tanned, which leather was in Thomas Laton's (12d) shop, and the said Thomas Laton told the said Roger Dey that he bought it from John Barker.
   Thomas Woodes (4d) for selling leather unsealed though well tanned.

229. This reference is the only one in these records to Roger Mollyneux of Rainhill.
230. The upper-right corner (about 7.5 cms × 5 cms) is torn off and the name of the other sealer of leather is missing. Evan Hearefoote served with Roger Dey for the court year 1646–47 and was described as 'sworn before' at the court that met in May 1646. Only Thomas Layton was nominated to serve as a sealer of leather for the court year 1644–45.

[f.15v, blank]
[f.16r: 19 cms × 29.5 cms²³¹]

AT THE COURT HELD FOR THE MANOR OF PRESCOT on Friday, the day after Corpus Christi, 6 June, 1645.

PRESENTMENTS BY ONE OF THE ALETASTERS, Thomas Browne, for the past year on the behest of himself and William Mollyneux, dec., 'his late Fellow.'

Broke the assize of ale (12d each; in total, 37s):

Thomas Parr	Jane Fennowe
William Sutton	Jane Swift
Henry Standish	Ralph Plumpton
Thomas Woodes	Richard Marshall
William Hough	James Houghton
Frances Bolton, wid.	Thomas Fletcher
Thomas Ackers	Alexander Rylandes
Roger Man	Edward Booth
Hamlet Whitfield	William Rose
Ralph Halsall	Henry Kirkes
William Futerill	Nicholas Marshall
Jane Bolton, wid.	Henry Parr
Henry Darbishyre	John Berchall
Thomas Walles	Richard Sumner
Richard Jackson	Ellen Bond
Isabel Hey	John Pendleton
John Poughten	Richard Litherland
John Wainright	Thomas Kenwricke
John Hoole	

Have sold bread and have broken the assize (12d each; in total, 6s):

John Poughten	Jane Greene
Jane Fennowe	Thomas Woodes
John Massie	Richard Jackson

                                          Tho Browne *[mark]*

[f.16v²³²]
[f.17r: 20 cms × 31 cms]

OFFICERS for 1645:

Constables	*[2]* Ralph Plumpton	sworn
	[1] Roger Dey	sworn
	[2] James Sadler	declined in scandalous words in open court; therefore 40s.

231. This folio has come loose.
232. Blank except for fewer than a dozen cancelled words that are unreadable.

Four Men	[1] Edward Stockley	sworn before
	[1] William Fletcher	sworn
	[1] Peter Kenwrick	sworn
	[1] Richard Litherland	sworn before
Coroner	[1] John Alcocke, sen.	sworn
Clerks of the	[2] Ralph Halsall	sworn before
market	[1] <Hamlet Whitfeild>	
	[2] John Parr, butcher	sworn before
Burleymen	[1] Robert Hatton	sworn
	[2] Hugh Ward	sworn
Sealers of	[1] Thomas Layton	sworn
leather	[2] Evan Hearfoote	sworn
Alefounders	[1] Thomas Knowles	sworn
	[2] Thomas Sumner	sworn
Streetlookers	[1] William Eaud	sworn before
	[2] Hugh Ward	sworn before
Leygatherer	[2] James Houghton	sworn
Affeerors of	[2] Edward Stockley	sworn
the court	[2] William Fletcher	sworn
	[2] Thomas Devias	sworn
	[2] Thomas Woodes	sworn

[f.17v]
Prescot. Court held there. 6 June 1645. Extract made and delivered.[233] Sum total within: £6 10d.

[Paper Book: DDKc/PC 4/41 [234]]

[f.1r: 15.5 cms × 20 cms]
[SUMMONS TO HOLD COURT]
    Thomas Wolfall, esq., steward of the manor, liberty and court of Prescot in the county of Lancaster, to Henry Parr,[235] bailiff of the said court, greeting: I do command that you forthwith warn the customary tenants of the said manor, both resident and non-resident, to be before me at the next court baron to be held at

233. Delivered by Edward Stockley, clerk of court, to Henry Parr, bailiff.
234. While the following material is in a separate paper document within the bundle DDKc/PC 4/41, all parchment data for 1645 are included in the one parchment roll DDKc/PC 4/105 described in note 203 *supra*.
235. Bailiff for, at least, 1645, 1647 and 1648, Henry also was an alehousekeeper, badger, tailor and husbandman. He participated less often in manorial offices than Thomas, his elder brother and predecessor as bailiff, and served only as burleyman (1634, 1651) and constable (1636). Between 1635 and 1643, his name appeared in nine call books, just slightly closer to the top of the list of undertenants than to the bottom, but in ten call books for 1645 to 1655 his name rose to the top 10 percent. Interestingly, his rise to near the top was contemporary with his service as bailiff. When he died in March 1657, his widow, Dorothy, assumed his alehousekeeping duties. LPRS, 114, p. 115; LRO: QSB/1/202/91, Midsummer 1638.

Prescot on Friday, 10 October, to do their suit and to execute all other things which to them shall appertain. And this you may not omit. Dated 19 September, 21 Charles, 1645.

> *[signed]* 'Examined' by me, Edw Stockley,
> clerk of the court of Prescot aforesaid [236]

(*Parchment*: **COURT BARON OF THE MANOR OF PRESCOT** in the county of Lancaster held there according to the custom of the manor aforesaid before Thomas Wolfall, esq., steward of the manor, liberty and court aforesaid, on Friday, 10 October, 21 Charles, 1645.)

[f.1v, blank]
[f.2r: 19 cms × 26 cms]
JURORS FOR THE LORD OF THE MANOR at the court held on Friday, 10 October, 1645:[237]

William Blundell	3s 4d	Thomas Woodes of Widnes	
William Fletcher	3s 4d	Henry Webster of Knowsley	sworn
Nicholas Marshall	sworn	William Aspe of Kirkby	3s 4d
William Parr of Cronton	sworn	Thomas Woodes of	
William Lyon of Thingwall	sworn	<Widnes>Whiston	sworn
James Houghton of Whiston	sworn	Richard Litherland	sworn
Edmund Webster	sworn	Peter Kenwricke, sen.	sworn
Edward Kenwricke	sworn	Hugh Ward	sworn
Thomas Devias	sworn	Willam Sutton	3s 4d
Robert Wainwright		Ellis Webster	
of Tarbock	sworn		

[f.2v, blank]
[f.3r: 20 cms × 31 cms]
Whereas at the court held on 2 June 1643 John Alcocke of Eccleston surrendered to the lord one messuage, tenement and tanhouse in Hall Lane now occupied by George Lyon, tanner, to the use of the said John Alcocke of Eccleston and his heirs. For want of such issue, to Thomas Alcocke, son of John Alcocke of Prescot. For want of such issue, to the right heirs of the said John Alcocke of Eccleston forever.

And at the same court surrendered to the lord two messuages and tenements in the lane leading from Mill Hill to the Town Moss, one occupied by Ralph Plumpton or his assigns and the other occupied by John Rigbie or his assigns, to the use of the said John Alcocke of Eccleston. For want of such issue, to William Alcocke, son of John Alcocke of Prescot. For want of such issue, to the right heirs of the said John Alcocke of Eccleston forever.

---

236. The 'Examined...aforesaid' note is in a different ink and possibly a different hand from the summons itself.
237. All names are in the same hand and ink.

With proviso in the said surrender that if the said John Alcocke of Eccleston pays to any of his 'Coozins' before named or to any other person 12d and in the presence of two or more credible witnesses declares his intent to revoke this surrender or any part thereof, then this surrender in whole or in part shall be void.

Now the jury says that the said John Alcocke of Eccleston on 9 October 1645 did <before and in the presence of> pay to Edward Stockley, William Parr and Edward Kenwricke 12d to the use of the above-named William Alcocke and Thomas Alcocke

[f.3v]
and did declare his intent to void the said surrender of the estate in the said messuage, tenement and tanhouse occupied by the said George Lyon, tanner, and the estate in those two messuages and tenements, one of them in the occupation of Ralph Plumpton and the other occupied by John Rigbie. And the said John Alcocke of Eccleston prays that his revocation may be presented at Prescot's manorial court and that the said John Alcocke of Eccleston[238] may be admitted tenant of the said three messuages, tanhouse and premises to hold forever.

'Witnes herof':   proclaimed   *[signed]* John Alcock
[signed] Edw Stockley   admitted
[signed] William Parr
[signed] Edw Kenwricke

(*Parchment*: The said John Alcock is admitted forever, paying yearly to the lord for the said messuage and tenement in the occupation of the said George Lyon the rent of 18d; for the said messuage and tenement occupied by Ralph Plumpton the annual rent of 13d; and for the said messuage and tenement occupied by John Rigbie the annual rent of 14d.)

[f.4r: 20 cms × 31 cms]
Court baron of the manor of Prescot held on Friday, 10 October 1645.

Afterwards[239] to this court came the said John Alcocke of Eccleston in open court before the steward and homage and for £47[240] already paid to him by John Lyon of Woolfall Heath, tanner, did surrender to the lord one messuage and tenement in Hall Lane, now occupied by George Lyon, tanner, father of the said John Lyon, and all buildings, tanhouses, tanpits, backhouses and premises. The lord to regrant to the said John Lyon forever. Paying yearly to the lord the rent of 18d.

Acknowledged in open   proclaimed   *[signed]* John Alcock
court before me: admitted
[signed] Tho Wolfall

(*Parchment*: The said John Lyon is admitted forever.)

[f.4v, blank]
[f.5r, blank: 20 cms × 30 cms]
[f.5v]
Court baron of Prescot held on Friday, 10 October, 1645.

238. Not in the parchment roll: 'of Eccleston'.
239. 'Afterwards' appears only in the parchment roll.
240. 'Fortie Seaven Poundes' was added in a blank in the same hand and ink as the surrender.

1646

[Paper Book: DDKc/PC 4/41]   [Parchment Roll: DDKc/PC 4/77²⁴¹]

[f.1r: 20 cms × 30 cms]

VIEW OF FRANKPLEDGE WITH COURT BARON OF PRESCOT in the county of Lancaster held there according to the custom of the manor and liberty of Prescot aforesaid before Thomas Wolfall, esq., steward of the manor and court aforesaid, on Friday, the day after Corpus Christi, 29 May, 22 Charles, 1646.

SUITORS OR CUSTOMARY TENANTS:

William Gerard, baronet
Henry Eccleston, esq.
Henry Ogle, esq.
John Lancaster, esq.
Henry Lathom, esq.
<Richard Eltonheade, gent.>
Thomas Wolfall, gent.   dead²⁴²
Thomas Sorrocold, gent.
o John Alcocke, sen., gent.
o John Alcocke, jun., gent.
o Edward Stockley
o William Blundell
o William Lyme
o Mris Elizabeth Smyth
  Mris Margaret Tyrer   out of the
                                county
  William Parr of Cronton
  Thomas Symond, gent.   out of the
                                county
  George Croston, gent.   out of the
                                county
o Henry Pinnington   essoined by H P
o William Lyon of Thingwall
  William Kenwricke   <out of the
                                county>
o Edward Kenwricke
o George Deane of Rainhill
  Robert Lyon of Eccleston
o John Lyon of Windle

o Thomas Woodes of Widnes
o James Houghton of Whiston
o Thomas Woodes of Whiston
o John Leadbeter
o John Lyon, tanner
o Henry Webster of Knowsley
o John Webster of Knowsley
o Edmund Webster of Knowsley
o Robert Wainwright of Tarbock
  William Leadbeter, jun.
o Henry Parr   out of the county
  Dorothy Mercer, wid.
  Richard Mollyneux
o William Aspia of Kirkby
  John Glover of Rainhill   out of
  George Tarleton of Liverpool
  John Torbocke of Windle
  Paul Orme of Tarbock
  Richard Woodes of Rainford
o Roger Billinge of Upholland
o Thomas Devias of Huyton
  George Cartwright
o William Fletcher
o George Lyon, jun.
o Peter Kenwricke, sen.
o Nicholas Marshall
o Richard Litherland
o Ellis Webster
o Hugh Ward

---

241. Three membranes with writing on all sides except the verso of the third. They measure 31.5 cms × 54.5 cms, 31.5 cms × 54 cms and 31.5 cms × 57 cms.
242. Of the Damhouse in Huyton, buried on 26 June 1645. LPRS, 85, p. 142.

o Hugh Ward
o William Sutton
o Ann Litherland
  Ann Lodge

[f.1v]
Undertenants and inhabitants:
  Hamlet Whitfeild   dead[243]
  Ralph Halsall   dead[244]
o Nicholas Anderton
o Janet Futerell
o Thomas Kenwricke
o John Pendleton
o <Thomas> Richard Somner
o John Birchall
o Henry Parr
o William Ewde
o William Rose
o Edward Booth
o Alexander Rylandes
o Thomas Moberley
o Robert Kenion
o Edward Finney
o John Huson, sen.
  Edward Bate
o Richard Wolfall
  James Parker
o James Houghton
  Ralph Hall
o Thomas Garnett
o John Houghton
o Henry Houghton
o William Coppow
o Thomas Somner
o Richard Ditchfeild
o Richard Marshall
  James Sadler
o Richard Banner
o Edward Webster
o Gilbert Heyes
  Thomas Fletcher

o Henry Kirkes
  John Sutton   out of
o Thomas Rainforth
o Thomas Litherland
o Thomas Walles
o Henry Darbishire
o Robert Knowles
o William Hough
o Thomas Knowles
  James Angsdale
o John Frodsham
o William Hardman
o Henry Standish
o Anthony Prescott
o Ferdinand <Anderton> Parker
o <William Sutton>
o Richard Jackson
  Thomas Parr   dead [245]
  Thomas Wood
o Robert Parr
  John Cowper
o Thomas Ackers
o William Birchall
  John Walker   infirm
  Edward Brundreath
o Thomas Aspe
o Evan Garnett
o Peter Hearefoote
o John Parr, butcher
o Michael Romley
o John Houghland
o Richard Jackson on the Hillock
o Edward Rylandes
  John Huson, jun.
o Peter Garnett
o Roger Dey
o Richard Chorleton
o Robert Hatton
o Richard Hoomes
[f.2r: 20 cms × 30 cms]
o John Oliverson

243. Of Prescot, blacksmith, buried on 11 March 1646. LPRS, 114, p. 96.
244. Of Prescot, blacksmith, buried on 11 February 1646. LPRS, 114, p. 96.
245. Of Prescot, yeoman and bailiff of Prescot's manorial court. Buried on 12 December 1645. LPRS, 114, p. 95. For his will, see LRO: WCW/Prescot/1647/ Thomas Parr.

○ John Poughten
  Robert Woosie
○ Peter Kenwricke, jun.
  John Wainwright
○ Richard Birch
○ Ralph Houghton
  <Widow Fenno>
○ John Tyrer
  Richard Angsdale
○ Thomas Browne
  Richard Higgonson

○ Ralph Plumpton
  John Massie
○ John Rigbie
○ Robert Boulton
  Thomas Webster
○ Henry Rigbie
  Henry Prescott
  Roger Mann
○ William Browne
  Thomas Horneby
  John Taylor

[f.2v, blank]
[f.3r: 20 cms × 30.5 cms]

JURORS FOR THE SOVEREIGN LORD KING AND LORD OF THE MANOR OF PRESCOT at court held on Friday, after Corpus Christi, 29 May, 1646:[246]

Thomas Sorrocold, gent.		Thomas Devias of Huyton	sworn
Edward Stockley	sworn	Thomas Woodes of Whiston	sworn
William Blundell	sworn	Robert Wainwright	
William Fletcher	sworn	of Tarbock	sworn
Nicholas Marshall	pardoned	Roger Billinge of Upholland	
George Deane of Rainhill	sworn	Richard Litherland	sworn
William Lyon of Thingwall	sworn	<Peter Kenwricke, sen.>	
James Houghton of Whiston	sworn	Hugh Ward	sworn
<Edward Kenwricke>		Ellis Webster	
<Thomas Woodes of Widnes>		John Lyon, tanner	
John Lyon of Windle	sworn	William Aspe of Kirkby	sworn
Henry Webster of Knowsley	sworn	doorkeeper, Richard Hoomes	sworn
Edmund Webster			
of Knowsley	sworn		

[f.3v, blank]
[f.4r: 20 cms × 30 cms]

OFFICIALS for 1646:[247]

Constables	Edward Booth	sworn	The said constables are adjourned until next 5 June on pain
	James Sadler	sworn	of 40s each.
Four Men	Edward Stockley		sworn

246. All names appear to have been written at the same time.
247. All names appear to have been written at the same time.

	William Blundell	sworn
	William Fletcher	sworn
	Nicholas Marshall	sworn
Coroner	John Alcocke, sen.	sworn before
Clerks of the	Nicholas Anderton	sworn
market	John Parr, butcher	sworn before
Burleymen	Robert Hatton	sworn before
	Hugh Ward	sworn before
Sealers of	Roger Dey	sworn
leather	Evan Hearefoote	sworn before
Alefounders	Thomas Knowles	sworn before
	Thomas Somner	sworn before
Streetlookers	Ralph Houghton	sworn
	Hugh Ward	sworn before
Leygatherer	James Houghton	sworn before
Affeerors of	Edward Stockley	sworn
the court	William Blundell	sworn
	<William Halsall>	
	William Fletcher	sworn
	Thomas Woodes	sworn

[f.4v, blank]
[f.5r: 20 cms × 30 cms]

VIEW OF FRANKPLEDGE *[PRESENTMENTS BY THE JURORS]*.
We present the following persons for default in appearance (6d each):

William Gerard, baronet
Henry Ogle, esq.
Henry Lathom, esq.
Thomas Sorocold, gent.
Dorothy Mercer, wid.
Richard Molyneux
George Tarlton

Paul Orme
Richard Woodes
Edward Bate
James Angsdale
Richard Angsdale
Richard Higginson

Whereas Thomas Litherland and Nicholas Anderton, constables for 1643, were at the last court ordered to make their accounts to the Four Men of all the money they have received for the town's use, at or before next 3 July on pain of 40s each, but they have neglected to perform. And it appears to us that during their time in office leys were laid and arrears delivered to them to be collected, amounting to £98 3s 10d or thereabouts. We now further order that the said Thomas Litherland and Nicholas Anderton shall pay the said pain of 40s each already forfeited. And further order that they shall give account to the present Four Men about how they have disposed of the said £98 3s 10d, at or before 1 <July> August next on pain of £5.

[f.5v]

We present that Thomas Parr, dec., late one of the surveyors of this town, had 11s 4d of the town's money which we order his son, his executor, to pay to the present surveyors before the last of this month on pain of 3s 4d.

'Whereas divers Complayntes have beene made of the multiplicitie of Alehowses in this towne upon which Mr steward and the Constables havinge taken it into Consideracon have agreed that the persons followinge shalbe allowed and none other.'

William Harrison	Henry Darbishyre
Ann Halsall, wid.	Isabel Fernes
John Pendleton	Jane Boulton
Henry Parr	Thomas Parr
Edward Booth	Robert Parr
Alexander Rylandes	Mrs Bolton
James Houghton	John Poughten
Thomas Garnett	Widow Fenney
Richard Marshall	Ralph Plumpton
Nicholas Marshall	Jane Swift
Ellen Bond	Richard Edwardson
Richard Litherland	John Waynwright
Thomas Wall	

'And have sent the names above menconed to be entered in our presentmentes which wee in obedience to the said Direction have done accordingly.'

And we order that all who keep an alehouse in this town other than those before named shall forfeit 6s 8d for every bushell of malt they shall brew contrary to this order.

[f.6r: 20 cms × 30.5 cms]

We present that diverse persons within this town have received and entertained undertenants to inhabit without consent of the Four Men contrary to former orders of this court. Those persons so entertained are:

Henry Bold	Roger Man
Richard Jackson	William Canner
Mr Leigh	Michael Rumley
Elizabeth Tarlton, wid.	Robert Parr
Mrs Bolton	Richard Williamson alias Edwardson
Thomas Cooke	John Waynwright
William Browne	Robert Boulton, hatter
John Taylor, currier	

'and some others. All which some have desyred the Consent of some of the 4 men and have not as yet geven securitie as they shold by former orders have done.' We order that all persons who have entertained or been entertained shall repair to the Four Men and procure consent and give security, as by former orders are required, at or before 1 August next on pain of 13s 4d each.

We present John Parr, butcher, for converting a shippon into a house of habitation, and he has forfeited 13s 4d.

We present that he has maintained the same as a cottage by suffering Katherine his sister to inhabit therein for one* month and has forfeited <for every month> 13s 4d <in toto for *[blank]* months>.

John Webster, nailer, has converted part of his two dwelling houses into two cottages for habitation and has received two tenants into them and for converting them has for each forfeited 13s 4d and for maintaining them for one* month 13s 4d for each month. In the whole, 53s 4d.

[f.6v]

William Rose has converted his house into several habitations and several dwellings. Therefore 40s.

Edmund Webster has converted a new house built by John Webster, dec., into a house of habitation. Thus 13s 4d.

The said Edmund Webster has maintained the same as a house of habitation by allowing Michael Rumley and his family to inhabit for one * month last past and has forfeited <for every month> 13s 4d; <in toto>.

William Fletcher[248] has erected four cottages in Hall Lane for habitations. Thus for each, 13s 4d; in total, 53s 4d.

The same cottages have been employed for habitations by him. One cottage has been inhabited by William Browne for one* month. Therefore the said William Fletcher is amerced 13s 4d.

Thomas Hornby has inhabited another cottage for one* month. The said William Fletcher is amerced 13s 4d.

John Taylor, currier, has inhabited another for one* month last past. The said William Fletcher is amerced 13s 4d.

Lawrence Man has inhabited one other cottage for one* month. The said William Fletcher is amerced 13s 4d.

---

*   The 'one' in 'one moneth' from here to the first line at the top of folio 7r was added in a blank in an ink different from the rest of each presentment.

248. Of Prescot, mercer. At the 1647 court jurors again presented William for these four cottages and in 1650 ordered Elizabeth Fletcher, daughter of the said William, now deceased, or the executor (William Glover) of his will, to pay 53s 4d yearly to the lord of the manor and 4s to the schoolwardens. These payments were in lieu of arrears for unpaid amercements for the said four cottages of 13s 4d a month per cottage since the first presentment and were to continue as long as the said four cottages were maintained as houses of habitation. In 1620 the court also amerced William 6s 8d for entertaining Margaret Webster, wid., without consent of the Four Men and in 1633 commanded him to remove out of Prescot 'Prettie Peg' whom he maintained. William's name appeared in the bottom 20 percent of tenants. He served as a presentment juror in 1621 and in every year from 1624 to 1647 except 1642 when he was nominated but not sworn. He also served as a juror at seven courts baron, as one of the Four Men eleven times, five years as affeeror, twice as surveyor of highways and as a witness for thirty surrenders. LRO: DDCs/Paper Books/1620 and 1650; DDKc/PC 4/161/Paper Book/1633. Also see note 297 *infra*.

Ralph Halsall, dec., did in his lifetime convert a part of his house, sometimes used as a smithy, into a house of habitation. Therefore 13s 4d.

The same has been inhabited by several tenants and is now inhabited by one Thomas

[f.7r: 20 cms × 30 cms]
who has lived there for one* month last past. Thus 13s 4d.

Whereas it appears that the town is indebted to Edward Stockley for money laid out for the highway and for a musket and furniture sold to Thomas Wall, constable,[249] in the amount of £3 7s 11d. And to William Fletcher for money laid out for the highway, 20s 10d. To the said Thomas Wall, 30s 11d. To Ralph Halsall, dec., for two muskets and furniture sold to Thomas Wall, 43s 4d. To Edward Darbishyre, 3s 4d. To Peter Heirefoote, late constable, 57s. Total is £11 3s 4d. We order that the Four Men shall assess a ley for payment thereof, and the constables shall collect and pay as due, and that the Four Men shall likewise examine all the arrears due and unpaid to the town and that those arrears shall be collected and paid. Those arrears that shall fall short to satisfy these debts, the constables shall pay out at the ley so laid.

We further order that all who do not pay their leys to the town shall forfeit double the unpaid amount and also 3s 4d for every default.

[f.7v[250]]
We order that the last constables, Roger Dey and Ralph Plumpton, shall perfect and deliver their accounts to the Four Men at or before next 14 July on pain of 40s each.

We order that the sum of 24s shall be paid to Ralph Plumpton which is due to him by the town for keeping one Clayton, a sick soldier, and his father for twenty-four days by the command of Peter Heirefoote, constable, who was commanded by Colonel Ashton's[251] warrant to provide for that soldier.

---

249. Thomas Walls was constable from June 1642 to June 1643. In 1632 jurors ordered the constables to pay Thomas 10s for keeping the town's arms for the past three years; and in 1636 the court ordered him to be paid 3s 4d a year for the past three years for oiling and keeping that armour. In this case the caretaker of Prescot's armour was a royalist. Those who assisted the king against Parliament could retain control over their property by 'compounding' (paying a fine), as Thomas Walle, an undertenant, did in 1646 for his messuage and garden in Prescot. A number of non-resident tenants also compounded, e.g., Richard Eltonhead, sen., of Sutton, gent.; Sir William Gerard of Brynn, baronet; John Lancaster of Rainhill, esq. (Thomas's landlord between 1629 and 1642); and Thomas Wolfall of Huyton, gent. LRO: DDKc/PC 4/161/Paper Book/1632 and DDKc/PC 4/66/Paper Book/ 1636; J.H. Stanning, ed., *The Royalist Composition Papers, Being the Proceedings of the Committee for Compounding, A.D. 1643–1660, So Far as They Relate to the County of Lancaster,* RSLC, xxvi (1892), p. 279; xxix (1896), pp. 51–71; xxxvi (1898), pp. 53–5; John Brownbill, ed., xcv (1941), pp. 250–1; xcvi (1942), pp. 330–4. Also see note 164 *supra.*
250. Pinned to this folio is a piece of paper (8 cms × 2.5 cms) with '1646 inhabitants within this Manor' written on it.
251. Ralph Assheton of Middleton (d. 1652) who 'was first a colonel, then a general, and finally the commander-in-chief of all the Parliament forces in Lancashire.' Beamont, *Warr in*

'Wheareas It appeareth to us by good evidence' that John Hoole, Eleanor his wife and Ellen Hoole their daughter have committed 'notorious abuses against dyvers of theire neighbors within this towne and soe thought unfitt to Continew in the towne.' We order that no person inhabiting within this manor shall permit the said John Hoole, his wife Eleanor or daughter Ellen Hoole to inhabit the town from next 24 June and that they shall depart from the town before that day on pain that everyone staying after that day to forfeit for every night 3s 4d and everyone who receives them or any of them to forfeit 3s 4d for every night.

[f.8r: 20 cms × 30.5 cms]

Diverse dunghills and other nuisances are offensive to this town and are to be taken into consideration, but which at this present for want of time and evidence cannot be perfected. We order the Four Men to perfect as they think fit and make presentment thereof at the next court.[252]

Whereas the walls of the shops under the court house are in decay and since there is disagreement over who shall repair them, we order the Four Men to view the walls and settle the difference. And the same shall be repaired in such sort and by such time and persons as the said Four Men shall order, or those defaulting to forfeit 3s 4d each.

We present that three of the feoffees for the money given to charitable uses by Lawrence Webster, dec.,[253] that is, William Alcocke, gent., Oliver Lyme and Edward Fynney, are dead,[254] and no new feoffees have been chosen; and the surviving feoffees, called to present others in their places, proposed William Blundell, William Fletcher and Evan Garnett. We now present the said William Blundell, William Fletcher and Evan Garnett to be feoffees of the said charitable money and to join with the vicar of Prescot, Edward Stockley and Nicholas Marshall in disposing thereof.

[f.8v, blank]
[f.9r: 20 cms × 30 cms]

Lancashire, p. 100, note 17. He was involved in the defence of Bolton in February 1643 and in the taking of Wigan in early April of the same year; he participated in the siege of Lathom House in early 1644 and in the battle of Preston in August 1648, as well as in other military engagements.

252. An offensive dunghill could be one that had been against the street side of a house longer than allowed by a by-law, or one so large that it hindered travellers when it became 'disordered' and 'spread' into the street, or even one on the waste that was deemed too large. See note 80 *supra*. Not surprisingly, during the war-torn 1640s public health violations did not greatly concern the residents of Prescot; then only 1.7 public health offenders annually were brought before the leet compared to 4.8 from 1615 to 1639, 4.1 during the 1650s and 6.7 between 1660 and 1700. As the century wore on, inhabitants became less tolerant of public health violations and became more inclined to punish than issue a warning. During the pre-Civil War period leet officers made 2.3 presentments for every order issued but 7.1 after 1660.

253. Yeoman, husbandman. At his death in May 1608, a dozen individuals owed him a total of £62 15s. LPRS, 76, p. 177; LRO: WCW/Prescot/1608/Lawrence Webster. In 1605 his age was recorded as about eighty-eight. TNA: DL 4/49/13/f.6v.

254. Alcocke, Lyme and Fynney were buried in April 1645, June 1631 and January 1645, respectively. LPRS, 76, p. 218; 114, pp. 93, 94.

PRESENTMENT AND INFORMATION of Mris Blundell and Mris Tyrer of Prescot against John Hoole, Eleanor his wife and Ellen Hoole their daughter.

The said Mris Blundell says that the said John Hoole when 'the Princes forces' were in the county did on the Sabbath at night bring with him to the house of William Blundell, gent., her husband, four soldiers of Sir Thomas Gardner[255] 'who in a voylent manner came into the howse and forced the said Mris Blundell out of her bedd, shee then lyinge in child bedd, and gave her base language callinge her Divell and Rounhead whore and Did plunder and take from the said Mris Blundell two silver spoones, one hatt and ijs in money and threatned her to carry her away prisoner before the Prince.'

She also says that Eleanor Hoole, wife of the said John Hoole, several times since has given bad language against the said Mris Blundell and much abused her by saying, 'Thou are a Parlyament queane' and with such other like words, and Ellen Hoole, her daughter, called the said Mris Blundell 'a Cutt with other scurrilous wordes.' Sworn in open court.

Mris Tyrer also says that the said John Hoole about a month ago met her in the street and said, 'Well I wilbee Revenged on thee whore' and that Eleanor Hoole, his wife, will not suffer the said Mris Tyrer to pass by her in the streets but calls her 'Parlyament whore'. Eleanor also threatened the wife of Ralph Houghton 'that shee should not bee left worth a groate for nursinge a Parlyament whores child' and also that Ellen Hoole gives threatening words against the said Mris Tyrer who is daily afraid for her life. The said Mris Tyrer also says that Margaret, wife of John Oliverson,[256] said she heard the said Ellen Hoole say that 'if ever the Cavelleers came againe shee would cutt throates as fast as ever shee cutt sheaves of bread.' Sworn in open court.[257]

[f.9v, blank]
[f.10r: 20 cms × 22 cms]
PRESENTMENTS by Roger Dey and Ralph Plumton *[constables].* [258]

Richard Jackeson, mercer (12d, Edward Brundereth), made a tussle on Katherine Ashton, and she (12d, John Ashton her husband) on him again.

255. Thomas was the son of Sir Thomas Gardiner (1591–1652), a royalist. Thomas the son was knighted by Charles I in early 1643 and died fighting for the king in late July 1645. Sir Leslie Stephen and Sir Sidney Lee, eds, *The Dictionary of National Biography*, 7 (London, 1921–22), pp. 865–6. This incident occurred between late May 1644 when Prince Rupert entered Lancashire from Cheshire and late June when he left the county on his way to York, or after his defeat on 2 July at Marston Moor when during July Rupert passed through Lancashire on his way to Chester (25 July) and further south. More precisely, it probably took place during the first three weeks of June when the Prince's forces successfully attacked Liverpool or around 22 July when Rupert was again at Liverpool. For William Blundell, see Introduction, p. liv, note 201.
256. For Margaret and John, see Introduction, p. lv, note 205.
257. For more on the Hooles, see Introduction, pp. liv–lvii.
258. Ralph was styled alehousekeeper, miller, tailor, husbandman and yeoman. Between 1638 and 1671 in twenty-five call books bailiffs entered Ralph's name, on average, in the bottom 10 percent of undertenants. He served in no parish office and in only a few manorial offices: juror-between-parties (1634), streetlooker (1638, 1660), aletaster (1641) and constable (1645). Being accused of only two breaches of the peace (1643, 1647) suggests that

Wife of Gilbert Hey, Ann, wife of Robert Kenion, and Katherine, wife of Richard Banner, made a tussle on Jennet Orrell and on her son John, and they against them. Everyone a pledge for themselves; amerced 12d each.

Richard Birtch (12d; for Bertch, Ralph Houghton) made a tussle against Richard Higgonson, and he (12d, William Canner) against him.

PRESENTMENTS by Roger Dey himself.[259]

Evan Hereffotte (3s 4d, John Taylor, currier) did 'flinge a Candlesticke' at Nicholas Anderton and broke his brow and drew blood. 'Nicholas was houlden and did not stricke.'

Mris Isabel Lyme (12d, herself) came into the house of Ralph Fletcher the elder and did give the said Ralph many blows, according to the said Ralph, and broke his head.

John Leadbetter (12d, Thomas Fletcher, son of Thomas) made a tussle on Elizabeth Stocke.[260]

[f.10v, blank]
[f.11r: 15 cms × 19.5 cms]
PRESENTMENTS by Roger Dey and Ralph Plumpton.[261]

We present Thomas Aspe (3s 4d) 'for eivell and slanderous words' and for claiming that we did demand more than was in the ley book and that he would affirm that one double ley was £5 and that the Four Men and constables 'did Chett and Cossen all the Towne.'

We present Eleanor (3s 4d[262]), wife of John Hoole, 'for diveres evell and slanderous words many tymes and such words as we Cannot well expres.'

We present Ellen Halsall, wid. (3s 4d), and Widow Mollineux (3s 4d) for the like.

A PRESENTMENT by Ralph Plumpton.

Ralph Parr, butcher (2s), did strike and abuse Edward Parr, son of Henry Parr, and did much wrong the said Edward Parr both by words and blows.

[f.11v, blank]
[f.12r: 16 cms × 27 cms]

he was less volatile and violent than many of his neighbours, as does his remarkable restraint in not retaliating against any of the many individuals accused at the 1646 court of physically and verbally abusing him. Ralph died in 1685. What little we know of Roger, shoemaker, suggests that his social standing and service in manorial offices paralleled those of Ralph. Roger's name commonly appeared in the bottom third of undertenants. As constable he served only this one time but did also function for six years as a sealer of leather. Although the parish register does not record his burial, Roger, who first appears in Prescot's manorial records in 1618, may have died during the 1650s when references to him cease. His wife Mary died in September 1653. LPRS, 149, p. 113; 114, p. 111.

259. Presentments by Dey are in the same hand and ink as the preceding by Dey and Plumton.
260. While much of the rest of the sheet is missing, enough of the left side survives to suggest that no text is missing.
261. The entire folio is written in the same hand and ink as the above presentments by Dey and Plumton and by Dey himself.
262. 'Elnor the wyf of John' is underscored, and the amercement is written above 'Elnor the wyf'.

PRESENTMENTS by Ralph Plumpton, one of the constables, 1645.[263]

John Massye (12d) for railing against the said Ralph Plumpton and uttering many threatening words against him in the execution of his office two times.

James Houghton (12d) for the same against the said Ralph one time.

Henry Parr (12d) for the same one time.

William Futerill (12d) for the same another time.

Elizabeth Poughten (6d) for denying to quarter a soldier who was imposed upon her husband.[264]

Thomas Walles (6d) for the like.

Richard Sumner (12d) and Ann his wife for railing against and striking both constables.

John Rainforth (2s) for drawing his knife and offering violence against the said Ralph Plumpton.

William Sutton[265] and Ann his wife for railing against the said Ralph Plumpton in collecting leys.

Edward Finney (6d) for refusing to quarter a soldier imposed upon him and for uttering many foul words against the said Ralph Plumpton.

William Rose (6d) for abusing the said Ralph by foul words.

Eleanor (6d), wife of John Hoole, for the like.

Thomas Kenwrick[266] (12d) for receiving into his house in the night time a strange woman of evil carriage and for abusing Margery, wife of the said Ralph Plumpton, who went with her husband to search for the said woman, and for breaking the lantern of the said Ralph Plumpton at that time.

[f.12v]

Nicholas Anderton (12d) for abusing Ralph Plumpton with evil words in the house of Jane Bolton and for offering to strike him.

Gregory Flitcroft, milner (3s 4d, Henry Ogle, gent.), for drawing blood on John Orrell.

John Orrell (12d, Thomas Sumner) for assaulting the said Flitcroft.

Edward Booth (12d) for entering the house of the said Ralph Plumpton on 4 March 1646 and abusing him both in words and deeds.

[f.13r: 20 cms × 30.5 cms]

263. These presentments, in a hand and ink different from the hand and ink on sheets 10 and 11, were not written by Ralph, who apparently could only make his mark. To judge by Roger's signature from 1651 and 1652, he, too, did not write these presentments. LRO: DDKc/PC 4/112/Paper Books/1651 and 1652.
264. Elizabeth's husband was John Poughten, cooper. Leet officials also amerced her 3d in 1635 for buying butter before it came to the market. They lived in a messuage rented from Henry Ogle of Whiston, esq. LRO: DDKc/PC 4/66/Paper Book/1635; for quartering soldiers during the Civil War, see Kenyon, *Civil Wars of England*, p. 130.
265. No amercement is given.
266. Thomas, an undertenant, was an alehousekeeper and shoemaker whose only leet offices between 1642 and 1675 were as sealer of leather four times and aletaster twice. He died in 1676. LPRS, 149, p. 97.

At the court held at Prescot on 29 May 1646.
PRESENTMENTS BY THE ALETASTERS, Thomas Sumner and Thomas Knowles.
For breaking the assize of ale (12d each):

Thomas Parr	William Futerill
Robert Parr	Jane Boulton
Frances Bolton, wid.	Richard Jackson
William Harrison	Isabel Hey
Ann Halsall, wid.	John Poughten
Henry Darbishire	John Waynright
Thomas Walles	John Hoole
Ralph Plumpton	Jane Fennow
Edward Booth	Jane Swift
Nicholas Marshall	Richard Marshall
Henry Parr	James Houghton
Ellen Bond	Thomas Fletcher
Richard Litherland	Alexander Rylandes
William Sutton	William Rose
Henry Standish	Henry Kerkes
Thomas Woodes	Edith Sugden, wid.[267]
William Hough	John Berchall
Thomas Ackers	Richard Sumner
Roger Man	John Pendleton
Elizabeth Tarlton, wid.	Thomas Kenwricke

For breaking the assize of bread (12d each):

John Poughten	Thomas Woodes
Jane Fennow	Richard Jackson
John Massie	Robert Bolton
John Cowper	Robert Knowle
Jane Greene	

Richard Jackson (2s) for uttering and selling unwholesome bread and such as was unfit to be sold.

'By us': Tho Sumner *[mark – first initial]*
Tho Knowles *[mark]*

[f.13v, blank]
[f.14r: 15 cms × 20 cms]
29 May 1646. **PRESENTMENTS BY THE STREETLOOKERS**, Hugh Ward and William Ewde.

---

267. There is no other reference to 'Idith Sugden, wid.', in Prescot's paper books and parchment rolls for the entire seventeenth century.

They present William Fletcher (12d) for laying straw in the street and watering the same at the watering pool.

They present Edmund Webster (12d) for the like.

[f.14v, blank]
[f.15r: 20 cms × 30.5 cms]

[SURRENDERS AND ADMITTANCES]

[1] On 26 May, 22 Charles, 1646 Hugh Ward and his wife Jane – Jane being solely and secretly examined by the steward – out of court came before William Blundell, Edward Stockley and James Houghton[268] and for good considerations surrendered to the lord that messuage or cottage which the said Hugh Ward now inhabits, together with a croft and parcel of land on the north side containing 'one Roode land of land of the large measure.' The lord to regrant the said messuage, croft and premises to the said Hugh Ward and his wife Jane for their lives and the life of the survivor. After their decease, to William Ward, son of the said Hugh Ward,[269] forever. Paying yearly to the lord the rent of 2d.[270]

Acknowledged before us: proclaimed   Hugh Ward *[mark]*
    [signed] Edw Stockley   admitted
    [signed] Will Blundell
    [signed] James Houghton
The said Jane solely examined before me:
    [signed] Tho Wolfall
(*Parchment*: The said Hugh Ward is admitted forever.)

[f.15v, blank]
[f.16r: 20 cms × 31 cms]

[2] On 18 December, 21 Charles, 1645 John Lyon of Eccleston near Knowsley, yeo., and Robert Lyon, son of the said John, out of court came before William Blundell, Edward Stockley and Nicholas Marshall, and for £8 10s paid by William Fletcher of Prescot, mercer, surrendered to the lord a messuage or cottage which Edward Brundreath, tailor, now inhabits, together with a garden on the south side. The lord to regrant to the said William Fletcher forever. Paying to the lord the annual rent of 12d.

Acknowledged before us: proclaimed   *[signed]* John Lyon
    [signed] Will Blundell   admitted   *[signed]* Robart Lyon
    [signed] Edw Stockley
    [signed] Nyc Marshall
(*Parchment*: The said William Fletcher is admitted forever.)

[f.16v]
   William Fletchere's surrender.

268. The names of WB, ES and JH were added in a blank in the same hand and ink as the surrender.
269. The parchment roll adds 'and Jane'.
270. 'ijd' was added in a blank. Marginated in the Abstract Book: 'Rent to lord 6d'. Both the paper book and parchment roll have 2d.

[f.17r: 20 cms × 30.5 cms]

[3] On 9 April, 22 Charles, 1646 George Cartwright out of court came before William Fletcher and Richard Litherland and for £10 paid by Richard Jameson of Huyton, blacksmith, surrendered to the lord a messuage or dwelling house now occupied by <James Taylor> Henry Standish. The lord to regrant the said messuage or dwelling house to the said Richard Jameson forever. Paying yearly to the lord the rent of 6d.

Acknowledged before us: proclaimed   George Cartwright *[mark]*
    William Fletcher *[mark – initials]*   admitted
    Richard Litherland *[mark – initials]*
(*Parchment*: The said Richard Jameson is admitted forever.)

[f.17v]
    Richard Jameson's surrender.

[f.18r: 27 cms × 33 cms]

[4] Ralph Halsall of Prescot, blacksmith, now possesses to him for the life of the said Ralph Halsall, his wife Ann, his son John Halsall and Elizabeth[271] his daughter, now wife of Thomas Heirefoote, and the longest liver of them or for some number of years determinable thereupon in the messuage and[272] dwelling house which the said Ralph Halsall now inhabits and in one barn standing on Mill Hill and two closes and parcels of land commonly called the Fall Acre and Fells Acre by the surrender of Richard Mercer, gent., dec., Dorothy his wife, and Roger Bryars,[273] gent.

Now on 20 November 21 Charles[274] the said Ralph Halsall out of court came before John Alcock, jun., and William Sutton and for good considerations surrendered to the lord the said messuage and dwelling house which the said Ralph now inhabits together with the said barn and the said two closes and parcels of land called Fall Acre and Fells Acre. The lord to regrant the said messuage, barn and closes to the said Ralph Halsall for forty years. After his death, to the said Ann, now wife of the said Ralph, 'during her Chast widowhood.' And after to the said John Halsall and his heirs. For want of such issue, to Thomas Halsall, brother of the said John, and his heirs. For want of such issue, to the said Elizabeth, now wife of the said Thomas Heirifoote, during the remainder of the said term of the said Ralph Halsall. And then to come unexpired so that the said John Halsall or the said Thomas Halsall or the said Elizabeth, respectively, within six months after the death of the said Ann[275] or next after their or any of their enjoying the said premises pays to Ellen Halsall, younger daughter of the said Ralph, £10 towards her preferment. And if default be made in payment thereof, then the said premises

                                              [signed] Raph Halsall

271. The parchment roll adds 'Halsall'.
272. The parchment roll has 'or'.
273. The parchment roll has 'Breres'.
274. 1645.
275. The Abstract Book has 'after the death of the said Raph Halsall and Ann his wife'.

[f.18v, blank]
[f.19r: 27 cms × 32.5 cms]
to be to the said Ellen Halsall until she shall of the profits of the said premises have levied £10 with interest or damages for forbearance at the rate of £8 per 100 until the said sum be raised. The parties before mentioned paying yearly to the lord 10s 8d and paying to the said Dorothy Mercer the annual rent of 29s 4d.

Provided that the said John Halsall may during the chaste widowhood of the said Ann enjoy the smithy belonging to the said messuages and the chamber adjoining to the said smithy and way thereto. And if the said Ann do marry again after the said Ralph's death, then the said John Halsall or his heirs or the said Thomas Halsall or his heirs or the said Elizabeth or her assigns shall, respectively, as they shall happen to be in possession of the said premises, pay yearly to the said Ann from the profits of the said premises 40s on the Nativity of St John the Baptist and the Birth of Our Lord in equal portions during the life of the said Ann.

Provided also that if the said Ralph Halsall pays to the said John Halsall or to any other person or persons 6d in the presence of two or more credible witnesses and declares his intent to void this present surrender, then this surrender shall be void.

Acknowledged before us:	proclaimed	*[signed]* Raphe Halsall
[signed] John Alcock Jn	admitted	
[signed] William Suttonn		

(*Parchment*: The said Ann Halsall is admitted.)

[f.19v, blank]
[f.20r: 19.5 cms × 31 cms]
View of frankpledge with court of Prescot held on Friday, after Corpus Christi, being *[sic]* day of May,[276] 22 Charles.

[5] To this court came William Aspe of Kirkby, yeo., and Thomas Parr of Prescot, sadler, in their own persons before the steward and homage and for good considerations surrendered to the lord a messuage or dwelling house which the said Thomas Parr now inhabits, late in the tenure or occupation of Thomas Parr, sen., dec., father of the said Thomas Parr, sadler, and one burgage or yard on the south side of the said house. The lord to regrant the said premises to the said Thomas Parr the son during the lives of the said Thomas Parr the son, Ellen his wife, and William Parr, brother of the said Thomas Parr the son, and during the life of the longest liver and during a term of twelve years beginning immediately after their deaths and then fully to be complete and ended. Paying yearly to the said William Aspe during the said term of three lives the rent of 17s; to the said William Aspe during the said term of twelve years after the said term of three lives has expired the annual rent of 2s; to the lord the annual rent of 2s 8d.

proclaimed	William Aspe *[mark]*
admitted	*[signed]* Thomas Parr

276. 29 May 1646.

[f.20v]

Provided that if the said William Aspe within three months after the decease of the above-mentioned three lives pays to the executors, administrators or assigns of the said Thomas Parr the son the full sum of £10, then this surrender to be void.

Howbeit the said William Aspe agrees that if the said Thomas Parr pays the yearly rent to the lord of the manor it shall be deducted from the 17s payable to the said William Aspe on the feast days of St Andrew the Apostle and Corpus Christi yearly.

Act of the court: William Aspe *[mark]*
    [signed] Tho Wolfall   *[signed]* Thomas Parr
(*Parchment*: The said Thomas Parr the son is admitted.)

[f.21r: 17 cms × 28 cms]

[6] At the court held on the day[277] after Corpus Christi[278] 1644, John Webster surrendered to William Webster of Eccleston, his brother, forever those messuages and cottages hereafter mentioned, that is, one messuage or cottage occupied by Richard Wolfall, another messuage or cottage occupied by John Huson the elder, a messuage or cottage occupied by Edward Bate and another messuage or cottage occupied by Robert Kenion. With a proviso in the same surrender that if the said John Webster pays to William Webster £23 4s on Corpus Christi in 1645, then the said surrender shall be void.

Now the jurors further say that the said William Webster did in the presence of the jury acknowledge that he had received full payment from the said John Webster, his brother,[279] for the said debt of £23 4s, whereupon the said surrender became void.

And hereupon the said John Webster asks to be admitted as in his former estate.

proclaimed
admitted

(*Parchment*: The said John Webster is admitted forever.)

[f.21v, blank]
[f.22r: 17.5 cms × 28 cms]

[7] The jury further says that Lawrence Mercer held forever one parcel of land near Mill Hill and adjoining to a messuage and[280] dwelling house now occupied by John Tyrer with a barn of two bays on the same, and also one shop or parcel of building late in the occupation of William Ackers.[281] The said Lawrence Mercer died[282] seised thereof before the last court. Henry Mercer is son and next heir of

277. The parchment roll has 'Friday'.
278. The parchment roll has 'xxi of June'.
279. Not in the parchment roll: 'his brother'.
280. The parchment roll has 'or'.
281. The Abstract Book has 'William Ackers butcher'.
282. All references to Lawrence in Prescot's records omit any mention of a manor or parish where he resided. Lawrence's son, Henry, is said in the manorial records of 1654–57 to be from Kirkby in the parish of Walton-on-the-Hill. Since the parish register for Walton has a gap in the burials for 1641–63, one can report only that Lawrence died between 6

the said Lawrence[283] and is of the age of eleven years or thereabouts[284] and asks to be admitted.

proclaimed

admitted

(*Parchment*: The said Henry Mercer is admitted forever.)

[f.22v, blank]
[f.23r: 20 cms × 30 cms]

   [8] On 26 May, 22 Charles, 1646 Henry Ogle, esq., out of court came before Nicholas Marshall and William Fletcher and, in consideration that Henry Kirkes of Prescot has at only his costs repaired a messuage and cottage which the said Henry now inhabits and heretofore was inhabited by Thomas Dichfield, now dec., surrendered to the lord the said messuage and cottage. The lord to regrant the said messuage and cottage to the said Henry Kirkes to hold for ninety-nine years to be ended if Margaret, wife of the said Henry Kirkes, and George Kirkes and Henry Kirkes, sons of the said Henry Kirkes, or any of them live so long. Paying yearly to the lord the rent of 2d and to the said Henry Ogle the annual rent of 2s 6d.
Acknowledged before us: proclaimed   *[signed]* Henry Ogle
   [signed] Nyc Marshall   admitted
   Willm Fletcher *[mark – initials]*
(*Parchment*: The said Henry Kirkes the father is admitted.)

[f.23v, blank]
[f.24r: 18 cms × 28 cms]

   [9] On 29 May, 22 Charles, 1646 Margaret Woodes, wid., and Thomas Woodes, her son, out of court came before Edward Stockley, George Lyon and John Lyon[285] and for £11 10s already paid by Thomas Halsall of Prescot, skinner, surrendered to the lord a messuage and tenement now in the tenure or occupation of the said Thomas Halsall and Thomas Woodes, butcher, or one of them; and one croft and parcel of land belonging thereunto containing 'one Rood land of land of the large measure' or thereabouts. The lord to regrant the said messuage and tenement to the said Thomas Halsall for the lives of the said Thomas Halsall, Thomas Hearefoote, son of Peter Hearefoote, and William Parr, son of Thomas Parr, dec., and the longest liver. Paying yearly to the said Margaret Woodes and Thomas Woodes the rent of <15s> 16s on the feasts of

[f.24v]
St John the Baptist and the Nativity of Our Lord and paying yearly to the lord the rent of.[286]

       June 1645 and 29 May 1646. LRO: DDKc/PC 4/112/Paper Books/1654–57; LPRS, 5, pp. 142 and 151.
283. The parchment roll adds 'Mercer'.
284. The parchment roll has 'is of the full age of twenty-one years and above', while the paper book has 'is of the age of xj yeares or theraboutes'.
285. The names of ES, GL and JL were added in a blank in the same hand and ink as the surrender.
286. Blank in the paper book, parchment roll and Abstract Book.

Acknowledged before us: proclaimed   Margrett Woodes *[mark]*
    [signed] Edw Stockley   admitted   *[signed]* Thomas Woods
    [signed] Geo Lyon Jn
    [signed] John Lyon of Windle
(*Parchment*: The said Thomas Halsall is admitted.)

[f.25r: 19.5 cms × 30.5 cms]
    [10] On 5 March, 21 Charles, 1646 Hamlet Whitfeild out of court came before
George Lyon the younger of Whiston and for good considerations surrendered to
the lord one messuage and tenement which the said Hamlet Whitfeild now inhabits and heretofore commonly called Potter's house. The lord to regrant the said
messuage and tenement to the said Hamlet Whitfeild for his life. After his death
to Margaret Whitfeild his wife for her life if the said Margaret happens to outlive
the said Hamlet Whitfeild her husband. After the death of the said Hamlet and
Margaret, then to his nephew and godson Richard Gregory, son of William
Gregory of Whiston, during the remainder of such term as the said Hamlet
Whitfeild has in the premises and is then unexpired. Paying to the lord the yearly rent of 12d.
This surrender acknowledged before me:
    [signed] Geo Lyon Junior
John[287] Alcocke of Eccleston pleaded in bar to the admission and a day was
given, that is, at the next court after the feast of St Michael the Archangel.
    John Alcocke of <Prescot> Eccleston on 2 October 1646 pleaded in bar. A day
was given for replying.

[f.25v]
    Provided that if the said Hamlet Whitfeild at any time during his life pays to
any two or more copyholders within this manor 6d in silver for the use of the said
Margaret Whitfeild and Richard Gregory and declares his will to void this present surrender, then this surrender is void.[288]

[f.26r: 17 cms × 28 cms]
    [11] To this court Richard Chorleton of Prescot and Ellen his wife, one of the
daughters of Evan Finney late of Prescot, dec., came in their own persons in open
court before the steward and homage and pray licence to enter one messuage or
cottage and garden on the south side of the said messuage heretofore built by the
said Evan Finney and by him enjoyed during his life. After his death Edward Finney
his son was admitted as tenant to hold to him and his heirs forever. And the said
Edward Finney is now dead,[289] and the said Richard Chorleton and Ellen his wife,
sister and coheir of the said Edward Finney, petition to hold the said messuage or
cottage and the said garden to them the said Richard and Ellen and the heirs of the

287. The remainder of folio 25r from 'John' onwards is only in the paper book.
288. Neither the paper book nor parchment roll contains a petition for admission or notice of
    admittance, and the Abstract Book has 'Noe addmittance herupon'.
289. Of Prescot, buried on 2 January 1645. LPRS, 114, p. 93.

said Ellen forever. Thereupon licence is granted to the said Richard and Ellen his wife by the steward with the consent of the homage to enter the said premises forever. Paying yearly to the lord 2d and to the schoolwardens of the school of Prescot and their successors for the use of the said school the rent of 8d.

proclaimed   Act of the court:
admitted   *[signed]* Tho Wolfall

(*Parchment*: The said Richard Chorleton and his wife Ellen are admitted forever.)

[f.26v, blank]
[f.27r: 17 cms × 28 cms]

[12] To this court Roger Dey of Prescot and Mary his wife, one of the daughters of Evan Finney, late of Prescot, dec., came in their own persons in open court before the steward and homage and request licence to enter into one messuage or cottage and one garden on the south side, which said messuage was built by the said Evan Finney and by him enjoyed during his life. After his death, Edward Finney his son was admitted as tenant forever.

And the said Edward Finney is now dead, and the said Roger Dey and Mary his wife, sister and coheir of the said Edward Finney, petition to hold the said messuage or cottage and garden to the said Roger and Mary and the heirs of the said Mary forever. Thereupon licence is granted by the steward with the consent of the homage to Roger Dey and his wife Mary to enter and hold the said messuage or cottage and garden forever. Paying yearly to the lord the rent of 2d and to the schoolwardens of the school of Prescot and their successors for use of the said school the rent of 16d.

proclaimed   Act of the court:
admitted   *[signed]* Tho Wolfall

(*Parchment*: The said Roger Dey and his wife Mary are admitted forever.)

[f.27v, blank]
[f.28r: 29.5 cms × 39.5 cms]

[13] To this court came Nicholas Marshall and in open court before the steward and homage surrendered to the lord a messuage and tenement now in the holding or occupation of the said Nicholas Marshall; another messuage and tenement now in the holding or occupation of Henry Marshall, son of the said Nicholas Marshall; a close and parcel of land commonly now called Nicholas Marshall's acre; a messuage and tenement in the holding or occupation of Peter Hearefoote; and another messuage and tenement now in the holding or occupation of Evan Garnett. The lord to regrant to the said Nicholas Marshall and his wife Margaret and the longer liver of them the said messuage and tenement occupied by the said Nicholas Marshall – the new bay only excepted – and the said close and parcel of land commonly called Nicholas Marshall's acre and the one bay of building adjoining to the house of Peter[290] Hearefoot with a garden stead on the backside, being all parcel of the premises. After their death, then to the said Henry Marshall and Ellen his wife for the life of the longer liver. After their death, to the male heirs

290. The parchment roll has 'said Peter'.

of the said Henry Marshall on the body of the said Ellen. For want of issue, to the male heirs of the said Henry Marshall. For want of such issue, to the right heirs of the said Henry Marshall forever. The lord further to regrant all the rest of the said messuages and tenements to the said Henry Marshall and his wife Ellen and the survivor. After their death, to the male heirs of the said Henry Marshall on the body of the said Ellen. For want of such issue, to the male heirs of the said Henry Marshall. For want of such issue, to the right heirs of the said Henry Marshall forever. They respectively paying yearly to the lord for the said messuage and tenement occupied by the said Nicholas Marshall the rent of 2s 6d; for the messuage and tenement occupied by the said Henry Marshall the annual rent of 2d; for the said close and parcel of land called Nicholas Marshall's acre, for the said messuage and tenement occupied by Evan Garnett, for the said messuage and tenement occupied by Peter Hearefoote and for the said bay of building and garden to the same messuage adjoining [291] the annual rent of 3s 4d; the whole is 6s.

    [signed] Tho Wolfall   proclaimed   *[signed]* Nyc Marshall
                                     admitted

[f.28v, blank]
[f.29r: 30 cms × 16.5 cms]
    Provided that the said Henry Marshall and his wife Ellen may have liberty, way and passage to use the kitchen belonging to the dwelling house of the said Nicholas Marshall for brewing and baking and other necessary uses and also passage to the backside as occasion may require without hindrance of the said Nicholas Marshall and his wife Margaret.

    Provided also that the said messuages and tenements before mentioned be charged with £20 to be paid by the owners and occupiers of the said lands unto Elizabeth Marshall, daughter of the said Henry Marshall, within one month after she shall attain the age of twenty-one. And if the said £20 shall not be paid to the said Elizabeth Marshall as aforesaid, then the lands before mentioned to the use of the said Elizabeth Marshall until she shall have of the said profits the said £20 with damages for forbearance at the rate of £8 per 100 until the said £20 be paid. Afterwards to remain to such several uses as mentioned herein.

                                      [signed] Nyc Marshall
(*Parchment*: The said Nicholas Marshall and Henry Marshall are admitted.)

[f.29v, blank]
[f.30r, blank: 20 cms × 31 cms]
[f.30v]
View of frankpledge with court baron held on Friday, 29 May, 1646. Extract made and delivered.[292] Sum total within: £23 5s 6d.

---

291. '[T]o same messuage adjoining' is only in the parchment roll.
292. Delivered by Edward Stockley, clerk of the court, probably to Henry Parr who was the bailiff in 1645, 1647 and 1648.

1647

[Paper Book: DDCs]   [Parchment Roll: DDKc/PC 4/165[293]]

[f.1r: 20 cms × 31 cms]

VIEW OF FRANKPLEDGE WITH COURT BARON OF PRESCOT in the county of Lancaster held there according to the custom of the manor and liberty of Prescot aforesaid before Thomas Wolfall, esq., steward of the manor and court aforesaid, on Friday after Corpus Christi, 18 June, 23 Charles, 1647.

SUITORS OR CUSTOMARY TENANTS:

William Gerard, baronet
Henry Eccleston, esq.
Henry Ogle, esq.
John Lancaster, esq.
Henry Lathom, esq.
○ Thomas Wolfall, gent.
Thomas Sorrocold, gent.
○ John Alcocke, sen., gent.
○ John Alcocke, jun., gent.
○ Edward Stockley, jun.
○ William Blundell
○ William Lyme
○ Elizabeth Smyth
○ Margaret Tyrer
○ William Parr of Cronton   pardoned
○ Thomas Symond, gent.   out of the county
○ George Croston, gent.   out of the county
○ Henry Pinnington   essoined
○ William Lyon of Thingwall   sick
○ William Kenwricke
Edward Kenwricke   dead[294]
○ George Deane of Rainhill
<Robert Lyon of Eccleston>
○ John Lyon of Windle
○ Thomas Woodes of Widnes
○ James Houghton of Whiston
○ Thomas Woodes of Whiston
○ John Leadbeter

○ John Lyon, tanner
○ Henry Webster
of Knowsley   essoined
○ John Webster of Knowsley
○ Edmund Webster of Knowsley
○ Robert Wainwright of Tarbock
○ Henry Parr   out of the county
○ Dorothy Mercer, wid.
○ Richard Mollyneux
○ William Aspia of Kirkby
○ John Glover of Rainhill   out of
George Tarleton of Liverpool
○ John Torbocke of Windle
○ Paul Orme of Tarbock   essoined
○ Richard Woodes of Rainford
○ Roger Billinge of Upholland
○ Thomas Devias of Huyton
○ Richard Jameson
○ William Fletcher
○ George Lyon, jun.
○ Peter Kenwricke, sen.
○ Nicholas Marshall   infirm
○ Henry Marshall
○ Richard Litherland
○ Ellis Webster
○ Hugh Ward
○ William Sutton   sick
○ Ann Litherland
○ Ann Lodge

---

293. Three membranes with writing on all sides; all measure 28 cms × 57 cms.
294. Of Eccleston, buried on 24 May 1647. LPRS, 114, p. 97.

[f.1v]

Subtenants and inhabitants:
- William Harrison
- John Halsall
- John Parr

   William Fewtrell
- Thomas Kenwricke
- John Pendleton
- Edward Darbishire
- John Birchall
- Henry Parr
- William Ewde
- William Rose
- Edward Booth
- Alexander Rylandes
- Thomas Moberley
- Robert Kenion
- Edward Finney
- John Huson, sen.
- Edward Bate
- Richard Wolfall
- James Parker
- James Houghton
- Ralph Hall
- Thomas Garnett
- John Houghton
- Henry Houghton

   William Coppow
- Thomas Somner

   Richard Ditchfeild
- Richard Marshall
- James Sadler

   Richard Banner
- Edward Webster
- Gilbert Heyes

   Thomas Fletcher
- Henry Kirkes
- John Sutton   out of the county
- Thomas Rainforth   essoined
- Thomas Litherland
- Thomas Walles
- Henry Darbishire
- Robert Knowles
- William Hough   sick
- Thomas Knowles

   James Angsdale
   John Frodsham
- William Hardman
- Henry Standish
- Anthony Prescott
- Robert Bolton
- Richard Jackeson
- Thomas Parr
- Thomas Wood
- Robert Parr
- John Cowper
- William Birchall
- John Litherland
- Roger Mann
- Thomas Aspe
- Evan Garnett
- Peter Hearefoote
- Michael Romley
- John Houghland
- Edward Rylandes
- John Huson, jun.
- Peter Garnett
- Roger Dey
- Richard Chorleton
- Robert Hatton
- Richard Hoomes
- John Oliverson
- John Poughten

[f.2r: 20 cms × 31 cms]
- Robert Woosie
- Peter Kenwricke, jun.

   John Wainwright
- Richard Birch
- Ralph Houghton
- John Tyrer
- Richard Angsdale
- Thomas Browne
- Richard Higgonson
- Ralph Plumpton
- John Massie
- John Rigbie
- Robert Boulton
- Thomas Webster
- Henry Rigbie
- Henry Prescott

John Taylor   William Browne
o Thomas Horneby   John Horneby

[f.2v, blank]
[f.3r: 20 cms × 31 cms]

JURORS FOR THE SOVEREIGN LORD KING AND LORD OF THE MANOR OF PRESCOT at the court held on Friday after Corpus Christi, 18 June, 1647:[295]

	Thomas Sorrocold, gent.	
– o	Edward Stockley	sworn
– ab[296]	William Blundell	sworn
– o	George Deane of Rainhill	sworn
dead[297]	William Fletcher	sworn
– o	James Houghton of Whiston	sworn
– ab	William Kenwricke	<6s 8d> sworn
	Henry Marshall	pardoned
	John Lyon of Windle	6s 8d
	Thomas Woodes of Widnes	6s 8d
– o	Edmund Webster	sworn
	Thomas Woodes of Whiston	6s 8d
	John Lyon, tanner	pardoned by the steward
– o	Robert Wainwright of Tarbock	sworn
– o	William Aspia of Kirkby	sworn
– o	Thomas Devias of Huyton	sworn
	George Lyon, jun., of Whiston	6s 8d
	Robert Lyon of Eccleston	'noe tenant'
– o	Hugh Ward	sworn
<ab o>	Ellis Webster	sworn
	Richard Mollyneux	6s 8d
– o	Richard Litherland	sworn
	Richard Hoomes, doorkeeper	sworn

9 July 1647 the jury adjourned to perfect their verdict until 1 October under pain of 6s 8d each.

1 October 1647 the jury further adjourned to perfect their verdict until 22 October under pain of 13s 4d each.

The jury further adjourned to perfect their verdict until 3 December under pain of 13s 4d each.

---

295. All names appear to be in the same hand and ink.
296. Absent.
297. Of Prescot, mercer, buried on 6 October 1647. LPRS, 114, p. 98. For his will, see LRO: WCW/Prescot/1647/William Fletcher. Also see note 248 *supra*.

[f.3v, blank]
[f.4r: 20 cms × 30.5 cms]
VIEW OF FRANKPLEDGE *[PRESENTMENTS BY THE JURORS].*
Owe suit to this court and have not appeared when called (6d each):

Sir William Gerard, baronet
Henry Eccleston, esq.
Henry Ogle, esq.
Henry Latham, esq.
Thomas Sorocold, gent.
George Tarlton of Liverpool
William Fewtrill
William Cappowe
Richard Dichfeild

Richard Banner
Thomas Fletcher, son of Thomas
James Angsdale
John Frodsham
John Waynwright
John Taylor
William Browne
John Hornby

We present that Thomas Litherland and Nicholas Anderton, late constables, were at the last court ordered to make account of moneys they had received for the use of the town unto the Four Men at or before next 1 August on pain of £5, which they have neglected to perform and therefore have forfeited the said £5.

[f.4v]
Whereas twenty-five persons of this manor were allowed by Mr Steward at the last court to brew ale and beer to sell and no one else to exercise the same. And whereas we are informed that others notwithstanding the said order have also brewed 'whose names wee know not for want of Informacon at present'. We therefore order the alefounders to present who these persons are at the next court so that they may be proceeded against.

Diverse undertenants have entered the town to inhabit without giving security as former orders and the order of the last court required. We now order all such persons as have come to inhabit this town contrary to the said orders to give security to the Four Men at or before 2 February next under pain of 13s 4d.

We present that John Parr, butcher, has maintained the cottage, for which he was presented at the last court, for twelve months since the last court, and he has forfeited 13s 4d a month or £8 total.

John Webster, nailer, has continued to maintain the two cottages, for which he was presented at the last court, for twelve months longer and has forfeited for either of them 13s 4d a month or £16 total for twelve months.

[f.5r: 20 cms × 31 cms]
Edmund Webster has maintained for twelve months longer the cottage for which he was formerly presented and has forfeited 13s 4d a month or £8 total for twelve months.

William Fletcher has maintained four cottages, for which he was presented at the last court, for twelve months since the last court and has forfeited for every one 13s 4d a month or £32 total for twelve months.

Thomas[298] Halsall has for twelve months maintained a cottage erected by his father and has forfeited 13s 4d a month or £8 total for twelve months.

We present that Robert Prescott has erected a cottage near 'Potters brooke' and has forfeited 13s 4d.

The said Robert Prescott has maintained the same for the past six months and has forfeited 13s 4d a month or £4 total.

According to the last court, the town is indebted to several persons for a total of £12 7s 4d. Also, there were diverse arrears due to the town which if collected would have more than satisfied the said debt 'with an overplus', but they remain uncollected 'soe as noe hope appeares for helpe that way to satisfy the said debt.' We therefore order the Four Men to assess leys to pay the said debt which the constables shall collect and pay to whom owed, on pain of 40s.

[f.5v]

Several persons are presented for erecting and maintaining cottages contrary to former order of this court, which if no remedy is found the same may prove very hurtful to the builders. We ask the steward 'to call to his assistance some of the Jury or other townesmen such as he shall please and to frame some way for puttinge an end to theise grevances for the present and to prevent the lyke heireafter.'

Thomas Litherland and Nicholas Anderton in his lifetime [299] were ordered to account for several sums of money they received as constables for the town's use but have not done so. We therefore order that the present constables 'shall take advyse of Councell' and request the said account forthwith 'as Councell shall advyse without delay', at the town's charges.

[f.6r: 20 cms × 31 cms]

John Hoole, Eleanor his then wife and their daughter Ellen Hoole were at the last court for several misdemeanours committed against their neighbours ordered to leave town by 24 June 1646 and for every night they inhabit thereafter to forfeit 3s 4d. We present that the said Eleanor and Ellen Hoole have since inhabited a house of Nicholas Marshall and his wife Margaret in the lower end of the street towards 'the holt' [300] for forty nights since the said 24 June 1646 and have thereby forfeited £6 13s 4d.

And it was then at the said last court also ordered that no one shall receive them to inhabit on pain for every night 3s 4d. We further present that because the said Nicholas Marshall and his wife Margaret allowed the said Eleanor Hoole and Ellen her daughter to inhabit their house for forty nights, they have forfeited for either of them 3s 4d a night or £13 6s 8d total.

298. When referring back to the presentments of 1646, the paper book of 1650 (LRO: DDCs/Paper Book/f.7r) has Ralph Halsall, as does that of 1646 (f.6v). Ralph died in February 1646, and Thomas, his son, was born in 1625. LPRS, 76, p. 83; see note 244 *supra*.
299. Nicholas was buried on 10 March 1647. LPRS, 114, p. 97.
300. 'The holt' is in Rainhill on the north side of the road to Warrington. Between 1590 and 1604 from 'the Hoult' came stones to repair the churchwall and the steps into the churchyard of the parish church in Prescot. Bailey, *Churchwardens' Accounts of Prescot*, pp. 114, 125, 134, 139, 146 and 147.

[f.6v]

Mr Ogle 'hath inclosed a greate parte of the hall lane with a wall and gate without consent of this Court' to the hindrance of the tenants of this manor. We order him to lay open the same and take away the wall and gate before the next feast of St Michael the Archangel. In default, his son Mr Henry Ogle who now enjoys that estate is to remove and lay open the same as formerly it was, on pain of either of them making default to forfeit 13s 4d.

The constables in their accounts have returned diverse inhabitants for unpaid leys 'which wee accompt to be asmuch the negligence of the Constables as otherwyse.' We therefore order no allowance of arrears to the constables henceforward, but they shall fully account for all leys that shall be laid 'without defaltacon of any arreres at all.'

[f.7r: 20 cms × 30.5 cms]

PRESENTMENTS BY THE CONSTABLES, James Sadler and Edward Booth.

They present an affray between Thomas Hearefoote (3s 4d) and Edward Finney (12d) with blood drawn from the said Finney.

They present an affray between Hugh Parr of Knowsley (6s 8d, John Parr, butcher) and Nicholas Lyme of Prescot (12d) with blood drawn from the said Nicholas from a cut on his face, but by which weapon is unknown.

They present that John Alcocke the younger entered the house of John Pendleton where the constables and Four Men 'were mett together aboute the townes busines'. The said John Alcocke gave 'some uncivill speeches' against them, especially against Edward Stockley, one of the Four Men. After some words between them, a tussle occurred between the said John Alcocke (3s 4d) and Edward Stockley (12d).[301]

They present an affray between Ralph Plumpton (3s 4d) and Richard Angsdale (12d) with blood drawn from the said Angsdale. Ralph Plumpton 'Run away' and Angsdale 'suffered imprisonment'.

They present a tussle between William Canner (12d) and Richard Asteley (12d). Pledge for Astley, John Pendleton.

[f.7v, blank]
[f.8r: 19 cms × 30 cms]

AT THE LEET OF PRESCOT, 18 June 1647. **PRESENTMENTS BY THE ALETASTERS**, Thomas Sumner and Thomas Knowles.

They present for selling beer and ale and breaking the assize (12d each; in total, 36s):[302]

Thomas Walles	John Halsall
William Harrison	Frances Bolton, wid.
Thomas Parr	Richard Edwardson

301. See Introduction, pp. lxii–lxiv.
302. In the left margin: '<37> 36 in number'.

Edward Booth
Alexander Rylandes
Robert Parr
John Poughten
Henry Darbishire
Edward Darbishire
Ellen Bond, wid.
John Pendleton
Richard Litherland
Henry Parr
John Birchall
Christian Jackson, wid.
Jane Boulton, wid.
William Futerill
Richard Marshall
William Rose

James Houghton
<Thomas Fletcher>
Jane Swift, wid.
Ralph Plumpton
Jane Fennow, wid.
David Catton
Isabel Hey, wid.
William Hough
Henry Standish
Thomas Woodes
Margery Ackers, wid.
Jane Greene, wid.
Evan Heirfoote
Roger Man
Jarvis Simonett

They present for breaking the assize of bread (12d each; in total, 8s):[303]

John Poughten
Jane Fennowe, wid.
John Massie
Robert Bolton the elder

Richard Banner
Christian Jackson, wid.
Thomas Woodes
Jarvis Simonett

They present John Birchall (2s) for selling ale not fit to be sold.

Thomas Sumpner *[mark]*
Tho Knowles *[mark]*

[f.8v, blank]
[f.9r: 20 cms × 31 cms]
PRESENTMENTS BY THE SEARCHERS AND SEALERS OF LEATHER,
Roger Dey and Evan Heirffoot.

We present Thomas Browne of Whiston, shoemaker (12d), for buying unsealed leather and bringing it to be curried within Prescot diverse times.

We present Edward Garnet, William Gregorye, John Casse, Henry Fairechild, Thomas Ackeres, <Edward> William Banner, Robert Whitlow of Rainhill, John Halland of Rainford, Henry Cowper of Knowsley and Henry Radcliff for the like (12d each).

We present the said Henry Cowper (12d) and Henry Radcliff (12d) for working unlawful leather.

We present Thomas Kenwricke of Prescot, James Mather and Henry Presscott for buying unsealed leather (12d each).

We present the said Henry Presscott (12d) for working leather not half tanned but claimed it was sufficient.

303. In the left margin: '8 in number'.

We present John Massye of Prescot, tanner (12d), for selling unsealed leather.
We present the said John Massye (12d) for selling badly tanned leather.
We present Thomas Kenwricke (12d) and Henry Presscott (12d) 'for Curringe of leather which doeth not belonge to theire Trade.'
'Theise are to give notice unto All whom it maye Concerne that yf any leather be Founde within this manor which is sould and bought and not sealled one parte doth belonge to the lord of the manor and one parte to the sealers and third part to the poore of Presscott Accordinge to the statute.'

[f.9v, blank]
[f.10r: 20 cms × 31 cms]
AT THE COURT OF PRESCOT held on 18 June 1647.
There has not been any presentment of the disposition of the money given to charitable uses by Lawrence Webster, dec., since the court held in 1627 when the then feoffees informed the court how the funds had been employed from 1608 to 1621 and did then further show that the account from that year to 1627 remained in the custody of Mr Aldem, then vicar of Prescot, and they prayed respite for any further account. Since then there has been no further account made. Now to this court came Edward Stockley and Nicholas Marshall, surviving feoffees of the said charitable gift, and William Blundell, William Fletcher and Evan Garnett, feoffees nominated at the last court. Their account shows that the increase of the said charitable gift from the last account until 1642 was kept by Mr Aldem, then vicar of Prescot, and at his death,[304] they believe, was delivered with his books to his son-in-law, Mr Hynd, and so they cannot give any account for those years. But for the time since, they show as follows:
- 1642–44: It was distributed to the poor of Prescot, Whiston, Rainhill and Eccleston.
- 1645: It was employed to bind a son of Thomas Horneby of Prescot apprentice to Thomas Knowles.
- 1646: It was employed to bind *[blank]* Leadbeter, son of Thomas Leadbeter, dec., apprentice to Robert Bolton, hatter.
- 1647: Employed to bind a son of Edward Webster of Prescot to William Markland of Eccleston.
And the feoffees show that for security of the £20 stock they have a conveyance of land from Evan Garnett of Prescot and pray approval or other direction of this court.

[f.10v, blank]
[f.11r: 20 cms × 31 cms]
18 June 1647. **OFFICERS CHOSEN** to serve for the following year:

| Constables | *[1]* William Harison | sworn |
| | *[2]* Richard Edwardson | sworn |

304. See note 143 *supra*.

Four Men	[1] Edward Stockley	sworn before
	[1] William Blundell	sworn before
	[1] William Fletcher	sworn before
	[1] Nicholas Marshall	sworn before
Coroner	[1] John Alcocke, sen.	sworn before
Clerks of the	[1] John Halsall	sworn <before>
market	[2] John Parr	sworn <before>
Burleymen	[1] John Poughten	sworn
	[2] Robert Hatton	sworn
Sealers of	[1] Roger Dey	sworn before
leather	[2] <Henry Radclyff>	
	[3] Evan Heirefoote	sworn before
Alefounders	[1] <John Birchall>	
	[2] Thomas Sumner	sworn before
	[3] Thomas Knowles	sworn before
Streetlookers	[1] <William Eaud>	
	[2] Hugh Warde	sworn before
	[3] Ralph Houghton	sworn before
Affeerors of	[1] Edward Stockley	sworn
the court	[1] William Blundell	sworn
	[3] George Deane	sworn
	[3] James Houghton	sworn

[f.11v, blank]
[f.12r: 19 cms × 29.5 cms]

[SURRENDERS AND ADMITTANCES]

[1] Em Nailor of Prescot, wid., now possessed, for a number of years not yet expired and determinable on her life, of a messuage, cottage, burgage or dwelling house lately inhabited by Thomas Nailor, dec., late husband of the said Em, of the yearly rent of [blank[305]] to the lord, and of the yearly rent of 13s 4d to James Sorocold, gent., dec., and his heirs, as by a surrender made by the said Thomas Nailor and acknowledged on 6 June 10 Charles.[306]

Now the said Em Nailor on 17 June 1647 for 50s to her the said Em paid by Thomas Lea, one of the sons of Richard Lea late of Rainhill, dec., and also for 5s by the said Thomas to be paid yearly on 25 December to the said Em during her life with the first yearly payment to be made on 25 December 1649 and not before, came in her own person before John Alcocke the younger and Nicholas Marshall [307] and surrendered to the lord the said messuage, cottage, burgage and dwelling house.

[f.12v]
The lord to regrant the said premises to the said Thomas Lea for the term that Em has therein according to the said surrender. Paying yearly to the lord the rent of

305. Blank in the paper book, parchment roll and Abstract Book.
306. 1634.
307. The names of JA and NM were added in a blank in a different hand and ink from the surrender.

[blank³⁰⁸] and to the heirs and assigns of the said James Sorocold the yearly rent of 13s 4d.

Acknowledged before us: proclaimed   Emm Nailor *[mark]*
    [signed] John Alcock Jn   admitted
    [signed] Nyc Marshall
(*Parchment*: 'And upon this came said.'³⁰⁹)

[f.13r: 20 cms × 30.5 cms]
    [2] On 24 August, 22 Charles, 1646 John Alcock of Eccleston near Knowsley, gent., out of court came before William Lyme and Henry Marshall and in consideration of the rent hereafter reserved surrendered to the lord that messuage or cottage which Ann Akars, wid., now inhabits. The lord to regrant the said messuage or cottage to Mary Akars, spinster daughter of the said Ann Akars, for the term of sixty years to be ended if the said Ann Akars and Mary Akars or either live so long. Paying yearly to the lord the rent of 8d and to the said John Alcocke the yearly rent of 6s 8d on the Nativity of Our Lord and the Nativity of St John the Baptist in equal portions. And the boon or yearly service of one day reaping corn with an able person during harvest time. The remainder after the said term ended to the said John Alcocke forever.
    Provided that if the said rent of 6s 8d or the said boon and service be unpaid or undone in part or whole to the said John Alcocke within twenty days after due, then the said John Alcock may repossess the said premises.
                                                      [signed] John Alcock

[f.13v]
Acknowledged by the within named   proclaimed
John Alcocke before us: admitted
    [signed] Wil Lyme
    [signed] Henry Marshall
(*Parchment*: The said Mary Akars is admitted.)

[f.14r: 19 cms × 29.5 cms]
    [3] Edward Kenwricke died³¹⁰ since the last court. At the time of his death he was seised of one shop and two rooms above the said shop late in the occupation of Thomas Eaton, shearman, and now occupied by Henry Eaton his brother, of the yearly rent to the lord of 12d. Richard Kenwricke is son and next heir of the said Edward Kenwricke and is nine years and more. The said Richard Kenwricke came in open court before the steward and homage and petitioned admission.
                                       proclaimed
                                       admitted

308. Blank in the paper book, parchment roll and Abstract Book.
309. There is no more in the parchment roll.
310. See note 294 *supra*.

William Kenwricke pleaded in bar to the said admittance and a day was given until the next court. On 1 October 1647 in court the said William Kenwricke pleaded nothing. Therefore he is admitted.
(*Parchment*: The said Richard Kenwricke is admitted forever.)

[f.14v, blank]
[f.15r: 15 cms × 24 cms]
[4] On 21 April, 23 Charles, 1647 Roger Billinge of Upholland out of court came before William Fletcher and Nicholas Marshall and for £12 to him paid by James Sadler of Prescot, buttonmaker, surrendered to the lord that cottage or dwelling house which William Coppall of Prescot now inhabits with a garden on the south side. The lord to regrant the said cottage and garden to the said James Sadler forever. Paying yearly to the lord the rent of 8d.

Acknowledged before us:	proclaimed	*[signed]* Roger Billinge
Wm Fletcher *[mark – initials]*	admitted	
[signed] Nicholas Marshall		

(*Parchment*: The said James Sadler is admitted forever.)

[f.15v, blank]
[f.16r: 24.5 cms × 30 cms]
[5] On 6 April, 23 Charles, 1647 Thomas Sorrocold, gent., out of court came before Edward Stockley and Richard Litherland and for £25 to him paid by Robert Parr of Prescot, hooper, surrendered to the lord the messuage or dwelling house which the said Robert Parr now inhabits, late in the tenure or occupation of William Hough of Prescot. The lord to regrant the said messuage and dwelling house to the said Robert Parr for the lives of the said Robert Parr, Elizabeth his wife and Katherine Parr their daughter and of the survivor. Paying yearly to the said Thomas Sorrocold the rent of 17s on 24 June and 25 December in equal amounts and to the lord the yearly rent of 4s.

Provided that if the said yearly rent of 17s is unpaid in part or in whole within twenty days after due, then the said Thomas Sorrocold may repossess and this surrender will be void.

Provided also that whereas £15 of the said £25 is unpaid to the said Thomas Sorrocold and is to be paid by the said Robert Parr on next 25 December. Both parties agree that if then unpaid, this surrender to be void.

Acknowledged before us:	proclaimed	*[signed]* Thomas Sorocold
[signed] Edw Stockley	admitted	
Richard Litherland *[mark – initials]*		

(*Parchment*: The said Robert Parr is admitted.)

[f.16v]
Robert Parr.

[f.17r: 24.5 cms × 30 cms]
[6] Henry Darbishire of Prescot, carpenter, is possessed for a number of years not yet completed, being determinable on the lives of Elizabeth Darbishire his

wife and Thomas Darbishire his son and survivor, of the messuage and tenement which the said Henry Darbishire now inhabits together with a croft or parcel of land on the north side; and of one acre or parcel of land in Churchley Field to the same messuage and tenement belonging. By the yearly rent of 9s to the lord and 41s to Henry Woodes, dec. As by a surrender made by the said Henry Woodes, Margaret then his wife and Thomas Woodes their son and presented by the jury at the court held on Friday, the day after Corpus Christi, 10 June, 7 Charles.[311]

Now the said Henry Darbishire on 9 February, 22 Charles, 1647 out of court came before Edward Stockley, William Fletcher and Richard Litherland and for £40 to him paid by Edmund Edmundes, late of Kexby in the county of York, husb., surrendered to the lord that messuage and tenement which the said Henry Darbishire now inhabits with the said croft or parcel of land on the north side and that one acre or parcel of land in Churchley Field belonging to the said messuage and tenement. The lord to regrant the said messuage, tenement and acre of land to the said Edmund Edmundes for sixty years to be completed if the said Edmund Edmundes lives so long. And the term and estate of the said Henry Darbishire shall therein so long continue in the same to all tenantly profits and commodities whatsoever. Paying

[f.17v, blank]
[f.18r: 24.5 cms × 30 cms]
yearly rent of 9s to the lord and 41s to the said Thomas Woodes.

Provided and it is agreed between the said Henry Darbishire and Edmund Edmundes that if the said Henry Darbishire shall maintain the said Edmund Edmundes 'with honest and sufficient meate, drinke and Lodginge, washinge and wringinge meete and convenyent' for the said Edmund Edmundes during the life of the said Edmund in the now house of the said Henry Darbishire in Prescot, then this surrender shall be void.

Provided also and it is agreed between both the said parties that the said Henry Darbishire may hold and peaceably enjoy the said messuage, tenement and other premises and take the profits to his own use during and until such time as the said Henry Darbishire shall neglect or fail to maintain the said Edmund Edmundes as aforesaid.

And the said Henry Darbishire agrees with the said Edmund Edmundes that if the term and estate of the said Henry Darbishire in the said premises shall end during the life of the said Edmund Edmundes, the said Henry Darbishire shall continue to maintain the said Edmund Edmundes as aforesaid during the said Edmund's life in the house of the said Henry Darbishire or in some other convenient house in Prescot.

Acknowledged before us: proclaimed   *[signed]* Henrie Darbisheire
  [signed] Edw Stockley   admitted
  Willm Fletcher *[mark – initials]*
  Richard Litherland *[mark – initials[312]]*
(*Parchment*: The said Edmund Edmundes is admitted.)

311. 1631.
312. While here the 'L' is inverted, at other times Richard's initials are right side up.

[f.18v]
9 February 1647. Surrender acknowledged by Henry Darbishyre to Edmund
Edmundes to be presented.

[f.19r: 24.5 cms × 30 cms]
[7] On 8 April, 23 Charles, 1647 Thomas Devias of Huyton and Ellen his wife
– the said Ellen being solely and secretly examined by the steward – out of court
came before William Fletcher, Nicholas Marshall and Richard Litherland and for
£20 paid by John Litherland of Prescot, butcher, surrendered to the lord that messuage or cottage with a small croft and a garden on the south side now or late in
the occupation of William Birchall of Prescot. The lord to regrant the said messuage or cottage, croft and garden to the said John Litherland and Margaret his
wife to hold to them and the survivor for the lives of the said John Litherland,
the said Margaret his wife and Thomas Parr, son of John Parr of Prescot, butcher,
and the survivor of them. Paying yearly to the said Thomas Devias rent of 2s on
the Nativity of St John the Baptist and the Nativity of Our Lord in equal portions
and to the lord the yearly rent of 3s on similar feasts in equal portions.
    And the said Thomas Devias covenants and agrees with the said John Litherland
that if the said John Litherland shall have a child or children lawfully begotten
and shall be minded to exchange the life of the said Thomas Parr for the life of
one of his children, then the said Thomas Devias and Ellen his wife shall, on
receipt of 5s from the said John Litherland and at his request and cost, execute
another surrender. That other surrender shall be of the said messuage, croft and
garden to the said John Litherland and Margaret his wife and and their assigns
for their lives and for the life of such child begotten by the said John Litherland
as the said John Litherland shall nominate instead of the life of the said Thomas
Parr. The said Thomas Parr is to be in full life at the time of such said acknowl-
edgment under the like rents and reservations as in this present surrender are mentioned.

The said Ellen solely examined by:	proclaimed	Ellen Devias *[mark]*
[signed] Tho Wolfall steward	admitted	*[signed]* Thomas Devias

[f.19v]
Acknowledged before us:
    William Fletcher *[mark – initials]*
    [signed] Nicholas Marshall
    Richard Litherland *[mark – initials]*
(*Parchment*: The said John Litherland and Margaret his wife are admitted.)

[f.20r: 19 cms × 30 cms]
At the view of frankpledge of Prescot, 18 June 1647.
    [8] John Alcocke of Eccleston near Knowsley, gent., by his surrender at the
court leet of 24 June 17 Charles,[313] in open court surrendered to the lord that
messuage and tenement then in the occupation of John Stevenson, gent., and

313. 1641; court met on 25 June. See f.19r for 1641 on p. 32 *supra*.

Nicholas Anderton, mercer, now dec. The lord to regrant to the said Nicholas Anderton to hold from 1 May then last past for twenty-one years under the yearly rent of 18d to the lord and of £4 to the said John Alcocke.

Now John Lightbowne, gent., administrator of the goods, chattels, rights and credits of the said Nicholas Anderton, on 18 June 23 Charles[314] came before Edward Stockley and William Blundell, gent., and for £6 paid to him by Henry Marshall of Prescot, mercer, surrendered to the lord that said messuage and tenement now in the holding or occupation of William Futerill and the said John Lightbowne.

[f.20v]
The lord to regrant the said messuage, tenement and premises to the said Henry Marshall to hold from the making of this present surrender during the remainder of the said term of twenty-one years. Paying yearly rent to the lord of 18d and to the said John Alcocke yearly rent of £4 on the feast of St Michael the Archangel.

Acknowledged before us: proclaimed   *[signed]* John Lightbown
    [signed] Edw Stockley   admitted
    [signed] Wil Blundell
(*Parchment*: The said Henry Marshall is admitted.)

[f.21r: 19 cms × 30.5 cms]
At the view of frankpledge with court of Prescot held on Friday after Corpus Christi, 18 June, 23 Charles, 1647.

[9] To this court William Kenwricke, younger son of Richard Kenwricke late of Eccleston, yeo., dec., came before the steward and homage and for good considerations to him the said William Kenwricke but mostly for £46 paid to him by Thomas Litherland of Prescot, yeo., surrendered to the lord that messuage and tenement heretofore occupied by Alice Miller and Ann Miller and that other messuage now occupied by Richard Marshall. The lord to regrant the said messuages and tenements to the said Thomas Litherland forever. Paying yearly rent to the lord of 2s.

                                proclaimed   *[signed]* William Kenwricke
                                admitted
(*Parchment*: The said Thomas Litherland is admitted forever.)

[f.21v, blank]
[f.22r: 19.5 cms × 30.5 cms]
View of frankpledge with court baron of Prescot held before the said steward on Friday after Corpus Christi, 18 June, 23 Charles, 1647.

[10] To this court came Edward Stockley and in open court before the steward and homage surrendered to the lord two messuages or cottages heretofore in several tenures or occupations of John Strettell, currier, and Richard Hoomes and now in

314. 1647.

the tenure of Robert Bolton, hatter. The lord to regrant the said two messuages or cottages to the said Robert Bolton for the lives of the said Robert Bolton and Mary[315] his wife and the survivor. Paying yearly during the said term to the said Edward Stockley rent of 30s[316] on the Nativity of St John the Baptist and the Nativity of Our Lord.

Provided that if the said yearly rent of 30s shall be unpaid in part or in all at any feast day within twenty days after due, then the said Edward Stockley may re-enter the said two messuages or cottages and this surrender to be void.

proclaimed
admitted

(*Parchment*: The said Robert Bolton is admitted.)

[f.22v, blank]
[f.23r: 18.5 cms × 30 cms]

[11] On 8 June, 23 Charles, 1647 Jane Pyke of Prescot, wid., Richard Litherland of Prescot, tailor, and Cecily his wife, lately called Cecily Pyke, out of court came before George Deane and Henry Marshall – the said Cecily being solely and secretly examined by the steward – and for good considerations surrendered to the lord that messuage and tenement which the said Richard now inhabits and those two closes or parcels of land commonly called Pyke's Higher Hey and Lower Hey containing about two acres of land. The lord to regrant the said messuage, tenement and premises to Thomas Litherland and Edward Darbishire of Prescot forever. Paying yearly to the lord the rent of 7s.

Acknowledged before us:　　　　proclaimed　　Jane Pyke *[mark]*
　[signed] Geo Deane　　　　　admitted　　　Ric Litherland *[mark – initials]*
　[signed] Hen Marshall　　　　　　　　　　Cicilie Litherland *[mark]*
The said Cecily was solely and secretly examined by:
　[signed] Tho Wolfall steward
(*Parchment*: The said Thomas Litherland and Edward Darbishire are admitted.)

[f.23v, blank]
[f.24r: 19 cms × 30 cms]

PLEAS AMONG OTHER THINGS AT VIEW OF FRANKPLEDGE WITH COURT[317] **OF PRESCOT** held there according to the custom of the manor of Prescot aforesaid before the said steward[318] of the manor and court aforesaid, on Friday after Corpus Christi, 18 June, 23 Charles, 1647.

[12] To this court came Evan Garnett and John Parr and in full court before the steward and homage complain against Thomas Litherland and Edward Darbishire in a plea of land, that is, of one messuage, one garden, one orchard and three acres of land in Prescot. And they have made protestation to prosecute their complaint

---

315. 'Mary' was added in a blank in a different hand from but the same ink as the surrender.
316. The amount was added in a blank in a different hand from but the same ink as the surrender.
317. The parchment roll adds 'baron'.
318. The parchment roll adds 'Thomas Wolfall esq.'

aforesaid in the form of a writ of entry upon disseisin in the post at the common law according to the custom of the manor aforesaid. And they have pledges, that is, John Doe and Richard Roe, to prosecute their plaint, and they request process against Thomas Litherland and Edward Darbishire which is granted.

But the said Thomas Litherland and Edward Darbishire are present in court and pray that the said Evan Garnett and John Parr, upon their said plaint in form of the said writ against them, may declare.

Whereupon the said Evan Garnett and John Parr declare against them and demand against the said Thomas Litherland

[f.24v]
and Edward Darbishire the said premises wherein the said Thomas Litherland and Edward Darbishire have no entry but by disseisin which Hugh Hunt has unjustly made to them the said Evan Garnett and John Parr within the past thirty years. They say that they have been seised of the said premises and bring their suit.

The said Thomas Litherland and Edward Darbishire appear and defend their right and call to warrant Richard Litherland of Prescot, tailor, and Cecily his wife, a daughter of Thomas Pyke late of Prescot, dec., who are in court and warrant. The said Evan Garnett and John Parr demand against the said Thomas Litherland and Edward Darbishire.

[f.25r: 19 cms × 29.5 cms]
The said Richard and Cecily come and defend their right and further call to warrant Edward Rylandes* who is also present in court and warrants. The said Thomas Litherland and Edward Darbishire demand against the said Edward Rylandes* and bring their suit.

The said Edward Rylandes* came and defends his right and says that the said Hugh Hunt has not disseised the said Evan Garnett and John Parr of the tenements aforesaid as the said Evan Garnett and John Parr by their said declaration have supposed. He puts himself on the country.

The said Evan Garnett and John Parr pray leave to imparl until the seventh hour in the afternoon. Granted. And the same hour is given to the said Edward Rylandes.*

Afterwards at the seventh hour the said Evan Garnett and John Parr return but the said Edward Rylandes* does not but defaults.

[f.25v]
The court decides that the said Evan Garnett and John Parr shall recover the said premises against the said Thomas Litherland and Edward Darbishire, and that the said Thomas Litherland and Edward Darbishire shall have of the lands of the said Richard Litherland and Cecily his wife to the value of, and so forth, and that the said Richard and Cecily shall have of the lands of the said Edward Rylandes.* The said Edward Rylandes* shall be amerced.

*   The name of Edward Rylandes was added in a blank in the same hand and ink as the rest of the document. In subsequent mentionings of ER, 'said' precedes the blank.

To the same court on the same day came the said Evan Garnett and John Parr who ask that a precept be directed to the bailiff of the manor of Prescot aforesaid – being minister of this court – in the nature of a writ at the common law, giving them full possession of the said property. Granted.

Afterwards the bailiff, Henry Parr, returns and certifies that, by virtue of the said precept directed to him, he has given full possession of the said premises to the said Evan Garnett and John Parr.

proclaimed   *[signed]* Tho Wolfall
admitted

(*Parchment*: The said Evan Garnett and John Parr came in full court before the steward and homage, ask to be admitted tenants and are admitted forever.)

[f.26r: 18.5 cms × 30 cms]

The jurors further say that the said recovery was of the said messuage and tenement called Pyke's house, Pyke's Lower Hey and Higher Hey in the said surrender recovered as above by the said Evan Garnett and John Parr by the name of one messuage, one garden, one orchard and three acres of land to the use of the said Richard Litherland forever.

Now the said Richard Litherland, Evan Garnett and John Parr came in open court before the steward and homage and for £70 to him Richard Litherland paid by Henry Lawton of Rainhill and Edward Pottes of Eccleston surrendered to the lord the said messuage and tenement and premises as recovered above by name aforesaid. The lord to regrant the said premises to the said Henry Lawton and Edward Pottes forever. Paying yearly

[f.26v]

to the lord the rent of. [319]

Provided that if the said Richard Litherland and Cecily his wife pay to the said Henry Lawton and Edward Pottes or either of them £70 within the next three years, the said messuage, tenement and premises immediately after such payment will remain to the said Richard Litherland and Cecily and the heirs of the body of Cecily by the said Richard. For want of such issue, to the heirs of the said Cecily. For lack of such issue, to the right heirs of the said Thomas Pyke forever.

proclaimed   *[signed]* Tho Wolfall
admitted

(*Parchment*: The said Henry Lawton and Edward Pottes are admitted.)

[f.27r, blank: 19 cms × 29.5 cms]
[f.27v]

Prescot court held there on 18 June 1647. Extract made and delivered.[320] Sum total within: £106 10s 6d.

---

319. The paper book, parchment roll and Abstract Book have a blank.
320. To Henry Parr, bailiff, delivered by Edward Stockley, clerk of the court.

1648

[Paper Book: DDCs]   [Parchment Roll: DDKc/PC 4/76[321]]

[f.1r: 20 cms × 31 cms]

VIEW OF FRANKPLEDGE WITH COURT BARON OF PRESCOT in the county of Lancaster held there according to the custom of the manor and liberty of Prescot aforesaid before Thomas Wolfall, esq., steward of the manor and court aforesaid, on Friday after Corpus Christi, 2 June, 24 Charles, 1648.

SUITORS OR CUSTOMARY TENANTS:

William Gerard, baronet		
o Henry Eccleston, esq.	within age	o George Deane of Rainhill
Henry Ogle, esq.	dead[322]	o John Lyon of Windle
<John Lancaster, esq.>		Thomas Woodes of Widnes
o Henry Lathom, esq.	infirm	o James Houghton of Whiston
o Thomas Wolfall, gent.	within age	o Thomas Woodes of Whiston
Thomas Sorrocold, gent.		o George Lyon of Eccleston infirm
o John Alcocke, sen., gent.		John Lyon, tanner
o John Alcocke, jun., gent.		o John Leadbeter
o Edward Stockley		o Henry Webster of Knowsley
o William Blundell		o John Webster of Knowsley
o William Lyme out of the county		o Edmund Webster of Knowsley
o Elizabeth Smyth		o Robert Wainwright of Tarbock
o Margaret Tyrer out of the county		o Henry Parr out of the county
o Thomas Symond, gent. out of the county		o Dorothy Mercer, wid.
		William Aspia of Kirkby
o George Croston, gent. out of the county		o John Glover of Rainhill
		infant George Tarleton of Liverpool
o William Parr of Cronton pardoned by the steward		infant John Torbocke of Windle
		o Paul Orme of Tarbock
		o Richard Woodes
		of Rainford essoined
o Henry Pinnington within age		Thomas Devias of Huyton dead[324]
William Lyon of Thingwall dead[323]		William Fletcher dead[325]
o Thomas Litherland		o Nicholas Marshall
o Richard Kenwricke within age		o Henry Marshall

---

321. Four membranes with writing on all sides except the verso of the last. Size: 28 cms × 74 cms; the last membrane is 1 cm narrower than the others.
322. Of Roby, buried on 16 March 1648. LPRS, 114, p. 99; Steel, *Prescot Churchwardens' Accounts*, pp. xv–xviii and *passim*.
323. Yeoman. Thingwall is a hamlet in the parish of Childwall whose parish register has a gap for burials from 1639 to 1653. LPRS, 106, p. 152.
324. Buried on 3 February 1648. LPRS, 85, p. 143.
325. See note 297 *supra*.

Henry Lawton
Edward Pottes
o James Sadler
Richard Jameson
o George Lyon, jun.
o Peter Kenwricke, sen.
o Ellis Webster
o Hugh Ward
William Sutton   dead [326]
o Richard Litherland
John Wall
o Ann Lodge

[f.1v]
Subtenants and inhabitants:

o William Harrison   out of the county
o John Parr
o John Halsall
o William Futrill
William Glover
o Thomas Kenwricke
o John Pendleton
Edward Darbishire
o John Birchall
o Henry Parr
o William Ewde
o William Rose
o Edward Booth
o Alexander Rylandes
o Thomas Moberley
o Robert Kenion
o Edward Finney
o John Huson, sen.
o Edward Bate
o Richard Wolfall

o James Parker
o James Houghton
o Ralph Hall
o Thomas Garnett
o John Houghton
o Henry Houghton
William Coppowe
o Thomas Somner
o Richard Ditchfeild
o Richard Marshall
Richard Banner
o Edward Webster
o Gilbert Heyes
o Thomas Fletcher
o Henry Kirkes
o John Sutton   out of the county
o Thomas Rainforth
o Thomas Walles
Henry Darbishire   dead[327]
o Robert Knowles

326. Of Prescot. A shoemaker, alehousekeeper, labourer, husbandman and yeoman, William's name commonly appears in the bottom 20 percent of tenants. Between 1630 and 1644 he served twenty-seven times in nine different manorial offices, witnessed twelve surrenders between 1627 and 1646 and served as a pledge in nineteen breaches of the peace by his neighbours between 1626 and 1645. He himself was accused of twenty-six breaches between 1625 and 1643. William was also a maltmaker who owned a kiln from which on 10 February and 9 June 1635 Alice Woodfall of Prescot stole malt, for which justices at the sessions of the peace found her guilty and ordered her to be whipped. William died in October 1647. LRO: QSB/1/154/22 and 53, Midsummer 1635; QSR/32, Ormskirk, Midsummer 1635; QJI/1/12, Midsummer 1635; LPRS, 114, p. 98.
327. Of Prescot, buried on 19 December 1647. LPRS, 114, p. 98.

○ Thomas Knowles
○ James Angsdale
○ John Frodsham
○ William Hardman
○ Henry Standish
○ Anthony Prescott
   Robert Bolton, hatter
   Richard Jackeson
○ Thomas Squeyre
○ Thomas Parr
○ Thomas Wood
○ Robert Parr
○ John Cowper
○ John Taylor
○ Thomas Horneby
○ William Browne
○ Evan Hearefoote
   John Litherland
○ William Birchall
○ Roger Mann
○ Thomas Aspe   sick
○ Evan Garnett
○ Peter Hearefoote
○ Michael Romley
○ John Houghland
○ Edward Rylandes

○ John Huson, jun.
○ Peter Garnett
○ Roger Dey
○ Richard Chorleton
[f.2r: 20 cms × 31 cms]
○ Robert Hatton   pardoned
○ Richard Hoomes
○ John Oliverson
○ John Poughtin
○ Robert Woosie
○ Peter Kenwricke, jun.
○ David Catton
○ John Wainwright
○ Richard Birch
○ Ralph Houghton
○ John Tyrer
○ Richard Angsdale
○ Thomas Browne
○ Richard Higgonson
○ Ralph Plumpton
○ John Massie
○ John Rigbie
○ Robert Bolton, schoolmaster
○ Thomas Webster
○ Henry Rigbie
○ Henry Prescott   infirm

[f.2v, blank]
[f.3r: 20 cms × 31 cms]

JURY TO INQUIRE FOR THE SOVEREIGN LORD KING AND LORD OF THE MANOR OF PRESCOT at the court held on 2 June 1648: [328]

	<John Alcocke, sen.>				Thomas Woodes	
– ○	Edward Stockley*	sworn			of Widnes	6s 8d
– ab	John Alcocke, sen.*	sworn	ab ○		James Houghton	
– out	William Blundell*	sworn			of Whiston	sworn
	of			– ○	Thomas Woodes	
	William Parr	pardoned by			of Whiston	sworn
	of Cronton	the steward			John Lyon, tanner	6s 8d
– ○	Thomas Litherland	sworn	– ○		Edmund Webster	
– ○	George Deane of Rainhill	sworn			of Knowsley	sworn
	Henry Lawton of Rainhill	6s 8d	– ○		Robert Wainwright	
– ab	John Lyon of Windle	sworn			of Tarbock	sworn

328. All names appear to be in the same hand and ink.
*   The parchment roll adds 'gent.'

– ○	George Lyon, jun.,		Henry Webster	
	of Whiston	sworn	of Knowsley	6s 8d
	William Aspia of Kirkby	6s 8d	John Webster of Knowsley	6s 8d
– ○	Henry Marshall	sworn	– ○ Hugh Ward	sworn
– ○	James Sadler	sworn		
	Richard Jameson			
	of Huyton	6s 8d		

Jury adjourned to perfect its verdict until 23 June on pain of 3s 4d each.
Jury further adjourned to perfect its verdict until 14 July on pain of 6s 8d each.

[f.3v, blank]
[f.4r: 20 cms × 31 cms]

JURORS PRESENT on their oaths for owing suit and service but this day default-ing in appearance (6d each):

Thomas Woodes of Widnes	William Glover
John Lyon, tanner	Edward Darbishire
Henry Lawton	William Coppowe
Edward Pottes	Robert Bolton
Richard Jameson	John Litherland

Thomas Devias died[329] since the last court seised at the time of his death of a messuage and tenement now in the holding of John Litherland, butcher, and that Henry Devias is his son and heir and of the age of,* and the said messuage and tenement are of the yearly rent of* to the lord. Proclaimed. Admitted.
(*Parchment*: The said Henry Devias is admitted forever.)
    William Sutton died[330] since the last court 'but of what Coppiehold estate he was seized this Jury are ignorant.'
    William Fletcher died [331] since the last court and in his lifetime acknowledged a surrender of all his copyhold lands in this manor to which this jury refer them-selves.

[f.4v]
    They present that Ralph Halsall, dec., did in his lifetime make two pits in Fall Lane to the impairing of the highway and danger of passengers and that John Halsall (3s 4d) his son has lately made another pit in the same lane which is a great annoyance.
    It is therefore ordered that the said John Halsall shall fill up and even the said pits before next 14 August on pain of 26s 8d.

329. See note 324 *supra*.
*   The paper book, parchment roll and Abstract Book have a blank.
330. See note 326 *supra*.
331. See note 297 *supra*.

They present that the profit of the money given by Lawrence Webster, dec., 'to pious uses' <by the last will of the said Lawrence> was last year distributed among the poor of the several towns to whom it is given.

Henry Chawner of Whiston (2s 6d) 'by his owne Confession' cut down and carried out of Prescot Wood two young saplings 'to make bowes for Baskett bottoms.'

Ralph Fletcher the elder (6s 8d) has received as inmates Edmund Edmundes and his wife.

It is further ordered that the said Ralph Fletcher shall remove the said Edmund Edmundes and his family before next 29 September on pain of 13s 4d.

The following have brewed ale and beer without consent of the steward (3s 4d each):[332]

David Catton	Ann Hough, wid.
Thomas Woodes	Thomas Squyre
Edward Darbishyre	Jane Greene, wid.
William Rose	Thomas Kenwrick
Margery Ackers, wid.	John Birchall
Roger Man	Evan Heirefoote
Edmund Edmundes	Eleanor Hoole
William Futerill	Jarvis Simonett

[f.5r: 20 cms × 31 cms]

We are informed that diverse alehousekeepers or innkeepers within this manor have contrary to the custom of this town obtained licences from justices of the peace for brewing or selling ale without the allowance of the steward of this court.

Those who have so done or will hereafter shall forfeit to the lord of this manor 13s 4d a time.

It is ordered that the Four Men shall inquire about those who have been received to inhabit contrary to former orders and to demand security. If default be made regarding the giving of security, then upon presentment by the Four Men, penalties will be inflicted according to former orders upon view thereof.

We continue an order made at the last court concerning the motion made to the steward for regulating cottages and the orders and penalties made for the same and desire that the steward would within the next month determine the same.

While Eleanor Hoole and Ellen her daughter were ordered by a former order of this court to leave this town, they have not. We further order them to leave before next 1 September and not return on pain of 26s 8d.

[f.5v]

At the last court it was ordered that the yate and wall placed in Hall Lane should be removed before last Michaelmas, but it is not yet done. It is further ordered that Henry Ogle, gent., shall remove said yate and wall and lay open the lane as formerly before next St Michael the Archangel on pain of 26s 8d.

---

332. Knowles, *Prescot Records*, p. 38, incorrectly has '15 persons' who are not named.

We order the constables at the town's expense to repair the walls of the water-ing pool and the court house stairs before next St Michael the Archangel on pain of 6s 8d.

Also they shall see that the way to the Lady Well be repaired at or before next 14 August so inhabitants may fetch water 'without lett', on pain of 3s 4d.

Thomas Parr shall remove the part of his midding that hinders the way to the said well at or before 14 August on pain of 3s 4d.

The owners and occupiers of the shops under the court house shall repair the court house at the oversight of the Four Men before next Michaelmas on pain of 13s 4d.

[f.6r: 20 cms × 31 cms]
We present that William Fletcher, now deceased, Edward Booth and William Webster have before this court laid muck on the Town Moss contrary to a former order of this court and to the prejudice of the inhabitants and their common of pasture and have each forfeited 6s 8d.

Because of 'the unseasonablenes of the weather', highways could not be repaired and are in decay and ditches could not be sufficiently scoured. It is therefore ordered that all who have hedges and ditches annoying the highway shall on notice by the surveyors cut their hedges and cleanse their ditches before next Michaelmas on pain of 6s 8d each.

We order that the constable<s> for last year, namely, Richard·Edwardson <and William Harrison> shall perfect and deliver in <their> his accounts for his receipts and payments as constable to the Four Men at or before next 18 August on pain of 40s.

William Harrison, the other constable, shall do likewise on pain of 40s.

We present that the said Richard Edwardson (6s 8d) and William Harrison (6s 8d), constables, have neglected to attend this jury and make their presentments.

We present Henry Wilson, one Birchall of Rainford, Thomas Darbishyre, Edward Molyneux, John Litherland and William Futerill for an assault one on another. Each 12d.

[f.6v]
We present that there are diverse sums in arrears owed to persons <amounting to £12> appearing at four courts and an order made for levying leys to satisfy the same. This was done, and 'the booke' offered to Richard Edwardson, constable, to collect the said leys which he has neglected and has forfeited 40s. We now fur-ther order that the constables for the following year shall collect the said leys and pay the same over accordingly and also pay to Ralph Plumpton 4s which he expended on a trip to Manchester about the town's business, on pain of 40s.

We present that James Angsdale (5s), 'much taken with Drinke' on the last fair day in the open streets in the presence of the steward and 'before the greatest part of the inhabitantes of this towne and many others', uttered reproachful terms to Mr Henry Ogle, to the breach of the peace and evil example of others.

We order that the said James Angsdale before next 1 September shall deliver to the constables a chain for the town's common bell. He about December 1643 took or caused to be taken that chain.

We order that none of the inhabitants shall lay any muck or dung near the churchwall or in the way to the vicarage or in the churchyard or allow their swine to depasture in the churchyard, on pain of 6s 8d for every offence.

[f.7r: 20 cms × 13.5 cms]
2 June 1648. **PRESENTMENTS BY THE CLERKS OF THE MARKET**, John Halsall and John Parr.

We present Edmund Edmundes (6s 8d) for selling beef not marketable because it was 'deade before of some desease.'

We present Henry Parr, butcher (2s), for stuffing and opening veal and mutton several times contrary to the custom of this market.

John Parr *[mark]*

[f.7v, blank]
[f.8r: 19.5 cms × 30 cms[333]*]*
2 June 1648. **PRESENTMENTS BY THE ALETASTERS**, Thomas Sumpner and Thomas Knowles.

They present alehousekeepers for breach of the assize of ale (12d each):

○ Thomas Walles	William Futerill
○ Richard Litherland	○ Frances Bolton, wid.
○ Ellen Bond	Ann Hough, wid.
○ Edward Booth	○ Alexander Rylandes
○ Thomas Parr	Thomas Squyre
○ Robert Parr	Thomas Woodes
○ William Harrison	Jane Greene
○ John Halsall	Edward Darbishire
○ Richard Edwardson	Thomas Kenwricke
○ Elizabeth Darbishyre	William Rose
David Catten	John Birchall
○ Jane Fennowe	Margery Ackers, wid.
○ Ralph Plumpton	Evan Heirfoote
○ Richard Marshall	Roger Man
○ Isabel Fearnes	Eleanor Hoole
○ John Poughten	Edmund Edmundes
○ Jane Bolton	Jarvis Simonett
○ John Pendleton	Henry Meade
○ James Houghton	

For selling bread and breaking the assize (12d each):

John Poughten	Robert Bolton
Jane Fennowe	James Houghton
John Massie	Richard Banner

333. Though once bound, sheet 8 has come loose and is now fastened to the paper book by a modern paper clip.

Edmund Edmundes	Elizabeth Houghton
Thomas Woodes	John Oliverson
Thomas Squire	Jarvis Simonett

by us: Tho Sumner *[mark]*
Tho Knowles *[mark]*

[f.8v³³⁴]

[JURORS ORDER AND PRESENT]

We order that <John> Thomas Rainforth shall before the end of next August take away and make up the door place at the further end of the said Rainforth's barn which opens on the back of Henry Marshall's housing, on pain of 13s 4d.

We present that the surviving feoffees, for the money given to charitable uses by Lawrence Webster, dec., have nominated to us Thomas Litherland to be one of the feoffees for the same gift in place of William Fletcher, dec., and we accept Thomas Litherland.

[f.9r: 20 cms × 30.5 cms]

OFFICIALS ELECTED to serve:³³⁵

Constables	*[1]* Edward Darbishyre	sworn <made default; therefore 40s> <further made default; therefore £5>
	[2] <Robert Parr>	
	[2] William Birchall	sworn <made default; therefore 40s> <made further default; therefore £5>
Four Men	*[1]* Edward Stockley	sworn
	[1] William Blundell	sworn
	[1] Thomas Litherland	sworn
	[1] Henry Marshall	sworn
Coroner	*[1]* John Alcocke, sen.	sworn before
Clerks of the	*[1]* Thomas Walles	sworn
market	*[2]* John Halsall	sworn
Burleymen	*[1]* John Poughten	sworn before
	[2] Robert Hatton	sworn before
Sealers of	*[1]* John Houghland	sworn
leather	*[2]* Evan Hearefoote³³⁶	sworn
Alefounders	*[1]* Thomas Sumner³³⁷	sworn before

334. Folio 8v is in the same hand and ink as the jurors' presentments.
335. This list of officers sworn, minus marginalia on defaults, also appears in the parchment roll.
336. The parchment roll has 'Herford'.
337. The parchment roll has 'Somner'.

	[2] Thomas Knowles	sworn before
Streetlookers	*[1]* William Eawde	sworn
	[2] Ralph Houghton	sworn
Affeerors of	*[1]* Edward Stockley	sworn
the court	*[1]* John Alcock	sworn
	[1] William Blundell	sworn
	[1] Thomas Litherland	sworn

[f.9v, blank]
[f.10r: 20 cms × 29.5 cms]
[SURRENDERS AND ADMITTANCES]
   [1] On 13 January 23 Charles,[338] Richard Molyneux came before Edward Stockley and Thomas Woodes out of court and for £3 9s paid to him by James Houghton of Prescot, tailor, surrendered to the lord that messuage or cottage in the upper end of the street in Prescot leading toward Eccleston heretofore in the occupation of William Molyneux, dec., late great uncle to the said Richard Molyneux. To the use of James Houghton of Prescot, tailor, forever. Paying yearly to the lord the rent of 8d and to the school of Prescot yearly the rent of 3s 4d.
Acknowledged before us: proclaimed   *[signed]* Rich Molyneux
   [signed] Edw Stockley   admitted
   [signed] Thomas Woods
(*Parchment*: The said James Houghton is admitted forever.)

[f.10v, blank]
[f.11r: 19 cms × 31 cms]
   [2] Ralph Halsall late of Prescot, blacksmith, dec., was in his lifetime possessed for the lives of the said Ralph Halsall, Ann then his wife, now also dec., John Halsall their son and Elizabeth their daughter, now wife of Thomas Hearefoote,* and the survivor for some number of years determinable of and in that messuage or mansion house which the said Ralph Halsall then inhabited and the said John Halsall now inhabits; and of one barn on Mill Hill and two closes commonly called the Fall Acre and Fells Acre.
   The said Ralph Halsall on 20 November 21 Charles[339] surrendered the said messuage, barn, closes and premises to the said Ralph Halsall during his life. Thereafter to the said Ann during her chaste widowhood. Thereafter to the said John Halsall. For lack of his heirs, to Thomas Halsall his brother, during the remainder of the said term, with several provisos in the same surrender mentioned.
   Now on 8 November, 23 Charles, 1647 the said John Halsall and Thomas Halsall his brother out of court came before Richard Litherland and Henry Marshall and for £16 to the said John Halsall paid by Peter Harforde* of Prescot, shearman, surrendered to the lord

                         John Halsall *[mark – last initial]*
                         Tho Halsall *[mark – first initial]*

338. 1648.
*   The parchment roll has 'Hairford'.
339. 1645.

[f.11v]
that said messuage or mansion house with the said barn and that close and parcel of land called Fells Acre. The lord to regrant to the said Peter Harforde* the said messuage, barn and close called Fells Acre for the lives of the said John Halsall and Elizabeth, wife of the said Thomas Harforde,* and the survivor. Paying yearly to the lord the rent of 2s – parcel of the rent of 10s 8d – reserved for the said messuage, barn and two closes.[340]

Provided that if the said John Halsall pays to the said Peter Harforde* £16 on 25 December 1649 and in the meantime pays the said rent of 2s to the lord yearly, then this surrender to be void.

Provided also that the said John Halsall shall have and enjoy the said messuage and barn as long as he and they shall free the said close called Fells Acre from being charged with the yearly rent of 29s 4d payable for all the said premises to Dorothy Mercer, wid., and of and from the said 10s 8d[341] rent to the lord, except the said 2s parcel thereof.

Acknowledged before us: proclaimed   John Halsall *[mark – last initial]*
Ric Litherland *[mark – initials]* admitted[342]   Thomas Halsall *[mark – first initial]*
  [signed] Henry Marshall

[f.12r: 19.5 cms × 30 cms]
[3] John Halsall of Prescot, blacksmith, and Thomas Halsall his brother or one of them are possessed to them for the lives of the said John Halsall and Elizabeth, wife of Thomas Herefoote⁺ lately called Elizabeth Halsall, and survivor or for some number of years determinable of and in that close and parcel of land commonly called Fall Lane Acre.

Now the said John Halsall and Thomas Halsall for £7 paid by Thomas Litherland of Prescot, yeo., came on 2 February 23 Charles[343] before John Alcock the younger and Richard Litherland and surrendered to the lord that said close and parcel of land commonly called Fall Lane Acre containing about one large acre. The lord to regrant the said close and premises to the said Thomas Litherland, holding from the making of this surrender for ninety-nine years to be ended if the said John Halsall and Elizabeth Herefoote⁺ live so long. Paying yearly to the lord the rent of.[344]

John Halsall *[mark – last initial]*
Tho Halsall *[mark]*

---

340. Marginated in a different ink and probably by a different hand: 'the Rent reserved must bee 3s 4d'.
341. The parchment roll has 'xs iiijd'.
342. The parchment roll contains no statement that Peter Harford asks to be admitted.
+   The parchment roll has 'Harford'.
343. 1648. The parchment roll incorrectly has 24 Charles.
344. The paper book, parchment roll and Abstract Book have a blank. Marginated in the paper book in the same ink and probably the same hand: 'a proporconable parte of the Rent to bee reserved'.

[f.12v]

Provided that if the said John Halsall pays to the said Thomas Litherland £7 11s 2d on 2 February 1649, then this surrender to be void.

Acknowledged before us: proclaimed John Halsall *[mark – last initial]*
   [signed] John Alcock Jn   admitted   Tho Halsall *[mark]*
   Richard Litherland *[mark – initials]*

(*Parchment*: The said Thomas Litherland is admitted.)

[f.13r: 20 cms × 31 cms]

[4] On 26 <April> May, 24 Charles, 1648 Cuthbert Ogle, esq., out of court came before Nicholas Marshall and Thomas Litherland[345] and for good consider-ations surrendered to the lord that one messuage or cottage with burgage hereto-fore in the tenure or occupation of John Sutton of Prescot. The lord to regrant the said messuage and burgage to Ellen Sutton, late wife of the said John Sutton, and Robert Sutton and William Sutton, sons of the said Ellen Sutton, and the longest liver for the lives of the said Ellen Sutton, Robert Sutton and William Sutton and the survivor. Paying yearly to the said Cuthbert Ogle the rent of 5s on the Nativity of St John the Baptist and the Nativity of Our Lord in equal portions and yearly to the lord the rent of.[346]

Acknowledged before us: proclaimed   *[signed]* Cuthbert Ogle
   [signed] Nic Marshall   admitted
   [signed] Thomas Litherland

(*Parchment*: The said Ellen Sutton *[and]* Robert and William, sons of the said Ellen, <is> are[347] admitted.)

[f.13v, blank]
[f.14r: 19.5 cms × 30.5 cms]

[5] On 26 November, 23 Charles, 1647 Margaret Tyrer, spinster sister of Richard Tyrer, clerk, out of court came before Henry Parr of London, gent., and John Walles the younger of Prescot, and for £29 to the said Margaret Tyrer paid by Thomas Litherland of Prescot, yeo., surrendered to the lord that messuage and tenement heretofore occupied by John Garnett, dec., late in the occupation of William Hough, dec., and Thomas Parr the younger and now in the holding or occupation of Ann Hough, wid. The lord to regrant the said messuage and tenement to the said Thomas Litherland forever. Paying yearly to the lord the rent of 2s.

Acknowledged before us: proclaimed   Margrett Tyrer *[mark – initials]*
   [signed] Henry Parr   admitted
   [signed] John Walles

(*Parchment*: The said Thomas Litherland is admitted forever.)

---

345. The names of NM and TL were added in a blank in the same hand and ink as the sur-render.
346. The paper book, parchment roll and Abstract Book have a blank.
347. Interlined in the parchment roll: 'Robert and William sons of the said Ellen are'.

[f.14v, blank]
[f.15r: 20 cms × 30 cms]

[6] William Lyon held forever two messuages or cottages with two gardens and one croft on the backside. One of the said messuages with a garden and the said croft are in the holding or occupation of Edward Finney, his undertenants or his assigns, and the other messuage or cottage with a garden is now occupied by James Parker. The said William Lyon at the court held on Friday after Corpus Christi, 19 James,[348] surrendered the said premises to himself for his life and afterwards to George Lyon, oldest son of the said William Lyon, and his male heirs.

The jurors further say that since acknowledging the said surrender the said William Lyon the father and George Lyon his oldest son are both dead.[349] The said George Lyon the son died about eleven years ago and the said William Lyon died since the last court. George Lyon the younger, oldest son of the said George Lyon, dec., is next heir of the said William Lyon, dec., and is seventeen years old and more and prays to be admitted tenant of the said two messuages or cottages.[350]

proclaimed
admitted

(*Parchment*: The said George Lyon, jun., is admitted forever.)

[f.15v, blank]
[f.16r: 20 cms × 31 cms]

VIEW[351] OF FRANKPLEDGE WITH COURT BARON OF PRESCOT in the county of Lancaster held there according to the custom of the manor of Prescot aforesaid before Thomas Wolfall, esq., steward of the manor and court aforesaid, on Friday after Corpus Christi, 2 June, 24 Charles, 1648.

[7] To this court came Richard Litherland of Prescot, tailor; Cecily his wife, lately called Cecily Pyke; Jane Pyke of Prescot, wid.; and Thomas Rainforth, son of John Rainforth of Prescot – the said Cecily being solely and secretly examined by the steward – and in open court before the steward and homage for good and valuable considerations, as recovered of a messuage and land hereafter mentioned, surrendered to the lord that one messuage and tenement now occupied by the said John Rainforth and Thomas Rainforth and one croft and parcel of land to the same messuage commonly called Leadbeter's croft. The lord to regrant the said messuage and premises

[f.16v, blank]
[f.17r: 20 cms × 31 cms]

348. 1 June 1621.
349. See note 323 *supra*. George, too, must have been buried during the period 1639–53 when a gap occurred in the parish register of Childwall. At this time in Prescot parish individuals with the name 'George Lyon' resided in Prescot, Eccleston, Whiston, Windle and Rainford.
350. While both the paper book and parchment roll fail to mention any rent, the Abstract Book notes in the margin that the annual rent to the lord is 4s 6d.
351. The parchment roll begins: 'Pleas among other things at the view of frankpledge....'

to the use of Henry Marshall of Prescot, mercer, and John Parr of Prescot, yeo., forever. Paying yearly to the lord the rent of 10d.

The said Cecily solely and secretly proclaimed   Jane Pyke *[mark]*
examined by the steward.   admitted   Ric Litherland *[mark – initials]*
   Witness: Cicely <Pyke> Litherland *[mark]*
   [signed] Tho Wolfall steward   Tho Rainforth *[mark]*
   The said Henry Marshall and John Parr are admitted forever.[352]

[f.17v, blank]
[f.18r: 20 cms × 31 cms]

PLEAS AMONG OTHER THINGS AT VIEW OF FRANKPLEDGE WITH COURT BARON OF PRESCOT held before the said steward on 2 June, 24 Charles, 1648.

[8] To this court came Thomas Litherland and Thomas Walles and in full court before the steward and homage complain against Henry Marshall and John Parr in a plea of land, that is, of one messuage, one garden and half an acre of land in Prescot. And they have made protestation to prosecute their plaint aforesaid in the form of a writ of entry upon disseisin in the post at the common law according to the custom of the manor aforesaid. And they have pledges, that is, John Doe and Richard Roe, to prosecute their plaint, and they request process against Henry Marshall and John Parr which is granted.

But the said Henry Marshall and John Parr are in court and pray that the said Thomas Litherland and Thomas Walles, upon the said plaint in form of the said writ against them, may declare. Whereupon the said

[f.18v, blank]
[f.19r: 20 cms × 31 cms]

Thomas Litherland and Thomas Walles do declare against them and demand the said premises wherein the said Henry Marshall and John Parr have no entry but by disseisin which Hugh Hunt has unjustly made to them the said Thomas Litherland and Thomas Walles within the past thirty years. They say that they have been seised of the said premises and bring their suit.

The said Henry Marshall and John Parr appear and defend their right and call to warrant Richard Litherland and Cecily his wife who are in court and warrant.

[f.19v, blank]
[f.20r: 20 cms × 31 cms]

The said Thomas Litherland and Thomas Walles demand against the said Richard Litherland and Cecily his wife who come and defend their right. The said Richard and Cecily further call to warrant Evan Chorlton who is also present in court and warrants.

The said Thomas Litherland and Thomas Walles demand against the said Evan Chorlton and bring their suit.

---

352. A note on admittance appears in both the paper book and parchment roll.

[f.20v, blank]
[f.21r: 20 cms × 31 cms]
The said Evan Chorleton came and defends his right and says that the said Hugh Hunt has not disseised the said Thomas Litherland and Thomas Walles of the tenements aforesaid as the said Thomas Litherland and Thomas Walles by their said declaration have supposed. He puts himself on the country.

The said Thomas Litherland and Thomas Walles pray leave to imparl until the second hour in the afternoon. Granted. And the same hour is given to the said Evan Chorleton. Afterwards at the second hour the said Thomas Litherland and Thomas Walles return but the said Evan Chorleton does not but defaults. The court decides that the said Thomas Litherland and Thomas Walles shall recover the said premises against the said Henry Marshall and John Parr, and that the same Henry Marshall and John Parr shall have of the lands of the said Richard Litherland and Cecily his wife to the value, and so forth, and that the same Richard and Cecily

[f.21v, blank]
[f.22r: 20 cms × 31 cms]
shall have of the lands of the said Evan Chorleton to the value, and so forth. The same Evan Chorleton shall be amerced.

To the same court on the same day came the said Thomas Litherland and Thomas Walles and ask that a precept be directed to the bailiff of the manor of Prescot aforesaid – being minister of this court – in the nature of a writ at the common law, giving them full possession of the said property. Granted.

Afterwards the bailiff, Henry Parr, returns and certifies that, by virtue of the said precept directed to him, he has given full possession of the said premises to the said Thomas Litherland and Thomas Walles.

And upon this the said Thomas Litherland and Thomas Walles came in full court before the steward and homage, ask to be admitted tenants

[f.22v, blank]
[f.23r: 20 cms × 31 cms]
and are admitted forever, paying 10d yearly to the lord.
proclaimed   admitted

Afterwards to this court came the said Thomas Litherland and Thomas Walles and the said Richard Litherland and Cecily his wife – the said Cecily being solely and secretly examined by the steward – in open court before the steward and homage. And whereas the said recovery was had of the said messuage and tenement now occupied by the said John Rainforth and Thomas Rainforth in the said first mentioned surrender and recovered as above by the said Thomas Litherland and Thomas Walles by the name of one messuage, one garden and half an acre to

[f.23v, blank]
[f.24r: 20 cms × 31 cms]
the said Richard Litherland and Cecily his wife forever.

Now the said Thomas Litherland and Thomas Walles at the request of the said Richard Litherland and Cecily for £16 5s paid to them by the said Thomas Rainforth surrendered to the lord the said messuage, tenement and premises recovered as above. The lord to regrant the said messuage and tenement to the said Thomas Rainforth forever. Paying yearly to the lord the rent of 10d.

The said Cecily solely and secretly proclaimed   *[signed]* Tho Litherland
examined by the steward.   admitted   *[signed]* Tho Walles
   Witness: Ric Litherland *[mark – initials]*
[signed] Tho Wolfall steward   Cicely Litherland *[mark]*
The said Thomas Rainforth is admitted forever.[353]

[f.24v, blank]
[f.25r: 29 cms × 39 cms]
[9] On or about 18 April, 24 Charles, 1648 James Houghton of Whiston, yeo., out of court came before William Lyme and George Lyon and for £40 paid to him by George Markland* as the marriage portion of Jane, daughter of the said George Markland* and now wife of Ralph Houghton, son and heir apparent of the said James Houghton, and in performance of an agreement made on 3 February 1646 between the said James Houghton and the said George Markland,* surrendered to the lord that one messuage and tenement lately inhabited by Richard Sumner[354] and then inhabited by Edward Darbishyre and another messuage and tenement then inhabited by John Birchall and now inhabited by William Futerell.[355] The lord to regrant the said messuage and tenement in the holding of Edward[356] Darbishyre to Ralph Houghton, son of the said James,[357] and Jane now his wife during their lives and the life of the survivor. Thereafter to the heirs of the said Ralph on the body of the said Jane. For lack of such heirs, to the heirs of the said Ralph. For want of such heirs, to the right heirs of the said James Houghton forever.

To the further intent that the lord would regrant the said other messuage and tenement to the same belonging now in the holding of John Birchall to the said James Houghton and Margaret his wife during their lives and the life of the survivor. Afterwards to the said Ralph Houghton and heirs. For lack of such heirs, to the right heirs of the said James Houghton forever. Paying to the lord for the said messuage and tenement in the holding of Edward Darbishyre the yearly rent of 1s <4d> 8d and for the other messuage and tenement in the holding of John Birchall the rent of 3s 4d.

Acknowledged before us: proclaimed
   [signed] Wil Lyme   admitted
   [signed] Geo Lyon Jn
(*Parchment*: The said James Houghton and Margaret his wife, Ralph Houghton and Jane his wife are admitted.)

353. A note on admittance appears in both the paper book and parchment roll.
*   The parchment roll has 'Martland'.
354. The parchment roll has 'Somner'.
355. The parchment roll has 'Fewtrill'.
356. The parchment roll has 'the said Edward'.
357. The parchment roll has 'James Houghton'.

[f.25v, blank]
[f.26r: 30 cms × 31.5 cms]
    [10] On 15 November, 23 Charles, 1647 Ellis Webster out of court came before John Alcock, jun., Henry Marshall and Richard Litherland and for £16 paid or secured to be paid to Ellis Webster by Edward Booth of Prescot, husb., surrendered to the lord those two messuages or cottages, one in the holding of the said Ellis Webster and the other in the occupation of Jane Webster, <'sester'> 'Kinswoman'[358] of the said Ellis, or either of their assigns, with a small garden on the south side of the said messuages or cottages. The lord to regrant the said messuages, cottages and other premises to the said Edward Booth forever. Paying yearly to the lord the rent of 6d.

Acknowledged before us: proclaimed   Ellis Webster *[mark – initials]*
   [signed] John Alcock Jn   admitted saving the right of Jane Webster,
   [signed] Henry Marshall   spinster
   Richard Litherland *[mark – initials]*

(*Parchment*: The said Edward Booth is admitted forever, saving always the right of Jane Webster, spinster, in the said premises.)

[f.26v]
    Edward Booth his surrender from Ellis Webster.

[f.27r: 29.5 cms × 37.5 cms]
    [11] William Sutton of Prescot, shoemaker, by a surrender dated 2 July, 7 Charles, 1631 surrendered to the lord that one messuage, tenement, burgage and dwelling house then and yet in the tenure, holding and occupation of the said William Sutton, to the use of himself the said William Sutton for his life.
    With proviso in the said surrender that if the said William Sutton shall at any time hereafter become indebted to any person or persons for an amount greater than his personal estate in goods will satisfy and which shall be his own proper debts – debts shall not be as surety for any person or persons – then the said William Sutton may surrender up to one half of the premises to any person for satisfaction of his just debts as aforesaid for such term and time for such of his said just debts which cannot otherwise be paid from the clear profits thereof.
    And whereas the said William Sutton is now indebted to Thomas Parr of Prescot for £4 2s 10d, to the executors or administrators of Thomas Whiteside for 20s and for four years' interest or damages for forbearance, to Henry Webster of Knowsley for 20s, to Thomas Walles for 12s or thereabouts, to Thomas Heirfoote[359] for 12s 6d, to William Webster for £5 9s 4d, and to John Poughten for 3s 8d.
    Now the said William Sutton on 30 September 23 Charles,[360] according to the power and liberty reserved to him in the said surrender that the said Thomas Parr

---

358. The paper book has 'sester' cancelled and 'Kinswoman' interlined, while the parchment roll has '*Consobrine*' for '*consobrinae*' or 'cousin'.
359. The parchment roll has 'Harford'.
360. 1647.

and George Lyon the younger of Whiston, yeo., may of the profits of the moiety or one half of the said messuage, tenement and burgage satisfy such debts as his personal estate in goods will not satisfy in such manner as the said Thomas Parr and George Lyon think fit, came before John Alcocke the younger and Henry Marshall and surrendered to the lord that moiety of the said messuage, burgage and tenement. The lord to regrant the said moiety of the said premises to the said Thomas Parr and George Lyon to hold for the next fifteen years.

[f.27v]
Paying yearly to the lord the moiety or one half of the rents due for the said messuage, burgage and tenement, that is.[361]

Provided that after the said debts and sums of money be satisfied from the profits of the hereby surrendered premises, then the said premises shall remain in the several uses according to the said surrender.

Acknowledged before us:	The word 'Seacond'	William Sutton *[mark]*[362]
[signed] John Alcock Jn	was interlined in one	
[signed] Henry Marshall	place, 'Septimo 1631' in	
	another place, 'three'	
	was 'raced out' and	
	'Five' interlined instead,	
	'ixs iiijd' interlined in	
	another place and 'all	
	before the acknowledg-	
	ment herof.'	
	Witnessed:	
	[signed] John Alcock Jn	
	[signed] Henry Marshall	
	proclaimed	
	admitted	

(*Parchment*: The said Thomas Parr and George Lyon are admitted to the said moiety.)

[f.28r: 29 cms × 39 cms]
　[12] Henry Darbishire of Prescot, carpenter, now possessed to him and his assigns by copy of court roll for term of the lives of Elizabeth Darbishire now his wife and Thomas Darbishire his son and the survivor of and in that messuage and tenement which the said Henry Darbishire now inhabits, with a croft or parcel of land on the north side; and of and in one acre in Churchley Field to the same messuage and tenement belonging. By and under the annual rent of 9s to the lord and yearly rent of 41s to Henry Woodes, dec., as by one surrender acknowledged by

361.　Blank in the paper book, parchment roll and Abstract Book.
362.　William, described as 'sick' in the call book of June 1647, was clearly ill on 30 September, thirteen days from his burial, when he made this mark consisting of two squiggles; between 1627 and 1646 he wrote his full name very legibly twenty times in manorial records. LPRS, 114, p. 98.

the said Henry Woodes, Margaret then his wife and Thomas Woodes their son and presented by the jurors and homage at the court held on Friday after Corpus Christi, 10 June, 7 Charles.[363]

Now the said Henry Darbishire on 15 December, 23 Charles, 1647 out of court came before Edward Stockley and William Blundell[364] and for good considerations, especially for the love and affection which he bears towards his wife and children and for their future maintenance, surrendered to the lord that said messuage and tenement which the said Henry Darbishire now inhabits, with one croft on the north side; and one acre in Churchley Field to the said messuage and tenement belonging. The lord to regrant the said messuage and tenement and acre to the said Henry Darbishire for life. After the decease of the said Henry Darbishire, then to Elizabeth Darbishire now his wife as long as she remains a widow. The said Elizabeth is to maintain Edmund Edmundes[365] – who now lives with the said Henry Darbishire – with meat, drink, lodging and washing during his life according to the agreement of the said Henry Darbishire with the said Edmund Edmundes.

And she also is to maintain Edward Darbishire, youngest[366] son of the said Henry Darbishire, with meat, drink, apparell, lodging and washing until he shall be provided for with a trade or some other settled way of preferment.

After the determination of the estate of the said Elizabeth Darbishire, then to the use of Thomas Darbishire,[367] oldest son

[f.28v, blank]
[f.29r: 29.5 cms × 19.5 cms]
of the said Henry Darbishire, during the term of the said Henry Darbishire in the said premises so as the said Thomas Darbishire[368] shall maintain the said Edmund Edmundes with meat, drink, lodging and washing during his life and also

---

363. 1631.
364. The names of ES and WB were added in a blank in a different hand from but the same ink as the surrender.
365. Edmund and his wife Ann and presumably their son John, baptized in October 1647, were received by Ralph Fletcher the elder as inmates according to Prescot's court in 1648 (f.4v). Edmund, a subtenant who in 1648 was for the first time styled alehousekeeper, died about 1660, and his widow, who lived until 1689, appears to have been poor. In 1682 Prescot's court amerced her 12d for being a fair brewer (a way to make some needed income), and in October 1682 justices of the peace ordered the churchwardens and overseers of the poor of the parish of Prescot to provide her with a 'weekly and competent allowance.' Henry Darbishire may have been providing assistance to Edmund and his family, and Henry was ill and would die a day or two after making this surrender and possibly wanted to ensure that his widow and son would maintain Edmund. Interestingly, Henry's widow, Elizabeth, was a recusant. THC: Paper Book/1682; LRO: QSR/76, Wigan, Michaelmas 1682; CRO: EDV 1/34 (f.51r); BIHR: V.1662–3/CB.2 (f.138r); LPRS, 114, pp. 39, 119–20; 149, p. 122.
366. The parchment roll incorrectly has 'oldest'. Henry was buried on 19 December 1647; his son Edward was baptized in 1633 and his sons Thomas and William in 1627 and 1630, respectively. Though not mentioned in this surrender of 1647, his son William was then alive. LPRS, 76, pp. 90, 97; 114, pp. 1, 98.
367. 'Thomas Darbishire' is not in the parchment roll.
368. 'Darbishire' is not in the parchment roll.

maintain Edward Darbishire, his youngest brother, with meat, drink, apparell, lodging and washing until he is bound to some trade or otherwise provided for with maintenance. They paying the rents that are due.

Acknowledged before us: proclaimed   *[signed]* Henrie Darbisheire
   [signed] Edw Stockley   admitted
   [signed] Will Blundell
(*Parchment*: The said Elizabeth Darbishire and Thomas Darbishire – the said Henry Darbishire being dead [369] – are admitted.)

[f.29v, blank]
[f.30r: 29.5 cms × 39.5 cms]
   [13] William Fletcher at the court held on Friday after Corpus Christi, 2 June, 19 Charles, 1643 in open court surrendered to the lord his copyhold messuages, cottages and lands, that is, one messuage or dwelling house then in the holding or occupation of James Parker; the messuage or cottage occupied by Margaret Goodicar; a messuage or cottage late in the occupation of Ann Ditchfeild; a messuage or cottage late in the occupation of Thomas Ackers, dec., and one barn adjoining; four cottages lately built and adjoining to the said barn; and one close and parcel of land called the Cow Hey containing two acres and 'three Rood land of land'. To the use of the said William Fletcher for his life and after his decease to the other uses noted in the said surrender.

   With the proviso in the same that if the said William Fletcher shall in the presence of two or more copyholders pay to the said copyholders 6d declaring his intent to void the said surrender, then the surrender is to be voided.

   Now the said William Fletcher on 22 September, 23 Charles, 1647 out of court came before Edward Stockley and William Blundell, gent., and not only paid to the said Edward Stockley and William Blundell 6d declaring his intent to void the said surrender but also for good considerations surrendered to the lord that said messuage or dwelling house heretofore in the holding or occupation of James Parker and now occupied by Thomas Garnett; the messuage or dwelling house in the holding or occupation of Margaret Goodicar, wid., and Thomas Goodicar, her son; the messuage or dwelling house heretofore in the holding or occupation of Ann Dicthfeild, spinster, dec., and now occupied by Frances Bolton, wid.; the messuage or dwelling house heretofore in the holding or occupation of Thomas Ackers, dec., and now occupied by Margery Ackers, wid.; 'and all that barne lyinge and neare adjoyninge to the said messuage in the occupacon of Margery Ackers';[370] those four cottages lately built being in the several holdings or occupations of John Taylor, currier, William Browne, Thomas Horneby and Thomas Rainforth;[371] a messuage or cottage lately purchased from John Lyon and <Thomas> Robert Lyon his son now in the holding or occupation of Roger Mann; and the said close and parcel of land called the Cow Hey containing two acres

---

369. See note 327 *supra*.
370. '[A]nd all that barne...Ackers' is not in the parchment roll.
371. The parchment roll has 'Rainford'.

and three rood land of land now in the holding or occupation of the said William Fletcher. The lord to regrant the said messuages, cottages and lands to the said William Fletcher for his life.

William Fletcher *[mark – initials]*

[f.30v, blank]
[f.31r: 30 cms × 39.5 cms]

After his decease, the moiety or one half to Elizabeth Fletcher, now wife of the said William Fletcher, during her life. After her decease, to Elizabeth Fletcher, daughter of the said William Fletcher, and her heirs. For lack of such issue, to William Marshall, son of Henry Marshall of Prescot. For lack of such issue, to Elizabeth Marshall, daughter of the said Henry Marshall. For lack of such issue, to Thomas Fletcher, son of John Fletcher of the Outwood within Pilkington. For lack of such issue, to the right heirs of the said William Fletcher forever.

And to the intent that the lord would regrant the other moiety of all premises after the death of the said William Fletcher to the said Elizabeth Fletcher, daughter of the said William Fletcher, and her heirs. For lack of such issue, to William Marshall, son of the said Henry Marshall. For lack of such issue, to Elizabeth Marshall, daughter of the said Henry Marshall. For lack of such issue, to Thomas Fletcher, son of the said John Fletcher of the Outwood within Pilkington. For lack of such issue, to the right heirs of the said William Fletcher forever. Paying yearly to the lord for the said messuage occupied by Thomas Garnett the rent of 1s; for the said close and parcel of land called the Cow Hey the yearly rent of 2s; for the said messuage occupied by Roger Mann the yearly rent of 1s; and for the rest of the premises the yearly rent of 19s 6d.

Provided that if the said William Fletcher at any time in the presence of two or more copyholders pays them 6d and declares that his intent is to void this surrender, then the surrender is void.

Acknowledged before us: proclaimed   William Fletcher *[mark – initials]*
[signed] Edw Stockley   admitted
[signed] Will Blundell

(*Parchment*: The said William Fletcher and Elizabeth his wife being dead,[372] the said Elizabeth Fletcher, daughter of the said William Fletcher, is admitted.)

[f.31v, blank]
[f.32r: 30 cms × 39.5 cms]

[14] William Fletcher is possessed by copy of court roll for the lives of Elizabeth Fletcher, now wife of the said William Fletcher, and Ellen Marshall, late wife of Henry Marshall and daughter of the said William Fletcher, and the survivor of and in one messuage and tenement which the said William Fletcher now inhabits; and of and in one barn in the upper end of the town leading toward Eccleston

---

372. For William, see note 297 *supra*. Elizabeth Fletcher of Prescot, wid., was buried on 7 February 1648. LPRS, 114, p. 99. For her will, see LRO: WCW/Prescot/1648/Elizabeth Fletcher.

containing three bays of building with a cottage and garden and two crofts and parcels of land on the east side of the said barn containing one acre of land of the large measure. By the yearly rent of 3s 2d to the lord, and 10s to John Glover of Rainhill, as by the surrender made to the said William Fletcher from the said John Glover.

The said William Fletcher at the court held on Friday after Corpus Christi, 2 June, 19 Charles, 1643 in open court surrendered to the lord that said messuage and tenement, barn, cottage and crofts to the use of the said William Fletcher for his life. After his decease, to several other uses in the said surrender mentioned.

With the proviso in the same that if the said William Fletcher at any time in the presence of two or more copyholders pays 6d to them and declares his intent to void the said surrender, then the said surrender to be void.

Now the said William Fletcher on 22 September, 23 Charles, 1647 out of court came before Edward Stockley and William Blundell, gent., and not only paid 6d to the said Edward Stockley and William Blundell and declared his intent to void the said surrender, but also for good considerations surrendered to the lord that said messuage and tenement which the said William Fletcher now inhabits and that barn containing three bays of building at the upper end of the street leading toward Eccleston with a cottage and garden and two crofts on the east side of the said barn.

The lord to regrant all premises to the said William Fletcher during his life. After his decease, to Elizabeth Fletcher his wife during her life. The said Elizabeth Fletcher bestowing yearly 30s during the said term for twelve coats for twelve poor children in Prescot, Eccleston and Sutton, namely, six coats in Prescot, three in Eccleston and three in Sutton to those whom she will judge to be the most poor and needy.

[f.32v, blank]
[f.33r: 30 cms × 40 cms]
After the death of the said Elizabeth Fletcher, then to Elizabeth Fletcher, daughter of the said William Fletcher, during the term of the said William Fletcher in the said premises. They and every of them respectively paying yearly to the lord the rent of 3s 2d and paying to the said John Glover the yearly rent of 10s.

Provided that if the said William Fletcher at any time in the presence of two or more copyholders pays 6d to them and declares his intent to void the present surrender, then the surrender to be void.

Acknowledged before us:[373]   Wm Fletcher *[mark – initials]*
    [signed] Edw Stockley
    [signed] Will Blundell

[f.33v]
Court held on 2 June 1648. Extract made and delivered.[374] Sum total within: £10 12s 10d.

---

373. The paper book has no 'proclaimed, admitted' and the parchment roll no 'Upon this came...prays to be admitted...and is admitted.'
374. To Henry Parr, bailiff, delivered by Edward Stockley, clerk of the court.

1649

[Parchment Roll: DDKc/PC 4/139bis [375]]

[m.1r: 28 cms × 72 cms]
**VIEW OF FRANKPLEDGE WITH COURT BARON OF THE MANOR
AND LIBERTY OF PRESCOT** in the county of Lancaster held there according
to the custom of the manor and liberty of Prescot aforesaid before Arthur Borron,[376]
gent., steward of the manor, liberty and court aforesaid, on Friday after Corpus
Christi, 25 May 1649.

INQUISITION TO INQUIRE FOR THE LORD OF THE SAID MANOR on
the oaths of:[377]

John Alcocke of Eccleston, gent.	Edmund Webster of West Derby
Thomas Litherland	John Lyon of Woolfall Heath
Henry Marshall	John Lyon of Windle
George Lyon, jun., of Whiston	Richard Jameson of Huyton
Ralph Houghton of Whiston	James Sadler
Thomas Woods of Whiston	Edward Booth
William Aspia of Kirkby	John Webster of Knowsley
Henry Webster of Knowsley	

sworn who present on their oaths that
[SURRENDERS AND ADMITTANCES]
[1] Henry Lathom late of Mossborough, esq., died[378] since the last court possessed of one messuage and tenement now occupied by Thomas Bridge [379] and
late in the occupation of Edmund Tunstall, one cottage now occupied by Margery

---

375. The paper book with presentments and orders is missing, and all material to the list of
officials elected inclusive comes from the parchment roll.
376. Steward from 1649 to 1655. His signature appears forty-two times in these manorial
records of 1650–55 and is identical to the signature of Arthur Borron of Warrington, gent.,
in the records of the quarter sessions. He seems to have had an unusually high interest
in the plague in Warrington in 1647 and in Prescot during the outbreak of 1652–53.
LRO: DDCs/Paper Book/1650; DDKc/PC 4/112/Paper Books/1651–55; QSB/1/1652/82,
Epiphany 1653; QSB/1/293/66, Midsummer 1647; QSR/47, Wigan, Epiphany 1654.
377. Because the parchment roll is the final verdict of the court, all names are in the same hand
and ink.
378. Mossborough is in Rainford. 'Henry Lathom, gen.', of Rainford was buried on 7 January
1649. LPRS, 114, p. 101.
379. This appearance in these records is the first by Thomas, an undertenant. An alehousekeeper, husbandman and shearman, in the following year he will be accused of bastardy
with Ann Naylar and ordered by justices of the peace to pay her 26s 8d annually in order
to avoid his son becoming chargeable to the parish of Winwick. Thomas may have left
Prescot after May 1654 when he last appeared in the manorial records. LRO: QSP/31/65,
Easter 1650; QSP/35/42, Midsummer 1650; QSB/1/336/26, Easter 1650; QSB/1/340/33,
Midsummer 1650; QSR/44, Ormskirk, Midsummer 1650.

Browne, wid., one messuage and tenement now occupied by John Tyrer and heretofore in the occupation of Thomas Carter, dec., and one parcel of building called 'Le Bay on the mylne hill' now occupied by Thomas Litherland. The jurors further say that William Lathom, esq., as the jurors understand, is son and next heir of the said Henry Lathom and is twenty-one years old and more.

The said William Lathom is admitted forever.

[2] Henry Prescott late of Prescot, dec., during his life held at the will of the lord one cottage built by the said Henry Prescott and a parcel of land including waste land on which the said cottage was built and to which the said Henry Prescott was admitted tenant. Paying yearly rent of 4d to the lord and of 2s to the school of Prescot.

Now the jurors say that the said Henry Prescott is dead [380] since the last court leet.

Anthony Prescott, oldest son of the said Henry Prescott, is admitted holding to him at the will of the lord of the manor under the annual rent of 4d to the lord and to the free school of Prescot the yearly rent of 2s.

[3] John Halsall and Thomas Halsall of Prescot by their surrender of 2 February 1648 surrendered to Thomas Litherland of Prescot, yeo., one close and parcel of land called Fall Lane Acre, late in the tenure or occupation of Ralph Halsall, dec., holding to him the said Thomas Litherland for ninety-nine years if the said John Halsall and Elizabeth, wife of Thomas Herford, or either of them live so long. Paying yearly to the lord the rent due on days and feasts usual in Prescot.

Provided that if the said John Halsall pays to the said Thomas Litherland £7 11s 2d on 2 February 1649, the said surrender to be void. He did pay, and the said surrender has been voided.

[4] On or about 7 May, 3 Charles, 1627 James Sorrocold, gent., dec., surrendered that cottage, burgage and dwelling house then and now in the tenure of John Cooper, weaver, to the said John Cooper for the term of ninety-nine years if the said John Cooper, Alice then and now his wife, and Robert Cooper their son, or any of them shall live so long, by the yearly rent of 10s paid to the said James Sorrocold on the Nativity of St John the Baptist and the Nativity of Our Lord in equal portions.

Now the said John Cooper on 24 March 1649[381] out of court came before Henry Marshall and Thomas Litherland and for £5 paid to him by Ralph Lea of Knowsley, yeo., surrendered to the lord that said messuage, cottage, burgage and dwelling house. The lord to regrant to the said Ralph Lea to hold from 25 March 1650 for twenty years, if the previously recited term continues in such a manner as he the said John Cooper will have occupied the premises. Paying the annual rent and services due.

The said Ralph Lea is admitted.

Provided that if the said John Cooper pays to the said Ralph Lea £5 8s on 25 March 1650 or 8s on that day and £5 8s on 25 March 1651, then this surrender to be void.

---

380. Of Prescot, buried on 19 June 1648. LPRS, 114, p. 100.
381. The parchment roll has '*vicessimo quarto die Martii Anno domini 1649*'.

Provided that if default be made in any of the said payments, the said John Cooper may, except for the croft or yard, enjoy the said premises and liberty to fetch water at the well therein during the said term, 'soe as they doe from tyme to tyme satisfy free and pay the said Rent of Tenn shillings and the Rent and services due to the lord of the mannor and all leyes gelds Taxacons imposicons and quartering of soldeires Charged or Chargable upon any parte of the herby Surrendred premisses.'

[5] On 23 March 1649 Edmund Webster, late of Knowsley and now of West Derby, blacksmith, son of Thomas Webster, late of Knowsley, dec., out of court came before William Parr and Thomas Litherland and in consideration of

[m.1v]
the annual rent hereafter reserved surrendered to the lord that messuage and tenement now inhabited by John Parr, butcher, and heretofore commonly called Webster's of the Well, with a barn to the same messuage belonging; the close and parcel of land on the back side to the same house commonly called 'The Close by the howse'; and those two closes and parcels of land near Sparrow Lane now possessed by the said John Parr. The lord to regrant the said messuage and premises to the said John Parr to hold the said messuage with barn from next 1 May for five years, and holding the said close and remaining said premises from last 2 February for five years. Paying yearly during the said last mentioned term to the lord the rent of *[blank* ³⁸²*]*, and to the said Edmund Webster the annual rent of £7 on 1 May and the feast of St. Martin the Bishop in Hyeme³⁸³ in equal amounts.

The said John Parr is admitted.

Provided that if the said Edmund Webster fails yearly to satisfy on Corpus Christi the leys and taxations, as the said John Parr shall expend as charged on the said premises, then the said John Parr may default out of the said rent and detain the leys or taxations that shall be laid out, and the said John Parr may default out of the rent of £7 the rent reserved to the lord yearly.

[6] On 27 March 1649 Edmund Webster of West Derby, blacksmith, son of Thomas Webster late of Knowsley, dec., out of court came before William Parr and Thomas Litherland and for £10 paid by Dorothy Corbett of West Derby, spinster, surrendered to the lord that messuage and dwelling house which Barbara Story, wid., now inhabits with a garden belonging to the same and those two burgages and parcels of land in Churchley Field containing half an acre of land of the large measure or thereabouts now occupied by Michael Romley. The lord to regrant the said messuage, garden, burgages and premises to the said Dorothy Corbett holding from next 2 February for a term of fifty years if she lives so long. Paying yearly to the lord the rent of 2s and also paying yearly to the said Edmund Webster the rent of 2s on 24 June. The remainder after the said term ended to the said Edmund Webster forever.

382. The Abstract Book is also blank.
383. 11 November.

The said Dorothy Corbett is admitted.

[7] On 8 December, 24 Charles, 1648 Henry Marshall of Prescot, mercer, out of court came before John Walles, jun., and Thomas Litherland and for £24 paid or secured to be paid by Henry Ratcliffe of Knowsley, shoemaker, surrendered to the lord that messuage and dwelling house heretofore inhabited by the said Henry Ratcliffe and lately inhabited by Thomas Dumbell, late schoolmaster of Prescot; that parcel of building called 'le new Bay' – so much at the south end as is set out for a range between the two doors only excepted – lately belonging to the messuage inhabited by Nicholas Marshall, father of the said Henry Marshall; that garden stead at the end of the said bay containing in length seven yards and in breadth six yards extending from the far side of the said bay; and liberty and passage through the lower floor of the dwelling house of the said Nicholas Marshall to the said bay in order to lay his muck in the midding stead belonging to the messuage of the said Nicholas Marshall. The lord to regrant the said beforementioned messuage, the bay of building, garden stead and premises to the said Henry Ratcliffe and Alice now his wife to hold during the lives of the said Henry Ratcliffe, Alice his wife and Ann Fairehurst, daughter of Alice Fairehurst, late of Hardshaw, wid., dec., and the life of the survivor. Paying yearly to the lord the rent of 2d and to Henry Marshall yearly rent of 5s on the Nativity of Our Lord and the Nativity of St John the Baptist in equal amounts.

The said Henry Ratcliffe is admitted.

Provided that if the said yearly rent of 5s be unpaid in part or in whole within twenty days after either said feast, then the said Henry Marshall may repossess the said premises.

[m.2r: 28 cms × 72 cms]

[8] John Halsall of Prescot, blacksmith, and Thomas Halsall, his brother, at the court held on Friday after Corpus Christi, 2 June 1648, surrendered to the lord that messuage or dwelling house lately occupied by Ralph Halsall, dec., late father of the said John Halsall; one barn on Mill Hill; and one close and parcel of land in Prescot called Fells Acre. The lord to regrant to Peter Harford of Prescot, shearman, during the life of the said John Halsall and Elizabeth, his sister and wife of Thomas Harford, and the survivor under the rent and services due.

With the proviso in the same surrender that if the said John Halsall pays to the said Peter Harford £16 on 25 December 1649 and to the lord the annual rent of 2s, then the said surrender to be void.

Also the said John Halsall and Thomas Halsall to this same court held on Friday after Corpus Christi in 1648 surrendered to the lord one close and parcel of land called Fall Lane Acre to Thomas Litherland of Prescot for ninety-nine years to be ended if the said John Halsall and the said Elizabeth Harford or either so long live, under the rent and services due.

With the proviso in the same surrender that if the said John Halsall pays to the said Thomas Litherland £7 11s 2d on 2 February 1649, the said surrender to be void.

Now on 14 December, 24 Charles, 1648 the said John Halsall and Thomas Halsall for £31 11s 2d, of which £8 thereof has already been paid, to the said John

Halsall paid by Henry Marshall of Prescot, mercer – the said Henry Marshall agreed to pay £7 11s 2d to the said Thomas Litherland on next 2 February for recovery of his estate in the said Fall Lane Acre and the said Henry Marshall agreed to pay £16, or the remainder of the said £31 11s 2d, to the said Peter Harford on 25 December 1649 for recovery of his estate – out of court came before Edward Stockley and Hugh Ward and surrendered to the lord the said messuage or dwelling house with the said barn on Mill Hill, that close called Fells Acre and that other close called Fall Lane Acre. The lord to regrant to the said Henry Marshall for ninety-nine years to be ended if the said John Halsall and Elizabeth Harford his sister or either live so long. Paying during the said term to the lord the annual rent of 10s 8d and to Dorothy Mercer, wid., the annual rent of 29s 4d.

Provided that if the said John Halsall or Thomas Halsall pays to the said Henry Marshall £33 7s 6d on 25 March 1650 and meanwhile pays the said yearly rent of 10s 8d to the lord and the said yearly rent of 29s 4d to the said Dorothy Mercer, then this surrender to be void.

John Halsall of Prescot, blacksmith, and Thomas Halsall, his brother, by their surrender of last 14 December surrendered to the lord that messuage or dwelling house lately occupied by Ralph Halsall, dec., late father of the said John Halsall; one barn on Mill Hill; one close and parcel of land called Fells Acre; and one other close and parcel of land called Fall Lane Acre. To the use of Henry Marshall of Prescot, mercer, for ninety-nine years to be completed if the said John Halsall and Elizabeth Harford, his sister, or either live so long. Paying yearly to the lord the rent of 10s 8d and to Dorothy Mercer, wid., the rent of 29s 4d.

With the proviso in the said surrender that if the said John Halsall or Thomas Halsall pays to the said Henry Marshall £33 7s 6d on 25 March 1650, pays to the lord the said annual rent of 10s 8d, and pays the said yearly rent of 29s 4d to the said Dorothy Mercer, then the said surrender to be void.

Now on 28 March 1649 the said John Halsall and Thomas Halsall out of court came before George Lyon, jun., of Whiston and Ralph Houghton and for valuable considerations relinquished forever to the said Henry Marshall that said messuage or dwelling house with the said barn on Mill Hill and the closes called Fells Acre and Fall Lane Acre.

Thus the said John Halsall and Thomas Halsall from all interest and claim in the said premises heretofore forever will be excluded.

[m.2v]
[9] Thomas Halsall of Prescot, whittawer, is possessed for the lives of the said Thomas Halsall, Thomas Harford, son of Peter Harford, William Parr, son of Thomas Parr, dec., and the life of the survivor of that messuage and tenement which Thomas Woods, butcher, now inhabits, and of one croft. Of the annual rent to the lord of *[blank³⁸⁴]* and of the rent of 16s to Thomas Woods, tanner, as by a surrender by the said Thomas Woods and Margaret Woods, wid., his mother, and presented to the court leet held on 29 May 1646.

384. Also blank in the Abstract Book.

Now on 3 August, 24 Charles, 1648 the said Thomas Halsall out of court came before George Lyon, jun., Henry Marshall and Thomas Litherland and for £12 10s paid by William Wood of Glugsmore in Eccleston and John Sutton, jun., of Sutton surrendered to the lord that said messuage and tenement which the said Thomas Woods, butcher, now inhabits. The lord to regrant the said messuage and premises to the said William Wood and John Sutton for the lives of the said Thomas Halsall, Thomas Harford[385] and William Parr and the life of the survivor. Paying yearly to the lord the rent of *[blank*[386]*]*and to the said Thomas Woods, tanner, the annual rent of 16s on the Nativity of Our Lord and the Nativity of St John the Baptist in equal portions.

The said William Wood and John Sutton are admitted.

Provided that if the said Thomas Halsall pays to the said William Wood and John Sutton £13 10s on 4 August 1649 for the only use of Elizabeth Marshall and William Marshall, children of Henry Marshall – 'the principall' being £12 10s, parcel of the money given to them by the last will and testament of Elizabeth Fletcher, wid., dec. – then this surrender to be void.

[10] On 4 April 1649 John Alcocke of Eccleston near Knowsley, gent., out of court came before William Lyme and Thomas Litherland and for good considerations surrendered to the lord of the manor those two messuages and tenements now in the tenure of Ralph Plumpton and John Rigby. The lord to regrant to the said John Alcocke and the heirs of his body. For lack of such issue, to John Alcocke, second son of John Alcocke of Prescot, gent., and the male heirs of John Alcocke the son. For lack of such issue, to Thomas Alcocke, his brother, and his male heirs. For want of such issue, to the right heirs of the said John Alcocke of Eccleston forever. Paying the rent of 13d yearly to the lord for the said messuage and tenement in the tenure of Ralph Plumpton, and for the other messuage and tenement in the tenure of John Rigby the rent of 14d.

The said John Alcocke of Eccleston is admitted.

Provided that if the said John Alcocke of Eccleston pays to the said John Alcocke the son or Thomas Alcocke 12d and declares his intent to void this surrender, then the same to be voided.

[11] On 7 November, 24 Charles, 1648 William Parr of Cronton, yeo., out of court came before William Lyme and Thomas Litherland and for £20 to the said William Parr paid by James Sadler of Prescot, buttonmaker, and Jane his wife surrendered to the lord that messuage, cottage and tenement which Thomas Knowles, tailor, now inhabits. The lord to regrant to the said James Sadler and Jane his wife forever. Paying yearly to the lord the rent of 3s.

The said James Sadler and Jane his wife are admitted forever.

[m.3r: 28 cms × 73.5 cms]

[12] John Litherland of Prescot, butcher, and Margaret his wife are possessed, by copy of court roll for the lives of the said John Litherland, Margaret his wife

---

385. The Abstract Book has 'Heirefoote'.
386. Also blank in the Abstract Book.

and Thomas Parr, son of John Parr of Prescot, butcher, and the survivor, of one messuage or cottage with a small croft and garden on the south side then occupied by the said John Litherland under the yearly rent of 2s to Thomas Devias, dec., and to the lord the yearly rent of 3s, as by a surrender made by the said Thomas Devias and Ellen his wife and presented at the court held on Friday, 18 June 1647.

Now on 3 April 1649 the said John Litherland and Margaret his wife – the said Margaret being solely and secretly examined by the steward – out of court came before Thomas Litherland and Henry Marshall and for £16 16s to the said John Litherland paid by Henry Ratcliffe of Prescot, shoemaker, surrendered to the lord the said messuage or cottage with a small croft and garden on the south side then occupied by the said John Litherland. The lord to regrant the said messuage or cottage, croft and garden to the said Henry Ratcliffe for the lives of the said John Litherland, Margaret his wife and Thomas Parr, son of the said John Parr, butcher, and the survivor. Paying yearly to the heirs and assigns of the said Thomas Devias, dec., rent of 2s and to the lord rent of 3s.

The said Henry Ratcliffe is admitted.

[13] John Halsall of Prescot, blacksmith, and Thomas Halsall, his brother, previously in consideration of £16 to the said John Halsall paid by Peter Harford of Prescot, shearman, surrendered that messuage, tenement and dwelling house lately inhabited by Ralph Halsall and now inhabited by the said John Halsall and that close called Fells Acre with one barn on Mill Hill. Holding during such term as they the said John Halsall and Thomas Halsall have in the same with redemption by payment of £16 at or about the next Nativity of Our Lord.

Now on 6 April 1649 the said John Halsall and Thomas Halsall out of court came before John Alcocke, jun., and Thomas Litherland and for 26s 8d, paid to them for the estate aforesaid by the said Peter Harford, not only released and quit claimed to the said Peter Harford[387] all estate and interest of the said John Halsall and Thomas Halsall or either of them but also all property, redemptions or agreements concerning the said premises.

Provided that the said John Halsall and Thomas Halsall may enjoy the said messuage with the barn on Mill Hill during such time as they shall satisfy the rent for all the said premises due to the owner of the inheritance of the said lands and also the rent due to the lord of the manor for the same, saving what is apportioned to be paid for the said Fells Acre by the surrender formerly made to the said Peter Harford.

[14] Richard Webster of Sutton, butcher, is now possessed, by copy of court roll for the lives of John Webster and George Webster, sons of the said Richard Webster, and the survivor, of one messuage and tenement heretofore in the tenure or occupation of William Fearnes, dec., and now in the tenure or occupation of the said Richard Webster under the yearly rent of 2s to George Deane of Rainhill, yeo., and of 2s yearly to the lord, as by a surrender made by the said George Deane and presented to the court held on Friday, 25 June 1641.

---

387. The Abstract Book has 'Hearefoote'.

Now on 8 May 1649 the said Richard Webster out of court came before John Alcocke, sen., and Edward Stockley, and for £12 paid to him by Edward Darbishire of Prescot, yeo., surrendered to the lord that said messuage and tenement heretofore in the tenure or occupation of the said William Fearnes, dec., and now in the tenure or occupation of the said Richard Webster, subtenant. The lord to regrant to the said Edward Darbishire for the lives of the said John Webster and George Webster, sons of the said Richard Webster, and the survivor. Paying yearly to the said George Deane the rent of 2s and to the lord 2s.

The said Edward Darbishire is admitted.

[15] On 22 March 1648 Elizabeth Smith of Knowsley, spinster, out of court came before Edward Stockley and Henry Marshall and for valuable considerations surrendered to the lord that one messuage or cottage in the tenure or occupation of John Parr, butcher, one garden, croft and parcel of land on the north side; two other messuages or cottages in the tenure or occupation of Alice Fletcher and Katherine Parr; and one other messuage or cottage occupied by Ann Mollyneux, wid. The lord to regrant the said premises to the said Elizabeth Smith for her life. After her decease to William Brettergh, second son of Nehemiah Brettergh of

[m.3v]
Aigburth in the county of Lancaster, esq., forever. Paying to the lord the yearly rent of *[blank³⁸⁸]*.

The said William Brettergh – the said Elizabeth Smith being dead ³⁸⁹ – is admitted forever.

Provided that the said William Brettergh shall permit Dorothy Lowe, his sister, to enjoy the messuage or cottage occupied by Ann Mollyneux during the life of the said Dorothy or until she shall be provided a better habitation.

[16] On 24 May 1649 Richard Woods of Rainford out of court came before John Lyon and Hugh Ward and for £8 paid by Paul Orme of Tarbock, yeo., surrendered to the lord that one shop now occupied by Henry Parr of Prescot, butcher. The lord to regrant the said shop to the said Paul Orme forever. Paying yearly to the lord the rent of 5d.

The said Paul Orme is admitted forever.

[17] Edmund Edmunds of Prescot, husb., and Elizabeth Darbishire of Prescot, wid., late wife of Henry Darbishire, dec., or one of them are possessed by copy of court roll for years determinable on the lives of the said Elizabeth Darbishire, Thomas Darbishire her son and the survivor of that messuage and tenement heretofore in the tenure or occupation of the said Henry Darbishire, dec., with a croft or parcel of land on the north side, and of one acre or parcel of land in Churchley Field to the said messuage and tenement belonging. Under the yearly rent of 9s to the lord and 41s to Henry Woods, dec., as by one surrender made by the said Henry Woods for the lives of Margaret then his wife and Thomas Woods their son and presented by the jurors and homage at the court held on Friday, 10 June, 7 Charles³⁹⁰ and by another surrender then made by the said Henry Darbishire.

388. Also blank in the Abstract Book.
389. Buried on 24 March 1649. LPRS, 85, p. 144.
390. 1631.

Now the said Edmund Edmunds and Elizabeth Darbishire on 9 August, 24 Charles, 1648 out of court came before Edward Stockley, John Alcocke, William Blundell and Thomas Litherland and for £20 paid to Edmund Edmunds by John Parr of Prescot, yeo., in satisfaction of the maintenance of the said Edmund Edmunds with meat, drink, lodging and washing during his life, surrendered to the lord the said messuage and tenement formerly in the tenure or occupation of the said Henry Darbishire and now in the tenure or occupation of the said Elizabeth Darbishire and of one Peter Beliall alias Cooke, one croft or parcel of land on the north side, and one acre or parcel of land in Churchley Field to the same messuage and tenement belonging. The lord to regrant the said messuage, tenement, croft and acre of land to the said John Parr for sixty years to be completed if the estate and term of the said Edmund Edmunds and Elizabeth Darbishire shall so long continue. Paying yearly the rent of 41s to the said Thomas Woods and 9s to the lord.

The said John Parr is admitted.

[18] On 26 August, 24 Charles, 1648 Thomas Darbishire, son of Henry Darbishire late of Prescot, dec., out of court came before Thomas Litherland and Henry Marshall and surrendered to the lord that messuage and tenement heretofore in the tenure or occupation of the said Henry Darbishire, dec., with a croft or parcel of land on the north side, and one acre or parcel of land in Churchley Field to the same messuage and tenement belonging. The lord to regrant the said messuage, tenement and premises to John Parr of Prescot, yeo., during the term and estate as the said Thomas Darbishire has in the same that is yet not expired. Paying yearly rent of 41s to Thomas Woods of Widnes and 9s to the lord.

The said John Parr is admitted.

[m.4r: 28 cms × 70.5 cms]

[19] On 18 January, 24 Charles, 1649[391] Ralph Fletcher, sen., of Prescot, Ralph Fletcher and Thomas Fletcher, sons of the said Ralph Fletcher, sen., and Robert Wainwright of Tarbock out of court came before James Sadler and John Walles and for £50 paid to them or any of them by Henry Marshall of Prescot, mercer, surrendered to the lord that one messuage and dwelling house which the said Ralph Fletcher, sen., Ralph Fletcher and Thomas Fletcher, his sons, now inhabit; one also with two bays of building, one small croft and one garden on the backside; and one cottage on or near Mill Hill with one garden on the backside late heretofore in the tenure or occupation of Thomas Fletcher, dec., brother of the said Ralph Fletcher, sen. The lord to regrant the said premises to the said Henry Marshall forever. Paying to the lord the yearly rent of 2s 4d.[392]

---

391. On 30 January 1649 Charles I was executed.
392. While the parchment roll contains no statement about admittance, the Abstract Book informs us that 'Admittance barred and afterwards he was Admitted.'

OFFICIALS ELECTED for serving for the manor of Prescot: [393]

Constables	William Glover	sworn
	Henry Marshall	sworn
Four Men	Edward Stockley	sworn
	William Blundell	sworn
	John Alcocke, sen.	sworn
	Thomas Litherland	sworn
Coroner	John Alcocke, sen.	sworn before
Clerks of the	Thomas Walles	sworn
market	Edward Darbishire	sworn
Burleymen	John Oliverson	sworn
	Robert Hatton	sworn
Sealers of	Henry Ratcliffe	sworn
leather	Roger Dey	sworn
Aletasters	Richard Marshall	sworn
	James Houghton	sworn
Streetlookers	William Eawde	sworn before
	Ralph Houghton	sworn before
Affeerors of	John Alcocke, sen.	sworn
the court	Thomas Litherland	sworn
	Henry Marshall	sworn
	George Lyon, jun.	sworn

[m.4v, blank]

[Paper Book: DDKc/PC 4/41[394]]

[f.1r]
VIEW OF FRANKPLEDGE WITH COURT BARON OF PRESCOT held according to the custom of the manor and liberty of Prescot aforesaid before Arthur Borron, gent., steward, on Friday after Corpus Christi, 25 May 1649.

To this court came Peter Harford of Prescot, shearman, and, having requested to be heard, says that the surrender of John Halsall of Prescot, blacksmith, and Thomas Halsall, his brother, acknowledged before Edward Stockley and Hugh Ward on 14 December, 24 Charles, 1648 to the use of Henry Marshall of a messuage, barn and parcel of land called Fells Acre should not be accepted by the steward of the manor aforesaid and that the said Henry Marshall as tenant thereof should not be admitted for the following reasons, namely, at the frankpledge with court baron of Prescot held before Thomas Woofall, esq., steward, on Friday after Corpus Christi, 2 June, 24 Charles, 1648.

---

393. All names were written at the same time.
394. Consists of six leaves that are of the same size (31 cms × 38 cms) and are in the same hand and ink. This material is not in the Abstract Book or parchment roll.

[f.1v, blank]
[f.2r]

INQUISITION TO INQUIRE FOR THE LORD on the oaths of:

Edward Stockley
John Alcocke, sen.
William Blundell
Thomas Litherland
George Deane of Rainhill
John Lyon of Windle
James Houghton of Whiston

Thomas Woodes of Whiston
Edmund Webster of Knowsley
Robert Waynewright of Tarbock
George Lyon, jun., of Whiston
Henry Marshall
James Sadler
Hugh Ward

The jurors say on their oaths that Ralph Halsall late of Prescot, blacksmith, dec., during his life was possessed for the lives of the said Ralph Halsall, Ann his then wife who is now also deceased,[395] John Halsall their son and Elizabeth their daughter, now wife of Thomas Hearefoote, and for the life of the longest liver of that messuage or mansion house which the said Ralph Halsall then did inhabit and the said John Halsall now inhabits and of one barn on Mill Hill and two closes

[f.2v, blank]
[f.3r]

commonly called Fall Acre and Fells Acre. The said Ralph Halsall on 20 November 21 Charles[396] did surrender the said messuage, barn, closes and premises to him the said Ralph Halsall during his life. After to the said Ann during her chaste widowhood. After to the said John Halsall and the heirs of his body. And for want of such issue, to Thomas Halsall his brother and his heirs. With several provisos in the said surrender.

Now the said John Halsall and Thomas Halsall his brother out of court came before Richard Litherland and Henry Marshall on 8

[f.3v, blank]
[f.4r]

November, 23 Charles, 1647 and for £16 to the said John Halsall paid by Peter Harforde of Prescot, shearman, surrendered to the lord the said messuage or mansion house with the said barn and that close called Fells Acre. The lord to regrant the said messuage, barn and Fells Acre to the said

[f.4v, blank]
[f.5r]

Peter Harforde to hold for the lives of the said John Halsall and Elizabeth wife of the said Thomas Harforde and the survivor. Paying yearly to the lord the rent of 3s 4d, parcel of the rent of 10s 8d, reserved for the said messuage, barn and two closes.

The said Peter Harforde is admitted.

395. For Ralph see p. 92 and note 244 *supra*. Ann (Ditchfield) was buried in January 1647; see LPRS, 114, p. 97.
396. 1645.

[f.5v, blank]
[f.6r]
The said Peter Harforde establishes further that the said messuage, barn and parcel of land called Fells Acre mentioned in the surrender aforesaid to which the said Peter Harforde was[397] admitted tenant and the messuage, barn and Fells Acre in the said surrender to which this plea is in bar are one and the same messuage, barn and parcel of land.

And the said John Halsall and Thomas Halsall in the said surrender acknowledged before the said Richard Litherland and Henry Marshall and the said John Halsall and Thomas Halsall in the said surrender acknowledged before Edward Stockley and Hugh Ward similarly are one and the same persons. And the said Peter Harford admitted tenant of the premises mentioned previously and the said Peter Harford in this plea are one and the same person. And this preparation is to defend against the said Henry Marshall.

[f.6v]
1640 to 1650, 1649.

[Paper Book: DDKc/PC 4/41[398]]

[f.1r: 29.5 cms × 37.5 cms]
COURT BARON OF THE MANOR OF PRESCOT in the county of Lancaster held on Friday, 6 July 1649.

To this court came Henry Marshall who says that the said Peter Harford in his said plea alleges that the surrender aforesaid of John Halsall and Thomas Halsall, acknowledged before the said Edward Stockley and Hugh Ward on the said 14 December 1648 to the use of himself Henry concerning the said messuage, barn and parcel of land called Fells Acre, should be accepted and that the said Henry should be admitted by the steward. He also says that the said surrender was made by the said John Halsall and Thomas Halsall to the said Peter Harford, and the said Peter as customary tenant of the said messuage, barn and Fells Acre was admitted by the steward under the proviso that if the said John Halsall pays to the said Peter Harford £16 on

[f.1v, blank]
[f.2r: 29.5 cms × 37.5 cms]
25 December 1649 and meanwhile pays the said rent of 2s to the lord yearly, then this present surrender to be void.

And the said Henry Marshall further says that the intention in the said surrender, made to the same Peter under the proviso aforesaid in the said surrender made

---

397. 'Is' ('*est*') was cancelled and 'was' ('*fuit*') interlined.
398. These three loose leaves, fastened by a modern paper clip at the top, are in the same hand and ink as the previous six leaves, and this material is likewise not in the Abstract Book or the parchment roll.

to himself Henry by the said John Halsall and Thomas Halsall, was that the said Henry Marshall would pay to the same Peter Harford the said £16 on the said 25 December 1649. Also, in this reservation in the said surrender made to himself Henry the intent was that the same said Henry, during the term in the same surrender, would pay yearly to the lord of the manor the rent of 10s 8d.

And the said Henry Marshall further says that the messuage, barn and Fells Acre in the said surrender made to the said Peter Harford and upon which the said Peter was admitted, and the messuage, barn and Fells Acre in the said surrender made to the said Henry Marshall are one and the same; that the said John Halsall and Thomas Halsall in the surrender made to the said Peter Harford, and the said John Halsall and Thomas Halsall in the surrender made to the said Henry Marshall similarly

[f.2v, blank]
[f.3r: 29.5 cms × 37 cms]
are one and the same persons; and that the said Peter Harford may be admitted tenant. And the said Peter Harford in his said plea is one and the same person. Likewise, however, Henry says that the said surrender made to himself Henry and the said surrender made to the said Peter Harford neither contradict nor prejudice the admission of himself Henry on his said surrender and of the said Peter on his said surrender because, he says as before, the said surrender to himself Henry was made and acknowledged with respect to the previous proviso in the said surrender to the said Peter Harford, and the said Peter was admitted as tenant to the said messuage, barn and Fells Acre.

The said Henry asks to be admitted and so forth.

[f.3v]
Prescot 1649.

[PRESENTMENTS AND ORDERS [399]*]*
An information against Ralph Angsdale by Mary Akers.

Henry Marshall or the occupiers of the close called Fall Acre are ordered to fill the pits in the highway before next 30 June on pain of 13s 4d.

Henry Ogle, gent. (26s 8d), for not removing the yate and wall out of Hall Lane.

Cuthbert Ogle, esq., farmer thereof, is ordered to remove the same before next Michaelmas on pain of 13s 4d.

Everyone who falls young saplings in the Wood shall forfeit 6s 8d for every sapling.

---

399. From the 'Paper Rowle', that is missing, as recorded in the Abstract Book.

GLOSSARY

affeeror: leet officer who assessed amercements

amercement: payment assessed by affeerors for misdemeanours

assize: regulation of the quality, quantity and price of ale and bread

backhouse: possibly a privy behind the principal dwelling

badger: middleman who bought and sold corn

bailiff: officer of the manorial court who collected rents and performed other duties

baronet: hereditary member of the nobility below baron but above knight; baronetcy was created in 1611

burgage: small parcel of land

Cavalier: a supporter of Charles I in the civil war between Royalists and Parliamentarians

chapman: small merchant

clerk: cleric; one who wrote records (clerk of the court); presentment officer (clerk of the market)

close: small enclosure

cooper: one who made and repaired barrels

cop: embankment

copyhold: manorial land held by copy of the court roll, with the copyholder retaining a copy of the entry in the roll

cossen: to cheat

croft: small enclosed field often adjacent to a house

cudgel: short heavy club

currier: one who soaked and coloured tanned hides

curry: to soak and colour tanned hides

cutt: term of abuse, possibly referring to drunk, tipsy

demesne: land held by the lord of the manor for his own use

disseisin, disseizin: wrongfully dispossessing a person of land

downdubb: outhouse

eavesdropper: one who under walls, windows or eaves listened to private conversations

enclosure: converting land held in common into private property by erecting fences or hedges

esquire: member of the English gentry ranked above gentleman but below knight

essoin: excuse for not attending the manor court

feoffee: a trustee of a charitable bequest

forestall: to purchase goods before they arrived at the market and later to resell for a profit

frankpledge: in medieval times a division of a community into ten men who shared responsibility for the behaviour of each other; in the seventeenth century the 'view of frankpledge' required inhabitants of a manor to assemble periodically at a court

furniture: military equipment including weapons

gelding: castrated animal, particularly a horse
gentleman: a man above the rank of yeoman who did no manual labour
glover: a maker or seller of gloves
groat: a coin worth four old pence

hatter: a maker and seller of hats
hayment: hedge
homage: the jury; all suitors attending court
hooper: one who made hoops and put them on barrels
husbandman: a farmer

imparl: court licence to parties in a dispute allowing time to talk and settle
inmate: someone unable or unwilling to provide for himself or herself and who lodged with an inhabitant or in an unoccupied building

knight: member of the gentry who ranked below baronet and above esquire

lay, ley: local tax on land and houses
linenwebster: linenweaver

mansion: large house
mercer: dealer in textile fabrics or small wares
messuage: dwelling house and adjacent land and buildings
midden, midding: dunghill or refuse heap
miln(e): obsolete form of mill
milner: miller or one who ground corn in a mill
moss or town moss: waste land on which tenants enjoyed common pasture, laid dung and removed clay and sand

ob: abbreviation for the Latin *obolus*; old halfpenny
oven house: bakehouse

plat(t): small bridge
plea in bar: a legal action to prevent admittance to land
plea of land: an allegation in a legal suit in order to recover land; see 'recovery'
pledge: person serving as surety for another
presentment: written accusation of wrongdoing delivered to the manorial court by jurors or other officers

pricks: wood used in thatching to hold straws in place

quit claim: a renouncing of any claim to a property

recovery: restoration of property by employing collusive actions
recusant: usually a Roman Catholic ('papist') who refused to attend the services
  of the Church of England
rental: register containing names of tenants and undertenants, their holdings and
  the rents due
rood: a unit of land measure equal to one-fourth of an acre
roundings: inferior pieces

sad(d)ler: one who made, repaired or sold saddles and other leather equipment for
  horses
shearman: a cutter of cloth
shew or show up: pile up, make compact
shippon: cattle pen
sink: a ditch for carrying away waste water
skinner: one who cured and dressed skins or hides
smithy: the workshop of a blacksmith
sough: gutter
steward: principal manager of a manor who also presided over the manorial court
stoop: a post
stound: wooden vessel
suit of court, suit and service: personal attendance that was required at the manorial court in order to answer to one's name
surety: one who provided security for the good behaviour of another
surrender: the return of land to the lord of the manor who in turn granted it back
  to the surrenderer or his or her designee
swynecoate: pigpen or pigsty

tanhouse: a building in which hides were tanned
tanner: one who tanned hides
tanpit: place where heat was produced by burning the bark of oak or other trees,
  in the process of tanning hides into leather
tinsel: twigs for hedges or fences
town moss: see 'moss'

underwood: underbrush

victualler: innkeeper
vintner: one who sold wine

waste: see 'moss'

watchman: person directed by constables to patrol the streets between sunset and
    sunrise or to guard a prisoner
webster: weaver
wheelwright: one who made and repaired wheels and wheeled vehicles
whittawer: saddler
windings: see 'pricks'
within age: under age

yate: gate
yeoman: small farmer below the rank of gentleman

INDEX OF PEOPLE

A name may appear more than once on a page.

INDEX OF PLACES

A place may appear more than once on a page.

Marston Moor (Yorkshire), lii, 99n.
Middlesex, xxviii
Middleton, 97n.
Mossborough (Rainford), 56, 149 & n.
Muchland, xliiin.

Naseby (Northamptonshire), lv
Newton, xxxiii
Newton-with-Scales, liii, livn.
Northamptonshire, lv

Ormskirk, xiiin., xvi, xxvii, xln., lii, liv

Parr, xxxivn., *l*, 15
Penketh, xxxivn.
Pilkington, the Outwood within, 59, 147
Prescot, *passim*; the Acre, 81; the Brook, 24;
    Brown's Croft, 31, 81, 82; Churchley
    Field, 30, 61, 75, 122, 144, 145, 151, 156,
    157; Churchleys, 25, 26; Church Street,
    xxxv; the close by the house, 151; the
    common, xix, 25, 34, 44n., 133; Cow Hey,
    12, 59, 60, 146, 147; Cross Croft, 31, 81,
    82; cuckstool pit, xlv; the Delves, 24;
    demesne 45, 46, 163; Eccleston Street, xlv,
    10n.; Fall Acre, 104, 136, 159, 161; Fall
    Lane, 6, 10n., 57, 131; Fall Lane Acre,
    137, 150, 152, 153; Fells Acre, 104, 136,
    137, 152, 153, 155, 158–61; Fletcher's
    Field, 82; Fletcher's two fields, 51, 73, 75;
    Goodicar's Acre, 57; Prescot Hall, xiv,
    lxiin.; town hall, xxix, xlii, *see also*
    INDEX OF SUBJECTS, Court: court
    house; Hall Lane, *l*, 57, 89, 90, 96, 116,
    132, 161; Hall Meadow, 71; High Street,
    14, 17, 18, 81; Higher Hey, 31, 81, 82; the
    Hillock, 7, 78, 83, 86, 92; the Holt, 115 &
    n.; Hough's well, xxxviii, 37; King's Arms
    Hotel, xlii; Lady Well, lvi, 10n., 133;
    Leadbeter's Croft, 74, 139; little cuckstool
    house, 30, 32; Lower Hey, 31, 81, 82;
    Lowest Field, 82; Lyon's yard, 17;
    Nicholas Marshall's Acre, 109, 110;
    Middle Croft, 31, 81, 82; Mill Hill, 56, 57,
    89, 104, 106, 136, 150, 152, 153, 155,
    157, 159; Nell Milner's crofts, 57;
    Museum, xiin.; New Hall, 34, 36; the
    Platt, 7, 164; Potter's Brook, 115; Potter's
    house, 108; Prescot Meadow, 61; Pyke's
    Higher Hey, 125, 127; Pyke's house, 127;

Pyke's Lower Hey, 125, 127; Royal Hotel,
    xlii; Sign of the Eagle and Child, 57;
    Slutterforth Well, 10 & n.; Sparrow Lane,
    xlv, 46, 57, 62n., 75, 151; Sparrow Lane
    Cottage and Meadow, 57; town moss,
    xxxii, xxxiii & n., xlv, 25, 26, 34n., 46,
    57, 89, 133; waste ground, xxxv, xliv, 25
    & n., 26n., 44 & n., 45n., 46, 98n., 150,
    165; watering pool, lvi, 57, 103, 133; John
    Webster's well, 10n., 32, 33, 38, 40, 43,
    67, 151; the Wood, xxxii, xxxvi, xlv,
    xlixn., *l*, 23 & n., 24 & n., 69, 84, 132, 161
Preston, xv, xxxvii, xlvii, 98n.

Rainford, xxxivn., lxii & n., 62n., 65, 77, 91,
    111, 117, 128, 133, 139n., 149n., 156
Rainhill, xxxi, xxxiii & n., xxxivn., xxxv,
    lviii, lx, 2, 19, 22, 23, 28, 31, 33, 38, 40,
    41, 51, 52, 55, 60, 62n., 77, 79, 86 & n.,
    91, 93, 97n., 111, 113, 115n., 117–19,
    127, 128, 130, 148, 155, 159
Ribble Valley, lii
Ribchester, xviin.
Rishton, xxxixn., liii & n.
Roby, 27, 128n.

St Ellens [St Helens] (Windle), 62n.
Salesbury, xxiiin., liii, livn.
Salford, liii
Scarisbrick, xvin., liiin.
Scotland, 15
Shropshire, xxviii
Speke, xlvii
Sutton, xxxi, xxxivn., 31, 42, 60, 61, 97n.,
    148, 154, 155

Tarbock, xiin., xxxi, 26, 38n., 41, 67, 77, 79,
    89, 91, 93, 111, 113, 128, 130, 156, 157,
    159
Thingwall, 2, 38, 40, 67, 77, 79, 89, 91, 93,
    111, 128 & n.
Thornley, xviin.

Upholland, xvin., xxn., xxvi, xxviin.,
    xxviiin., xli, xlii, xliii & n., xliv & n.,
    xlvn., xlvin., xlviii, lxi & n., lxii & n., 76,
    77, 91, 93, 111, 121
Urmston, liii, livn.

Walton-le-Dale, xviin., xliv & n., liii

INDEX OF SUBJECTS

A subject may appear more than once on a page.

Bread, lv, 99; assize of, xxxix, xl; broke
assize of, xl, liii, 11, 28, 44, 64, 72, 73,
87, 102, 117, 134, 135; other offences, xl,
lvi, 72, 102; baker, xl; breadbaker, xiv,
72. *See also* Overseers of the weights of
bread and measures of beer
Bridle, xlvin.
Burgage, 12, 15, 30, 48, 56, 61, 75 & n.,
105, 119, 138, 143, 144, 150, 151, 163
Burleyman, xxix, xxxii, lvn., lx, 13n., 71,
88n.; nominees, liii, 11, 29, 46, 65, 69,
88, 94, 119, 135, 158; presentments, 10
& n., 28, 44, 71; responsibilities,
xxxviii
Butcher, xiv, xxviii, 9, 23, 27, 31, 42n.,
47n., 56, 62, 64, 65, 67, 78, 84, 88, 92,
94, 96, 100, 106n., 107, 114, 116, 123,
131, 134, 151, 153–6
Butter, 9, 101n.
Buttonmaker, xiv, 121, 154

Candlestick, li, 100
Carpenter, xiv, 121, 144
Catholicism—*see* Recusant, recusancy
Cattle, xlv, 9n.; bull, xxxiiin.; calf, xxxiiin.,
xxxviii, lvi, 9, gelding, 65; cow, xxxiiin.,
xxxviii, 43. *See also* Meat
Cavaliers, lv, 99, 163
Challenge, place of, lxin.
Chapman, xiv, 16, 37, 48, 163; petty, 13n.
Charitable bequests, xvi, xxxii, xxxiii & n.,
xxxiv & n., livn., lviii, lxii, 98, 118, 132,
135; charity, welfare, xxxiii, xxxiv, 13n.
See also Churchwarden; Overseers of the
poor; Poor
Charter: of 1447, xi, xxviii; of 1614, xi &
n., xiii
Chest, town, xxii, xxiii & n., xxiv, xxv & n.,
xxxvi, xlviii, 24, 45, 46; keys, xxiii, xxiv,
xxv & n., xxxvi, 24, 45, 46. *See also*
Clerk of the court
Childbed, liv, lvn., 99
Church: bells, lin., lvii; bishop of Chester,
xvi; churchwall, 115n., 134; churchyard,
30n., 47n., 57, 83, 115n., 134;
Communion, liin., 62n.; gate, 30 & n.;
leys, xxxivn., livn.; parish church, xiv,
xxviii, xxxiv & n., xxxv, lin., liv, lxii &
n., 12, 23n., 51, 62n., 115n.; rectory, xi,
xxvii; vestry, xxiii

Churchwarden, xix, xxxivn., 62n.; accounts,
xvi, xxxiiin., xxxivn., xxxvn., livn., lxiin.;
election, xxxiv & n.; executing orders for
punishment, xliv; ordered to maintain
individuals, xxxvn., 6n., 145n.
Civil war, xxvi, xxviii, xxxviin., xlix–lxi,
livn., 98n., 101n.
Clay, 29
Clerk, xiv, 1, 12, 15, 19, 30, 38, 41, 51, 52,
62, 73, 77, 79, 138, 163
Clerk of the court, xvi & n., xxiii, xxiv,
xxviii, xxxii & n., xxxv, livn., lvn., lxii;
assistant clerk, xxxiiin., 46; delivered
records to the bailiff, 32n., 36n., 50n.,
66n., 73n., 88n., 110n., 127n., 148n.;
enrolled records, xvi, xx, xxiv, xxv, xlviii,
14n., 18n., 24, 46, 163; possessed key to
town chest, xxiii, xxiv, 46;
responsibilities, xvi, xx, xxii, xxiv, xxv;
summons to hold court, 33, 88, 89
Clerk of the market, xxxii, lviiin., lx, 28n.,
47n., 163; nominees, lii, 11, 29, 46, 65,
69, 88, 94, 119, 135, 158; presentments, 9
& n., 28, 43, 64, 65, 71, 134;
responsibilities, xxxviii, 9n. *See also*
Weights and measures
Clerk of the parish church, xxxiv, xxxv
Close, 12, 31, 51, 57, 59–61, 73, 75, 81, 82,
104, 109, 110, 125, 136, 137, 146, 147,
150–3, 155, 159, 161, 163
Clothmaker, 62n.
Coal, xxvn., 45; collier, xiv, 4, 27; mineral
rights, xxv
Coats for the poor, 60, 148
Coffee, lxii
Common land or pasture, 25 & n., 26n., 34,
44n., 133
Common law, 35, 126, 127, 140, 141
Commonwealth, xviii, lx
Compounding, 97n.
Constable, xxix, xxxii, xxxiii, xxxvi, li, livn.,
lviii, lx, 13n., 45n., 47n., 62 & n., 67n.,
88n., 93, 99n., 100n.; accounts, xiiin., xvii
& n., xxxii, xxxvi, xxxvii, xxxviiin., xli,
xlv, livn., 62, 85, 94, 97, 114–16, 133;
assistants, xxxii, xxxiii, xliv, 71;
attendance at quarter sessions, xiii & n.;
discharge from office, liiin.; election,
xxxvin.; financial problems, xxxvii & n.,
xxxviii & n.; met with Four Men, xxix,